Slovenia

the Bradt Travel Guide

Robin & Jenny McKelvie

www.bradtguides.com

Bradt Travel Guides Ltd, UK
The Globe Pequot Press Inc, USA

914.97
MCK

edition
2

AUSTRIA

Lake Bled
page 101

Ljubljana
page 47

Kranjska Gora

2208m
Mt Rombon

2884m
Triglav

Vrba

Bled   Begunje

Bovec

Lake Bohinj   Radovljica   Brezje

Savica Falls   Stara Fužina   Kropa

Kobarid   Ribčev Laz   Bohinjska Bistrica

Mt Vogel 1922m   *Mt Kobla 1227m*   Kranj   Kamnik

Tolmin   Crngrob

Cerkno   Škofja Loka   Šuha

ITALY

Goriška Brda

Šmartno   Spodnji Idrija   **LJUBLJANA** ■   Litija

Dobrovo   Idrija

Nova Gorica   Vrhnika   *Ljubljanica*

Grosuplje

Ajdovščina

Vipava Valley   **SLOVENIA**

Štanjel   Vipava

Postojna

Ribnica

Lipica   **Škocjan Caves**

TRIESTE ●   Mahovnik

*Adriatic
Sea*

Ankaran

Stunjan   Izola

Piran   Koper   Hrastovlje

Portorož   Šmarje

*Sečovlje
Salina NP*

Škocjan Caves
page 141

Piran
page 153

HUNGARY

Murska Sobota

Radenci

Dravograd

Maribor

Slovenj Gradec

Ptuj

Velenje

Pragersko

Ptuj
page 206

Celje

Hrastnik

Sevnica

Brestanica

Trebnje

Kostanjevica Na Krki

Novo Mesto

Metlika

Črnomelj

CROATIA

N

Bradt

0   20km
0   10 miles

Slovenia
Don't
miss...

**Historic towns
and cities**
Skofja Loka
(STB) page 86

Mountains
Logarska Dolina
(RM) page 203

Ljubljana
Slovenia's beguiling
capital
(RM) page 47

Winelands
Vipava Valley vineyard
(RM) page 140

**The Slovenian
Riviera**
Izola
(RM) page 151

top   **The banks of the Ljubljanica**
(AG) page 69

above **Buildings in Ljubljana**
(JS) page 47

left   **Flower market in Ljubljana**
(RM) page 67

top left   **Franciscan Church of the Annunciation and Ljubljanica** (RM) page 79

top right   **Celica Hostel — stay in a converted prison!** (RM) page 52

above left   **Art Nouveau rooftop and Ljubljana Castle** (RM) page 68

above right **City Door, St Nicholas's Cathedral, Ljubljana** (RM) page 79

top   **Traditional costumes at a festival in Ljubljana** (JS) page 36
above   **Festival masks in Ptuj, Štajerska** (RM) page 210

AUTHORS

Robin McKelvie (*www.robinmckelvie.com*) has been a full-time travel writer and photographer since 1997. He has written about more than 200 European towns and cities – including co-writing *Ljubljana: The Bradt City Guide* – and travelled to over 80 countries worldwide. He first visited Slovenia in 1992, and since then has covered the region extensively, writing on Slovenia, Croatia and Montenegro. Robin has published thousands of magazine and newspaper articles around the world, with his work appearing in publications including the *Independent on Sunday*, *The Independent*, *Sunday Herald*, *The Scotsman*, *Scotland on Sunday*, *The Guardian*, the *Daily Mail* and the *Sunday Post*. Robin is also easyJet's 'Man in Ljubljana', writing destination reports on a monthly basis for their in-flight magazine.

Jenny McKelvie (*www.jennymckelvie.com*) is also a full-time travel writer. Her job has taken her to destinations around the world and she has specialist knowledge of central and eastern Europe. Her writing credits include *TravelMail*, *Guardian Online*, *Ryanair Magazine*, *easyJet Magazine*, *Highstyle*, *European Businessman* and the *People's Friend*. Jenny also co-wrote *Ljubljana: The Bradt City Guide*.

AUTHORS' STORY

When Robin first visited Slovenia back in 1992 it was a country that was almost completely undiscovered. Jenny herself didn't visit until 1997. Since those first trips we have returned to Slovenia dozens of times, and while the country now welcomes around 2.5 million foreign tourists every year, it remains a relative secret. A unique country that boasts vaulting alpine peaks, tumbling rivers, glacial lakes, swathes of unspoiled countryside and a stretch of balmy Adriatic, Slovenia more than deserves the 'Europe in Miniature' clichés that are lavished upon it.

Back in 1992 Slovenia was just starting to emerge from five decades of Yugoslav socialism which, despite its relative freedoms, still kept a tight rein on the country's economy and political set-up. Even then Slovenia was an impressive country. Far from fulfilling images of communist deprivations it was a place whose citizens were affluent, optimistic and progressive. Then there was the scenery, something that never fails to blow us away no matter how many times we visit. For us a visit to Slovenia is all about getting active amongst its skyscraping mountains, dining on boat-fresh seafood in the restaurants that dot its laidback Mediterranean coast, retreating to the rural homesteads of the interior or letting our hair down in the country's vibrant towns and cities. Whether it is strolling by the banks of the Ljubljanica River in the capital on an autumnal day, heaving yourself up onto the summit of a peak in the Julian Alps and feeling like you are on top of Europe, or simply just relaxing with a glass of chilled Slovenian Chardonnay in a waterfront restaurant by the coast, we have a sneaking suspicion that you may just end up loving Slovenia as much as we do.

PUBLISHER'S FOREWORD   *Hilary Bradt*

The first Bradt travel guide was written in 1974 by George and Hilary Bradt on a river barge floating down a tributary of the Amazon. In the 1980s and '90s the focus shifted away from hiking to broader-based guides covering new destinations – usually the first to be published about these places. In the 21st century Bradt continues to publish such ground-breaking guides, as well as others to established holiday destinations, incorporating in-depth information on culture and natural history with the nuts and bolts of where to stay and what to see.

Bradt authors support responsible travel, and provide advice not only on minimum impact but also on how to give something back through local charities. In this way a true synergy is achieved between the traveller and local communities.

* * *

After reading Robin and Jenny's evocative manuscript I wondered why on earth I'd never been to Slovenia. It seems to have everything I like: beautiful mountain scenery, a beguiling capital, vineyards and the Adriatic coast. Come to think of it, isn't this what almost everyone likes?

Second edition May 2008
First published May 2005
Bradt Travel Guides Ltd, 23 High Street, Chalfont St Peter, Bucks SL9 9QE, England.
www.bradtguides.com
Published in the USA by The Globe Pequot Press Inc, 246 Goose Lane,
PO Box 480, Guilford, Connecticut 06475-0480

Text copyright © 2008 Robin & Jenny McKelvie
Maps copyright © 2008 Bradt Travel Guides Ltd
Illustrations © 2008 Individual photographers and artists (see below)

The authors and publishers have made every effort to ensure the accuracy of the information in this book at the time of going to press. However, they cannot accept any responsibility for any loss, injury or inconvenience resulting from the use of information contained in this guide.

British Library Cataloguing in Publication Data
A catalogue record for this book is available from the British Library

ISBN-10: 1 84162 211 7   ISBN-13: 978 1 84162 211 8

Photographs Alan Grant (AG), Robin & Jenny McKelvie (RM), Jonathan Smith (JS), Slovenia Tourist Board (STB)
Front cover Church of the Assumption, Lake Bled, Jon Arnold Images/Alamy
Back cover Dragon Bridge, Ljubljana (RM)
Title page Logarska Dolina (RM); Piran and the Adriatic (RM); Façade of Co-operative Bank, Ljubljana (RM)
Illustrations Carole Vincer   **Maps** Kevin Baverstock

Typeset from the authors' disc by Wakewing
Printed and bound in India at Nutech Photolithographers

ACKNOWLEDGEMENTS

In Ljubljana special thanks go to Petra Stušek at the Ljubljana Tourist Office for her unfaltering and invaluable help in the city she helped us love as much as she does, and to her predecessor Petra Čuk, now with Hoteli Bled, who offered her expert knowledge as well as her generous hospitality. Our thanks also go out to Brina Čehovin of the Slovenian Tourist Board, as well as Nina Turuk, Miha Kovačič, Janis Skok, Janez Fajfar and Eva Ferjan, Matjaž Kos, Štefan Čelan, Marija Lah, Vesna Male, Marko Lenarčič, Boštjan Burger and Studio Breza. Then there are the countless other Slovenes around the country who helped brighten up our research trips with their humour and unerring friendliness.

In the UK we would especially like to thank Mary Stuart-Miller, the Slovenian Tourist Board's UK public relations contact, who deserves a special mention for her enthusiasm and assistance.

We would also like to thank readers for their feedback on the first edition and look forward to hearing your continued comments.

FEEDBACK REQUEST

Every guidebook is a snapshot in time. New hotels open, restaurants change hands, tour operators come and go – and prices change. The authors and publishers would appreciate any feedback you may have from your travels, whether to tell us about somewhere new that you have discovered or to share your experience of places mentioned in the guide. Such feedback will make a huge difference when it comes to the next edition, and will ensure that the guide continues to evolve and broaden its scope for future readers.

Please send your feedback to Bradt Travel Guides at e info@bradtguides.com, or by post to 23 High Street, Chalfont St Peter, Bucks SL9 9QE, England.

Contents

	Introduction	**VII**

PART ONE   GENERAL INFORMATION   I

Chapter 1   **Background Information**   **3**
Geography and climate 3, History 4,
Government and politics 7, Economy 8, People 9,
Language 10, Religion 11, Education 11,
Natural history and conservation 12

Chapter 2   **Practical Information**   **13**
When to visit (and why) 13, Highlights 14,
Tour operators 16, Red tape 18,
Embassies 18, Getting there and away 19, Health 21,
Safety 23, Disabled visitors 24, Family travel 24,
Gay and lesbian travellers 24, What to take 25,
Money matters 25, Budgeting 28, Getting around 29,
Accommodation 31, Eating and drinking 32,
Public holidays and festivals 34, Shopping 37,
Arts and entertainment 37,
Media and communications 40, Business 42, Buying
property 42, Cultural etiquette 43, Local charities 43

PART TWO   THE GUIDE   45

Chapter 3   **Ljubljana**   **47**
History 47, Getting there 49, Getting around 50,
Tourist information/local tour operators 51,
Where to stay 52, Where to eat 56,
Entertainment and nightlife 61, Shopping 65,
Other practicalities 67, What to see 68

Chapter 4   **Gorenjska**   **83**
Kamnik 83, Ljubljana to Bled – off the tourist highway 86,
Škofja Loka 86, Around Škofja Loka 90, Suha 91,
Škofja Loka to Kropa 92, Radovljica 92, Kropa 94,
Kranj 96, Brezje 101, Bled 101, Bohinj 107,
Activities around Bled and Bohinj 112,
Day trips around Bled and Bohinj 116,
Kranjska Gora 117, Over the Vršič Pass to Primorska 120

Chapter 5	**Primorska**	**123**
	Bovec 123, Kobarid 128, Tolmin 131, Goriška Brda 132,	
	Idrija 134, Around Idrija 138, Vipava Valley 140,	
	The Karst (Kraš) 141, Lipica 142, Štanjel 144,	
	Elsewhere in the Karst 145	

Chapter 6	**The Slovenian Adriatic**	**147**
	Koper 147, Izola 151, Piran 153, Portorož 158	

Chapter 7	**Notranjska**	**163**
	Postojna Caves 163, Postojna Town 167,	
	Other caves near Postojna 168, Predjama Castle 168,	
	Predjama Cave 168, Lake Cerknica 169,	
	Križna Cave 170, Snežnik Castle 170,	
	Park of Military History 171	

Chapter 8	**Dolenjska and Bela Krajina**	**173**
	Kočevje and Kočevski rog 173, Dolenjske Toplice 175,	
	Novo Mesto 176, Back towards Ljubljana 178,	
	Abbeys and castles east of Novo Mesto 179,	
	Kostanjevica na Krki 180, Kostanjevica Cave 180,	
	Terme Čatež 181, Mokrice Castle and Golf Course 181,	
	Bela Krajina 182, Metlika 182, Črnomelj 185	

Chapter 9	**Štajerska and Prekmurje**	**189**
	Maribor 189, Maribor Pohorje 196,	
	Zreče and Rogla 198, Velenje 199, Celje 200, Laško 204,	
	Logarska Dolina 205, Robanov Kot and Matkov Kot 206,	
	Ptuj 206, Štajerska castles 211, Terme Radenci 212,	
	Prekmurje 213	

Chapter 10	**Koroška**	**219**
	Slovenj Gradec 219, Kope 223, Dravograd 223,	
	Podzemlje Pece 224	

Appendix 1	**Language**	**225**
Appendix 2	**Further Information**	**231**
Index		**244**

LIST OF MAPS

Bled	102	Notranjska	164
Bohinj	108	Novo Mesto	178
Celje	202	Piran	154
Dolenjska & Bela Krajina	172	Primorska	122
Gorenjska	84	Ptuj	208
Koper	148	Škofja Loka	87
Koroška	218	Slovenia	colour section ii–iii
Kranj	97	Slovenian Adriatic	146
Ljubljana	46	Slovenj Gradec	220
Ljubljana centre	54–5	Štajerska & Prekmurje	188
Maribor	190		

Chamois

Introduction

The first time I (Robin) visited Slovenia back in 1992 it was a country that it seemed virtually no-one had heard of. Those who did know it were surprised that I was travelling there as their only experience of Slovenia was from television news reports of the fighting that had erupted in 1991 during the break-up of Yugoslavia. The reality, though, was that even in 1992 Slovenia was completely safe to visit. Its only direct involvement in the regional conflicts had been a ten-day skirmish with the Yugoslav National Army (JNA) a year earlier as it quickly secured its independence.

Since that first visit I have been back to Slovenia, a unique hideaway squeezed between Italy, Austria, Hungary and the Balkans, over 20 times with Jenny accompanying me on most occasions since we met in 1997. This is a country that more than justifies all the 'Europe in Miniature' clichés. Even though its epic sweep of scenery, everything from alpine peaks and tumbling rivers in the north to the balmy Adriatic coastline and vineyards in the south, garners increasing praise in the travel pages of magazines and newspapers, the country still remains largely 'unspoilt'.

Part of the reason for Slovenia's relative anonymity may lie in the fact that many people, including famously a certain US president, tend to get it confused with Slovakia, once part of Czechoslovakia. True, there is only a slight difference in the spelling and they sound very similar, not to mention the fact that they also have identikit flags, but Slovenia is thoroughly unique. This tiny nation of two million people was not ever behind the Iron Curtain, as many people presume, as it was part of Yugoslavia, an independent socialist state that gave its citizens passports and freedoms that the dissidents of the Prague Spring could only have dreamt of.

In just over a decade Slovenia has transformed itself from an unwilling appendage of Yugoslavia into a modern and successful European democracy. In 2004, Slovenia joined both NATO and the European Union, something no other state in the old federation has yet done and it became the first of the 2004 accession states to adopt the euro in 2007. It is hard not to be impressed by the Slovenes, who seem to have a natural aptitude for just buckling down and getting on with it. Instead of getting immersed in ethnic strife and conflict they have focused on building up their economy, putting their tiny country on the map and infiltrating the previously closed shops of NATO and the EU.

Despite its move towards greater integration with Europe Slovenia still retains a real independent spirit that manifests itself in so many ways. In Ljubljana there is the outdoor market right in the heart of the city where, in a defiant stand against the world of supermarket hegemony, old ladies sell their homemade honey and the city's citizens peddle vegetables plucked straight from their gardens. It also comes out in the long lazy lunches and languorous early dinners that many people take, with a nonchalance that is far more Mediterranean than central European. The

Slovenes themselves hate being labelled or categorised – they see themselves as independent citizens of their country, not as eastern Europeans, nor central Europeans and certainly not as belonging to the Balkans.

If you are not a 'mountain person' you may just about manage not to be affected by some of the most dramatic skyscraping peaks in Europe, which rise improbably all around this tiny country, but then surely the Mediterranean light of the coast would beguile you, or maybe just the rolling farmland and trim villages of much of the interior, or perhaps some of Europe's wildest forests where bears and wolves still roam wild. Increasingly Slovenia is also emerging as an adrenaline junkie's paradise where you can throw yourself off on a bungee, raft a grade five rapid or tumble downhill on a mountain bike.

Fitting into the sweep of landscape are Slovenia's towns and cities, sometimes dwarfed by the scenery but each offering something different. The capital, Ljubljana, is a neat and appealing city of around 330,000 inhabitants which manages to pack an incredible amount into a very compact and easily navigable space, but which rarely feels crowded or hectic. Every time we visit there seems to be a new bar, restaurant or café and the place appears to take on even more of a buzz. The same can be said of Maribor, the second city, with its near neighbour Ptuj one of the most attractive towns we have visited in the region. Then there are Kranj, Piran, Koper and Novo Mesto, or what about Izola, Kropa or Kamnik?

The Slovenia that we are writing about today is a very different one from that which emerged from the break-up of Yugoslavia at the start of the 1990s. Its epic scenic appeal, of course, still entrances, but these days along with the natural attractions tourism is starting to take off with improved transport facilities, better hotels, first-rate restaurants and an attempt to give visitors what they want rather than just relying on the beauty of the mountains and the sea. Concerns that Slovenia will be swamped by mass tourism and the hegemony of the EU do, though, seem a touch unfounded. This is a country that has, after all, managed to survive centuries of domination by the Venetians, Austro-Hungarians and Yugoslav communists, before it recently managed to extricate itself from the biggest armed conflict on the continent since World War II.

Where Slovenia will be in ten or 20 years' time is anyone's guess, but this plucky little nation has shown a remarkable tenacity and determination to succeed no matter what the odds over the centuries. Tourism may change Slovenia, but we are confident that one of our favourite countries will always boast the myriad charms, both immediately obvious and also more subtle, that keep drawing us back year after year.

Part One

GENERAL INFORMATION

REPUBLIC OF SLOVENIA AT A GLANCE

Location Central Europe, between Italy, Austria, Hungary and Croatia, and with a small stretch of Adriatic coastline
Area 20,273km^2
National parks Triglav National Park
Highest peak Mt Triglav, 2,864m
Forest 10,124km^2
Vineyards 216km^2
Coastline 46.6km
Climate Average temperature in winter −1°C, spring 10°C, summer 20°C and autumn 10°C
Population 2 million
Capital Ljubljana (population 328,499 – Statistical Office of the Republic of Slovenia, June 2006)
Other major towns and cities Maribor, Celje, Koper, Kranj, Novo Mesto, Velenje
Currency Euro and cents
Rate of exchange €1 = £0.75/US$1.47/AS$1.60/C$1.49 (March 2008)
Language Slovene
Religion Majority Roman Catholic
International dialling code +386
Time Central European Zone (GMT +1)
Electricity 220V/50Hz, two-pin plug with round prongs
Weights and measures Metric
National flag Horizontal stripes of white-blue-red with the Slovenian coat of arms located towards the top left corner
National anthem The 7th stanza of 'Zdravljica' ('A Toast') by national poet France Prešeren
Public holidays 1 & 2 January, 8 February, Easter Monday, 27 April, 1 & 2 May, Pentecost, 25 June, 15 August, 31 October, 1 November, 25 & 26 December (see page 34)

Background Information

GEOGRAPHY AND CLIMATE

The Republic of Slovenia is one of Europe's smallest countries, with a territory that covers just 20,273km^2, making it similar in size to Wales. Located in central Europe, Slovenia shares borders with Croatia, Italy, Austria and Hungary. Ljubljana is at the heart of the country and is within a three-hour drive of even the most distant parts of the country. This compact size means that the country's dramatic mountains, underground caves, forests, Adriatic coast, lakes and rivers are all within easy reach of the capital.

Slovenia has a climate that reflects its diverse landscape. Primorska in the southwest of the country enjoys a Mediterranean climate, with temperatures in the coastal towns of Portorož, Izola, Piran and Koper being especially pleasant. In the summer temperatures hover around the mid 20s and rarely fall below 6°C in the winter.

The rest of Slovenia's lowland, including Ljubljana, has a continental climate with mild and often hot summers, but cold winters. Again July and August are the

WHEN IS A REGION A REGION?

Trying to delineate Slovenia by region is a difficult and thankless task. Officially there are no regions as such, but many Slovenes regard the regions that were developed under the Austro-Hungarian Empire as an important part of the history of their country and still talk about the likes of Notranjska (or the Inner Carniola region), Dolenjska (Lower Carniola), Gorenjska (Upper Carniola), Štajerska (Styria) and Koroška (Carinthia). During the Austro-Hungarian era the regions of Štajerska and Koroška extended into modern-day Austria, with the greater part of the historical areas of Carinthia and Styria also located there today. Of these historical regions, Lower, Upper and Inner Carnolia (Dolenjska, Notranjska and Gorenjska) are widely considered to be the most 'Slovenian', as the name 'Carniola' was used prior to Habsburg rule, originating from the Latin name for Kranj. The majority of Slovenes will also identify two other regions, Prekmurje and Tržaška (Trieste region), the former, located on the extreme northeast, used to be in the Hungarian part of the Austro-Hungarian Empire, while Tržaška is now almost entirely in Italy.

This book has been organised in line with these historic regions – areas with many common features and shared histories – with which many Slovenes still identify today. If you want to be a stickler they do not exist and the country must be split up into over 190 municipalities, which makes things a lot more complex. So here we have stuck with the unofficial regions, though of course you will almost certainly come across people who will want to argue the boundaries of Dolenjska or Primorska or subdivide things further still.

warmest months, with an average temperature of 20°C and highs hovering around 25°C. Days in May, June and September are often pleasantly warm with average temperatures of 14–17°C, and maximums that can regularly exceed 20°C. April and October, which traditionally mark the beginning and end of the tourist season, are slightly colder with average temperatures of 10°C and highs of 15°C. December, January and February are the coldest months, with an average temperature of −1°C. In January and February the mercury can plummet as low as −5°C and rarely rises above 2°C. Temperatures in Slovenia's Alps are obviously colder and winters here are characterised by frequent snowfalls.

Away from its Adriatic coast, which is drier, Slovenia has high levels of precipitation, with the weather in the spring months particularly changeable; therefore it is wise to bring waterproof clothing or an umbrella at any time of year.

HISTORY

A MIXED BAG Situated at the heart of Europe on a crossroads between east and west, and providing central Europe's access to the Mediterranean Sea through the Adriatic, Slovenia has long attracted a diverse range of settlers and invaders. You should always, though, take any recent stab at Slovenian history with a pinch of salt as over the last decade the country has been free for the first time to really explore and – as some critics would suggest – rewrite its history and heritage. It is, however, not always wise to challenge the highly subjective version of history you hear from an animated local in this part of the world.

HUMBLE BEGINNINGS Historical evidence suggests that Slovenia was first inhabited during the Neolithic period – sometime between 4000BC and 3400BC – with human remains, artefacts and dwellings discovered between the Pannonian plains and the Karst. These Stone Age residents were followed by pile dwellers, who lived in stilt-houses built on marshland, including the Ljubljansko Barje (Ljubljana Marshes). Life for the country's earliest settlers was dominated by agriculture and this continued through the Bronze Age into the early Iron Age (8th to 4th century BC), a period that was also characterised by the production of cast-iron objects – remnants of which are proudly displayed at museums throughout the country – and the growth of hilltop settlements such as those in Most na Soči, Rifnik, St Vid, near Stična, and Vače.

THE CELTS AND THE ROMANS In the 4th and 3rd centuries BC Celtic tribes from western Europe rumbled into the region and established the state of Noricum. By the beginning of the 2nd century BC, the Noric Celts had established trade links with Rome – a relationship that was to turn sour when the Romans began attacking the territory and finally annexed the state in 10BC. This first Roman era was characterised by the construction of roads and the development of urban settlements that subjugated those in the countryside. It also saw the establishment of the Roman towns of Emona (Ljubljana), Celeia (Celje) and Poetovio (Ptuj), with the last becoming the most important Roman settlement on Slovenian land.

For many of the country's inhabitants everyday life under Roman rule was good, save for the frequent attacks by barbarian Huns and central Asian Avars. The capitulation of the Romans in AD452 saw the country's residents even more exposed to attacks by barbarians and Germanic tribes.

THE SLAVS Historians dispute the timescale of the arrival of the first Slavic settlers in Slovenia, but most sources reckon that Slavs from the north migrated here early in the 6th century AD. What is certain is that by the 7th century the Slavs had become the dominant people in Slovenia, establishing the first independent Slavic or Slovenian state, Carinthia, in AD746, which later fell under Frankish control. This Frankish period was characterised by a mass conversion to Christianity and the watering down of Slavic identity.

In the 9th century Slovenia was subsumed into the Holy Roman Empire, while the early 10th century saw the writing of the Freising Manuscripts – three religious texts widely believed to be the oldest documentation in the world to be written in a Slavic language – which many in Slovenia regard as the true origin of the nation's distinctive national and cultural identity. Perhaps unsurprisingly their current preservation in the Munich National Library is a bone of contention for many Slovenes.

AUSTRO-HUNGARIAN DOMINANCE

AUSTRO-HUNGARIAN DOMINANCE Six hundred years of Austro-Hungarian rule was, arguably, the most defining period in Slovenia's history. In the 14th century the Habsburg dynasty took control of most of Slovenia's territory, with the Counts of Celje holding out until 1456, and they were to remain in power until World War II, with one brief exception when Napoleon usurped their authority. This period of Austro-Hungarian dominance was not without other problems, with Ottoman incursions widespread in the 15th and 16th centuries. Popular uprisings in protest at ineffectual defences against Turkish attacks and against high taxes also resulted in well-supported peasant uprisings in 1572 and 1573, which were violently suppressed.

This general dissatisfaction with Austro-Hungarian rule also asserted itself in more peaceful ways with Protestantism, which rose to the fore in the late 16th century, playing a significant role in shaping the nation's psyche over the next 200 years. A key characteristic of this time was the embracing of the Slovene language and Slovenian traditions. One of the most significant events was the 1550 publication of the first book written entirely in Slovene, Primož Trubar's *Catechismus in Abecedarium*. Around 50 further titles were also published in Slovene including a translation of the Bible by Jurij Dalmatin and Adam Bohorič's book of Slovenian grammar.

This flourishing of Slovene literature was muted by the suppression of Protestantism by the Catholic Church in the early 17th century, something that was happening all over Europe. By the 19th century the picture had turned on its head, with the Catholic Church being the main champion of the preservation of Slovene identity, language and culture. Influential figures in the evolution of Slovenia's cultural, national and literary identity who rose to the fore during this period, include the satirical writer Ivan Cankar (1876–1918) and the romantic poet France Prešeren (1849–80).

A period of suppression and strict religious direction was replaced with a period of relative freedom as the Enlightenment swept though central Europe under the reign of Emperor Josef II (1765–90). During this time compulsory schooling was established, the Slovene language was introduced into primary schools and the Slovene literati became increasingly active.

AN UNLIKELY CHAMPION OF SLOVENIA

AN UNLIKELY CHAMPION OF SLOVENIA The beginning of the 19th century afforded the Slovenian people a brief respite from what was still autocratic Austro-Hungarian rule, when Napoleon made a brief invasion into the Balkans, making Ljubljana the capital of his Illyrian Provinces between 1809 and 1813. During this short-lived period of Napoleonic rule the Slovene language flourished more openly, the taxation system was reformed and the distinctive national identity that had been suppressed by the Austro-Hungarians came to the fore. Napoleon's downfall saw the redrawing of the map of Europe and the return of Slovenia to Austro-Hungarian rule at the 1815 Congress of Vienna. It was here that the Habsburg Prince Klemens von Metternich agreed to join the Holy Alliance.

WAR CLOUDS AND A NEW NATION World War I heralded the collapse of the Austro-Hungarian Empire and it also saw Slovenia suffer heavy casualties, particularly on the bloody Soča Front (see box, *Chapter 5, The Soča Front*, page 126). The fear that the 1915 London Pact would result in the distribution of Slovenian territory among various countries, combined with the rise of the regional pan-Slavic movement which had been growing through the 19th and early 20th centuries, led Slovenes, Croats and Serbs to lobby for a common kingdom in 1917. The plea to Vienna fell on deaf ears, but after the Habsburg monarchy lost the war and disintegrated, Slovenia was in 1918 incorporated into the new Kingdom of Serbs, Croats and Slovenes, which adopted another title, the Kingdom of Yugoslavia, in 1929.

THE DARK DAYS OF WORLD WAR II In 1939, war engulfed Europe once again. After staying on the sidelines for over a year the kingdom entered the fray and was soon swallowed up by the Axis powers, with Germany, Italy and Hungary dividing Slovenia among them. This dark period in Slovenia's history was clouded by massacres, the suppression of Slovenian identity, the collaboration of the Slovenian Home Guard and the murder of thousands of the latter by partisans in the denouement of the war, an event whose full horror only really came to light in the 1970s.

TITO'S YUGOSLAVIA A dramatically different Slovenia emerged from the rubble of World War II, and in 1945 Ljubljana took its place as one of the six capitals of Tito's new Yugoslavia. The federation's other capitals were Belgrade in Serbia, Zagreb in Croatia, Sarajevo in Bosnia and Herzegovina, Skopje in Macedonia and Titograd (Podgorica) in Montenegro. For almost half a century what was by now known as the People's Republic of Slovenia (which became the Socialist Republic of Slovenia in 1963) found itself under the rigid control of the Yugoslav socialist regime, which was characterised by dictatorial leadership from Serbia and the shared ownership of property.

Slovenia was the most prosperous part of the federation (with per-capita GDP around 2½ times higher than the other Yugoslav states), but under the socialist system the wealth was redistributed to less developed regions such as Serbia and Montenegro, a siphoning off of resources that was to turn many Slovenes against the idea of Yugoslavia. This animosity grew amidst recurrent stories of government corruption, nepotism and attempts to suppress Slovenian identity, and was further intensified by Tito's death in 1980. With the man who had welded the disparate parts of Yugoslavia gone, the stage was set for the break-up of the federation.

INDEPENDENT AT LAST By the end of the 1980s political parties that opposed the Belgrade-based regime had emerged and gained popular support in Slovenia, with calls for an independent state first officially coming in 1989 under the auspices of the May Declaration. Just over a year later, on 23 December 1990, an overwhelming majority of voters (88%) asserted their desire to leave the Socialist Federal Republic of Yugoslavia and become an independent country.

After a delay of six months, independence was officially declared on 26 June 1991, a move that led to a ten-day war with Yugoslav government troops. Mercifully this brief conflict was relatively bloodless. Over 2,000 soldiers from the Yugoslav National Army (JNA) were ordered to seize the country's border stations, but blockades prevented many from leaving their barracks and the well-organised Slovenian domestic forces proved themselves a match for the confused and demoralised JNA troops (some of whom were actually Slovenes), many of whom voluntarily surrendered. After ten days of skirmishes and threats to attack Brnik Airport and Ljubljana itself – a menace that never materialised – the JNA backed down and a ceasefire took effect on 6 July 1991.

Slovenia's independence was recognised by the EU on 15 January 1992, and by the USA on 17 April 1992. The country then set about developing its economy and building political and economic relationships with the rest of the world. Slovenia's integration into the European fold was complete in 2004 when it joined both the EU and NATO. Becoming the first of the 2004 EU member countries to adopt the euro in 2007 and holding the EU presidency for the first half of 2008 cemented for many Slovenes their rightful place as they see it at the heart of Europe. Potential political problems do remain, such as the lingering dispute with Croatia over territorial waters in the Adriatic and the fate of the stateless refugees who came north from other parts of Yugoslavia in the 1990s, but for the fledgling nation of Slovenia the future does look as bright as it ever has during any point in its history.

GOVERNMENT AND POLITICS

The political history of modern-day Slovenia is a relatively short one, which begins with the assertion of independence in 1991 (see *History* above). One of the biggest tasks that confronted the newly independent country was the implementation of a new constitution, which materialised in December 1991 under the guidance of the country's first democratically elected prime minister, Lojze Peterle. This new constitution established a democratic parliamentary political system, which clearly delineated the roles of separate judicial, legislative and executive powers. Under this model of government the Državni Zbor (National Assembly), which is the Upper House of the Parliament and has the final say in legislative issues, is the most powerful institution. Slovenia's National Assembly comprises 90 officials who are elected through proportional representation and stay in office for four years.

Slovenia's Državni Svet (National Council) – which is the Lower House of the Parliament, representing the interests of the city and its workforce – has the power to challenge legislation passed by the National Assembly and can also initiate legislative change, although it rarely does so. The 40 elected officials – 22 of whom represent Slovenia's municipalities, four of whom represent the employers' organisation, four the employees' union, four farmers and craftsmen and six representing education, science, health and similar professions – serve a five-year term. In principle the referendums held by the National Assembly create a transparent political process that directly involves the people. Past referendums have included ballots on membership of the EU and NATO, as well as one on weekend opening hours for retail outlets. Some Slovenes now feel many of these numerous referendums are a waste of money and that state funds could be used more prudently. Others cast aspersions on the authenticity of this process, claiming that the majority of Slovenes did not want to join NATO and yet the result was overwhelmingly in favour of this.

Slovenia's judicial system comprises four different types of court – district, regional, higher and supreme – with the last being the most powerful. District Court judges deal with lesser offences, while those in Regional Courts deal with minors, business law and land registration. Higher Court judges are responsible for repeat offenders and appeals made against the rulings of the District and Regional courts.

The principal role of the Supreme Court is that of reviewing appeals, settling disputes over jurisdiction and regulating the legal profession. Judges are independent but accountable to the National Assembly, which elected them. Another independent institution, the Bank of Slovenia, is also accountable to the National Assembly.

Slovenia's government holds executive powers, and the country's current government is led by Prime Minister Janez Janša, leader of the Slovenian Democratic Party (SDS), who took up his post in December 2004, two months after the October elections. The other three parties of the government are New Slovenia Party (NSi), the Slovenian People's Party (SLS) and the Pensioners' Party (DeSUS). In addition to the prime minister the government has 14 cabinet members. Slovenia's other political parties include the Liberal Democratic Party (LDS), the United List of Social Democrats (ZLSDS), the Slovene National Party (SNS), the Slovenian Youth Party (SMS) and the Greens of Slovenia.

Dr Janez Drnovšek, Slovenia's second prime minister, served as president from December 2002 until December 2007. Danilo Türk took over this role in January 2008 after a decisive victory in the November 2007 election. According to the Slovenian Constitution the president is the country's commander-in-chief and is restricted to a maximum of ten years in office (two five-year terms). Presidential duties include calling elections, nominating a candidate for prime minister and appointing ambassadors and other state officials. Although Drnovšek had held prominent political office since 1992, it was not always plain sailing for him. In May 2000, while he was still prime minister, a vote of no confidence forced him to resign his post, and Dr Andrej Bajuk of the NSi took over. Six months later parliamentary elections returned the LDS to power and Drnovšek to his role as prime minister. In recent years the political stage in Slovenia has been dominated by the rapid privatisation of business and preparation for EU membership, which this young country achieved with impressive speed and efficiency on 1 May 2004, giving Slovenia access to an internal trade market of over 450 million people. Since 1991, Slovenia has also joined the United Nations, the Council of Europe and NATO, as well as becoming a non-permanent member of the United Nations Security Council. In January 2007, Slovenia adopted the euro as its national currency.

ECONOMY

Slovenia has a strong and growing economy, which has gone from strength to strength since joining the EU in May 2004. Far from being an impoverished new member Slovenia's economy is doing well, with the country's GDP witnessing a steady annual growth since 1991. Inflation has also been falling in recent years, standing at 9.1% in 1991 and just 2.8% in 2006. The number of unemployed people in Slovenia has also been declining since the late 1990s, and the country had an unemployment rate of 5.9% in September 2006.

Slovenia's service industry is vital to the country's economy, as it accounts for around 60% of GDP. Manufacturing accounts for 31%, construction 5.8% and agriculture just 3% of GDP. Important service industries include education, health, finance, retail, service industries and tourism. The last suffered a serious decline as Yugoslavia began to disintegrate in 1991, but it has been making a steady recovery ever since and is set to boom now that Slovenia is part of the EU. In terms of manufacturing, Slovenia's main products, and exports, include kitchen appliances, Renault cars, car components, electromechanical mechanisms, furniture, pharmaceuticals and transport services. Slovenia is also a world leader when it comes to manufacturing niche products including Elan − one of the world's largest ski producers − and the Seaway yacht. There are some concerns amongst Slovenes that these manufacturing companies will struggle to survive in the open market of the EU, but the adoption of the euro in 2007 has already simplified business deals for Slovenian companies.

The agricultural sector is a small and relatively insignificant part of Slovenia's economy, with the main activity here centred on the growth of potatoes, cereal and sugar beet, beef production, dairy farming and fishing. Slovenia's mining industry, which formerly played a vital role in the country's economy, has fallen into decline, with many of the remaining mines set to shut down under a phased closure programme. At one time the mining of coal, zinc, lead and uranium was a mainstay of Slovenia's economy and that of Yugoslavia; however, the country's only uranium mine has been closed for some years. Gas and oil are also drilled near Lendava, but in experimental quantities only.

The only clouds on the economic horizon are the structural economic legacies of socialism (such as the powerful trade unions) and the rising domestic costs that have already led some international companies to seek new and more cost-effective bases elsewhere in the expanded EU. Little economic turbulence has resulted from the switch to the euro in 2007, which has enabled more transparency in international trade.

PEOPLE

Trying to tie down who exactly the Slovenes are is a bit tricky given that they have only had their own country since 1991 and that they share land borders with four European countries. Many Slovenes will tell you that they have no idea what exactly constitutes a Slovene. This in a sense is part of the country's attraction as no-one wants to ram down your throat why their nation is the strongest, smartest and most important country in this often volatile part of Europe, something that some of the countries further south could perhaps take a lesson from.

Although it is difficult to pin down what makes someone Slovene, Slovenia is actually one of the most ethnically homogeneous countries in Europe with an overriding majority of people declaring themselves ethnically Slovene. This, though, does not take into account the full picture as many people have at least one parent who is Italian, Hungarian, Croatian or Austrian. Nationalities are fluid in Slovenia, but mercifully not normally a source of conflict.

If you have to generalise about a 'typical Slovene' you could say they have instilled in them a deep sense of the importance of nature, whether or not they live in the countryside. They like nothing better than heading out into the mountains and do so at every opportunity, as you will soon discover with the weekend traffic jams in and out of Ljubljana and Maribor. This back-to-the-earth approach crosses over into their diets as they, unusually for Slavs, enjoy healthy fresh fruit and vegetables and organic produce is much sought after.

THE LINDEN TREE

One of Slovenia's national symbols is the leaf of the linden tree, or *lipa* in Slovene. For Slovenes, and other south Slavs, the tree is a symbol of life, therefore villages have traditionally been constructed around now ancient linden trees. At the geographical centre of a village, the *lipa* also became the heart of the local community's social life, with villagers meeting at the tree. As well as being planted all over the country, the linden tree pops up in music and literature, in the form of poems and children's songs. It was also used in a campaign to promote tourism in the former Yugoslavia in the late 1980s.

With so little acknowledgment of Slovenia on the global political map and with world leaders getting it confused with Slovakia it is perhaps not too surprising that sporting success has become something of an obsession for many Slovenes. The country may not be heralded on television news programmes around the world, but it has certainly managed to force itself onto the sports bulletins by qualifying for both the European Football Championships in 2000 and the Football World Cup in 2002. The European Championships in 2004, though, proved disastrous as Slovenia narrowly missed out on qualifying in a play-off against arch-rival and neighbour Croatia by a single goal. Then there is Primož Peterka, double ski-jumping World Cup winner, and Davo Karničar, the man who managed the first-ever ski descent of Mount Everest in 2000, a sure sign that Slovenes will go to any length to get noticed. In 2004, Celje also became European handball champions. The country secured Olympic golds at the Sydney 2000 games in the rowing and although no golds were won in Athens in 2004 Slovenia rated fifth on the medal table going by a medals-to-population ratio (the Bahamas with their solitary gold came first!). The Slovenes further demonstrated their sporting prowess in 2004 by seeing off the mighty Italians in a football qualifying match in Celje for the 2006 World Cup.

Slovenes tend to be quietly self-confident, which can be mistaken for arrogance. In terms of temperament they have a reputation for being calmer and more rational than some of their more hot-headed 'Balkan brethren' further south. Having said that, once inflamed they can dig their heels in and be intensely stubborn and once offended they stay offended rather than just laughing things off with the clink of a glass so beware of ruffling their feathers. The oft-quoted 'Don't mess with the little guy' line that Slovenes like to trot out has a lot of truth to it.

LANGUAGE

Slovene is the country's official language, although English is also used widely, especially by the younger generation. In the north German is an important language, as is Hungarian in Prekmurje and Italian in Primorska. In different regions 'foreign' words creep into Slovene depending on the proximity to the borders with Austria, Croatia, Hungary or Italy.

Language is still a politically charged subject in the former Yugoslavia. The Croats and Serbs for example speak a very similar language that each passionately claim as their own with steps being taken to 'invent' new words and find differences to separate the two. Slovene, while more different from Serbian and Croatian than they are from each other, is still in the Slavic family of languages and travellers around many of the countries of the 'old east' will recognise more than a few words and have a major advantage when it comes to pronunciation.

Today Slovene is spoken by most of the two million people in the country as well as perhaps up to a million of the Slovene diaspora. People speak Slovene with pride, as it was a language that was suppressed for centuries, but the Austro-Hungarians, Mussolini and Tito were unable to snuff out this tongue. If you take the effort to learn a few Slovene words it will be amply rewarded with smiles of appreciation, though be aware that your pronunciation will probably be so bad, and your effort so unexpected, that you may often just elicit a blank stare as your listener tries to decipher what language you are talking. For an introduction to the basics of Slovene see *Appendix 1*, page 225.

RELIGION

According to the 2002 census 57.8% of Slovenes are Roman Catholic, although many do not adhere strictly to the principles of their faith. From the census data, the next biggest religion in Slovenia is Islam (2.4%), followed by the Christian denominations of Serb Orthodox (2.3) and Evangelist (0.8%). Catholicism and Protestantism (Evangelism) are Slovenia's two domestic faiths, and while a small minority of the country's population adhere to the latter, historically it played an important role in the development of the Slovene language. Today the Protestant minority live mainly in the region of Prekmurje, an area that fell outside the Roman Catholic influence of the Habsburgs, and in some larger cities.

In this same census 10.1% of respondents reported that they were agnostic, 7.1% said they did not know what religion they were, 3.5% said they had no religious affiliation and 16.1% did not disclose information about their faith. Despite the relative homogeneity of the population, there are a further 30 registered religious societies in Slovenia. Given the divisions, hatred and violence with which religion has become synonymous within the Balkans, Slovenes as a rule are pretty tolerant when it comes to religion, though seriously bad publicity was generated thanks to a bid a few years back to block the construction of Ljubljana's first mosque.

There are signs that Catholicism is strengthening its hold on the country, with a conservative cardinal elected in 2006 and proposals to make Catholic teaching compulsory in schools.

EDUCATION

Education is very important to most Slovenes and the country has one of Europe's highest adult (over 15) literacy rates at 99.6% (based on 2001 figures). The main language of education is Slovene. Nine years of elementary school education is compulsory and free from the ages of six to 15. All children between the ages of one and six are entitled to attend pre-school. At the end of their compulsory schooling students have a variety of choices, including continuing in general secondary education until age 18 or 19 or completing vocational training for up to three years. In terms of universities the University of Ljubljana is the oldest in the country, established in 1919. It has since been joined by the University of Maribor and, the newest arrival, the University of Primorska in Koper. Students generally begin university when they are 19 years old and spend three to six years studying. A system of post-graduate education also operates within the country. For the majority of students choosing this path, the starting age is 23. For more information see the Slovenian Ministry for Education website (*www.mszs.si*).

THE NATIONAL FLAG OF SLOVENIA

The Slovenian national flag is a tricolour of white, blue and red, from top to bottom, with a small image of Mount Triglav in the top left-hand corner. It does strongly resemble both the Russian and the Slovakian flags, which has helped cause confusion in the past, especially with 'Slovakia' being so similar in both sound and spelling to 'Slovenia'. There have been calls from some quarters recently for a new national flag to differentiate Slovenia more clearly and ease the confusion, though no consensus has yet emerged on what a new flag would look like. Other unofficial symbols of the country are the ubiquitous *kozolecs* (hay racks) that you will see dotted all over the place, and the traditional beehive panels that you will also see throughout the countryside, particularly in Gorenjska.

For such a small territory Slovenia has an outstanding geographical diversity and biodiversity, with the Pannonian Plains (a large flat plain extending across central and southeastern Europe, found in the east of Slovenia), alpine mountains and Dinaric mountains (the term 'Dinaric' is taken from the Dinara mountain range which forms a border between Slovenia and Croatia in the south; it also separates Croatia from Bosnia and Herzegovina) each comprising 30% of the land, with the Mediterranean covering the remaining 10%. This diversity brings significant changes in altitude – from sea level to 2,864m – and dramatic climate differences (see page 3), where annual rainfall is around 3,000mm on the Alps in the west of the country, yet is just 700mm in the east. To cap it all, around 54% of Slovenia is forested – making it the third-most forested country in Europe – and this compact nation supports more than 7,000 underground Karst caves. Perhaps unsurprisingly, this incredibly varied landscape is home to an enormous number of animal and plant species.

After gaining independence in 1991, Slovenia acted swiftly to protect and conserve the country's natural heritage – which had been threatened (and still is) by pollution from industry and increased road traffic, as well as urban and agricultural development – and passed a number of regulatory laws. One of the most important, as far as visitors are concerned, is the Nature Conservation Act (1999) which prohibits removing or harming plants and animals in the wild; the law also protects their habitats and stipulates the need for responsible tourism when visiting Slovenia's fragile natural attractions, such as the Škocjan Caves and Triglav National Park.

The Slovenian government is proactive in the work of UNESCO, the United Nations Environment Programme (UNEP), the Council of Europe and the EU. Although Slovenia has only one national park – Triglav – it also protects a large proportion of its landscape through regional and landscape parks, nature reserves and the official identification of natural monuments. The Slovenian Ministry of the Environment and Spatial Planning (*www.sigov.si/cgi-bin/wpl/mop/en/index.htm*) is responsible for conservation.

SLOVENIAN WILDLIFE

Gerard Gorman

Slovenia is essentially a land of mountains but, as it sits in a zone where four distinct regions meet – the Carpathian Basin, the Adriatic Sea, the Alps and the Dinaric Mountains – it has a surprising range of wildlife habitats. The country's only national park, Triglav, protects over 800km^2 of high mountain terrain in the Julian Alps. The park's mammals include alpine ibex, chamois, mountain hare and alpine marmot, and there are a few brown bears, wolves and lynxes. Slovenia's population of brown bears has increased over the last 50 years, currently numbering between 500 and 700 individuals, though a certain number can be hunted each year. There are perhaps a few hundred wolves and around 50 lynxes. Key birds in the park are ptarmigan, rock partridge, three-toed woodpecker, alpine accentor, alpine chough and wallcreeper. Elsewhere, avian highlights include hazel grouse, various owls, wallcreeper, citril finch and snowfinch.

Alongside the salt pans of the Sečovlje Salinas, on the Adriatic coast, are tidal mudflats, saltmarsh, reedbeds and scrub. This is an important place for breeding, wintering and passage birds: of the 200 species recorded, 80 have nested in the area.

Adapted from 'Central and Eastern European Wildlife' (see page 232)

2

Practical Information

WHEN TO VISIT (AND WHY)

There really is no bad time to visit Slovenia. In early May, when the spring showers have largely ceased and the temperature often rises above 20°C, blossoming trees, blooming flowers and fresh green leaves give the country's dramatic landscape an ethereal beauty. From spring through to October you can indulge in the diverse range of outdoor activities on offer, from white-water rafting on grade five rapids, hang-gliding and canyoning through to hill walking and mountain climbing. At this time of year the country also offers alfresco living with cafés, bars and restaurants exploding onto the streets in a flurry of tables.

In autumn when the country's bountiful trees start to change colour and shed their leaves Slovenia is an incredibly romantic place to be as you kick your way through the leaves by the Ljubljanica River or take a bracing stroll through some of the most stunning landscapes in Europe. Many of Slovenia's pavement cafés keep their tables out. September vies with May for being the best month to visit many parts of the country, as the chill of winter still seems a long way off.

Winter is the season that tends to put off many would-be visitors, worried that they will be frozen by the ravages of a continental European winter. True, the mercury can plummet, but the weather can also be glorious with clear blue skies accompanying walks across the crisp fresh snow. October to late April are also great months for winter-sports enthusiasts, with ski resorts in the north and west offering exhilarating runs that are largely undiscovered by the rest of Europe. The myriad winter sports on offer at this time include ice-climbing, snow trekking, tobogganing, tubing and snowboarding, as well as both downhill and cross-country skiing.

Slovenia's historic cities, towns and villages are enjoyable places to visit at this time of year, with a host of winter festivals livening up the atmosphere. In the run-up to Christmas seasonal markets spill onto the streets and if you follow the

SLOVENIA GOLF

A recent drive to promote Slovenia as a golf destination has seen standards rise at the country's golf courses. At present there are 18-hole courses at Bled, Olimje, Moravske Toplice, Ptuj and Mokrice Castle, as well as the country's newest course in Ljubljana. Three further 9-hole courses are located in Otočec, Slovenske Konjice and Lipica.

Contact details: **Otočec** (*www.krka-terme.com*); **Lipica** (*www.lipica.org*); **Bled** (*www.golf.bled.si*); **Trnovo** (Ljubljana) (*www.golftrnovo.com*); **Mokrice Castle** (*www.terme-catez.si*); **Ptuj** (*www.golf-ptuj.com*); **Moravske Toplice** (*www.terme3000.si*); **Olimje** (*www.agolf.si*); **Zlati Grič** (Slovenske Konjice) (*www.zlati-gric.si*).

A LONG WEEKEND Ljubljana and day trip to Bled and/or Bohinj.

ONE WEEK Start in Ljubljana, loop up to Bled, Bohinj, Kranjska Gora and over the Vršic Pass to Primorska, coming back north via Škofja Loka to Ljubljana. Alternatively strike out northeast from the capital to Logarska Dolina.

TWO WEEKS Same as one week but continue south to the coast and explore Piran, Portorož, Izola and Koper before heading back to Ljubljana via Lake Cerknica and either the Postojna or the Škocjan caves. An alternative route that heads east/northeast to Celje, Logarska Dolina, Maribor and Ptuj, one of the oldest towns in Slovenia, is also recommended.

ONE MONTH Same as two weeks, but head east through the Kočevski Rog to Novo Mesto. Explore Bela Krajina before striking north for Maribor, Ptuj and Prekmurje. Then head back west through Slovenj Gradec to Logarska Dolina before dropping down through Kamnik to Ljubljana.

On the longer trips there is plenty of time for stopping off at a *terme*, seeking out a rural *gostilna* or indulging in adventure sports.

locals and wrap up warm, bring a brolly and pepper your visit with plenty of glasses of warming mulled wine, then you will really get into the festive spirit. At New Year, Ljubljana is engulfed by a giant street party.

Slovenia's lively cultural and artistic scene also ensures that there is always plenty to do, with a string of events and festivals taking place year round (see *Public holidays and festivals*, page 34).

HIGHLIGHTS

The 'Europe in Miniature' eulogies of the tourist office and many travel writers do for once really ring true. You could quite easily spend a month in Slovenia and only scratch the surface. When planning a trip to Slovenia it is essential not to underestimate how much there is to see and do and then to let its compact size and good transport infrastructure work with you to get the best out of your trip.

Ljubljana is a must-do, and a holiday that uses the city only as a brief entry and exit point will be all the poorer for it. Allow at least two or three days here, more if you can, especially from May to September when the days are long and the pavement café tables are out.

Then there's the rest of the country's towns and cities. Maribor is well worth a visit for its culture and Old Town, while Ptuj is remarkably attractive. Celje and Novo Mesto may not be as aesthetically cohesive, but still have their charms and plenty to see and do, while the list of worthwhile historic towns would not be complete without mentioning Kamnik, Radovljica, Slovenj Gradec and, of course, the striking Venetian town of Piran on the coast.

It is the countryside that many people come for and there is much more on offer than a quick day trip to Bled hints at. The Julian Alps and Triglav National Park are the blockbusters and simply must not be missed, with the famous lake at Bled and the equally impressive alpine stretch of water at Bohinj. Also try venturing into the Kamniške Savinje Alps, down the Soča Valley and through the wild expanse of the Kočevski Rog, one of Europe's wildest forests. Then there is

Logarska Dolina, a superlative-defying alpine valley that you will simply never forget, while the Adriatic coastline offers another world altogether.

Admiring the scenery is one thing but make sure, if you are fit and able, to hurl yourself into it: scale the peaks, ride the rapids, fling yourself off a bungee jump or tumble down a mountain on two wheels. Slovenia is an adventure-lover's paradise with Bovec, Kranjska Gora and Kobarid all good bases for adrenaline junkies.

It may be small in size, but below ground the country delves on and on with over 7,000 caves. The Postojna Caves are well and truly on the tourist map and deservedly so, but the Škocjan Caves are if anything more stunning, a Tolkienesque netherworld that delights and intrigues in equal measure. Many of the smaller caves around Slovenia lie virtually untouched by tourists.

Culture vultures will not be disappointed by the first-class museums in all of Slovenia's major cities, with Ljubljana being the obvious highlight. You will also find ancient monasteries, rural churches with stunning Gothic frescoes and unusual museums (like the bee-keeping museum in Radovljica) sprinkled around the country. Slovenes love their music, literature and art; this is after all a country with a holiday dedicated to the national poet France Prešeren, so there is plenty of intellectual stimulus on offer too.

Then there are the castles, with hundreds scattered around the country acting as a constant reminder of Slovenia's rich and chequered history. Highlights include the sturdy fortress in Ljubljana and the picturesque ramparts high above Bled, not to mention the chance to actually spend the night in your very own castle at Mokrice or Otočec. When all the sightseeing gets too much then there are always the countless spas, or *terme*. Here bubbling hot water gushes from the earth and you can join Slovenes frolicking around in the regenerative waters, maybe popping off for a massage afterwards. This is a country where spas are no mere fad.

After a dip in the spa an epicurean treat awaits. This is one of Europe's most underrated wine-producing countries and you can savour a wide range of quality reds and whites, not to mention some good sparkling wines and some fiery *digestifs*. On the plate there is the bountiful seafood of the Adriatic, the *pršut* (air-dried ham) of the Karst and the tempting desserts of Prekmurje. Once you have travelled around and tried Slovenia's myriad attractions, you may just want to pop back for another visit, as there is always something to see in a corner of Europe that manages to cram so much in, making it hard to believe its small size.

HIKING IN SLOVENIA

Walkers from around the globe are drawn to Slovenia by the myriad opportunities that the country offers to hike amidst a dramatic landscape of forests, hills and mountains. One of the most difficult questions facing ramblers though is where to go. The *Hiking in Slovenia* brochure produced by the Slovenian Tourist Board (see *www.slovenia.info* for your nearest office) is a good starting point for anyone who wants to plan an independent walking holiday in the country. It gives an overview of 33 trails around the country, which range from the challenging 2,864m ascent of Mount Triglav to easy circular walks through the Vintgar Gorge in Gorenjska to the 15km walk along the Brežice mountain path in Dolenjska. Slovenia's mountains are much higher than those in the UK and anyone planning high-level walks should consider hiring a mountain guide – contact the **Slovenian Mountain Guides Association** (*www.zdruzenje-gvs.si*) for more information.

TOUR OPERATORS

The Slovenian Tourist Board can provide a full list of tour operators based in your country of residence. Contact details for your closest office can be found at their website (*www.slovenia.info*). Kompas is a Slovenian company with representatives at various offices around the globe, but only those in Slovenia itself, and in Croatia and Switzerland, work directly with the general public.

UK A large number of UK travel agents offer package holidays and city breaks in Slovenia. They can also assist with independent travel arrangements. In the UK flights commonly leave from Gatwick, Heathrow or Manchester, although some serve other regional airports.

Balkan Holidays Sofia Hse, 19 Conduit St, London W1S 2BH; ☎ 0845 130 1114; www.balkanholidays.co.uk. Regional specialists with both package deals & hotel- or flight-only options.

Crystal Holidays Kings Pl, 12–42 Wood St, Kingston upon Thames KT1 1JY; ☎ 0870 888 0252; e lakesres@crystalholidays.co.uk; www.crystalholidays.co.uk

Exodus Travels Grange Mills, Weir Rd, London SW12 0NE; ☎ 0845 863 9600; e info@exodus.co.uk; www.exodus.co.uk

First Choice ☎ 0871 200 7799; www.firstchoice.co.uk. The company have started selling skiing holidays in Slovenia online & through their network of travel shops.

Holiday Options 3rd Floor, 49 The Martlets, Burgess Hill, West Sussex RH15 9NJ; ☎ 0844 477 0451; e info@holidayoptions.co.uk; www.holidayoptions.co.uk

Inghams Travel 10–18 Putney Hill, London SW15 6AX; ☎ 020 8780 4400; www.inghams.co.uk

Just Slovenia Woodlands End, Mells, Frome, Somerset BA11 3QD; ☎ 01373 814230; e info@justslovenia.co.uk; www.justslovenia.co.uk. Tailormade holidays from hotels to farmstays.

Major Travel Plc Fortress Grove, London NW5 2HB; ☎ 0871 855 3030; e sales@majortravel.co.uk; www.majortravel.co.uk

Regent Holidays Mezzanine Suite, Froomsgate Hse, Rupert St, Bristol BS1 2QJ; ☎ 0845 277 3387; f 0117 925 4866; e regent@regent-holidays.co.uk; www.regent-holidays.co.uk. Well-established operator offering city breaks, group tours & fly-drive options, as well as tailor-made holidays.

W A Shearings Miry Lane, Wigan, Lancs WN3 4AG; ☎ 01942 824824; e res@washearings.com; www.washearings.com

Slovene Dream PO Box 49926, London SE5 8WS; ☎ 020 7737 3054; f 020 7738 4911; e info@slovenedream.com; www.slovenedream.com

Solo's Holidays 54–58 High St, Edgware HA8 7EJ; ☎ 0870 499 2233; e travelsolos@ solosholidays.co.uk; www.solosholidays.co.uk

Thermalia Travel 1a Stanmore Hill, Stanmore, Middx HA7 4BL; ☎ 0870 165 9420; e sales@thermalia.co.uk; www.thermalia.co.uk

Vamos Travel 2 Styles Close, Leamington Spa, Warwks CV31 1LS; ☎ 0870 762 4017; f 0870 762 1016; e info@vamostravel.com; www.vamostravel.com

IRELAND

Crystal Holidays 18–19 Duke St, Dublin 2; ☎ +353 01 433 1010; f +353 01 670 8910; e info@crystalholidays.ie; www.crystalholidays.ie

Falcon Holidays Block 5, Westland Sq, Pearse St, Dublin 2; ☎ +353 01 850 946 164; www.falconholidays.ie

---

MOUNTAIN HUTS

For hikers and mountaineers Slovenia also has a network of around 170 mountain huts, which are dotted at high altitudes around the country. As a rule of thumb huts are open between June and October, although those at lower levels may open for an additional month or so. Staying overnight at a hut costs from €10 per person. For a list of mountain huts check the website of the Slovene Alpine Association (*www.pzs.si*), who also publish this information in printed form.

Topflight Jervis Hse, 3rd Floor, Jervis St, Dublin 1;
📞 +353 01 240 1700, f +353 01 240 1707;
e info@topflight.ie; www.topflight.ie

AUSTRIA

ESTA Europe A-1030 Wien; 📞 +43 01 378 2835;
f +43 01 378 2329; www.esta.net
Gruber Reisen Idlhofgasse 5–7; A-8020 Graz;
📞 +43 0316 7089–0; f +43 0316 7089–71;
www.gruberreisen.at

Reisebüro Idealtours GmbH Marktstrasse 6B,
A-6230 Brixlegg; 📞 +43 053 376170;
www.idealtours.at
Ruefa Reisen Dresdnerstrasse 81–85, A-1200
Wien; 📞 +43 0810 300400; www.ruefa.at

GERMANY

Berge & Meer Touristik GmbH Andreestrasse
27, 56578 Rengsdorf; 📞 01805 671 010;
www.berge-meer.de
Eberhardt Travel GmbH Zschoner Ring 30,
01723 Kesselsdorf; 📞 +49 035 2049 2112; f +49
035 2049 2115; e info@eberhardt-travel.de;
www.eberhardt-travel.de
Reisebüro Eberhardt GmbH Bahnhofstrasse 2,
75172 Pforzheim; 📞 +49 072 3138 0243; f +49 072
3138 0218; www.reisen.eberhardt-travel.de
Fit Reisen GmbH 📞 +49 069 405 8850;
www.fitreisen.de

Gemainsam Schöner Reisen GmbH 📞 0800
119 6959; www.gsr-urlaub.de
ITS Reisen GmbH 📞 +49 018 0500 2344;
www.its.de
Neckermann Reisen Thomas-Cook-Platz 1,
61440 Oberursel; 📞 +49 061 716 500; f +49 061
7165 2125; www7.neckermann-reisen.de
SEITZ Reisen GmbH Ruchelnheimerstrasse 15,
63743 Aschaffenburg-Obernau; 📞 +49 060 288 011;
f +49 060 285 809; e busreisen@seitz-ab.de;
www.seitzreisen-ab.de

ITALY

Agestea Srl Via Liside 4, 70126 Bari; 📞 +39 080
595 8111; f +39 080 592 8200; www.agestea.net
Aurora Viaggi Srl Via Milano 20, 34122 Trieste;
📞 +39 040 631 300; f +39 040 365 587;
e info@auroraviaggi.com; www.auroraviaggi.com

Aviomar 📞 +39 02 583 944; www.aviomar.it
Firma Via Nuova Circonvallazione 67, 47900
Rimini; 📞 +39 0541 760 311; f +39 0541 760 300;
www.firmatour.it

SWITZERLAND

Kompas Travel Tour Operating Alpenstrasse 1,
6004 Lucerne; 📞 +41 041 418 8030; f +41 041 418
8036; e mail@kompastravel.ch;
www.kompastravel.ch

Unique Travel Lerchenstrasse 16, 8027 Zürich;
📞 +41 043 344 3232; f +41 043 344 3233;
e welcome@uniquetravel.ch; www.uniquetravel.ch
Walliser-Reisen AG Weiernstrasse 20, CH-8355
Aadorf; 📞 +41 052 245 1777; f +41 2 245 1779;
e info@walliserreisen.ch; www.walliserreisen.ch

Practical Information TOUR OPERATORS

2

RED TAPE

Slovenia adopted the Schengen agreement at the end of 2007. Theoretically it is possible to travel between fellow Schengen countries without a passport. For most visitors Slovenia's border formalities are nominal and the majority simply need a valid passport for stays of less than three months. Citizens from EU countries and those from Croatia and Switzerland can enter Slovenia for up to 30 days with a national identity card. Visa requirements for those travelling to Slovenia from a country that has not signed the Schengen agreement vary. At present those from Australia, New Zealand, Canada and the USA can stay for up to 90 days without a visa, while South Africans need a visa to enter Slovenia. Visa requirements are subject to change and non-EU citizens are advised to check the Slovenian Ministry of Foreign Affairs website (*www.mzz.gov.si*).

In accordance with EU regulations, citizens from EU member states can freely bring tobacco and alcohol into Slovenia for personal use. For non-EU members duty-free rules still apply. These restrict the import of tobacco to 200 cigarettes or 250g of tobacco, or 50 cigars; 2l of wine, 1l of spirits, 50g of perfume and 250ml of eau de toilette can also be imported.

Ⓔ EMBASSIES

SLOVENIAN EMBASSIES OVERSEAS

Australia Level 6, St George's Bldg, 60 Marcus Clarke St, Canberra, ACT 2601; ☏ +61 02 6243 4830; f +61 02 6243 4827

Austria Nibelungengasse 13, A-1010 Vienna; ☏ +43 01 586 1309; f +43 01 586 1265; e vdu@gov.si

Belgium Av Louise 130A/VI, 1050 Brussels; ☏ +32 02 643 4950; f +32 02 644 2079

Canada 150 Metcalfe St, Suite 2101, Ottawa, Ontario K2P 1P1; ☏ +1 613 565 5781; f +1 613 565 5783; e vot@mzz-dkp.gov.si

Denmark Amaliegade 6, 2nd Floor, 1256 Copenhagen; ☏ +45 33 730 120; f +45 33 150 607

France 28 rue Bois-le-Vent, 75116 Paris; ☏ +33 01 44 96 50 71; f +33 01 45 24 67 05

Germany Hausvogteiplatz 3–4, 10117 Berlin; ☏ +49 030 206 145/0; f +49 030 206 145/70; e vbn@mzz-dkp.gov.si

Ireland Morrison Chambers, 2nd Floor, 32 Nassau St, Dublin 2; ☏ +353 01 670 5240; f +353 01 670 5243; e vdb@mzz-dkp.gov.si

Italy Via Leonardo Pisano 10, I-00197 Rome; ☏ +39 06 8091 4310; f +39 06 8081 471; e vri@mzz-dkp.gov.si

Russia ul Mala Dimitrovka 14/1, 127006 Moscow; ☏ +7 495 737 6355; f +7 495 69415 68; e vmo@gov.si

Spain Hermanos Becquer 7–2, 28006 Madrid; ☏ +34 091 411 6893; f +34 091 564 6057; e vma@mzz-dkp.gov.si

Switzerland Schwanengasse 9/II, 3011 Bern; ☏ +41 031 311 4421; f +41 031 310 9000; e vbe@mzz-dkp.gov.si

UK 10 Little College St, London SW1P 3SH; ☏ +44 020 7222 5700; f +44 020 7222 5277; e vlo@gov.si

USA 1525 New Hampshire Av NW, Washington, DC 20036, ☏ +1 202 667 5363; f +1 202 667 4563; e vwa@gov.si

OVERSEAS EMBASSIES AND CONSULATES IN SLOVENIA

All of the embassies and consulates listed below are located in Ljubljana.

Australian Consulate Trg Republike 3/XII; ☏ 01 425 4252; f 01 426 4721

Austrian Embassy Prešernova 23; ☏ 01 479 0700; f 01 252 1717; e austroamb@austrianembassy.si; www.austriantrade.si

Belgian Embassy Trg Republike 3; ☏ 01 200 6010; f 01 426 6395

Canadian Consulate Miklošičeva 19; ☏ 01 430 3570; f 01 430 3575

Danish Embassy Tivolski 48; ☏ 01 438 0800; f 01 431 7417

French Embassy Barjanska 1; ☏ 01 479 0400; f 01 424 0465; e info@ambafrance.si; www.ambafrance.si

German Embassy Prešernova 27; ✆ 01 479 0300; f 01 425 0899

Irish Embassy Poljanski nasip 6; ✆ 01 300 8970; f 01 282 1096; e ljubljanaembassy@dfa.ie

Italian Embassy Snežniška 8; ✆ 01 426 2194; f 01 425 3302; e amblubiana@siol.net

New Zealand Consulate Verovškova 57; ✆ 01 580 3055; f 01 568 3526; e janja.bratos@lek.si

Russian Embassy Tomšičeva 9; ✆ 01 425 6875; f 01 425 6878

South African Consulate Pražakova 4; ✆ 01 200 6300; f 01 200 6434

Spanish Embassy Trnovski pristan 24; ✆ 01 420 2330; f 01 420 2333

Swiss Embassy Trg Republike 3/VI; ✆ 01 200 8640; f 01 200 8669

UK Embassy Trg Republike 3; ✆ 01 200 3910; f 01 425 0174; e info@british-embassy.sil; www.british-embassy.si

USA Embassy Prešernova 31; ✆ 01 200 5500; f 01 200 5555; e email@usembassy.si; www.usembassy.si

✈ GETTING THERE AND AWAY

BY AIR Ljubljana's Jože Pučnik Airport (*Zgornji Brnik 130A, 4210 Brnik-Aerodrom;* ✆ *04 206 1981;* f *04 202 1220;* e *info@lju-airport.si; www.lju-airport.si*), located 23km northwest of the city centre, is small by European standards, though it is rapidly expanding as tourist and business demand grows. Facilities in the departures hall are, at present, better than those in arrivals, with an ATM, car rental, currency exchange, bar, telephone-operated hotel booking system, restaurants, telephones, toilets and shops. The airport terminal is well served by taxis and bus services. A growing clutch of airlines fly to Jože Pučnik providing the city with direct connections to the likes of Amsterdam, Belgrade, Berlin, Brussels, Budapest, Copenhagen, Dublin, Frankfurt, Helsinki, Istanbul, London, Manchester, Moscow, Munich, Ohrid, Paris, Podgorica, Prague, Priština, Sarajevo, Skopje, Split, Tel Aviv, Tirana, Vienna and Zürich. Charter flights also serve the capital's airport.

There are now two budget connections to the UK, with easyJet and Ryanair (see below). Adria Airways has responded to the new competition by making its prices more competitive and by constantly reviewing its routes. The airline currently flies direct to Ljubljana from Gatwick, Manchester, Birmingham and Dublin.

Adria Airways Zgornji Brnik 130A, 4210 Brnik-Aerodrom; ✆ 04 259 4245; www.adria-airways.com

Austrian Airlines Zgornji Brnik 130A, 4210 Brnik-Aerodrom; ✆ 04 202 0122; www.aua.com

Czech Airlines Zgornji Brnik 130A, 4210 Brnik-Aerodrom; ✆ 04 206 1750; www.czechairlines.com

easyJet Zgornji Brnik 130A, 4210 Brnik-Aerodrom; ✆ 04 206 1677; www.easyJet.com

JAT Airways Slomskova 1, 1000 Ljubljana; ✆ 01 231 4340; www.jat.com

Malév Zgornji Brnik 130A, 4210 Brnik-Aerodrom; ✆ 04 206 1676; www.malev.hu

Turkish Airlines PO Box 76, Zgornji Brnik 130A, 4210 Brnik-Aerodrom; ✆ 04 206 1680; www.thy.com

In June 2007, Ryanair (*www.ryanair.com*) began operating flights from London Stansted to Maribor Airport (*Letališka 10, Orehova Vas;* ✆ *02 629 1175;* f *02 629 1253;* e *info@maribor-airport.si; www.maribor-airport.si*). This has really opened up the east of the country and Slovenia's second city for visitors from the UK.

⚍ BY TRAIN Slovenian Railways (*Slovenske Železnice;* ✆ *01 291 3332;* e *potnik.info@ slo-zeleznice.si; www.slo-zeleznice.si*) operates Slovenia's train services and the rail network connects the country to the rest of Europe via Germany, Italy, Austria, Switzerland, Hungary and Greece, as well as countries that were formerly part of Yugoslavia. Key international services include the *Mimara* (Munich–Zagreb via Salzburg, Villach, Jesenice and Ljubljana), the *Emona* (Vienna–Ljubljana via Graz), the *Simplon Express* (Geneva–Zagreb via Ljubljana), the *Citadella* (Budapest–

Ljubljana), the *Drava Express* (Budapest–Venice via Ljubljana) and the *Pohorje* (Graz–Ljubljana). The high-speed *Casanova* travels between Ljubljana and Venice (Mestre and Santa Lucia) once daily, missing out the Trieste switchback and cutting journey times by 90 minutes to around four hours. There are also frequent rail services to Slovenia from Belgrade, Karlovac, Milan, Pula, Rijeka, Rome, Skopje, Thessaloniki, Trieste and Zürich.

Slovenske Železnice have invested in their rolling stock in recent years and the majority of their trains are comfortable and modern, with sleeping berths available on some overnight services. Buying a ticket within Slovenia should be straightforward as many sales agents speak English. However, one way to avoid confusion is to write down the departure time and the train number listed on the timetable before buying your ticket or making a reservation.

Rail passes/ticket discounts Standard rail tickets for international services to and from Slovenia are not as expensive as those in many western European countries, but are still not cheap. They are more expensive than the bus, when you consider the distance travelled. A direct train from Ljubljana to Zagreb costs around €12 (2½ hours), Ljubljana to Munich €68 (6½ hours) and Ljubljana to Budapest €59 (8 hours).

A single-country Inter-Rail Pass is available for three–eight days' travel in one month. Standard fees charged in the UK are £24–57 for those aged 12–25 and £36–87 for over 26s. Global Inter-Rail Passes valid in all the countries participating in the scheme are available from five days' travel out of ten up to a month of unlimited use. Prices range from £117 to £292 for those aged 12–25 and £182 to £438 for over 26s. Discounted passes are available for the under 12s. For further information contact **Rail Europe** (↘ +44 08708 371 371; *www.raileurope.co.uk, or www.raileurope.com for the USA and Canada).*

🚐 **BY BUS** Ljubljana's bus station (*Avtobusna postaja; Trg Osvobodilne fronte 4;* ↘ *090 934 230 (€0.78 per min);* **e** *avtobusna.postaja@ap-ljubljana.si; www.ap-ljubljana.si;* ⏲ *05.30–21.00 daily)* is served by an extensive number of national and international services, with connections to destinations all over Slovenia and neighbouring Croatia. There are also a large number of routes operating from the other states in the former Yugoslavia – Bosnia and Herzegovina, Macedonia and Serbia and Montenegro. International services also link the Slovenian capital to Austria, Hungary, Denmark, Sweden, Germany, France, Belgium and Italy.

Croatia and Slovenia are particularly well connected with coaches from Rijeka, Pula, Rovinj and Poreč in Croatian Istria running to Koper, Piran and Portorož on Slovenia's Adriatic coast, these services being more frequent during the summer months. A limited number of international services also operate between other destinations in Slovenia and Croatia; these include services to and from Varaždin in Croatia, from Celje, and Ptuj. The Croatian capital, Zagreb, is also accessible by bus from Ptuj and Maribor.

Bus fares are reasonably priced, but not cheap: a 2½-hour journey to Zagreb from Ljubljana costs approximately €15 and a 2½-hour journey to Trieste from Ljubljana €10, while an eight-hour journey to Belgrade from the Slovenian capital will set you back around €40.

🚗 **BY CAR** Slovenia is easily accessible by car from much of mainland Europe. The key routes from Austria include the E651 which links Ljubljana to Villach, the E652/E61 from Klagenfurt and the E57/E59 from Graz. From Italy the E61/E70 connects Trieste to Ljubljana, while the E70 serves Zagreb in neighbouring Croatia and the E57/E71 extends to Budapest in Hungary. Since Slovenia became part of the EU in 2004 procedures at its borders with Italy, Austria and Hungry have become more relaxed, although you still need to make sure that you have a valid passport or national identity card, the correct papers for your car and international vehicle insurance (meaning that those with cars registered outside the EU need to purchase a Green Card). If you are planning to travel to Slovenia from the UK you will obviously have to cross either the North Sea or the English Channel, with the former providing the most direct route.

Some typical road distances from Ljubljana include: Klagenfurt 79km, Trieste 110km, Zagreb 135km, Graz 202km, Venice 249km, Salzburg 290km, Vienna 395km, Munich 430km, Budapest 491km and Belgrade 507km.

BY SEA Marinas in Portorož, Izola and Koper have facilities for yachts. During the tourist season two passenger catamaran services, Prince of Venice and Venezia Lines, run between Venice and the Slovenian coast.

Prince of Venice services operate from March to October, shuttling passengers between Venice and Izola (approximate journey time 2½ hours; price €45–70). Tickets can be purchased from Kompas travel agents in Slovenia.

The Venezia Lines service from Venice docks at Piran. Tickets for this service can be purchased online, from the company's call centre or from Atlas Express travel agents. Tickets cost from €43 single and €85 return.

If you arrive in Slovenia at either Izola or Piran you can take a local bus to Koper from where regular train and bus services connect the coast to Ljubljana.

Marina Portorož Cesta Solinarjev 8, 6320 Portorož; ☎ 05 676 1100; f 05 676 1210; e marina.portoroz@marinap.si; www.marinap.si
Marina Izola Tomažičeva 10, 6310 Izola; ☎ 05 640 0250; f 05 641 8346; e info@marinaizola.com; www.marinaizola.com
Marina Koper Kopališko nabrežje 5, 6000 Koper; ☎ 05 662 6100; f 05 662 6161; e info@marina-koper.si; www.marina-koper.si
Prince of Venice PE Portorož, Obala 41, 6320 Portorož; ☎ 05 617 8000; f 05 674 7258;

e portoroz@kompas.si; www.kompas-online.net/ pages/CruisesFerries/prince.aspx
Venezia Lines ☎ +39 041 520 5473; f +39 041 277 8335; e info@venezialines.com; www.venezialines.com
Kompas (for Prince of Venice services) Pražakova 4, Ljubljana; ☎ 01 200 6111; e info@kompas.si; www.kompas.si
Atlas Express (for Venezia Lines services) Obala 55, Portorož; ☎ 05 674 6772; f 05 674 5597; e atlas.portorz@siol.net

✚ HEALTH *with Dr Felicity Nicholson*

There are no specific vaccine requirements for visitors to Slovenia. However, it is advisable to ensure that you are up to date with tetanus, diphtheria and polio which comes as the all-in-one vaccine Revaxis which lasts for ten years. Vaccination against hepatitis A is also recommended. For those visiting more rural parts of Slovenia, typhoid vaccine may also be recommended. Whilst tap water is deemed safe to drink, if you have any concerns it is still wise to be cautious and drink bottled water to avoid an upset stomach. Every large town or city in Slovenia has a health centre, generally open 07.00–19.00 Monday–Friday, and a pharmacy (*lekarna*) open 07.00–20.00 Monday–Friday, 08.00–13.00 Saturday. If you urgently require medication the prescribing doctor should be able to help you find a reasonably close 24-hour pharmacy.

Emergency medical care for EU citizens is free upon the production of a valid **European Health Insurance Card (EHIC)**. UK residents can apply for the EHIC card online at the Department of Health website (*www.dh.gov.uk/travellers or www.ehic.org.uk*). It can also be obtained from the post office with form T7. For UK citizens a passport is sufficient, as long as treatment is given in a state-funded hospital or health centre. Other non-emergency treatment or consultations and medicine must be paid for. Citizens from Croatia, Romania and Bulgaria are also entitled to free emergency medical care in Slovenia.

Visitors from countries that do not have a reciprocal healthcare agreement with Slovenia must pay for all of their medical treatment, including emergency care. Your national health ministry can tell you if any mutual agreements exist. Regardless of any health agreements that may be in place, all international visitors to Slovenia should take out travel insurance with an adequate level of medical cover before travelling to the country. This is important in case you need emergency repatriation.

A few simple precautions before you leave for Slovenia will help you safeguard your health during your trip. If you take prescribed medication make sure you pack it and keep a separate note of the drug's generic name and not just its brand. This will make replacement easier. Those who are travelling for a long time should consider going for a dental check-up. Taking an adequate supply of contact lenses or a spare pair of glasses is also advisable.

In Slovenia itself one of the biggest risks to your health is the sun. It can get surprisingly hot in the cities and along the coast during the summer months, making it essential to pack light clothing that allows your skin to breathe, sunglasses that provide protection against UV rays, a sunhat and plenty of suntan lotion. If you forget any of these items you will be able to buy them in any town or city.

Those who are intending to travel in the countryside, particularly in forested areas, need to consider the following health risks.

TICK-BORNE ENCEPHALITIS Tick-borne encephalitis is a viral infection, transmitted by ticks found in densely forested parts of Slovenia, which affects the central nervous system. Vaccination against tick-borne encephalitis may be available in the UK (on a named-patient basis) and comprises a series of three injections that can be administered over three to four weeks. Take advice from your doctor or a reputable travel clinic. If you are planning on spending a prolonged time in forested areas you should seek appropriate medical advice before leaving. Other precautionary measures include avoiding tick-infested areas from April to August when the risk of infection is at its highest, wearing clothing that covers your skin (including tucking trousers into boots and wearing a hat) and wearing an insect repellent containing DEET (N, N diethyl-m-toluamide). Permethrin-based insect repellents can also be applied to your clothing and camping gear, although this should never be put onto your skin. These repellent agents are also effective against Slovenian mosquitoes, which can give you painful bites but do not carry malaria. You can also get tick-borne encephalitis from unpasteurised dairy products and these should be avoided. Ticks should ideally be removed as soon as possible as leaving ticks on the body increases the chance of infection. They should be removed with special tick tweezers that can be bought in good travel shops. Failing that you can use your fingernails by grasping the tick as close to your body as possible and pulling steadily and firmly away at right angles to your skin. The tick will then come away complete as long as you do not jerk or twist. If possible douse the wound with alcohol (any spirit will do) or iodine. Irritants (eg: Olbas oil) or lit cigarettes are to be discouraged since they can cause the ticks to regurgitate and therefore increase the risk of disease. It is best to get a travelling companion to check you for ticks and if you are travelling with small children remember to check their heads, and particularly behind the ears. If you think you have been bitten by a tick then seek medical advice locally.

LYME DISEASE Lyme disease is a bacterial infection transmitted by ticks that have fed on an infected host animal. Again the risk of infection is at its highest in forested areas between April and August. Symptoms associated with Lyme disease include a red abrasion at the site where the tick bit, which can be up to 7.5cm in diameter and is often clear in the centre. Fever, headaches, a stiff neck, muscle pain, inflamed joints and extreme lethargy are also amongst the symptoms. If you have any of these symptoms or think you have been bitten by a tick you should always seek medical advice as soon as possible, as Lyme disease is treatable with antibiotics.

HEPATITIS A The hepatitis A virus attacks the human liver and, while it is rare, can affect anyone. After an incubation period of three to five weeks, infected individuals display flu-like symptoms and experience fever, abdominal pains, nausea, lack of appetite, physical exhaustion and jaundice. The length of illness and convalescence varies and can be prolonged, but the majority of patients make a complete recovery. The disease is transmitted through food or water contaminated with human faeces, so it is essential to maintain a high level of personal hygiene when travelling. Restaurants in Slovenia conform to high standards, so visitors do not normally need to worry about what they are eating or drinking. Hikers or climbers intending to drink water from streams should either boil it or treat it with purifying tablets. If you have any doubts about the quality of the water that you are drinking opt for bottled mineral water. Vaccination against hepatitis A is usually recommended for those who travel frequently. Injections are administered in two stages. The first dose gives protection for about one year, and a subsequent booster dose extends this to around 25 years. Those who have already suffered with hepatitis A are immune to the disease.

RABIES Rabies is a viral disease transmitted in the saliva of an infected animal via a bite or a lick on an open wound. Although it is extremely rare, rabies does occur in Slovenia. Untreated rabies is always fatal. The best defence against rabies is prevention, making it essential to avoid handling wild or stray animals. If you are bitten, scratched or licked over an open wound by any warm-blooded animal, wash the wound immediately with soap and water and apply an antiseptic. Go immediately for medical help to get post-exposure treatment. For those who intend to work with animals or for anyone who is more than 24 hours away from medical help then pre-exposure vaccine is recommended. Three doses of vaccine can be given over a 21-day schedule and makes post-exposure treatment much easier. Whether or not you have had the pre-exposure vaccine you should always seek medical help as soon as possible.

TRAVEL CLINICS AND HEALTH INFORMATION A full list of current travel clinic websites worldwide is available from the International Society of Travel Medicine on www.istm.org. For other journey preparation information, consult www.tripprep.com. Information about various medications may be found on www.emedicine.com.

SAFETY

Slovenia is a safe country. Crime rates in its urban and rural areas are low, especially when compared with those in most European countries, and violent crimes are rare. Travellers should take sensible precautions to safeguard their valuables, as tourists occasionally fall prey to pickpockets and handbag snatchers. Simple and effective deterrents against crime include not leaving valuables unattended, keeping purses and wallets in inside pockets, and carrying any bags securely while holding them so that they are not facing the road. Anyone unfortunate enough to become a victim of crime must report it to the police immediately; this is especially important if you intend to make a travel insurance claim when you return home. National embassies or consulates can also provide useful help and information.

Slovenia is a small country and all generations are used to foreign visitors. Although some older people may think that it is strange for women to travel alone they will always be treated politely and with respect. Female travellers should not experience any specific difficulties, but sensible precautions should be taken to avoid potentially dangerous situations, eg: not meeting strange men in secluded places. The usual precautions should also be taken against sexually transmitted diseases.

DISABLED VISITORS

Visitors with disabilities will find that the facilities available to them, as in any country in the world, will vary greatly from town to town and from hotel to hotel. Disabled parking spaces and bedrooms are becoming increasingly commonplace, particularly in bigger towns and more expensive properties including Slovenia's thermal spas. Many public telephones have also been adapted for disabled users and pedestrian lights frequently beep when it is safe to cross the road. It is less common, however, to find disabled toilets in restaurants, cafés and bars. Disabled visitors are advised to contact the local tourist information centre in the destinations that they are planning to visit in order to explain any special needs that they have and to check what facilities are available to them locally.

FAMILY TRAVEL

Slovenia is a great family destination, particularly for those travelling with older children. The great outdoors offers opportunities for everything from pony trekking, gentle walks and cycling to more adventurous sports like rafting, mountain biking and hill walking. Slovenia's thermal spas have also been created or renovated with families in mind and it is common to find children's pools and waterslides alongside the thermal pools and therapies.

Accommodation in family hotel rooms, private rooms, apartments and tourist farms can be reasonably cost effective. Children and families are also frequently given discounts on everything from transport and museum entrance fees to ski passes and skiing lessons. While children are more than welcome in most restaurants don't expect to find a kids' menu. Most restaurateurs won't mind if smaller children share a meal and will provide an extra plate.

GAY AND LESBIAN TRAVELLERS

The gay and lesbian scene in Slovenia is not as prominent as in many European countries but there is one, and while attitudes towards homosexuality amongst the older generation are often far from enlightened, being gay or lesbian is becoming more socially acceptable. Although attitudes are improving, especially in the big cities, public displays of affection between gay or lesbian partners are still not the norm.

The first Ljubljana Gay and Lesbian Pride Parade was staged in 2000, and this annual event has been credited with changing attitudes in the city. The gay and lesbian communities in Ljubljana showed that they were not willing to be pushed around during the so-called 'water protest' a few years ago when the new owner of Galerija decided to axe it as a gay bar. For months the gay community showed its resolve by occupying the money-spinning outdoor tables and ordering only water. This defiant face of gay and lesbian culture was given a very visible face by Sestre (Sister), the transvestite trio who won the contest to represent their country at the 2002 Eurovision Song Contest, much to the chagrin of the more conservative elements of Slovenian society.

WHAT TO TAKE

Slovenia is a modern and prosperous country where you can buy almost anything that you might need. Therefore your only essentials are a valid passport or acceptable national identity card, a visa (if necessary), transport tickets, travel insurance documents, money (debit or credit cards, travellers' cheques or euros), EHIC or other documentation showing an entitlement to healthcare, driving licence (national or international depending on country-specific requirements) and, if appropriate, student discount cards and a Hostelling International (international youth hostel) card. It is also a good idea to keep photocopies of important documents such as passports, visas and travel insurance policies in case they need to be replaced.

It is advisable to pack for the weather, sticking to light clothes that let your skin breathe in the summer, with sunscreen, sunglasses and a hat all essential items. In the winter you will need a warm and waterproof coat, and a lighter jacket in the spring and autumn. It is also sensible to take a light waterproof raincoat or an umbrella at any time of year. Ljubljana, Maribor and the Adriatic coast have a buzzing nightlife scene, so you might want to pack your favourite clubbing gear. Anyone intending to dine out in some of the country's more expensive restaurants should pack smart casual clothes, though formal wear is not normally required except for specific business functions.

Plug sockets in Slovenia are of the two-pin, round-pronged European variety; if you are travelling with electrical items you may want to take an adapter with you. While you will be able to buy them at your departure airport, they are hard to come by once in Slovenia.

$ MONEY MATTERS

CURRENCY On 1 January 2007, the euro replaced the tolar (SIT) as the official currency of Slovenia. The euro is a decimal currency and there are 100 cents in a euro. Euro notes come in denominations of ten, 20, 50 and 100. There are also one, two, five, ten, 20 and 50 cent coins. It remains to be seen whether the introduction of the euro will lead to the hike up in prices that some countries have reported on adoption of the currency, a move that would obviously affect tourists.

Exchange rates Exchange rates current in March 2008:

£1 = €1.31
US$1 = €0.66
A$1 = €0.61
C$1 = €0.67

BANKS Most towns and cities in Slovenia have at least one centrally located bank. Most open 08.30–12.30 and 14.00–17.00 Monday–Friday and many open from

Ariadne Van Zandbergen

EQUIPMENT Although with some thought and an eye for composition you can take reasonable photos with a 'point-and-shoot' camera, you need an SLR camera if you are at all serious about photography. Modern SLRs tend to be very clever, with automatic programmes for almost every possible situation, but remember that these programmes are limited in the sense that the camera cannot think, but only make calculations. Every starting amateur photographer should read a photographic manual for beginners and get to grips with such basics as the relationship between aperture and shutter speed.

Always buy the best lens you can afford. The lens determines the quality of your photo more than the camera body. Fixed fast lenses are ideal, but very costly. A zoom lens makes it easier to change composition without changing lenses the whole time. If you carry only one lens, a 28–70mm (digital 17–55mm) or similar zoom should be ideal. For a second lens, a lightweight 80–200mm or 70–300mm (digital 55–200mm) or similar will be excellent for candid shots and varying your composition. Wildlife photography will be very frustrating if you don't have at least a 300mm lens. For a small loss of quality, tele-converters are a cheap and compact way to increase magnification: a 300 lens with a 1.4x converter becomes 420mm, and with a 2x it becomes 600mm. Note, however, that 1.4x and 2x tele-converters reduce the speed of your lens by 1.4 and 2 stops respectively.

For photography from a vehicle, a solid beanbag, which you can make yourself very cheaply, will be necessary to avoid blurred images, and is more useful than a tripod. A clamp with a tripod head screwed onto it can be attached to the vehicle as well. Modern dedicated flash units are easy to use; aside from the obvious need to flash when you photograph at night, you can improve a lot of photos in difficult 'high contrast' or very dull light with some fill-in flash. It pays to have a proper flash unit as opposed to a built-in camera flash.

DIGITAL/FILM Digital photography is now the preference of most amateur and professional photographers, with the resolution of digital cameras improving all the time. For ordinary prints a 6 megapixel camera is fine. For better results and the possibility to enlarge images and for professional reproduction, higher resolution is available up to 16 megapixels.

Memory space is important. The number of pictures you can fit on a memory card depends on the quality you choose. Calculate in advance how many pictures you can fit on a card and either take enough cards to last for your trip, or take a storage drive onto which you can download the content. A laptop gives the advantage that you can see your pictures properly at the end of each day and edit or delete images, but a storage device is lighter and less bulky. These drives come in different capacities up to 80GB.

08.30–12.00 on Saturday. In bigger towns and cities some remain open during the lunch period. Most banks exchange foreign currency and travellers' cheques.

ATMS Banks with ATMs (automated teller machines) that accept Maestro, Cirrus, Visa and MasterCard can be found in any of Slovenia's larger villages, towns and cities. This is the easiest way to get money in the country and banks generally give a good exchange rate, although it is worth checking how much your bank will charge for each transaction that you make when you are in Slovenia.

Bear in mind that digital camera batteries, computers and other storage devices need charging, so make sure you have all the chargers, cables and converters with you. Most hotels have charging points, but do enquire about this in advance. When camping you might have to rely on charging from the car battery; a spare battery is invaluable.

If you are shooting film, 100 to 200 ISO print film and 50 to 100 ISO slide film are ideal. Low ISO film is slow but fine grained and gives the best colour saturation, but will need more light, so support in the form of a tripod or monopod is important. You can also bring a few 'fast' 400 ISO films for low-light situations where a tripod or flash is no option.

DUST AND HEAT Dust and heat are often a problem. Keep your equipment in a sealed bag, stow films in an airtight container (eg: a small cooler bag) and avoid exposing equipment and film to the sun. Digital cameras are prone to collecting dust particles on the sensor which results in spots on the image. The dirt mostly enters the camera when changing lenses, so be careful when doing this. To some extent photos can be 'cleaned' up afterwards in Photoshop, but this is time-consuming. You can have your camera sensor professionally cleaned, or you can do this yourself with special brushes and swabs made for the purpose, but note that touching the sensor might cause damage and should only be done with the greatest care.

LIGHT The most striking outdoor photographs are often taken during the hour or two of 'golden light' after dawn and before sunset. Shooting in low light may enforce the use of very low shutter speeds, in which case a tripod will be required to avoid camera shake.

With careful handling, side lighting and back lighting can produce stunning effects, especially in soft light and at sunrise or sunset. Generally, however, it is best to shoot with the sun behind you. When photographing animals or people in the harsh midday sun, images taken in light but even shade are likely to be more effective than those taken in direct sunlight or patchy shade, since the latter conditions create too much contrast.

PROTOCOL In some countries, it is unacceptable to photograph local people without permission, and many people will refuse to pose or will ask for a donation. In such circumstances, don't try to sneak photographs as you might get yourself into trouble. Even the most willing subject will often pose stiffly when a camera is pointed at them; relax them by making a joke, and take a few shots in quick succession to improve the odds of capturing a natural pose.

Ariadne Van Zandbergen is a professional travel and wildlife photographer specialising in Africa. She runs the Africa Image Library. For photo requests, visit www.africaimagelibrary.co.za or contact her on ariadne@hixnet.co.za.

CURRENCY EXCHANGE
Cash can be exchanged in banks, many post offices, exchange offices, higher-grade hotels, some petrol stations, tourist agencies and even supermarkets; however the same outlets will not necessarily accept travellers' cheques. Sterling and US dollars are the most easily converted currencies.

CREDIT AND DEBIT CARDS
American Express, Diners Club, MasterCard/Eurocard and Visa credit cards and Visa, Electron, Plus, Maestro and Cirrus debit cards are accepted in most shops, restaurants and hotels. It is also possible to

withdraw cash from most ATMs using your credit or debit card, as long as you have a valid PIN number. With the majority of cards you can also withdraw money inside the bank if you don't know your PIN or the ATM is broken. Cash withdrawal fees and exchange rates vary between banks and credit card companies, so check these before you leave home. Credit and debit card transaction charges can be kept down by withdrawing larger sums of money, although there will be an upper limit on the amount you can extract.

If you are travelling with credit cards it is sensible to keep a record of the issuer's international telephone number for reporting lost or stolen cards. In the case of loss or theft your credit card company should help you arrange emergency cash if necessary. You can also get assistance with damaged, lost or stolen cards in Ljubljana.

American Express Trubarjeva 50; ✆ 01 438 0850
Diners Club Dunajska 129; ✆ 01 589 6111
MasterCard/Eurocard Nova Ljubljanska Banka,

Trg republike 2; ✆ 01 425 0155, or SKB Banka, Ajdovščina 4; ✆ 01 433 2132
Visa A Banka, Slovenska 58; ✆ 01 471 8100

TRAVELLERS' CHEQUES Travellers' cheques are much safer than carrying cash. Euro or US dollar travellers' cheques can be exchanged at banks, exchange offices, travel agencies and some post offices. Banks offer the best rate with commissions ranging from zero to 1%. Remember that you will need a valid passport or identity card to cash your cheques.

WIRING MONEY If you need emergency cash this can be wired via Western Union (*www.westernunion.com*) agents Nova Ljubljanska Banka at any branch.

BUDGETING

Slovenia is more affordable than many western European countries, although any notions of a poverty-stricken eastern European nation with rock-bottom prices will soon be dispelled. However, there are options to suit all budgets with hostel accommodation and camping typically costing under €15 per person, while a bed in a hostel dormitory costs €10–15. Meanwhile private accommodation costs €15–35 for a double room. A double room in a mid-range hotel would typically cost €60–80, with luxurious four- and five-star accommodation coming in at €150+. Restaurants likewise cater to a broad range of budgets. Regardless of your budget there are a couple of things to bear in mind: prices in the capital and the country's popular tourist resorts, like Lake Bled, will be more expensive than in other areas. Accommodation costs can also be significantly reduced if you are travelling with a partner or friends, as splitting the cost of double, triple or quadruple rooms works out cheaper.

ROCK BOTTOM You can get by on €35 a day if you camp or stay in a youth hostel dormitory and buy food from a market or fast-food stands. This budget will also allow you to eat one meal in a pizzeria or student eatery and to buy drinks from a supermarket. If you are planning to travel on a tight budget it is essential that you book your accommodation in advance.

MODEST Being savvy about where you stay will allow you to eat two meals in modestly priced but good-quality restaurants and enjoy four or five drinks in cafés and bars for €50–70 a day. Again if you want to keep your accommodation costs down then it is advisable to book a hostel or private room in advance.

FUN For €80–120 a day you can afford single occupancy in a mid-range hotel, eat two reasonably priced meals and not have to worry about what you drink.

INDULGENT Spend €180–200 a day and stay in good three- or four-star hotels and eat out twice, choosing from the majority of Slovenia's restaurants. You will also be able to pay entrance fees to the sites of your choice and enjoy a night out.

EXTRAVAGANT From €200 a day upwards you will be able to stay in four- or five-star hotels, eat in Slovenia's most exclusive restaurants and spend the day as you choose, eg: relaxing in cafés, drinking in bars or sightseeing. Again a budget of this size means that you can go out at night without having to watch the euros.

GETTING AROUND

BY CAR Slovenia's compact size and its good network of roads lend themselves to exploration by car. Driving also gives you easy access to Slovenia's more remote villages and dramatic rural scenery. Car hire costs from around €200 a week for a budget model, and a litre of unleaded petrol costs around €0.85. To hire a car you must be over 21 years old (those under 25 have to pay additional insurance premiums of around €5 a day) and have held a clean driving licence for at least a year. You also need your national driving licence, passport, a valid credit card and nerves of steel.

Many Slovenes have a fairly haphazard attitude to driving and almost everyone, from compact cars to articulated lorries, seems to drive above the mandatory speed limit. Speed is not the only problem, though, as many drivers assume that they always have the right of way, while others pull out from side streets and then look to see if there is anything coming. One favourite pastime is zigzagging in and out of the traffic to either undertake or overtake. At night the roads take on additional perils, as many of the best bars and restaurants are located in rural areas and drinking and driving is often still an accepted part of the culture.

However, traffic outside of urban centres is light, making driving in the countryside a straightforward and pleasant experience.

BY BUS Slovenia has a good bus network and it is possible to travel by bus to most of the country's towns and cities from its capital city, although smaller villages are less accessible and usually require local connections. Slovenes like their cars so the frequency of services varies greatly between destinations. Vehicles that service national routes are generally modern, with air conditioning. In addition they often represent the most straightforward and direct way of reaching some destinations such as Bled, the Julian Alps and the regions of Notranjska, Dolenjska and Koroška.

Fares are calculated by the distance covered, allowing you to travel 25km for €2.50–3, 50km for €5–6, 100km for €10–12 and 200km for €20–24. With short distances between destinations the fare will never be that high (see road distances from Ljubljana below). You can buy bus tickets from any *avtobusna postaja* (bus station), or just turn up and pay as you board the bus. For a nominal charge seat reservations can be made a day in advance.

Some typical road distances from Ljubljana include: Kranj 26km, Bled and Postojna 53km, Novo Mesto 73km, Celje 77km, Črnomelj 91km, Koper 117km, Bovec 125km, Maribor 133km, Ptuj 136km and Kranjska Gora 221km.

Bus timetables *Vozni red* (timetables) are usually displayed in bus stations, but can be difficult to understand. Some are colour coded; as a rule of thumb a black or

Traffic in Slovenia drives on the right. Mandatory speed limits are usually 130km/h on motorways, 100km/h on main highways, 90km/h on regional roads outside residential areas and 50km/h in built-up areas. You will often see signs for 70km/h, 60km/h and even 40km/h – these are usually on very winding sections of road, or when workmen are at the side of the road. Many Slovenes do not stick to the speed limits, but you should, as the police are vigilant and issue fines and penalty points to speeding drivers. It is illegal to overtake a school bus, seat belt use is compulsory and dipped headlights should be kept on at all times while driving. The last is a fairly new law so the police may just remind drivers to turn their lights on, although they can issue a fine. The legal alcohol blood level is 0.05% or 0.5g/kg, but it is much safer to avoid alcohol when driving.

For more information on driving in Slovenia contact the country's national automobile club, Auto-Moto Zveza Slovenjie (*AMZS; Dunajska 128, 1000 Ljubljana;* \ *01 530 5300;* f *01 530 5410; www.amzs.si*). Their emergency roadside number is \ 1987.

white text indicates that the service is daily, blue indicates Monday–Friday, green and orange are for daily excluding Sundays, yellow means during school hours and red is for on Sundays and holidays. Those that have letters to indicate the frequency of service are coded as follows:

V   daily
D   Monday–Friday
D+   daily, excluding Sundays
N   Sundays
NP   Sundays and holidays
ŠP   during school hours

Those that run only on certain days of the week take the first two letters of the spelling for the day, eg: Torek (Tuesday) is To. For the Slovene words for all the days of the week, see *Appendix 1, Time, days and months,* page 230.

Staff at the information window or ticket office will also help you decipher complex timetables.

Roundy Bus Running from Ljubljana the Roundy Bus operates four services, with single-day tours of Gorenjska (Monday, Wednesday, Friday and Sunday), Primorska (Tuesday, Thursday, Saturday and Sunday), the Soča Valley (Emerald River; Tuesday, Thursday and Saturday) and the hop-on and off West Roundy (Monday, Wednesday and Friday). The Gorenjska tour visits Bled, Vintgar Gorge, Bohinj and Škofja Loka; the Primorska tour visits Predjama Castle, Škocjan Caves, Piran, Lipica and a typical Karst wine cellar. Meanwhile Emerald River circuit takes in the Vršič Pass, Bovec and Kobarid. The West Roundy lets passengers choose where to start (Ljubljana, Bled, Bohinj, Bovec, Kobarid, Štanjel, Lipica, Piran or the Škocjan Caves) with passengers able to complete the circuit in two–30 days. Fares depend on routes, optional excursions and entrance fees and whether you book accommodation with the company etc.

Roundabout Savlje 89, Ljubljana; \ 05 142 7624; f 01 561 1039; e info@roundabout.si; www.roundabout.si. Booking is also available through tourist information centres, hotels & travel agencies.

BY TRAIN Slovenia's rail network extends over 1,200km of track operated by Slovenian Railways (*Slovenske Železnice;* ☎ *01 291 3332;* e *potnik.info@slo-zeleznice.si; www.slo-zeleznice.si*), and both track and rolling stock are in good condition. Travelling by train in Slovenia can be frustrating, though, as one enduring legacy of socialist Yugoslavia is few direct routes between towns and cities, with most journeys requiring connections through Ljubljana; for example it is quicker to travel from Maribor to Novo Mesto (which is almost due south) via Ljubljana in the west of the country. Lengthy journeys and the need to backtrack probably explain why it is cheap in terms of price per kilometre to travel by rail, with a 100km journey costing around €6.

Understanding some of the codes on train timetables makes it easier to navigate the system. A boxed R indicates that an advance reservation is needed in order to board the train, while an R that is not boxed simply indicates that reservations are available. The abbreviation IC denotes a faster but more expensive intercity route, although the supplement is less than €2. When there is no reservation required it is possible to simply board the train and pay the conductor, although this costs an additional €2 per person.

ACCOMMODATION

In 2007, the Slovenian Tourist Board introduced a new central reservations system. This allows visitors to book registered accommodation throughout the country. In many cases you can now book accommodation online through the tourist board's website (*www.slovenia.info*), or at least make an enquiry.

HOTELS Slovenia has a total accommodation capacity of around 80,000 beds, of which approximately 35% are in hotels. Hotels are classified from one to five stars, with the former meeting basic standards and the latter being the most luxurious accommodation. Most of the country's accommodation is in three-star properties, although the number of good-quality four- and five-star hotels is growing slowly. Hotels in Slovenia are not as cheap as you might expect, especially during high season. Increasingly, good-value deals are available through the internet. Many hotels offer beds in triple and quadruple rooms, which reduces the cost further.

Double room per night

Exclusive	$$$$	€150+
Upmarket	$$$$	€100–150
Mid range	$$$	€60–100
Budget	$$	€25–60
Shoestring	$	up to €25

Rates are usually inclusive of breakfast.

THERMAL SPAS *Terme* (thermal spas) are one of Slovenia's most appealing features and a large component of its tourism industry. At present over a dozen *terme* across the country offer curative and preventative health programmes, recreational facilities constructed around natural thermal spas, gyms, beauty parlours and aqua-parks. These resorts also have their own hotel accommodation. The quality of the facilities and accommodation varies greatly, with some being ultra-modern and others throwbacks from Slovenia's socialist era. A large amount of money is being invested in upgrading *terme* throughout the country. For more information visit Slovenian Spas website (*www.terme-giz.si*).

PRIVATE ROOMS Privately owned rooms and apartments are available throughout Slovenia, although capacity in Ljubljana is limited. You can go directly to the owner, who will be displaying a *sobe* (rooms) sign, usually with a picture of a bed. In more tourist-orientated areas these may be accompanied by signs in other languages, with the German *zimmer frei* being the most common. Alternatively tourist offices and tourist agencies can help you book private accommodation. Like hotels, private accommodation is graded and a one- to four-star classification system is used. Properties with one star are basic and often have shared facilities, while a four-star property is the most luxurious and will be en suite. Charges vary according to location and classification with single rooms costing €10–40 (average €20), double rooms €20–60 (average €35) and apartments sleeping two to six people €35–120. Many enterprising landlords have a presence on the internet, enabling you to book accommodation directly with them before you leave for Slovenia. Some owners will not take guests who want to stay for less than three days, while others might levy a surcharge of up to 30% per night for this.

YOUTH HOSTELS The Maribor-based Hostelling International Slovenia (*PZS; Gosposvetska 84, 2000 Maribor;* ✆ *02 234 2137;* f *02 234 2136;* e *info@youth-hostel.si; www.gaudeamus.si/hostelling*) has more than 30 HI-affiliated hostels located across the country. The majority of these hostels open year round and nightly rates start at €10 for a dormitory bed. June–August and December are busy months for Slovenia's hostels and you are advised to make advance bookings during these months.

CAMPING Over 50 official *kamps* (campsites) are registered with the Slovenian Tourist Board. Located at or close to some of the country's main attractions, these offer cost-effective accommodation. Most campsites are seasonal and open April–October. Visitors without tents may find that they can rent either a tent or a bungalow. Facilities on offer in each campsite vary, although many offer recreational activities and, perhaps more importantly for those spending a long time in Slovenia, self-service laundries. As a guide camping costs €6–15 per person. You will pay the top-end price for campsites at *terme*. This higher price generally includes access to swimming pools. At some sites, extra fees are often charged for cars, caravans, tents, camper vans, pets, refrigeration, hook-ups and even hot water.

TOURIST FARMS More than 200 farms in rural areas of Slovenia offer accommodation; endearingly these are called 'Tourist Farms' which conjures up quite an unusual image. To really get away from it all and experience traditional Slovenian hospitality these can be a good option. Tourist farms can be viewed and booked through the Slovenian Tourist Board website (*www.slovenia.info*). There is also a small network of traditional houses (country estates and rural homesteads) – *Hiše s tradicijo* (Houses of Tradition) – that have been renovated to a high standard in order to attract tourists (*Mala 8, Ljubljana;* ✆ *01 434 2660;* f *01 434 2664;* e *info@hisetradicijo.com; www.hisestradicijo.com*).

✘ EATING AND DRINKING

FOOD Forget any anachronistic images that you may harbour of communist-era culinary deprivations as Slovenia is fast developing into something of an eating and drinking oasis. It is difficult to say exactly what constitutes definitive Slovenian cuisine as the country wholeheartedly embraces Austrian, Hungarian,

Croatian and Italian influences, then tops them all off with a generous helping of genuine Slovenian hospitality.

In the hinterland, particularly the mountains, hearty meat dishes and a wide variety of grilled sausages and black pudding dominate the menu. Here sweet doughnuts and dumplings are also traditional. Fresh seafood is prevalent on the Adriatic coast, while freshwater fish, especially trout, are typically found on menus in areas close to rivers and lakes, particularly in Gorenjska. Each region of Slovenia has its own distinctive dishes. From Prekmurje there is goulash and the *gibanica* – pastry filled with poppy seeds, walnuts, apple and cottage cheese then topped with cream – the country's favourite sugary treat. Then there are sour soups from Pohorje and potato- and bean-based soups from Gorenjska and Primorska. Influences seep from the Balkans with the fast-food *burek*, an artery-clogging pastry with meat or cottage cheese.

One constant in Slovenia's restaurants is the quality of the ingredients. Fresh produce is paramount and the daily specials that are recommended by waiters are usually the preferred option of local diners. This is a country where the 'slow food' movement and organic food reign supreme, and where sitting down to a good meal is regarded as a God-given right rather than a luxury.

Venues are very loosely divided between *gostilnas*, *gostišče*s and *restavracijas*. In practice these definitions are very blurred, but generally a *gostilna* is an inn that serves drinks and traditional food. The *gostišče* is very similar and also specialises in Slovenian-style dishes, while a *restavracija* tends to be a more formal set-up with a more innovative, modern or international menu. In recent years it has become quite trendy to call your new restaurant a *gostilna* or *gostišče* as diners are seeking to re-explore traditional food, further blurring the lines. Another constant is the lack of formality and there are few places in Slovenia where you will feel out of place in casual dress. Handily almost all eating venues have English-language menus and multi-lingual staff.

Over the last few years a number of more exotic cuisines have been sneaking into Slovenia with the likes of Mexican, Japanese and Chinese all now in the mix. In the days before independence in 1991 tucking into a bowl of *sushi* would have been unimaginable, but today Ljubljana's first *sushi* restaurant is still one of its most fashionable spots. The most established 'foreign' cuisine is Italian, with pizza a staple of many Slovenian diets, and the country's myriad pizzerias offer excellent pizza that would not be out of place in Naples.

For most locals the day starts with a light breakfast, increasingly taken on the move with a quick coffee and pastry. Lunch is usually quite a low-key affair except on weekends when it can go on all afternoon and even extend into the evening, especially if you are at a *gostilna* or *gostišče* out in the countryside. Dinner is the main meal of the day and if you are meeting friends you should not plan to do much else afterwards. Slovenes like to take their time over dinner, so if you are lucky enough to snare an invite to dine with a Slovene, settle in for a long haul and remember to wish all of your dining companions '*dober tek*' (*bon appétit*).

Slovenia offers good value when it comes to eating out, though prices do vary markedly from the cheap and cheerful places through to the increasing array of top-end options.

WINE People have been making wine here for almost 2,500 years and Slovenia has more than 200km² of vineyards with an estimated annual production of around 80 million litres. This wine is grown in three main regions: Podravje, Posavje and Primorska. Popular wines include a semi-dry white Sauvignon Blanc with a straw colour, and Cviček, a blend of red and white wines that is not quite a rosé, and whose acidity renders it an acquired taste. Modra Frankinja

TEN GREAT RESTAURANTS

Špazja Ljubljana (see page 57)
JB Ljubljana (see page 57)
Smrekarjev Hram Ljubljana (see page 57)
Neptun Piran (see page 156)
Plesnik Logarska Dolina (see page 205)
Gostilna Pri Lojzetu Zemono Dvorec, Vipava Valley (see page 141)
Kendov Dvorec Spodnja Idrija (see page 135)
Restaurant Topli Val Kobarid (see page 130)
Kotlar Kobarid (see page 130)
Ribič Ptuj (see page 207)

meanwhile is a full-bodied red wine with a deep colour and a harsh taste. At the other end of the scale Laški Rizling is a sweet white. Other good whites include Chardonnay, always a safe option, and Beli Bizeljčan, a full-flavoured dry wine with a flowery taste, which locals often mix with sparkling mineral water to make a spritzer. Slovenia also has its own brand of sparkling wine, with good brands on a par with champagne. Slovenes are divided about which brand of sparkling wine is the most superior, with some rooting for Zlata Radgonska Penina and others going for those produced by the Istenič family. Many of Slovenia's wine areas have dedicated wine routes where you can drive or cycle between the different producers – see the individual regional chapters in this book or ask at local tourist offices.

PRICES

Food You can pick up a pastry and a hot drink for around €2. In terms of price there is little to differentiate lunch and dinner when ordering à la carte, although a growing number of cafés and restaurants offer three-course fixed-price menus that start at around €7 and rarely sneak above €15.

Average price of main course

Expensive	$$$$$	€15+
Above average	$$$$	€10–15
Mid range	$$$	€6–10
Cheap and cheerful	$$	€4–6
Rock bottom	$	€1–4

Drinks Soft drinks, mineral water and beer (both on draught and in bottles) come in at around €2–3 per drink, while tea and coffee are generally a little cheaper at €1–2. Decaffeinated coffee has finally arrived in Slovenia, though it tends to cost a little more than straight coffee. A 10cl glass of wine starts at around €1.40, although in practice most wine drinkers order double measures. If you order a full bottle of wine, this will usually cost upwards of €15.

PUBLIC HOLIDAYS AND FESTIVALS

PUBLIC HOLIDAYS

1 and 2 January	New Year Holiday
8 February	Slovene Cultural Day (also known as Prešeren Day)
Easter Monday	
27 April	Resistance Day

1 and 2 May	Labour Days
Pentecost	
25 June	Slovenia Day
15 August	Feast of the Assumption
31 October	Reformation Day
1 November	All Saints' Day
25 December	Christmas Day
26 December	Independence Day

FESTIVALS AND SPECIAL EVENTS
Spring
Slovenian Musical Days Organised by Festival Ljubljana (*www.festival-lj.si*), showcasing contemporary music by Slovenian and European composers. Ljubljana, April.

Izola Theatre and Dance Marathon Izola, April.

Arboretum Spring Flower Show Vločjo Potok, April–May.

Exodos (*www.exodos-festival.si*) This festival of contemporary performing arts has been an annual event in Ljubljana for over a decade. Past performers have included Japanese drummers, Vietnamese puppet theatre and a performance of *Thumbelina*. Main venue Cankarjev Dom. Ljubljana, May.

Internautica (*www.internautica.net*) Five-day international boat show. Portorož, May.

World Cup International Dressage Competition Lipica, May–June.

Druga Godba (*www.drugagobda.si*) The outdoor Križanke theatre is the main venue for a five-day festival of alternative and ethnic concerts by international performers. Founded in 1985 and a local favourite, the name literally means 'alternative bands'. The diverse music on offer ranges from modern jazz and ethno-electronic to folk music and African beats. Ljubljana, June.

Summer
Museum Summer Night An open-door event that gives access to museums, exhibitions and galleries in Ljubljana. Free workshops, tours, concerts, film screenings, performances, lectures and presentations also take place on this day. Ljubljana, June.

Ana Desetnica International Street Theatre Festival (*www.anadesetnica.org*) One of Europe's largest street-theatre festivals. Ljubljana, June.

Bled International Music Festival Bled, June–July.

Lent Festival (*http://lent.slovenija.net*) A 16-day annual summer fair with theatrical performances, concerts and firework displays. Maribor, June–July.

Summer in Celje Celje, late June–September.

Brežice Festival of Early Music Brežice, June–August.

Ljubljana Jazz Festival (*www.ljubljanajazz.si*) This event, which has been running for almost half a century, spans three evenings with performances from Slovene and international musicians. Ljubljana, June/July.

Mediterranean International Folklore Festival Piran, early July.

International Folklore Festival Maribor, July.

Bled Days & Bled Nights Lighting displays and fireworks come to this beautiful setting. Bled, July.

Kranj Fest (*www.kranfest.com*) Two nights packed with cultural events. Kranj, July.

Primorska Summer Festival (*www.portoroz.si*) This festival has been going strong since 1993, bringing theatre, music and other performance art to indoor and outdoor venues in Koper, Izola, Portorož and Piran throughout July.

Ljubljana Summer Festival (*www.ljubljanafestival.si*) The capital's biggest festival is organised by Festival Ljubljana and dates back to 1953. The city's stages fill with performers from around the world and its population swells as visitors flock to the festival. Musical, theatrical and dance performances take place in the Slovenian Philharmonic Hall, Cankarjev Dom, Križanke Summer Theatre, Ljubljana Castle and the Cultural and Congress Centre. Concerts are also staged in churches and squares throughout the city. Ljubljana, July–August.

Mini Summer Festival (*www.mini-teater.si*) This children's festival with its puppet shows and children's theatre is a perfect complement to the Ljubljana Summer Festival. Ljubljana, July–September.

Mediterranean Festival and **Fisherman's Festival** Izola, August.

Trnfest (*www.kud-fp.si/index.php/Projekt:Trnfest*) A month-long celebration of alternative culture including video, dance, music, theatre, exhibitions and events for children. Ljubljana, August.

Kamfest (*www.kamfest.org*) Kamnik town festival. Kamnik, mid August.

Autumn
Musical September International festival of chamber music. Maribor, September.

Medieval Days (*www.mini-teater.si*) Highlights of the festival, which re-enacts life in the Slovene capital during the Middle Ages, include medieval and Renaissance musical renditions, a medieval market and jousting knights. Ljubljana Castle is a spectacular venue. Ljubljana, September/October.

Ljubljana Marathon (*www.ljubljanskimaraton.si*) This annual sporting event caters to varying abilities, with a half-marathon, 10km run and various fun runs that span four days. Ljubljana, October.

Borštnik Festival The second city's stages fill with first-rate theatre performances for a two-week period. Maribor, mid–late October.

Ljubljana International Film Festival (*www.liffe.si*) Films from around the world are screened at the Cankarjev Dom, Kinodvor, Kino Kimuna and Kinoklub Vič during this two-week festival. Ljubljana, November.

Ljubljana Gay and Lesbian Film Festival This week-long festival celebrated its 23rd anniversary in 2007. Films are screened at the Slovenska Kinoteka. Ljubljana, November

Winter
December in Ljubljana Seasonal festivities throughout the city including Christmas markets, with food, mulled wine and seasonal gifts, along the banks of the Ljubljanica and on Kongresni trg. Impressive street lighting brings the city centre to life, making Ljubljana a great place to get into the festive spirit. Ljubljana, December.

Christmas and New Year Fairs Seasonal gifts and food. All main towns and cities, December–January.

New Year's Eve Join in the revelry on Kongresni trg, Prešernov trg and Mestni trg and watch the fireworks as they explode over Ljubljana Castle at midnight.

Ski World Cup Women's Slalom Races Maribor, January.

Dog Sled Race Kranjska Gora, January/February.

Kurentovanje Festival (*www.kurentovanje.net*) Traditional festival designed to fend off evil winter spirits and welcome spring, where the town's young men dress up in extravagant costumes and masks to chase out the devils. Ptuj, February–March.

World Championship Ski Flying and Ski Jumping Planica, March.

SHOPPING

Lace, basketry, wooden utensils, pottery and ceramics, crystal cut glass, gold jewellery, beeswax, Slovenian wine, wrought iron and woodcarvings are all good souvenirs. The majority of shops open 08.00–19.00 Monday–Friday and 08.00–12.00 Saturday, although an increasing number are staying open on Saturday afternoons and opening on Sundays. Department stores in big cities may also open on Saturday afternoons, with the enormous BTC city shopping and entertainment complex in Ljubljana opening from 09.00–20.00 on Saturdays and until 13.00 on Sundays.

ARTS AND ENTERTAINMENT

ART Much of Slovenia's early art was brought to the region by the various civilisations that breezed through, with the Romans leaving their early traces. There is a wealth of Gothic treasures, such as Hrastovlje's *Dance of Death* murals and the frescoes in the Church of St John the Baptist in Bohinj. The big names of Slovenian painting emerged in the 19th century with the Romantic works of Matevž Langus and Josip Tominc. As the 19th century moved into the 20th century a new phase of Impressionism took over with Rihard Jakopič and Ivan Gohar at the forefront. Even within the confines of Yugoslav socialism Slovenian art produced some very good work with the sculptors Jakob Savinšek and Lojze Dolinar excelling. After Tito's death the avant-garde strain that had always been evident throughout the history of Slovenian art rose up in the Neue Slowenische Kunst (NSK or New Slovenian Art) movement, where it was a case of the more challenging and thought-provoking the better. Today you can delve into this period in the Modern Art Gallery in Ljubljana.

Zoran Mušič, Jože Plečnik (whose work is covered in more detail in the Ljubljana chapter of this book), Boris Podrecca and Marko Ivan Rupnik are amongst Slovenia's most famous 20th-century artists. Zoran Mušič (1909–2005) was born in Slovenia, but spent most of his life in France. Boris Podrecca, who was born in Belgrade in 1940, but whose family came from the Primorska region of Slovenia, another of Slovenia's great artists, is heralded as one of the greatest contemporary Slovenian architects, adopting a style that is heavily influenced by Plečnik. The Slovene artist Marko Ivan Rupnik came to the attention of art lovers around the world when he was commissioned, in 1999, to decorate the walls of the Pope's Chapel of the Saviour's Mother in Vatican City. He rose to the challenge with a contemporary mosaic.

HANDICRAFTS Until the 19th century the majority of Slovenes were country folk, with few attending institutes of higher education or coming into contact with the higher art forms, therefore it is perhaps no surprise that Slovenian handicrafts have themselves flourished as an art form over the centuries. Woodwork is the strongest medium with the brightly painted beehive panels, mainly associated with the Gorenjska region, a fine example of expressive handicrafts. Today throughout the country at local markets you can pick up unique wooden souvenirs, whether it be miniature beehive panels or simple ladles, usually with excellent workmanship and quality wood. If you want to delve further into the history of the beehive panels head for the dedicated bee-keeping museum in Radovljica (see page 94).

LITERATURE The history of Slovenian literature can be traced back as far as the 10th century with the publication of the three Freising Manuscripts, though a Slavic oral tradition is said to have pre-dated this first Slovene Slavic text. The first book entirely in Slovene was published in 1550 – Primož Trubar's *Catechismus in Abecedarium*. Some 50 other titles were also published in Slovene around this time, including a translation of the Bible by Jurij Dalmatin and Adam Bohorič's book of Slovenian grammar. Slovene as a literary language still struggled and the most comprehensive series of books on the country written before the 20th century (perhaps ever), Janez Vajkard Valvasor's *The Glory of the Duchy of Carniola*, was not even written in Slovene.

Under the Austro-Hungarians the poet Valentin Vodnik and the playwright Anton Tomaž Linhart rose to the fore, with the former publishing the country's first newspaper between 1797 and 1800 and the latter writing a history of the Slovenes. However, Vodnik and Linhart pale into insignificance compared with Slovenia's most famous writer, poet France Prešeren, who emerged in the 19th century (see box, *Chapter 4*, page 99). His 1847 publication *Poezije* was especially influential. Slovenia's increasing taste for the avant-garde grew in the 20th century with the poet Oton Župančič and novelist-playwright Ivan Cankar, whom many Slovenes rate as the greatest-ever writer in the Slovene language. The post-World War II years witnessed, on the one hand, socialist realism in service to the regime, but, on the other, existentialism. One particularly notable dissident voice was Edvard Kocbek, who fought the Germans as a partisan but turned against the regime in his later work.

Slovenia's most important and most translated contemporary writer, Drago Jančar (b1948), is celebrated for his analysis of modern society and illuminating

JANEZ VAJKARD VALVASOR

In his own way Valvasor was every bit as influential as France Prešeren, certainly in terms of shaping the way we look at Slovenia's history, landscape, flora and fauna. Born in Ljubljana in 1641 Valvasor was, for a man of his time, quite an accomplished traveller, having spent time in many European countries as well as making forays into Africa. His seminal work was *The Glory of the Duchy of Carniola*, an impressively detailed multi-volume account of the country around him. Like Prešeren, Valvasor died (in 1693) with little real idea of the esteem in which he would be held one day, and in tragic circumstances as by then he was virtually penniless. He was recognised to some extent in his lifetime for his explanation of the until-then unfathomable, intermittent Lake Cerknica in Notranjska. Today Valvasor is eulogised as the man who wrote perhaps the greatest-ever study of Slovenia; he was also a member of the British Royal Society.

Vladimir Bartol's *Alamut* is arguably the most famous Slovenian book in the world today. Published in the late 1930s, the book is set in Iran during the Midldle Ages and focuses on the subjugation of the minority Shiite population by Seljuk Sunni Turkish leaders, and in particular the character of Hasan. As Hasan's ambition grows, he stoops to new lows in his degradation of and efforts to control those beneath him, including the use of drugs to command and manipulate his own private army. Many modern analyses of the book cast the main character in the role of an Islamic terrorist and regard it as a prediction of the type of fundamentalist terrorism that has risen to the fore in the 21st century. When it was first released, however, many interpreted it as an allusion to totalitarian domination in Europe, with characters in the book being likened to Hitler, Stalin and members of the SS. The casting of Hasan as an out-of-control megalomaniac has seen his character most strongly associated with Benito Mussolini, with suggestions that Bartol originally wanted to dedicate the book to the Italian fascist dictator, but was prevented from doing so. *Alamut* has been translated into Spanish, French and most recently English (see *Appendix 2, Further Information*).

essays about central Europe and Slovenian society. For Slovenes his work is as significant as that of the Czech writer Milan Kundera, with his book titled *Mocking Desire* (see *Appendix 2, Further Information*) in English held in particularly high esteem. The Trieste-based writer, Boris Pahor, is another influential Slovene writer, and he has had his works translated into both French and Italian.

MUSIC Much of Slovenia's early musical heritage dates back to the ecclesiastical style practised in the country's churches and monasteries during the 15th century, a style that remained popular for around 300 years. One of the most famous composers of this style of music was the Cistercian Monk Jakob Gallus (1550–91), often referred to as Jacob Handl. Gallus's most famous piece, *Opus Musicum*, is still performed by choirs around the world. The Ljubljana-based Academia Philharmonicorum Labacensium (which became the Filharmonija in 1794) was established in 1701 at a time when secular music had fallen out of fashion, and while choir singing remained an intrinsic component the focus was shifting to orchestra-led performances. Jakob Zupan (1734–1810) broke with tradition when he penned the first opera written by a Slovene in 1780. Throughout the 19th century the classical music scene in Slovenia was dominated by a Romantic school of composers such as Benjamin Ipavec (1829–1908), whose work includes the *Serenade for Strings*, with Blaž Arnic (1901–70), who wrote nine symphonies during his lifetime, continuing this legacy.

Ljudska glasba (folk music) has always been a popular facet of music in Slovenia. Most of what you hear will be accordion-laden reels and jigs piped out of speakers on Sunday afternoons at *gostilnas* across the land, but you may chance upon the real thing. Bela Krajina has a reputation as a hotbed of traditional music so if you are interested venture there and enquire at the tourist office in Metlika about what is on. Alternatively there are often concerts on in Ljubljana and Maribor so check with their tourist offices. Traditional instruments include the *frajtonarica* (accordion), *okarina* (flute) and *trstenke* (reed pipes). Among Slovenia's most influential folk musicians are the Avsenik brothers (*www.avsenik-sp.si*), who hail from Begunje. Other big names to look out for these days include Katice, an excellent female vocal group, and Terra

The Slovene kings of accordion oompah are the four Avsenik brothers – Slavko, Vinko, Janez and Majda – who formed the Avsenik Brothers Quintet in 1953. In a career that spanned almost half a century, they recorded more than 50 albums and sold over 31 million records. The folk music crafted by the Avsenik brothers is particularly popular in Upper Carniola (Gorenjska) and therefore appeals to Slovenes, Austrians and Germans from this historic region. The Avsenik brothers have achieved acclaim on an international stage, playing to an audience of 80,000 at a stadium in western Berlin back in 1961, and touring North America in the same year. Their impressive collection of awards includes 31 gold, two diamond and one platinum disc. The brothers stopped recording in 1990.

Folk, a cross-genre ensemble who utilise a variety of instruments and incorporate musical styles from Gypsy songs to Balkan pop.

Slovenia produced some interesting punk bands in the 1970s in the form of Pankrti and Laibach (the Austrian name for Ljubljana), whose lead singer later committed suicide. For a time Laibach were huge in Yugoslavia and behind the Iron Curtain. What little pop and rock music is produced domestically today tends to be heavily influenced by American and British bands, though some of the groups belting out at powerful gigs at the Metelkova squat in Ljubljana are more original. One growing field of music is dance, with Slovene DJs hitting the decks in Ljubljana, Novo Mesto and along the coast alongside big European names, garnering valuable experience and in the process getting some much-needed exposure for a musical genre that is the choice of many of today's teenagers and young adults.

During the 20th century a number of Slovenes achieved international acclaim in the field of classical music and opera, including the mezzo-sopranos Marjana Lipovšek (b1946), Bernarda Fink (b1955) and pianist Dubravka Tomšič-Srebotnjak (b1940). The voice of Ljubljana-born Marjana Lipovšek, daughter of composer Marijan Lipovšek, has been appreciated by opera-goers around the world, as she has taken the leading role in venues like Vienna, Hamburg, Munich and Paris, won various awards for her singing and worked alongside various orchestras. Born in Buenos Aires, Argentina, to Slovene parents, Bernarda Fink has enjoyed the same kind of success in her career as Marjana Lipovšek, performing with internationally acclaimed orchestras and at classical music festivals around the world. The repertoire of Dubravka Tomšič-Srebotnjak, who performs with internationally renowned orchestras at prestigious venues around the world, is also remarkable.

MEDIA AND COMMUNICATIONS

PRESS Slovenia has four daily newspapers, printed in Slovene and available on the internet: the Ljubljana-based *Delo* (Work; *www.delo.si*), *Dnevnik* (Daily; *www.dnevnik.si*) and *Ljubljanske Novice*, and the Maribor-based *Večer* (Evening; *www.vecer.si*). There is also a diverse range of weekly, fortnightly and monthly newspapers and magazines on sale.

English-language publications include the weekly *Slovenia News* (*http://slonews.sta.si*), the monthly *Slovenia Times* (*www.sloveniatimes.com*), the quarterly *Ljubljana Life* whose website (*www.geocities.com/ljubljanalife*) contains the *Slovenia Bulletin*, a weekly review of the stories in Slovenia's mainstream press, and the quarterly *Slovenija Magazine* (*www.zdruzenje-sim.si*). Sources of business news include the quarterly *Slovenian Business Report* (*www.sbr.si*) and the online *Slovenia Business Week* (*www.gzs.si*). In addition the government's Public Relations and Media Office (*www.uvi.si/eng*) is an official source of English-language news.

The *Guardian International, International Herald Tribune, USA Today* and the *Financial Times* are also widely available in hotels, bookshops and at kiosks throughout Ljubljana. Higher-class hotels and thermal resorts frequently have a limited supply of foreign-language publications.

RADIO Radiotelevizija Slovenija (RTV Slovenia; *www.rtvslo.si*) transmits three national radio channels, regional radio channels that include tourist broadcasts in foreign languages and one radio channel each for the country's Italian and Hungarian minorities. Around 100 stations in Slovenia also transmit commercial and non-commercial programmes. Turistični Radio (Tourist Radio) is available on 87.6MHz, 89.2MHz, 91.1MHz, 102.4MHz and 102.8MHz.

You can also access English-language broadcasts of the BBC World Service (*www.bbc.co.uk/worldservice*) and Voice of America (*www.voa.gov*).

TELEVISION RTV Slovenia transmits two national television channels and two regional channels – Koper-Capodistia in Koper and another in Maribor. Pro Plus operates the commercial channels Kanal A and Pop TV, which air a mixture of domestic and international programmes, while TV3 has a mixed Croatian–Slovenian ownership. Most of Ljubljana's better hotels have CNN, BBC World and other satellite channels such as Discovery, MTV and Eurosport.

⊖ INTERNET CAFÉS Home internet use is widespread in Slovenia so few locals need internet cafés, but there is still a sprinkling of places to get online, concentrated in urban centres. Many hotels and hostels provide internet points for guests. Where internet access is available the fee charged ranges from free to €3 an hour.

⊠ POST OFFICES Every city and town has at least one post office, as do most villages. Post offices are easily identifiable by the black horn against a yellow background and the word *Pošta*. You can buy stamps, phonecards and postcards, bank your money and exchange currency in most post offices. Those located in tourist areas often sell a range of souvenirs. Opening hours are generally 08.00–19.00 Monday–Friday and 08.00–12.00 Saturday, although smaller offices may close earlier. The postal service in Slovenia is comparable to any western European service with next-day delivery on internal first-class mail, and a quick airmail service to other destinations. Expect letters or cards sent to the UK to take around four to five days to arrive.

✆ TELEPHONES Telekom Slovenije (*www.telekom.si*) operates the country's telephone network and has a useful online directory available in Slovene and English. Only magnetic phonecards (*telekartica*) can be used in public phones; these are sold in 25, 50, 100 and 300 unit denominations and are sold at post offices and some newspaper kiosks. Prices start at €3.

Dialling To call Slovenia from outside the country dial the exit code of the country you are in, followed by Slovenia's country code, 386. When calling from overseas the first 0 of the regional code needs to be omitted before dialling the rest of the number – eg: instead of 01 for Ljubljana you just dial 1. When making international calls from Slovenia the exit code is 00. GSM networks cover the

2

whole country, so as long as you have an international roaming agreement with your mobile telephone company you should have no problems using your handset. Remember to dial the city code in full. Mobile networks include SIMobil (Vodafone), Vega and Mobitel. If you call a mobile number from inside Slovenia make sure you dial all of the digits. Dialling codes for Slovenian mobile phones begin 041, 040 or 070.

Useful telephone numbers

Police	113	Directory enquiries	1188
Fire	112	International directory enquiries	1180
Medical emergency	112	International operator	115
Automobile Association of Slovenia		Time (in Slovene)	195
(AMZS) roadside assistance	1987		

Regional telephone codes

Štajerska	02	Slovenian Adriatic	05
Prekmurje	02	Notranjska	05
Koroška	02	Dolenjska	07
Gorenjska	04	Bela Krajina	07
Primorska	05		

City telephone codes

Ljubljana	01	Kranj	04
Maribor	02	Koper	05
Murska Sobota	02	Nova Gorica	05
Celje	03	Novo Mesto	07

BUSINESS

Since becoming independent in 1991 Slovenia has quickly established itself as an efficient and stable democracy. As such business enterprises in Slovenia operate to the same high standards as other Western countries, official statistics show that the country's accession to the EU has opened up trade links with other member states and to attract more international investors to the country. Key benefits for prospective investors include a highly skilled workforce, the majority of which are proficient in English, and a central European location. The adoption of the euro in early 2007 should also further simplify business transactions with foreign companies.

For those conducting business in Slovenia a few common courtesies will ensure that everything runs smoothly. These include wearing smart business dress, making an appointment to see people and arriving on time for meetings. You will be expected to exchange business cards, so make sure that you have an ample supply. The majority of businesspeople in Ljubljana will have a high level of fluency in English or German, whilst those close to the Italian border are also likely to speak Italian. Business may be conducted in the office or over lunch or dinner. Office hours are generally from 08.00 to 16.00 or 17.00 Monday–Friday. You should expect a meeting that includes a meal to last longer, as Slovenes like to take time over their meals and will not want to appear rude by rushing you.

Slovenia has a growing number of venues for MICE (meetings, incentives, congress and exhibition) events. In Ljubljana the city's four- and five-star hotels provide conference and business facilities. For larger groups the Cankarjev Dom Congress and Cultural Centre (*www.cd-cc.si*) has ten halls which can accommodate a maximum of 1,400 delegates; it also has four additional conference rooms. The five-star Habakuk Hotel in Maribor, hotels and conference centres in Bled, and thermal spas are also excellent MICE venues. Meanwhile activities on offer in resorts like Kranjska Gora, Bovec, the Pohorje and Logarska Dolina are great for team-building events. The Slovenian Chamber of Commerce and Industry (*www.gzs.si*), the website InvestSlovenia–Tipo (*www.investslovenia.org*), *Slovenia Business Week* (*www.gzs.si/eng/news/sbw*) and commercial advisors at foreign embassies in Slovenia can all provide useful information for prospective investors.

BUYING PROPERTY

Many would-be foreign investors are surprised at how high property prices are in Slovenia, with a small centrally located apartment in Ljubljana costing upwards of £150,000 and prices in the Lake Bled region coming in at around £300,000 for a four-bedroom house. This property boom is the cumulative result of a healthy national economy, EU membership and the 2007 introduction of the euro. Some of Europe's most dramatic mountain scenery, a balmy Adriatic coast, properties that are large when compared with their UK counterparts, prices that (despite being reasonably high) still compare favourably with many parts of the UK and budget flights to Ljubljana and Maribor also help make Slovenian property an attractive option.

It is relatively straightforward to purchase property in Slovenia as long as you use a licensed real estate agent and a lawyer familiar with all the vagaries of Slovenian property law. One thing that buyers should be aware of is that the 10% deposit required to secure a purchase is non-refundable if you later renege on the agreement. If you keep your property for ten years you are not liable to pay Capital Gains Tax. SKB Banka (*www.skb.si*) offers an Overseas Buyer's Mortgage on up to 50% of the property price.

CULTURAL ETIQUETTE

Slovenes consider it polite to shake hands, especially when meeting for the first time. Those on business are also expected to exchange business cards. When clinking glasses and toasting say '*Na zdravje*' (pronounced 'noz-drav-yee' and meaning 'cheers'), make sure you look everyone in the group in the eye and then take a sip before returning your glass to the table.

Slovenes expect the same standards of behaviour in public as most other western European countries. It is illegal to smoke in cinemas, theatres and waiting rooms, or on public transport, and a complete smoking ban is mooted for introduction sometime in 2008, so check before lighting up.

Be polite and considerate to cyclists as cycling is part of the culture; you will seldom win an argument with anyone on two wheels even if they have just tried to cut you in half on a pedestrian crossing.

LOCAL CHARITIES

Slovenian Red Cross (Rdeči Križ Slovenije) Mirje 19, 1000 Ljubljana; ☏ 01 241 4300; f 01 241 2344; e rdeci.kriz@rks.si; www.rks.si

Caritas Slovenia (Slovenska Karitas) Kristanova 1, 1000 Ljubljana; ☏ 01 300 5960; f 01 232 3186; e info@karitas.si; www.karitas.si

Part Two

THE GUIDE

200m
200yds
0
0

Žale, BTC City

Orto Bar

GRABLOVIČEVA

BOHORIČEVA

Maveto Založka

ZALOŠKA

Ljubljanica

BIT Centre,
Ljubljana
Youth Hostel,
Hotel Stil,
Architectural
Museum

VILHARJEVA

MASARYKOVA

Railway Station

Slovenian Youth Theatre

Fairgrounds

Metelkova Mesto

Celica Hotel

Slovenian
Ethnographic
Museum

Dijaški
Dom Tabor

Church of
St Peter

TABOR

Park

TRUBARJEVA

Dijaški Dom
Ivana Cankarja

Gostilna
Noble

ŽARNIKOVA

VIDOVDANSKA

Čerin

Ali Baba

Meson
Don Felipe

Drog Art

Kinodvor

Kratochwill

ČUFARJEVA

TRG OSVOBODILNE FRONTE

Nobel

KOLODVORSKA

Slovenska
Kinoteka

JB

TRDINOVA

MIKLOŠIČEVA

See pages 54–5

TRUBARJEVA

ADAMIČ LUNDROVO NABREŽJE

CIRIL METODOV TRG

VODNIKOV TRG

NABREŽJE

Church of
St Florian

Taverna Tatjana

GORNJI TRG

OLD TOWN

Špajza

LPP Kiosk

Grand Union
Hotel Garni

Pasta Nona

Lesari

CIGALETOVA

DALMATINOVA

Park

SLOVENSKA

MIKLOŠIČEVA

NAZORJEVA

ČOPOVA

ŠTRITARJEVA

WOLFOVA

MESTNI TRG

STARI
TRG

Church of
St James

Gruber
Palace

Trta

Railway
Museum

Domino Media,
Ljubljana Hotel

KURILNIŠKA

M Hotel...

Resort, Central

DUNAJSKA

Klub K4

KERSNIKOVA

VOŠNJAKOVA

Lev

TIVOLSKA

ŽUPANČIČEVA

GOSPOSVETSKA

Rusalka

Figovec

CANKARJEVA

TOMŠIČEVA

ŠUBIČEVA

BEETHOVNOVA

KNAFLJEV PREHOD

KONGRESNI
TRG

DVORNI
TRG

HRIBARJEVO NABREŽJE

CANKARJEVO NABREŽJE

BREG

NOVI TRG

SLOVENSKA

Haramabaša

Okrepčevalnica

Pri Škofu

VRTNA

Manna

EIPPROVA

Sax Pub

REČNA

KRAKOVO

KARUNOVA

Church of
St John the Baptist

Architectural Museum
Plečnik

KUD France Prešeren

Union Brewery,
Brewery Museum

CELOVŠKA

Horse
Burger Stand

Cankarjev
Dom

TRG
REPUBLIKE

ERJAVČEVA

GREGORČIČEVA

RIMSKA

Old Roman
House

Roman
Wall

Vila
Veselova

Plečnik
Pyramid

TRNOVO

Breskvar
Fun Factory

Gradaščica Canal

Airport, M Hotel, Dijaški Dom Bežigrad,
Dijaški Dom Šiška, AA Lipa, Vila Minka,
Bežigrad 1&2, Latino Klub Cuba, Vegedrom

National Museum of
Contemporary History

AŠKERČEVA

PREŠERNOVA

TIVOLSKA

Tobacco
Museum

Tivoli Park

Tivoli
Mansion

Zoo

Mons
Hotel

N

Bradt

3

Ljubljana

Recent years have seen Ljubljana increasingly hailed as the 'new Prague', but comparisons like these do not do the Slovenian capital justice. Perhaps the tendency to compare the city comes from the fact that it is not as widely known as big city-break players like Prague, Paris and London, but it may also be because it does take some of the most attractive features from other cities and weaves them into a truly unique mix. At times walking around Ljubljana does feel a bit like Prague or Vienna, but also Amsterdam, Riga or Salzburg, making Ljubljana a sort of 'greatest hits' of European architecture and city planning.

No introduction to Ljubljana would be complete without an immediate mention of the man responsible for much of the way the city looks and is ordered today: Jože Plečnik (see page 48). Perhaps it should be 'Prague, the new Ljubljana' as the seminal Slovene architect honed his skills in Ljubljana before heading off to work on Prague Castle. His work in the Slovenian capital is perhaps even more impressive as he remoulded much of the city, bringing in the Triple Bridge across the Ljubljanica, giving the river new banks as it travelled through the centre of the city, adding the colonnades by the Central Market and turning Tivoli Park into a landscaped park in the grand European tradition. Everywhere you look in Ljubljana the hand of Plečnik can be seen.

While Plečnik shaped the core of the city, Ljubljana has also been heavily influenced by the other nations and ideologies that have rumbled through this strategic hub over the centuries. In Ljubljana an Italianate church rests comfortably beside a functional socialist-era office block and a lavish Art Nouveau façade sidles up to a sharp new steel and glass hotel. The Hungarians, Austrians and Italians are amongst those who have left their indelible marks. Other older civilisations have also left their stamp with the remnants of the old Roman walls sneaking out as a permanent reminder of the city's days as Emona. These eclectic influences permeate many aspects of city life such as its food and drink so that enjoying an Italian-style ice cream by the river is as much part of the Ljubljana experience as savouring hearty Hungarian goulash or quaffing a hoppy pilsner in a beer cellar.

For all its myriad influences Ljubljana is also very Slovenian – a neat, tidy and organised city, with green spaces never far away. Ljubljana was always a cultural hub in the former Yugoslavia, with an aggressively avant-garde reputation, and this vivacity still ripples through the city today with its artistically literate population and a large and active student community. One-off cultural performances and various 'happenings' are all the rage and you are as likely to hear local students talking through the latest experimental theatre as you are their favourite cutting-edge DJs.

HISTORY

According to local legend, Ljubljana's first inhabitants came straight from the pages of Greek mythology when, after being tricked into stealing a golden fleece that belonged to King Aeetes, Jason and his Argonauts fled from Colchis. The *Argo* then transported the ancient warriors on their epic adventure from the Black Sea to the Danube, onward to the Sava River and finally into the Ljubljanica. Having successfully escaped the wrath of Aeetes, the Argonauts were confronted by a formidable fire-breathing dragon which, during a fierce battle, the brave Jason managed to slay. In commemoration of this courageous act the city's coat of arms bears a picture of the beast. The Ljubljana dragon can also be found throughout the city, on the castle's tower, the town hall and railings along the banks of the Ljubljanica, as well as standing proud on the eponymous bridge and, of course, on a wealth of tourist souvenirs.

While it may not be full of colourful characters from Greek mythology, Ljubljana's recorded history is no less intoxicating. Historical evidence suggests that Ljubljana's first inhabitants were pile dwellers from the Copper Age, who lived in stilt-houses built on marshland. Next came the Illyrians, who settled near Ljubljana in the late Bronze Age. Cave paintings near the capital depict members of this ancient tribe engaged in battle and sporting events, enjoying great feasts and conducting ritual sacrifices. Around the 3rd century BC Celtic tribes rumbled into the region.

The arrival of the Romans in the 1st century BC saw Ljubljana's status elevated from a rough tribal settlement to a military base and later to a city. Under the Romans Ljubljana was called Emona and remnants of the Roman settlement can still be found on the left bank of the Ljubljanica, including reconstructed sections of the Roman walls. For its residents life in Emona was good save the frequent attacks by the barbarian Huns and the central Asian Avars, but the Romans finally capitulated in AD452.

By the 7th century the Slavs had become the dominant people in Slovenia, establishing the first independent Slavic or Slovenian state, Carinthia. In AD746, Carinthia fell under the auspices of the Bavarian Dukes. Ljubljana next emerged as a significant city in medieval times, with its Austrian name Laibach (a name that it kept until 1918) first appearing in written documents in 1144. In 1335, under the Austro-Hungarians, Ljubljana became the capital of the province of Carniola, and the Austro-Hungarians remained the dominant force in the city until the end of World War I.

In 1511, a devastating earthquake felled much of Ljubljana. While reconstruction after the earthquake helped shape the city's physical appearance, Protestantism, which rose to the fore in the late 16th century, played a significant role in shaping the city's psyche over the next 200 years. By the 19th century, however, the Catholic Church had become an influential force in the shaping of Ljubljana's (and Slovenia's) cultural and linguistic identity. Today Primož Trubar, Ivan Cankar and France Prešeren remain writ large on the national consciousness of modern Ljubljana. More than 150 years after his death in 1849, a looming statue of Prešeren still watches protectively over Ljubljana's residents.

At the beginning of the 19th century Napoleon made a brief incursion into the region, which left Ljubljana as the capital of the French emperor's Illyrian Provinces from 1809 to 1813. With Austro-Hungarian rule restored by the 1814–15 Congress of Vienna, the other defining events in Ljubljana's history were the construction of the Vienna–Trieste railway, which was completed in 1857 and brought new cultural influences to the Slovenian capital, and a second devastating earthquake in 1895. The rebuilding of the city in the late 19th and early 20th centuries gave rise to the stunning Art Nouveau (or secessionist) buildings found on Ljubljana's historic left bank.

World War I heralded the end of four decades of peace in Europe and the collapse of the Austro-Hungarian Empire. In 1918, Slovenia became part of the Kingdom of Serbs, Croats and Slovenes. The inter-war years saw the city take on much of its iconic architecture under the guiding hand of Jože Plečnik. At this time the biggest skyscraper in Yugoslavia, the Nebotičnik, was constructed. Currently closed due to a legal wrangle brought on by the process of denationalisation, the skyscraper still stands on Slovenska as an enduring testimony to the grand ambitions of this newly independent pan-Slavic country.

A dramatically different Slovenia emerged from the rubble of World War II, and in 1945 Ljubljana took its place as one of the six capitals of Tito's new Yugoslavia. For almost half a century the Slovenian capital found itself under the rigid control of a socialist regime, characterised by dictatorial leadership and the shared ownership of property, which was ended by the declaration of Slovenian independence on 26 June 1991.

In the period since independence Ljubljana has come of age as a capital city. In 2004, Slovenia joined both NATO and the European Union, heralding in a new phase for Slovenia and Ljubljana. The physical appearance as well as the political importance of the city is changing too, as new office buildings and houses spring up and older buildings are given much-needed refurbishment. Ljubljana today is a dynamic and rapidly evolving city that is becoming increasingly popular with both businesspeople and tourists from the rest of the EU and beyond.

GETTING THERE

BY AIR Located 23km northwest of Ljubljana's city centre, Ljubljana Jože Pučnik Airport (*Zgornji Brnik 130A, 4210 Brnik-Aerodrom;* \ *04 206 1981;* f *04 202 1220;* e *info@lju-airport.si; www.lju-airport.si*) is well served by taxis and bus services.

Airport transfers Buses leave Jože Pučnik for Ljubljana city centre on the hour between 05.00 and 20.00 Monday–Friday, and every two hours from 10.00–20.00 at the weekend, with an additional service at 07.00. Buses leave the main bus station for the airport at 05.20 and then at ten minutes past the hour from 06.10–20.10 Monday–Friday. At weekends they leave at 06.10 and then every two hours from 09.10 to 19.10. Journey time is 45 minutes; the one-way fare is €4.

Markun (✆ 04 252 1016) operate a private bus service between the airport and Ljubljana bus station. These depart Jože Pučnik Airport daily at 07.30, 09.55, 11.30, 13.45, 15.00, 16.00, 18.10, 21.50, 23.00 and midnight. Buses for the airport leave Ljubljana at 05.20, 06.15, 10.25, 12.15, 14.10, 15.30, 17.00 and 22.30. Journey time is 30 minutes; the fare is €5. Taxis to and from the city centre cost around €28–30. Watch out for unscrupulous drivers cranking the meter up to the highest possible rate.

BY BUS Ljubljana bus station (*Trg Osvobodilne fronte 4;* ✆ *090 934 230* (€ *0.78 per min);* e *avtobusna.postaja@ap-ljubljana.si; www.ap-ljubljana.si;* ⏱ *05.30–21.00*) is easily accessible by bus from towns and cities across Slovenia including: Kamnik (35 minutes), Škofja Loka (40 minutes), Kranj (40 minutes), Postojna (1 hour), Novo Mesto (1 hour 10 minutes), Idrija (1½ hours), Bled (1 hour 20 minutes), Celje (1 hour 35 minutes), Ribčez Laz for Lake Bohinj (2 hours), Kranjska Gora (2 hours), Koper (2 hours 20 minutes), Nova Gorica (2½ hours), Piran (2 hours 40 minutes), Maribor (2½ hours) and Murska Sobota (4 hours).

BY RAIL Regular train services link the capital railway station (*Trg Osvobodilne fronte 6;* ✆ *01 291 3332;* e *potnik.info@slo-zeleznice.si; www.slo-zeleznice.si*) to the rest of Slovenia; services tend to be less frequent and a little slower than buses. Available routes include: Kamnik (50 minutes), Postojna (1 hour), Novo Mesto (1 hour 40 minutes), Maribor (2½ hours), Črnomelj (2½ hours), Koper (2½ hours), Metlika (2½ hours) and Ptuj (2½ hours).

GETTING AROUND

BICYCLE HIRE From April to October bicycle hire is available from €0.83 an hour to €4.17 a day from nine locations within the city centre that are part of the Ljubljana Bike (*Ljubljansko kolo*) scheme. You need photo ID to rent a bike under this scheme; a small refundable deposit will also be charged. The city also has commercial hire outlets, including **Café Maček** (*Krojaška 5;* ✆ *01 425 3791*), and many hotels offer bicycle hire to guests.

Ljubljana Bike locations

Tir café bar, Ljubljana railway station, Trg Osvobodilne fronte 7
Podmornica café-bar, Miklošičeva
Sladoledni vrt, Nazorjeva
Slovenian Tourist Information Centre (STIC), Krekov trg 10

Pod Lipo, Rimska
Le Petit Café, Trg Francoske Revolucije 4
Parlament café-bar, Plečnikov trg (in front of the Maximarket department store)
Celica Hostel, Metelkova
Park Hotel, Tabor 9

BY BUS The city bus service run by Ljubljanski Potniški Promet (LPP) is useful if you are staying outside the city centre. Most of the 21 routes operate from 05.00 to 22.30, although some run from 03.15 until midnight. You can pay with cash (€1.25) or *žetoni* (metal tokens), which are available for €0.79 from newsstands, kiosks and anywhere displaying a *žetoni* sign. Tokens and daily or weekly passes can also be purchased at the bus station or directly from LPP.

LPP Information Centre (also lost & found) Celovška 160; ✆ 01 582 2420; e mail@lpp.si; www.lpp.si

LPP Information Centre Trdinova 3; ✆ 01 434 3248
LPP Information Centre Slovenska 56; ✆ 430 5174

BY TAXI Taxi ranks are located near the Ljubljana tourist information centre on Adamič-Lundrovo nabrežje, outside the Slon Hotel on Slovenska, at the railway station and near Mestni trg. At night taxis also wait on Prešernov trg. Taxis are metered, but rates vary between companies, and are also affected by the time of day and method of booking. As a guide the flagfall and the per-kilometre rate should be around €1. Reputable operators include:

- **Intersiti** ☎ 01 541 5800 or 📱 041 445 406
- **Intertours** ☎ 01 520 9704 or 📱 031 311 311
- **Rumeni** 📱 041 731 831

BY RAIL Ljubljana has a limited local route, which includes services north to Ježica, Črnuče and Vižmarje, east to Polje and southeast to Rakovnik.

CAR HIRE Car hire is available at the airport, in central Ljubljana and at some of the city's hotels. Central locations include:

- **Avis** Čufarjeva 2; ☎ 01 430 8010; f 01 430 8014; e lji@avis.si; www.avis-alpe.si; ⊕07.00–19.00 Mon–Fri, 07.00–13.00 Sat, 08.00–12.00 Sun, or Hotel Lev, Vošnjakova 1; ☎ 01 438 3250; f 01 438 3255; e lj3@avis.si; www.avis-alpe.si; ⊕08.00–15.00
- **Budget** Grand Hotel Union, Miklošičeva 3; ☎ 01 421 7340; f 01 421 7344; e ljubljana.dt@budget.si; www.budget.si; ⊕08.00–16.00 Mon–Fri, 08.00–12.00 Sat/Sun
- **Europcar** City Hotel, Dalmatinova 15; ☎/f 01 234 9170; ⊕08.00–18.00 Mon–Fri, 08.00–13.00 & 18.00–20.00 Sat, 08.00–13.00 Sun

- **Hertz** Trdinova 9; ☎ 01 434 0147; f 01 434 0148; e ljubljana@hertz.si; www.hertz.si.; ⊕07.00–19.00 Mon–Fri, 08.00–13.00 Sat, 08.00–12.00 Sun
- **National Car Rental** Dunajska 10; ☎ 01 589 0850; e national@avantcar.si; www.nationalcar-slovenia.com; ⊕08.00–22.00
- **Sixt** Trg Osvobodilne fronte 7; ☎ 01 430 1666; f 01 430 266; www.sixt.si; ⊕08.00–22.00

TOURIST TRANSPORT The year 2007 saw the opening of the new funicular (*adult/concession €2/€1.50 return, €1.50/€1 single; ⊕09.00–23.00 daily*) which ferries passengers between Krekov trg and Ljubljana Castle. An alternative way to get up to the castle without walking is to hop on the tourist train that runs from Prešernov trg on the hour (*adult/concession €2.50/€1.70; ⊕May–Sep 09.00–21.00 & Apr–Oct 10.00–19.00 (weather dependent)*). The return train leaves the castle at 20 minutes past the hour.

TOURIST INFORMATION/LOCAL TOUR OPERATORS

🛈 **Ljubljana Tourist Information Centre** Adamič-Lundrovo nabrežje 2; ☎ 01 306 1215; e info@ljubljana-tourism.si; www.ljubljana-tourism.si or www.ljubljana.si; ⊕Jun–Sep 08.00–21.00 daily, Oct–May 08.00–19.00 daily. Staff at Ljubljana's main tourist information office dish out a wealth of information about the city. They can also help you book accommodation & sightseeing tours on foot, by bicycle, by boat & even by hot-air balloon.

🛈 **Tourist Information Centre at the railway station** Trg Osvobodilne fronte 6; ☎ 01 433 9475; e ticzp@ljubljana-tourism.si; www.ljubljana-

tourism.si or www.ljubljana.si; ⊕Jun–Sep 08.00–22.00 daily, Oct–May 08.00–19.00 daily

🛈 **Slovenian Tourist Information Centre** Krekov trg 10; ☎ 01 306 4575/76; f 01 306 4580; e stic@ljubljana-tourism.si; www.slovenia.info; ⊕Jun–Sep 08.00–09.00 daily, Oct–May 08.00–19.00 daily

🛈 **Jože Pučnik Tourist Information Point** Zgornji Brnik 130A; e ticairport@Ljubljana-tourism.si; www.ljubljana-tourism.si or www.ljubljana.si. Hours vary to meet flights.

Kompas Slovenska 36; ☎ 01 200 6222; www.kompas.si. Offering a variety of excursions from Ljubljana. They can also help you to arrange accommodation & onward travel.

Globtour Trg Republike 1; ↘ 01 236 4400; www.globtour.si. Full service tourist agency offering the same services as Kompas.

Skok Sport Centre Marinovseva 8; ↘ 01 512 4402 or 📱 040 218 000; e info@skok-sport.si; www.skok-sport.si. Adventure specialist located 7km from the city centre. Kayaking (10hr course; € 150), rafting (€ 15–30), mountain biking & beach volleyball are all on offer. Raft, kayak & mountain-bike hire is also available.

Label Trubarjeva 47; 📱 051 200 743; www.label.si. Outdoor sports specialists organising everything

from paintball, rafting & kayaking to mountain biking & wakeboarding. Bicycle hire is also available.

Balonarski Centre Barje Flandrova 1; ↘ 01 512 9220; e balon@siol.net. A unique way to see Ljubljana is from the air aboard a hot-air balloon. The centre organises flights out across the Ljubljana marshes with unforgettable views of the city & surrounding mountains.

Lifetrek Adventures Near Cobbler's Bridge; ↘ 04 578 0662; e ziva@lifetrek.si; www.lifetrek-slovenia.com. Organising everything from canyoning & rock climbing to scuba diving, via ferrata & rafting from their offices in Bled, Kranj & Ljubljana.

🏠 WHERE TO STAY

🏠 **Alibi Hostel** (15 rooms) Cankarjevo Nabrežje 27; ↘ 01 363 666; f 01 251 1245; e info@alibi.si; www.alibi.si. Beds at this new hostel, which enjoys a prime Old Town location on the banks of the Ljubljanica, fill up fast so book ahead. Rates are pp. ⑤

🏠 **Antiq** (10 rooms) Gornji trg 3; ↘ 01 421 3560; f 01 421 3565; e info@antiqhotel.si. Opened in 2006, the Antiq boasts a central location & rooms with a real atmosphere & sense of history. The lavish old building housing the Antiq sits at the heart of the Old Town. All rooms are designated suites, with period furniture, satellite TV, large beds, bathtubs & corner sofas; some also have private terraces. ⑤⑤⑤⑤⑤

🏠 **Celica Hostel** (29 rooms) Metelkova 8; ↘ 01 230 9700; f 01 230 9714; www.souhostel.si. 5 mins' walk from the bus & train stations, this bright & funky hostel offers 92 beds in 2 14-person rooms. Housed in a former prison & military barracks of the Yugoslav army, the best rooms are the 20 renovated prison cells that sleep 2 or 3 people. Each of these individual & local-artist-designed cells retains its original window & cell bars. If you stay in a cell then bathroom facilities are shared, although the hostel's 9 other rooms have private bathrooms. A range of outdoor adventures can also be booked at the hostel. It is essential to book in advance. Rates are pp. ⑤

🏠 **City Hotel** (220 rooms) Dalmatinova 15; ↘ 01 234 9130; f 01 234 9140; e info@cityhotel.si; www.cityhotel.si. Impressively renovated 3-star hotel with en-suite, AC rooms; some of the new rooms boast castle views. Free internet. On-street parking, HB & FB rates & bicycle hire (for guests only) are also available. ⑤⑤⑤⑤

🏠 **Dijaški Dom Tabor** (120 rooms) Vidovdanska 7; ↘ 01 234 8840; f 01 234 8855; e ddtabor-lj@guest.arnes.si; www2.arnes.si/~ssljddta4. From late Jun to late Aug these centrally located student dorms offer accommodation in sgl, twin & dbl rooms & 10-bed dormitories. Rates are pp. ⑤

🏠 **Emonec** (26 rooms) Wolfova 12; ↘ 01 200 1520; f 01 200 1521; e hotelemonec@siol.net; www.hotel-emonec.com. Free internet access, a great location & reasonable prices all combine to make this 2-star hotel a good option. ⑤⑤⑤

🏠 **Fluxus** (3 rooms) Tomšičeva 4; ↘ 01 251 5760; e info@fluxus-hostel.com; www.fluxus-hostel.com. Bright & friendly hostel with 2 dorms & a dbl room. Rooms & dorms have en-suite showers, but the toilet is shared. Dorm rates pp ⑤, dbl ⑤⑤

🏠 **Grand Hotel Union Business** (139 rooms) Miklošičeva 3; ↘ 01 308 1170; f 01 308 1914; e hotel.business@gh-union.si; www.gh-union.si. The modern wing of the Grand Hotel Union has an unattractive exterior compared with its illustrious relation next door. However, guestrooms are furnished to the same high standards as rooms in the Executive & guests have access to all of the facilities detailed in the listing below. There is a modest gym & a small swimming pool. ⑤⑤⑤⑤–⑤⑤⑤⑤⑤

🏠 **Grand Hotel Union Executive** (191 rooms) Miklošičeva 1; ↘ 01 308 1270; f 01 308 1015; e hotel.union@gh-union.si; www.gh-union.si. Housed in a stunning Art Nouveau building dating from 1905, Ljubljana's most attractive hotel is just a min's stroll from Prešernov trg. Classically decorated rooms feature satellite TV, minibars, fluffy bathrobes & slippers. Meeting facilities, good-quality restaurants & garage parking are also on offer. Guests can use the leisure facilities at the hotel's Business sibling. ⑤⑤⑤⑤–⑤⑤⑤⑤⑤

🏠 **Grand Hotel Union Garni** (74 rooms) Miklošičeva 9; ☎ 01 308 4300; f 01 230 1181; e hotel.garni@gh-union.si; www.astralhotel.net. This centrally located hotel attracts a mainly business crowd. Large guestrooms are comfortable & equipped with all the amenities that you would expect to find in a 4-star hotel. The hotel also has its own restaurant, bar, relaxation centre with sauna, conference facilities & a hard-to-beat location, 10 mins' walk from the main bus & railway stations & 500m from the Old Town. $$$$

🏠 **Lev** (189 rooms) Vošnjakova 1; ☎ 01 433 2155; f 01 230 2578; e info@hotel-lev.si; www.hotel-lev.si. The 'Lion' is Ljubljana's only 5-star hotel, a place aimed firmly at businesspeople, though there are often good deals at weekends to attract leisure travellers as well. The best deals are often available on their website. Rooms are spacious, classically styled & comfortable. Some of the city-side rooms on the higher levels have castle views & others overlook Tivoli Park. $$$$–$$$$$

🏠 **Park** (122 rooms) Tabor 9; ☎ 01 433 1306; f 01 433 0546; e hotel.park@siol.net; www.hotelpark.si. The Park is located 800m from the main bus & railway stations & is one of the few moderately priced hotels in Ljubljana. It may have recently undergone something of a makeover, but it still feels pretty basic. Housed in a tower block it has clean en-suite rooms. The 2- & 4-bed hostel rooms on the top floor are a more affordable option. Hotel $$$, hostel $

🏠 **Pension Pri Mraku** (30 rooms) Rimska 4; ☎ 01 421 9600; f 01 421 9655; e mrak@daj-dam.si; www.daj-dam.si. This old school guesthouse has a

good location on an attractive street near the Križanke theatre, so if you are here for a concert or for the summer festival this is the place to stay. Despite their Old World feel, guestrooms are fairly large & have modern facilities including internet access & cable TV. $$$–$$$$

🏠 **Slon Best Western Premier** (176 rooms) Slovenska 34; ☎ 01 470 1131; f 01 251 7164; e sales@hotelslon.com; www.hotelslon.com or www.bestwestern.com. The Slon has one of the best locations in the city. In addition to comfortable AC rooms, the Slon offers internet access in the lobby & a ground-floor deli, café & restaurant. Good rates are often available through the Best Western website. At the time of going to press the hotel was in the midst of a revamp. $$$$–$$$$$

🏠 **Tour As** Mala 8; ☎ 01 434 2660; f 01 434 2664; e info@apartmaji.si; www.apartmaji.si. Agency co-ordinating stays in apts. All properties are fully furnished, have telephones, satellite TV & internet connections. Ensure that you know the exact location of your apt before booking if you want to avoid long walks or buses into town; a handy map on the company's website will help you do this. Prices depend on location & the number of people that the apt will sleep. 2-person apt $$$, 6-person apt $$$$$

🏠 **Vila Veselova** (5 rooms) Veselova 14; ☎ 059 926 72; f 031 640 965; e desk@v-v.si; www.v-v.si. This traditional villa close to Ljubljana's museums & Tivoli Park offers accommodation in dormitories, a dbl & an apt. Dorm rates pp $, dbl $$, apt $$$

OUTSIDE THE CITY CENTRE

🏠 **AA Lipa** Celovška 264; ☎ 01 507 4590; f 01 507 4960; e aa-lipa@siol.net; www.aa-lipa.si. Bus 1 direction Vižmarje, bus 15 direction Medvode or bus 16 direction Gameljne to Dravlje stop. Located on busy Celovška not far from the M Hotel (about 3km out of town), the AA Lipa offers basic motel-style accommodation in an unappealing tower block. $$

🏠 **Bit Centre** (39 rooms) Litijska 57; ☎ 01 548 0055; f 01 548 0056; e hotel@bit-centre.net; www.bit-center.net. Bus 5 or 9 direction Štepansko naselje & bus 13 direction Sostro to Emona stop. On the same site as the Ljubljana Youth Hostel this budget hotel is a step up from dormitory accommodation. Rooms are basic & small with satellite TV & private bathrooms with shower. Guests can use the facilities at the adjoining sports centre. $$

🏠 **Dijaški Dom Bežigrad** (70 rooms) Kardeljeva ploščad 28; ☎ 01 534 0061; f 01 534 2864; e dd.lj-bezigrad@guest.arnes.si; www.hostel-ddb.si. Bus 6 direction Črnuče, bus 8 direction Ježica or bus 21 direction Beričevo to Mercator stop. In Jul & Aug the student dormitories in Bežigrad provide budget accommodation for groups in sgl, dbl & trpl rooms. Rates are pp. $

🏠 **Dijaški Dom Ivana Cankarja** (180 rooms) Poljanska 26; ☎ 01 474 8600; f 01 432 0369; e dic@dic.si; www.dic.si. Bus 5 direction Štepansko naselje or bus 13 direction Sostro to Roška stop. The student dorms are just 10 mins' walk from central Ljubljana, close to Castle Hill. This part-time hostel has 480 beds in sgl, dbl & trpl rooms from late Jun to late Aug. The residence also has its own parking spaces, sports stadium, football pitch & basketball courts. Rates are pp. $

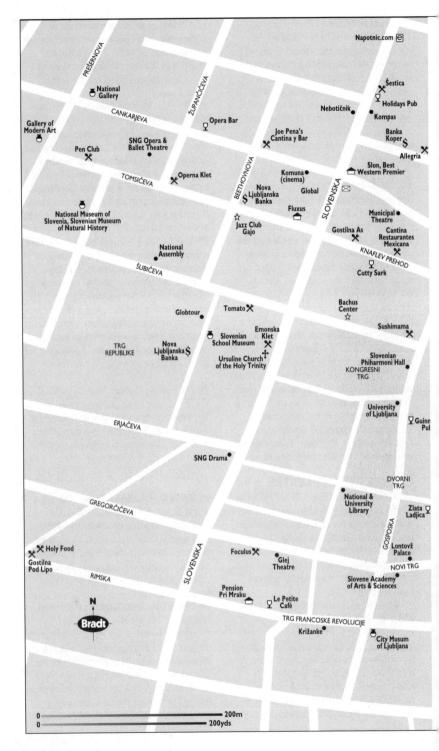

Napotnic.com

National Gallery

PREŠERNOVA

ŽUPANČIČEVA

CANKARJEVA

Opera Bar

Gallery of Modern Art

SNG Opera & Ballet Theatre

Pen Club

Joe Pena's Cantina y Bar

Šestica

Nebotičnik

Holidays Pub

Kompas

Banka Koper

Allegria

TOMSIČEVA

Operna Klet

BEETHOVNOVA

Komuna (cinema)

Nova Ljubljanska Banka

Global

Slon, Best Western Premier

SLOVENSKA

National Museum of Slovenia, Slovenian Museum of Natural History

Fluxus

Municipal Theatre

Jazz Club Gajo

Gostilna As

Cantina Restaurantes Mexicana

National Assembly

KNAFLEV PREHOD

ŠUBIČEVA

Cutty Sark

Globtour

Tomato

Bachus Center

TRG REPUBLIKE

Nova Ljubljanska Banka

Slovenian School Museum

Emonska Klet

Sushimama

Ursuline Church of the Holy Trinity

Slovenian Phiharmoni Hall

KONGRESNI TRG

University of Ljubljana

Guinn Pul

ERJAČEVA

SNG Drama

DVORNI TRG

GREGORČIČEVA

National & University Library

Zlata Ladjica

GOSPOSKA

Lontovž Palace

NOVI TRG

Holy Food

Foculus

Glej Theatre

Gostilna Pod Lipo

SLOVENSKA

Slovene Academy of Arts & Sciences

RIMSKA

Pension Pri Mraku

Le Petite Café

N

TRG FRANCOSKE REVOLUCIJE

Bradt

Križanke

City Musum of Ljubljana

0   200m
0   200yds

54

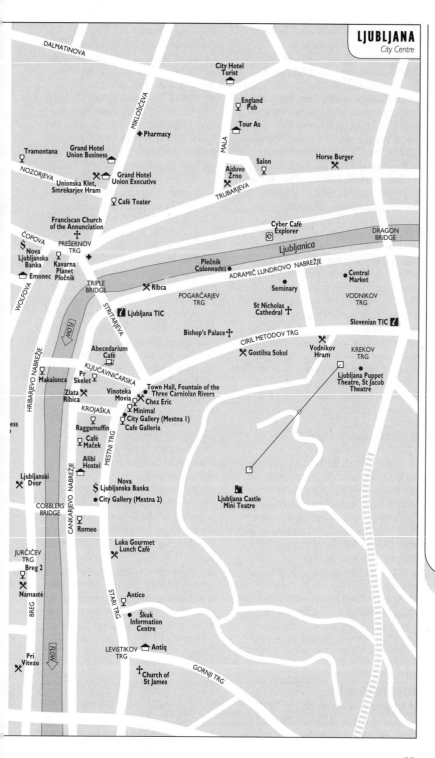

DALMATINOVA

City Hotel
Turist

England
Pub

Tour As

MIKLOŠIČEVA

+ Pharmacy

MALA

Salon

Horse Burger

Tramontana

Grand Hotel
Union Business

NOZORJEVA

Ajdovo
Žrno

Unionska Klet,
Smrekarjev Hram

Grand Hotel
Union Executive

TRUBARJEVA

Café Teater

Franciscan Church
of the Annunciation

Cyber Café
Explorer

DRAGON
BRIDGE

ČOPOVA

Nova
Ljubljanska
Banka

PREŠERNOV
TRG

Ljubljanica

Emonec

Kavarna
Planet
Pločnik

Plečnik
Colonnades

ADRAMIČ LUNDROVO NABREŽJE

Central
Market

WOLFOVA

TRIPLE
BRIDGE

Ribca

POGARČARJEV
TRG

Seminary

VODNIKOV
TRG

STRITARJEVA

FLOW

Ljubljana TIC

St Nicholas
Cathedral

Slovenian TIC

Bishop's Palace

CIRIL METODOV TRG

HRIBARJEVO NABREŽJE

Abecedarium
Café

Gostilna Sokol

Vodnikov
Hram

KREKOV
TRG

KLJUČAVNIČARSKA

Pr
Skelet

Makalonca

Ljubljana Puppet
Theatre, St Jacob
Theatre

Zlata
Ribca

Vinoteka
Movia

Town Hall, Fountain of the
Three Carniolan Rivers

Chez Eric

KROJAŠKA

Minimal

City Gallery (Mestna 1)

Cafe Galleria

Raggamuffin

MESTNI TRG

Café
Maček

CANKARJEVO NABREŽJE

Alibi
Hostel

Ljubljanski
Dvor

Nova
Ljubljanska Banka

City Gallery (Mestna 2)

Ljubljana Castle
Mini Teatre

COBBLERS
BRIDGE

Romeo

Luka Gourmet
Lunch Café

JURČIČEV
TRG

Breg 2

Namasté

BREG

STARI TRG

Antico

Škuk
Information
Centre

LEVISTIKOV
TRG

Antiq

FLOW

Pri
Vitezu

Church of
St James

GORNJI TRG

🛏 **Dijaški Dom Šiška** (50 beds) Aljaževa 32; ☎/f 01 500 7802; e info@ddsiska.com; www.ddsiska.com. Bus 1 direction Vižmarje, bus 3 direction Litostroj, bus 5 direction Podutik, bus 8 direction Brod, bus 15 direction Medvode or bus 16 direction Gamelnje to Stara Cerkev stop. Student dormitory located in Šiška, open from the beginning of Jun to the end of Aug. Accommodation takes the form of simply furnished twin rooms. This seasonal hostel also has a TV room, café-bar, currency-exchange facilities & a car park. Rates are pp. $

🛏 **Domina Media Ljubljana Hotel & Spa** (213 rooms) Dunajska 154; ☎ 01 588 2500; f 01 588 0599; e grandmedia.ljubljana@domina.it; www.dominahotels.it. Bus 6 direction Črnuče, bus 8 direction Ježica or bus 21 direction Beričevo. Comfortable dbls & junior suites offer broadband internet connections, free email, pay TV & computer games. In many rooms huge plasma TV screens also provide on-screen newspapers, books, films & even virtual sightseeing tours of Ljubljana. Additional facilities include the Sense wellness centre & spa, with its indoor pool, sauna, gym, casino, restaurants, bars, convention centre, meeting rooms & video conferencing. The only bugbear is that the hotel is located 3km out of the city centre, which means you will need to catch the hotel's shuttle bus, a taxi or municipal bus to & from town. Good rates are often available on the internet. $$$–$$$$

⛺ **Ljubljana Resort** Dunajska 270; ☎ 01 568 3913; f 01 568 3912; e ljubljana.resort@gpl.si; www.ljubljanaresort.si. Bus 6 direction Črnuče or bus 8 direction Ježica to Ježica stop. Located 3km from the city centre the campsite has electricity points, hot water, showers, laundry & dishwashing facilities, as well as its own restaurant & a snack bar. There is the option of renting a bungalow equipped with a telephone & TV. Onsite facilities include a skittle alley, gym, sauna, games courts & 3 swimming pools. Camping $, sgl bungalow $$, dbl/trpl bungalow $$$

🛏 **Ljubljana Youth Hostel** Litijska 57; ☎ 01 548 0055; f 01 548 0056; e hotel@bit-centre.net; www.yh-ljubljana.com. Bus 5 or 9 direction Štepansko naselje or bus 13 direction Sostro to

Emona stop. Affiliated with HI & providing accommodation in 2-, 3- & 10-bed rooms. Guests can use the sporting facilities located on the same site. The hostel also has a car park & a summer terrace bar. Shared bathrooms. Rates are pp. $

🛏 **M Hotel** (157 rooms) Derčeva 4; ☎ 01 513 7000; f 01 519 7090; e info@m-hotel.si; www.m-hotel.si. Bus 1 direction Vižmarje, bus 5 direction Podutik, bus 8 direction Brod, bus 15 direction Medvode or bus 16 direction Gamelnje to Šiška stop. Don't let your first glimpse of the M Hotel put you off. The hotel is not, as it may at first appear, totally immersed in a jungle of concrete high-rises & busy roads. Rooms at the front overlook a quiet tree-lined street & Tivoli Park. With friendly staff & modern rooms the M Hotel is arguably Ljubljana's best 3-star property. $$$$

🛏 **Mons Hotel** (114 rooms) Pot za Brdom; ☎ 01 470 2700; e info@hotel.mons.si; www.hotel-mons.com. This stylish design hotel – a box-like green & glass structure that was designed by the famous Slovenian-born architect Boris Podrecca. Rooms are comfortable & high-tech. The hotel also has a wine bar, fitness centre, snooker room, 2 restaurants & a conference centre. The hotel runs a free shuttle bus to Kongresni trg. $$$$

🛏 **Hotel Stil** (24 rooms) Litijska cesta 188; ☎ 01 548 4343; f 01 548 4344; e hotel@hotel-stil.si; www.hotel-stil.si. Bus 13 direction Štepanja Vas. The location just off the city's bypass may not sound too appealing, but the room rates are more attractive. Rooms feature satellite TV, minibars & wireless internet. Rooms $$$, apts (with kitchen) $$$$–$$$$$

🛏 **Vila Minka** Kogovškova 10; ☎ 01 583 0080; f 01 507 4691; e minka@vilaminka.si; www.vilaminka.si. Bus 5 direction Podutik or bus 22 direction Kamna Gorica stop Koseze. Located 3km from the city centre in the suburb of Koseze, just north of Tivoli Park, Vila Minka has spacious rooms & apts. Facilities include satellite TV, internet access & car parking. Apts for 1–5 people also have small private kitchens, while those staying in sgl or dbl rooms can use the communal cooking area. Car & bicycle hire is also offered. Rooms $$–$$$, 1-person apt $$–$$$, 5-person apt $$$$

✕ WHERE TO EAT

TOP-END DINING

✕ **Breskvar** Cesta na Loko 28; ☎ 01 282 8833; www.breskvar.com; ⏱ 12.00–22.00 Mon–Fri. A good 15-min walk south of the canal in Trnovo, a visit to

this cosy traditional restaurant is worth the effort. The owners like to steer you towards their favourite wines & dishes, which is no bad thing in this case, with starters like cuttlefish risotto married with lightly grilled octopus & rocket. Fish is the highlight of the main courses; the sea bream is a particularly good. **$$$$$**

✕ **Chez Eric** Mestni trg 3; ☎ 01 251 2839; www.delices.si; ⊕ 12.00–16.00 & 19.00–23.00. For sheer class & top-end French cuisine Chez Eric is hard to beat. The decadent interior & professional waiting staff ensure a quality experience & the food certainly does not disappoint. A flurry of 6 oysters to start is a popular option or perhaps you'd like to try some foie gras? The mains feature the like of veal medallions & beef tournedos, while a delicious crêpe Suzette awaits to finish things off, before you are caressed reluctantly back outside into reality. **$$$$$**

✕ **Gostilna As** Knaflev prehod 5a; ☎ 01 425 8822; www.gostilnaas.si; ⊕ 12.00–midnight daily. This is the place for a meal amongst Ljubljana's cognoscenti with top-quality cuisine & fine wine, but make sure to dress up smart. The outdoor covered terrace has more of a buzz & is less formal. Both venues concentrate on excellent seafood with a shared Adriatic platter to die for, as well as some creative options presented with lashings of flair. **$$$$$**

✕ **JB** Miklošičeva 17; ☎ 01 433 1358; www.jb-slo.com; ⊕ 11.00–23.00 Mon–Fri, 17.00–23.00 Sat. For slick international cuisine served up in smooth fine dining surrounds JB is hard to beat. Slightly off the beaten tourist track this is the place to bring anyone you want to impress. The wine list is one of the best in the city & signature dishes include sea bass topped with fresh black truffles. Well-sourced domestic ingredients are the key at JB so the menu changes regularly. **$$$$$**

✕ **Lesar** Gosposvetska 2; ☎ 01 438 2420; ⊕ 09.00–23.00 Mon–Fri. Another Luka Gourmet effort, this time a fine-dining restaurant in a charming historical building. **$$$$$**

✕ **Manna** Eipprova 1; ☎ 01 283 5294; www.kulinarika-manna.com; ⊕ 12.00–midnight Mon–Sat. Increasingly sophisticated Slovene restaurant in the fashionable suburb of Trnovo. Well worth the 10-min stroll south of the centre. **$$$$$**

✕ **Operna Klet** Župančičeva 2; ☎ 01 252 7003; ⊕ 11.00–23.00 Mon–Fri. Hiding away by the opera house in a small cellar is one of Ljubljana's best seafood restaurants. The dark wood fish swimming across the old stone walls & hardwood panelling make Operna Klet easy on the eye, but you will soon be concentrating on the plate with the likes of

crab croquettes & tartar sauce & grilled squid with garlic to start. Grilled fresh fish is the highlight of the main menu. **$$$$**

✕ **Pen Club** Tomsičeva 12; ☎ 01 251 4160; ⊕ 13.00–midnight Mon–Fri. Traditionally the meeting place for the Slovene literati, this intimate venue has a menu that changes daily. With décor that has a discernible 1970s edge, the Pen Club is pleasingly kitsch. Starters typically include pasta laced with white truffles or homemade ravioli stuffed with spinach. The fish dishes are the stand outs amongst the mains with fresh fish brought for inspection before cooking, with huge sea bass – usually more than enough for 2 – a speciality. **$$$$**

✕ **Pri Vitezu** Breg 20; ☎ 01 426 6058; www.privitezu.com; ⊕ 12.00–23.00 daily. This riverside brasserie & wine bar fuses Italian & Slovenian cuisine. . A favourite with locals taking someone out for a traditional treat. The 2 major downsides are that service can be patchy (we once had 4 main courses served at different times) & the unconventional owner who occasionally swaggers in & ruins diners' meals as happened on one occasion when we were there. **$$$$$**

✕ **Restavracija Unionska Klet** Miklošičeva 10; ☎ 01 308 1968; ⊕ 18.00–midnight Mon–Fri, 12.00–15.00 & 18.00–midnight Sat/Sun. Sample hearty Slovenian dishes in the Grand Hotel Union's elegant new cellar restaurant. **$$$$**

✕ **Rusalka** Vosnjakova 1; ☎ 01 433 2155; ⊕ 12.00–23.00 daily. The Rusalka is that all too rare beast: a hotel restaurant whose food matches the quality of the Lev Hotel's 5-star bedrooms. The speciality is venison laced with pepper & tart cranberries, served in spring with dandelion. Regular promotions bring in the likes of *sushi*. The dining space is light & simple with window tables where you can sit & watch the street outside. The weekday lunch buffet is superb value at €5. **$$$$**

✕ **Smrekarjev Hram** Nazorjeva 2; ☎ 01 308 1975; ⊕ 12.00–23.00 Mon–Fri. The signature restaurant at the Grand Union Hotel has been at the top of the tree for years. With an ambience & appearance more reminiscent of a grand 1920s' ocean liner than a Ljubljana hotel, Smrekarjev Hram still delivers on the plate, with the likes of pasta with truffles or *pršut* ham to start & grilled sole or venison with maraschino cherries amongst the mains. **$$$$$**

✕ **Špajza** Gornji trg 28; ☎ 01 425 3094; ⊕ 12.00–midnight Mon–Sat. Špajza is the archetypal

Slovenian upmarket restaurant, managing to conjure up first-class cooking, fresh ingredients & a cosy, informal ambience where jeans are perfectly acceptable. The wine list is reasonable value, but Špajza is definitely a candidate for the most expensive restaurant in the city. Well worth it though as you settle into one of the cosy tables for a night of pleasant excess. **$$$$$**

✗ **Taverna Tatjana** Gornji trg 38; ☎ 01 421

MID RANGE

✗ **Ali Baba** Poljanska 11; ☎ 01 230 1787; ⏱07.00–23.00 Mon–Fri, 10.00–22.00 Sat. Eclectic Arabian fare is the order of the day in one of the finest ethnic eateries in the city. **$$$**

✗ **Allegria** Nazorjeva 8; ☎ 01 426 7402; www.allegria.si; ⏱ 10.00–midnight Mon–Thu, 10.00–01.00 Fri, 12.00–01.00 Sat, 12.00–17.00 Sun. Right in the heart of the city centre, this is a classy Italian option. As good for lunch as it is for dinner daily specials join a sturdy Tuscan menu that is backed up by some equally sturdy Italian wines. **$$$$**

✗ **Cantina Restaurantes Mexicana** Wolfova 4, entrance on Knaflev prehod; ☎ 01 426 9325; ⏱11.00–23.00 Mon–Fri, 11.00–01.00 Sat/Sun. Offering passable fajitas & burritos in pleasant surrounds. The candlelit terrace is the place to be in summer, while the well-thought-out interior also looks the part. **$$$**

✗ **Figovec** Gosposvetska 1; ☎ 01 426 4410; www.figovec.si; ⏱09.00–midnight Mon–Fri, 12.00–17.00 Sat/Sun. One of the oldest coaching inns in the city serves up a menu that will have vegetarians diving for cover & décor that takes you back in time. Horsemeat comes in various permutations & there are the likes of pigs' trotters for the adventurous. More mainstream Slovenian dishes include grilled Adriatic squid & Prekmurje-style goulash. **$$$$**

✗ **Gostilna Sokol** Ciril Metodov trg 18; ☎ 01 439 6855; ⏱07.00–23.00 daily. A bustlingly popular *gostilna* close to the central market serving lashings of hearty traditional food including goulash, wild boar, Slovenian blood sausage & chunky vegetable broth, all washed down with generous carafes of wine. They also produce their own very palatable beer. **$$$**

✗ **Joe Pena's Cantina y Bar** Cankarjeva 6; ☎ 01 421 5800; www.joepenas.com; ⏱ 10.00–01.00 Mon–Thu, 10.00–02.00 Fri/Sat, 12.00–midnight Sun. This lively bar-restaurant is a good place to head with a group of friends for good Mexican food

0100; ⏱ 14.00–midnight Mon–Sat. The décor in this fish restaurant is pleasingly homely with little booths & a variety of seating options, including a small garden terrace in summer. For the best dining experience stick to fresh Adriatic fish (including bream, sea bass & sole), which you can view before it is cooked. Tatjana is often overpriced (save the fresh fish) & they don't take credit cards. **$$$$$**

amidst an unpretentious crowd of locals & expats. It can be raucous on weekend nights. **$$$**

✗ **Julija** Stari trg 9; ☎ 01 425 6463; ⏱08.00–midnight Mon–Sat, 10.00–midnight Sun. The perfect venue for an unrequited love affair as it is named after the girl that Slovenia's national poet, France Prešeren, fell hopelessly in love with. The restaurant itself was refurbished a few years ago with an informal feel & equally informal menu that ventures across the border into Italy more than once with the likes of *carpaccio* or *caprese* salad to start & pasta or risotto to follow. In summer there are tables out on busy Stari trg. **$$$**

✗ **Meson Don Felipe** Strelšika 22; ☎ 01 434 3862; www.donfelipe.net; ⏱ 10.00–12.00 daily. Spain comes to Ljubljana in the form of this warm & welcoming tapas bar/restaurant. Enjoy a smooth bottle of Spanish red wine as you tuck into a range of enticing tapas dishes, which range from salty *manchego* cheese & sizzling *chorizo* cooked in wine, through to a decent stab at tortilla & some sturdier main options. **$$$**

✗ **Namasté** Breg 8; ☎ 01 425 0159; restavracija-namaste.si; ⏱ 17.00–23.00 Mon, 10.00–23.00 Tue–Fri, 11.00–23.00 Sat/Sun. This Indian restaurant is a breath of fresh air on the Ljubljana dining scene using fresh local ingredients to concoct delicious sauces. The menu delivers staples like chicken curry & biriyanis with some aplomb, backed up with the freshly baked roti & naan breads. Wash it down with an Indian beer & you complete an experience as close to the subcontinent as you will find anywhere in Slovenia. **$$$**

✗ **Sushimama** Wolfova 12; ☎ 01 426 9125; ⏱11.00–23.00 Mon–Sat. Styling itself as 'modern Japanese cooking', this funky central restaurant was the first in the city to serve up fresh *sushi* & it does not disappoint. There are also meat dishes such as beef *teriyaki* on the menu in what is one of Ljubljana's hottest restaurants. They have Japanese beer too, including the excellent Asahi, which goes very well with *sushi*, though steer clear of the saki if

you want to emerge walking in a straight line. **$$$**
✕ Vodnikov Hram Vodnikov trg 2; ☎ 01 234 5268;
www.gpl.si; ⏰07.00–20.00 Mon–Fri, 07.00–17.00 Sat.
This traditional *gostilna*, located at the foot of the
funicular & opposite the market, serves up warming
Slovenian soups & hearty meat dishes. During the
day it buzzes with local colour as Slovenes pop in for
coffee or a meal once they've finished their
shopping. **$$$**
✕ Zlata Ribica Cankarjevo nabrežje 5; ☎ 01 241

BUDGET
✕ Ajdovo Zrno Trubarjeva cesta 7; ☎ 01 690 478;
⏰09.00–20.00 Mon–Fri, 11.00–16.00 Sat. This is as
close as Ljubljana gets to paradise for visiting
vegetarians & is also a great antidote to the usual
hearty local diet. This cosy retreat in a quiet
courtyard just off Trubarjeva offers a self-service
buffet laden with healthy treats. You can detox too
with one of their freshly squeezed fruit juices. Not
exactly a place to linger in, but for fresh & healthy
food it cannot be beaten. Bright & friendly staff too.
$$
✕ Emonska Klet Plečnikov trg 1; ☎ 01 421 9300;
www.emonskaklet.com; ⏰08.00–03.00 Mon–Fri,
12.00–03.00 Sat/Sun. A big favourite with the local
student crowd this cavernous underground venue
just off Kongresni trg buzzes in the evening,
especially at weekends. With few pretensions most
punters here come to scoff the filling Slovene
cuisine, washed down with some equally hearty
domestic beer. **$$**
✕ Gostilna Pod Lipo Borstnikov trg 3; ☎ 01 422
4110; www.podlipo.si; ⏰11.00–23.00 Mon–Fri,
12.00–23.00 Sat, 12.00–18.00 Sun. A cosy traditional
gostilna where you can dine like a local on typical
Slovene dishes with a heavy emphasis on meat-based
dishes. **$$**
✕ Harambaša Okrepčevapnica Vrtna 8; 📱 041
843 106; ⏰10.00–22.00 Mon–Fri, 12.00–22.00 Sat,
12.00–18.00 Sun. 'Welcome to Sarajevo' reads the
sign as you enter & this popular grill restaurant really
does offer a slice of Bosnia in a thoughtfully
refurbished house in Krakovo. The simple menu
offers *čevapčiči* (meat balls), *pleskavica* (meat pattie) &
sudukice (thin sausages), which come served with
fluffy Balkan bread, crispy onions & creamy kajmak
cheese. Okrepčevapnica's décor is themed without
being tacky with old photos of Sarajevo, football
strips & Bosnian magazines. **$$**
✕ Holy Food Igriska 5; 📱 041 323 719;
⏰09.00–18.00 Mon–Sat. For fans of fresh, simple &
healthy food this unpretentious eatery is a popular

2680; www.zlataribica.si; ⏰08.00–midnight. This
refurbished riverside restaurant in the heart of the
Old Town serves a mix of hearty Slovenian meat
dishes, Italian-influenced cuisine & vegetarian meals.
Its waterside terrace has good views & makes a
pleasant dining space on warmer days. Not as cheap
as it was before its revamp, but still reasonable value,
with the likes of baked sea bass laced with shrimps
coming in at around €15. **$$$**

choice near the university. Pizza, burek & sandwiches
all tempt from the menu. For those with a sweet
tooth there is a range of pancakes to choose from.
Everything is cooked from scratch. The student meal
deal is a real bargain at around €3. **$**
✕ Luka Gourmet Lunch Café Stari trg 9; ☎ 01
251 2575; ⏰09.00–23.00 Mon–Sat, 12.00–23.00 Sun.
Run by the people behind Pri Vitezu you can sample
the same quality ingredients here that make the
restaurant such a success. On sunny days the tables
outside are the perfect place to enjoy the
ridiculously good-value set menus, which include
soup to start followed by a green salad & a main
course which could be prawn & dill pasta, or grilled
beef with hand-cut chips & tomato.
✕ Pasta Nona Gosposvetska 2; ☎ 01 438 2420;
⏰09.00–23.00 Mon–Fri. For great-value pasta dishes
Pasta Nona is very hard to beat. A new creation of
Luka Gourmet, lunch is a highlight with daily specials
& meal deals. **$$**
✕ Pri Škofu Rečna 8; ☎ 01 426 4508;
⏰08.00–midnight Mon–Fri, 12.00–midnight
Sat/Sun. There is no menu as such with bright,
young waitresses gaily recanting the day's offerings,
usually a choice of soup to start, including a heart-
pumping ginger concoction, before a main course
of seafood risotto, roasted turkey or the house
speciality, plump beefsteak cooked with a
peppercorn crust. **$$**
✕ Ribca Tržnica Jožeta Plečnika; ⏰08.00–16.00
Mon–Fri, 08.00–14.00 Sat. For budget seafood Ribca
is hard to beat. Located beneath Plečnik's colonnades
just by the fish market, the fish could not be much
fresher or better value. The terrace is pretty no-frills
with plastic chairs, but there are views out over the
river & back towards Prešernov trg. Take the steps
that descend from the shops beneath the
colonnades. **$$**
✕ Šestica Slovenska 40; ☎ 01 242 0850; www.gp-
vic.si/sestica.asp; ⏰10.00–23.00 Mon–Fri,
12.00–23.00 Sat. Huge portions & cheap prices have

punters still piling into one of the city's oldest *gostilnas* after all these years. The building dates to 1670, with the first inn opened on the site in 1776. Back then it was at No 6 (hence the name) & these days it is on the map thanks to its hearty soups, spicy goulash & chunky risotto. $$

✗ **Tomato** Šubičeva 1; ✆ 01 252 7555; ◷ 07.00–22.00 Mon–Fri, 08.00–16.00 Sat. Fresh & healthy food is on offer at this massively popular take-away restaurant. They make sandwiches for many of the city's cafés & it is easy to see why, with fresh, inventive toppings & generous portions. There are over 30 sandwich permutations & also plenty of scope for choosing your own. $$

✗ **Vegedrom** Vodnikova 35; ✆ 01 513 2462; www.vegedrom.com; ◷ 09.00–22.00 Mon–Fri, 12.00–22.00 Sat. Just northwest of Cesta na Bellevue the road becomes Vodnikova, where you will find one of Ljubljana's 2 vegetarian restaurants. A real gem, this homely oasis serves tempting soups, sandwiches, vegetarian plates for 2, tofu, gnocchi & risotto alongside spicy Indian mains & vegan dishes. $$

PIZZA Given Ljubljana's proximity to Italy it is no surprise that pizza is ubiquitous here. For those on a tight budget Ljubljana's generous pizzas can be a lifesaver. Ask any local where the best pizza is on sale and you will get a different reply, with the main contenders:

✗ **Čerin** Trubarjeva 52; ✆ 01 232 0990; ◷ until 23.00. Dependable & centrally located pizzeria serving thin-crust pizzas. Flexible staff allow you to design your own topping & free internet access keeps you busy while you wait. $$

✗ **Foculus** Gregorčičeva 3; ✆ 01 251 5643; ◷ 10.00–midnight Mon–Fri, 12.00–midnight Sat. 'Probably the most popular pizzeria in Slovenia' scream the flyers & its large & bustling interior, with big tables & ceiling paintings, is certainly a bit of a surprise on this sleepy street. The pizza list is extensive with over 50 choices that include all the usual suspects, while at weekends families rule as kids are brought along for a treat. $$

✗ **Ljubljanski Dvor** Dvorni trg 1; ✆ 01 251 6555; ◷ 12.00–midnight Mon–Sat. A spacious outdoor terrace, with unrivalled views back across the river to Ljubljana's Old Town & the castle, make this restaurant & pizzeria an enduring favourite with visitors & locals alike. The pizzas are enormous – do not even contemplate ordering anything bigger than the gigantic *classico*. The back of the restaurant on Kongresni trg serves up take-away pizza & ice cream, while upstairs is a 'proper' restaurant serving an extensive menu of international dishes. $$

✗ **Trta** Grudnovo nabrežje 21; ✆ 01 426 5066; www.trta.si. This pizzeria is a little further out than the others in the suburb of Prule, opposite Trnovo in an old artistic district of the city by the river. The pizzas here are huge & you may want to ask for 2 plates & share one with a companion. In summer there is a terrace by the river & a smattering of wooden benches around the side. $$

FAST FOOD

✗ **Tržnica Central Market** ◷ 08.00–15.00 Mon–Sat. The sprawling market offers a range of affordable culinary goodies every day bar Sun. There are vans dispensing fresh Adriatic seafood as well as a network of stalls offering fresh fruit & vegetables. Amidst the colonnades is a sprinkling of more permanent shops that sell excellent bread, meats, pastries & *burek*. $

✗ **Hot Horse** Just as it sounds, this particular local 'treat' consists of a huge burger bun stuffed with horsemeat, various relishes & vegetables. Ljubljana's late-night drinking set insist you have not been on a real night out until you have topped it off with a horseburger from the stand at the northern side of Tivoli Park (◷ 08.00–01.00 *daily*) across from the Lev Hotel. The Hot Horse take-away at Trubarjeva 31 (◷ 08.00–01.00 *daily*) is more central, but for the real authentic experience Tivoli is the place to go. $

✗ **Nobel** Miklošičeva 30; ◷ 08.00–midnight *daily*. The southern Balkan staple *burek* is an instantly filling & very popular snack. It basically consists of a wrap of moist pastry that is stuffed with either meat or soft cheese, with a worryingly high fat & calorie content. Nobel is arguably the best place to try *burek*, but as long as it is piping hot & has not been sitting around it is the sort of comfort food that you cannot go too wrong with anywhere. $

For a small city, Ljubljana has a decent supply of theatre venues – with high-quality acting and vivid productions often transcending the language barrier. Throughout the year it bustles with the arts, ranging from small-scale street theatre and outdoor concerts, right through to grand opera performances, classical music recitals and the granddaddy of them all, the Ljubljana Summer Festival. Then there are the cafés, bars and nightclubs.

Ljubljana's café and bar scene is becoming increasingly sophisticated. Alongside the Old World cafés and grungy bars is an array of bright new drinking venues, complete with guest DJs, funky décor and waiting staff who would not look out of place in a glossy fashion magazine. Closing times are often the only thing that really differentiate cafés from bars. The majority of the cafés wind down before midnight during the week, while bars generally stay open until 01.00, some as late as 03.00. New places arise and shut down with alarming regularity and the best advice is to tap a local to find out where the newest hip venue is. At weekends the key is to start late and build up gradually with the action not really getting going until after 21.00.

Whatever your taste there is something to suit everyone. All of Ljubljana's tourist offices hand out the free monthly 'Where To' leaflet, with a good listings rundown, as well as a free sheet detailing events on a weekly basis. For more alternative and small-scale events and happenings ask in trendy bars like Café Maček or Fraga. *Major Events in Ljubljana* is an annual publication that allows for a bit of advance planning if you can get hold of it.

THEATRE

Café Teater Miklošičeva 2; ☎ 01 252 7108; www.cafe-teater.si. Staging musicals & comedy productions, with some performances in the Križanke theatre.

Cankarjev Dom Prešernova 10; ☎ 01 241 7299; www.cd-cc.si; booking office ⊕ 11.00–13.00 Mon–Sat, 15.00–20.00 Mon–Fri & for 1 hr before performances start. One of Slovenia's largest venues, covering everything from theatre to classical music, dance & opera.

Gledališče Glej (Glej Theatre) Gregorčičeva 3I; ☎ 01 251 6679. This is renowned as an avant-garde venue with a daring programme geared towards more experimental material. Closed Jul & Aug.

Križanke Trg Francoske Revolucije I; ☎ 01 241 6026. This wonderful outdoor arena in a sculpture-laden old monastery is at the crux of the Ljubljana Summer Festival. The Križanke complex dates back to the 13th century, with church & monastery buildings from that era still standing today. Outside of the festival, performances continue to take place in the outdoor arena, the Knights Hall & the anteroom.

Lutkovno Gledališče Ljubljana (Ljubljana Puppet Theatre) Krekov trg 2; ☎ 01 300 0970; www.lgl.si. Not just for children, the theatre's ambitious programmes range from *Winnie the Pooh* to Shakespeare. Also hosts Ljubljana's biennial International Puppet Theatre Festival.

Mestno Gledališče (Municipal Theatre) Čopova 14; ☎ 01 251 0852; www.mgl.si. The spectrum of performances on offer at the city's theatre includes satirical plays, comedies & modern theatre productions.

Mini Teater Ljubljana Ljubljanski Grad; ☎ 01 430 3143; www.mini-teater.si. Ljubljana Castle provides an unusual & romantic setting for theatrical performances. The Mini Theatre also organises the city's Medieval Day with Renaissance music, puppet shows, battle re-enactments & plays.

Šentjakobsko Gledališče (St Jacob Theatre) Krekov trg 2; ☎ 01 231 2860; www.sentjakobsko-gledalisce.si. The performance list of this alternative theatre group includes Monty Python's *Life of Brian*, Jules Verne's *20,000 Leagues Under the Sea* as well as the work of Ivan Cankar.

Slovensko Mladinsko Gledališče (Slovenian Youth Theatre) Vilharjeva 11; ☎ 01 231 0610; www.mladinsko-gl.si. The Slovenian Youth Theatre prides itself on its eclectic range of mainstream & experimental productions. Past performances include works by Chekhov, Dostoyevsky, Lewis Carroll & T S Eliot.

🎭 Slovensko Narodno Gledališče Drama (SNG Drama) Erjačeva l; ☎ 01 252 1462; www.sngdrama-lj.si. Slovenia's national theatre company is enviably housed in this lavish Art Nouveau building.

🎭 Teater Komedija (Comedy Theatre) Šmartinska 152; ☎ 01 585 1320; www.btccity.com. By night the BTC City Convention Hall takes on a new ambience as it plays host to comic productions.

CINEMA Ljubljana's cinemas generally screen films in their original language with Slovene subtitles, and mainstream cinemas show the predictable range of Hollywood films, though the local appetite for all things alternative spills over at the Slovenska Kinoteka and the Kinodvor. In November each year the city plays host to the Ljubljana International Film Festival (LifFe; *www.liffe.spletnastran.com*) and the Ljubljana Gay and Lesbian Film Festival.

Kinodvor Kolodvorska 13; ☎ 01 434 2544; www.kinodvor.si. Shows contemporary art-house films that have received wide critical acclaim such as Sue Brooks's *Japanese Story*. During the summer the cinema also screens Slovene-language films with English subtitles.

Kolosej Šmartinska 152; ☎ 01 520 5500; www.kolosej.si. Part of the suburban BTC City complex, Slovenia's first multiplex cinema has 12 screens, a bar, restaurant and confectioner.

Komuna Cankarjeva l; ☎ 01 241 8401; www.kolosej.si. Screening Hollywood films in a central location.

Slovenska Kinoteka Miklošičeva 38; ☎ 01 434 2500; www.kinoteka.si. This cinema specialising in art-house productions is something of a local legend. Come here to enjoy a film or just to talk cinema at the on-site café bar.

MUSIC Ljubljana's music venues are as diverse as the concerts held in them and include the Centralni Stadion (Central Stadium), Križanke, the Slovenian National Opera and Ballet Theatre and the Slovenian Philharmonic Hall, as well as a range of nightclubs. Big one-off events include the Ljubljana Summer Festival, Ljubljana Jazz Festival and the Druga Godba Festival (see *Chapter 2, Public holidays and festivals*, page 34). Tickets can be purchased from venue box offices and, increasingly, over the internet. The ŠKUC Information Centre (*Stari trg 21; ☎ 01 121 3142*) also sells tickets for pop and rock concerts.

Classical and opera venues
♬ Slovenska Filharmonija (Slovenian Philharmonic Hall) Kongresni trg 10; ☎ 01 241 0800; www.filharmonija.si. One of the most atmospheric venues in the country is home to the Slovenian Philharmonic Orchestra & the Slovenian Philharmonic Choir.

♬ Slovensko Narodno Gledališče Opera in Balet (Slovenian National Theatre Opera & Ballet) Župančičeva l; ☎ 01 241 1740; www.opera.si. Traditional & contemporary opera & ballet productions grace the stage of this Old World theatre.

Rock, pop and jazz venues
♬ Centralni Stadion (Central Stadium) Dunajska. This tatty suburban football stadium occasionally hosts larger concerts.

♬ Jazz Club Gajo Beethovnova 8; ☎ 01 425 3206; www.jazzclubgajo.com. This centrally located jazz club has regular live performances & weekly informal jam sessions, with the latter generally held on Mon evenings. Check the monthly schedule online.

♬ KUD France Prešeren Karunova 14; ☎ 01 283 2288; www.kud-fp.si. This popular youth venue prides itself on promoting alternative culture, with the calendar dominated by music performances, theatre & art that veer away from the mainstream.

♬ Metelkova Mesto (see *Nightclubs* later in this chapter). Everything from *banghra* & African tribal groups, through to nu-metal & rap. Multiple venues in the squat mean that there is always something happening. Drop by the night before to check what is on as information is not always posted around town & the venues tend to be deserted during the day.

♬ Orto Bar Grabloviceva l; ☎ 01 232 1674; www.orto-bar.com. Hosting everything from blues & jazz to punk & trash. If you like your nights out down

The Ljubljana Summer Festival (*www.ljubljanafestival.si*) has been going strong since 1952 and now embraces most of the city's performance spaces in a cultural extravaganza that rumbles through July and August. The key venue is the Križanke, but Ljubljana Castle, Cankarjev Dom and the Slovene Philharmonic Hall all come into play with myriad events. In 2006, guests included the New York Philharmonic Orchestra and the Vienna State Ballet. Neighbouring countries are also embraced with the likes of Croatian National Theatre and the National Theatre of Belgrade performing in recent years. The latter's choice of *Dr Jekyll and Mr Hyde* seemed strangely apposite to many locals who have lived through the Yugoslav wars of the 1990s and Serbia's recent struggle to change from a hardline Slobodan Miloševic-run state to a modern democracy.

& dirty with a liberal smattering of grunge, this is the place to come.

♪ **Sax Pub** Eipprova 7; ✆ 01 283 9009. This Trnovo mainstay serves up a solid menu of live jazz every Thu evening. The cosy interior feels more like a music lover's bedroom than a pub. Arrive early if you want a seat when there is music. At other times this is a relaxed place for a drink among a slightly older crowd.

Cafés and bars
The Ljubljančani are a sociable bunch and the capital has a large number of drinking venues for a city of its size.

🖵 **Abecedarium Café** Ribji trg; ✆ 01 426 9514. This café lays dual claims to being located in the oldest house in the city & the former home of Primož Trubar. Just a stone's throw from the river it has a good choice of coffees & beers & some decent snacks & light meals too.

🖵 **Antico** Stari trg 17; ✆ 426 5628. Less pretentious than many of the new arrivals in this part of town, this relaxed café is an ideal venue for flicking through a guidebook or newspaper. Wonderfully moist *tiramisu* & a decent choice of Slovenian wines invite a longer stay.

♀ **AS Lounge** Knaflev prehod 5a. On busy nights this subterranean retreat buzzes with energy as students & the pre-club set work themselves up for a big night. When there are live DJs the bar area can become a throbbing mass of dancing bodies.

♀ **Breg 2** Breg 2. There are various one-off events in this increasingly popular café/bar. After a recent makeover it seems to be finally establishing a regular clientele. The food is reasonable, but it is the wine you should come for with produce from all the various wine-producing areas of the country.

♀ **Café Galerija** Mestni trg 5; 📱 041 676 660. One of the city's most chic drinking dens would not look out of place in a spread for a fashion magazine. Delve through the modest foyer, itself used for various happenings, art exhibitions & catwalk-style shows, & you enter a world of

candlelit glamour, awash with mirrors, bountiful sofas & Ottoman décor.

♀ **Café Maček** Krojaška 5; ✆ 01 428 3791. For years the 'Cat' has been *the* place to be down on the riverside. 'When the weather allows the main action is outside where rampant people-watching & river breezes are perfect company for a cold glass of Union or Laško or a heart-starting *macchiato*. Maček also offers an excellent range of single malt Scottish whiskies including Lagavulin & Laphroaig. In winter a heated & covered terrace tempts. When Maček is too busy in summer just pop next door to **Boheme**, which has a similar terrace set-up.

♀ **Cutty Sark** Knaflev prehod; ✆ 01 425 1477. Within easy staggering distance of Prešernov trg, Cutty Sark seems to have a magnetic hold for Ljubljana's expat community. All the home comforts are here in a decent stab at a British pub with a big bar area, bar service & a range of beers & ales including Guinness & Kilkenny.

♀ **England Pub** Mala 8. A new arrival in 2006 hopes to capitalise on Ljubljana's seemingly insatiable appetite for British & Irish theme bars. Perhaps not the venue for red-blooded Scotsmen as the photos of 'England' include a piper standing by Eilean Donan Castle in Scotland. The draught Guinness & Union, though, are worth hanging around for & it is a good place to meet locals who are there to meet people like you.

Ljubljana ENTERTAINMENT AND NIGHTLIFE

3

The main brewers in Slovenia are Union in Ljubljana and Laško from the eponymous town in the east of the country. Traditionally, Ljubljančani have stayed loyal to Union (*www.pivo-union.si*), whose gigantic brewery is unmissable on the edge of the city centre by Tivoli Park, while Laško (*www.pivo-lasko.si*) has increasingly come to dominate outside the capital and expanded into other countries in the region, including Croatia and Montenegro. The picture has been muddied recently with a tussle over ownership of Union, which has seen Laško taking a majority stake. Worries amongst loyal Union drinkers that the flavour and even the brand may disappear have so far proved unfounded.

Both Union and Laško have a variety of different tipples to suit all tastes. The main Union product is simply called Union and comes in a trademark red can or bottle. It is backed up by Union 1964 lager, a dark beer (Črni Baron) and a Pilsner. A newer product is Smile, a beer with lemon that is very popular with the younger inhabitants of the city and is sold in many clubs and bars. There are tours of the brewery (see *What to see*, page 71).

Laško's most famous product is Zlatorog, a refreshing beer, usually in 50cl bottles. They also do a dark beer (Temno), a low-alcohol beer (Gren) and an ever-increasing range of other brews. In parallel with Union, a newer product is Roler, a beer with a twist of lemon.

♀ **Guinness Pub** Gosposka 3. This decent stab at the Irish theme bar concept serves up decent pints of the eponymous Irish stout. The late opening attracts the non-clubbing drinking crowd, though nights tend to end a bit abruptly when they unsubtly switch off the lights to force stragglers out.

♀ **Holidays Pub** Slovenska 36. This busy little pub is a good stand-by on Slovenska. The cosy British-style pub interior is often a largely male preserve, but the bar staff are friendly & there are leather seats & tables where you can dodge the serious drinkers propping up the bar.

♀ **Kavarna Planet Pločnik** Prešernov trg. When the mercury is up this is the place to be, in the shadow of the statue of France Prešeren right at the heart of the city by the river. A sprinkling of tables & chairs wrap around a brightly lit bar. Powerful heat lamps ensure that the people-watching stretches on late into the night.

♀ **Kratochwill** Kolodvorska 14; ☎ 01 433 3114. Kratochwill is the city's only micro-brewery pub. The *svetlo* & *temno* (light & dark beers), available in 20cl, 30cl, 50cl & huge 1l glasses, may not suit all tastes as they are both decidedly sour.

🍺 **Le Petite Café** Trg Francoske Revolucije. If you are taking in any shows at the Križanke theatre or are attending the Summer Festival this friendly café is the perfect pit stop. Packed in summer, this is a good place to meet a few locals in an environment that never seems to get too touristy.

♀ **Makalonca** Hribarjevo nabrežje 19. In summer this is the place amongst the colonnades on the right bank of the river. Follow the candles down the stairs by the wooden footbridge from where Ljubljana's only tour boat is berthed & you will enter a busy bar space. Inside, the small bar area is perfect for those not enjoying the river breezes.

♀ **Minimal** Mestni trg 4. As minimal as the name suggests, the interior is practically polar with white, white & more white. Do not let the beautiful staff & artsy ambience put you off, though, as this is a relaxed venue for a coffee or something stronger.

♀ **Opera Bar** Cankarjeva 12. Trendy Australian bar in the city centre where the local beautiful people come to see & be seen. They do reasonable food too to help keep you sober whilst you enjoy the cocktails.

♀ **Pr' Skelet** Ključavničarska 5; ☎ 01 252 7799. Delve below street level in the Old Town & you will soon be surrounded by an army of skulls & skeletons in this cellar bar. Once you get over the novelty of the horror theme it is not too disturbing & during the colder months this is a cosy retreat for a glass of mulled wine.

♀ **Raggamuffin** Krojaška 4. Jamaica comes to town in the shape of Ljubljana's stab at a reggae bar. Black-&-white posters of Bob Marley may line the walls, but that distinctive smell is conspicuously absent & the interior is surprisingly bright & airy.

♀ **Romeo** Stari trg 6; ☎ 426 9011. Beyond the pink neon sign, inside the high chairs are as funky as the music, while outside there is a sprinkling of tables & chairs that lead down towards the nearby river & an awning-covered wooden decking area. The food is good here too.

♀ **Salon** Trubarjeva 23; ☎ 01 439 8760. One expat that we spoke to described it as 'lounge bar meets camp hairdressing salon', a remarkably apt summation.

♀ **Vinoteka Movia** Mestni trg 1; ☎ 01 425 5448; www.movia.si. This cosy wine bar next to the town hall has wines stacked high up the wall behind the bar. They also have some tapas-style nibbles.

♀ **Zlata Ladjica** Jurčičev trg 1. This popular bar by the Cobbler's Bridge suffers from schizophrenia – by day it is a mellow outdoor café, but at night the action moves inside to a maritime-themed bar that is often one of the most raucous in the city – no wonder with Tennent's Super, the lethal-strength Scottish beer, on draught.

Nightclubs

☆ **Bachus Centre** Kongresni trg 3; ☎ 01 241 8244; www.bachus-center.com. Central & well-designed complex with a café, bars, restaurant & even a pool hall, as well as a basement dance floor. On a good night Bachus buzzes, but on busy weekends it can seem to be full of underage drinkers & big egos clad in ill-fitting R 'n' B clobber.

☆ **Fun Factory** Industrijska zona Rudnik, Jurčkova 224; ☎ 01 428 9690; www.funfactory.si. Bus 19 direction Livada. South of the city centre in Rudnik is one of Ljubljana's biggest clubs. Here you will find all the things you expect in a large venue, such as chill-out rooms, multiple bars & separate dance floors.

☆ **Global** Tomšičeva 2; ☎ 01 426 9020; www.global.si. Take the elevator from street level at the Nama department store & less than a minute later you will be in this modern nightlife oasis with sweeping views of the city centre & the castle. The terrace is open during the day as a café/restaurant, but the real action is inside at night on the single dance floor. The music policy is a bit hit & miss, so check ahead if you don't want to find yourself at a weird & wacky theme night.

☆ **Klub K4**; ☎ 01 431 7010; www.klubk4.org. K4 was pumping out cutting-edge sounds when Global & Bachus were only pipe dreams & it is still going strong well over a decade since it first opened its doors. The dingy & grungy rooms echo the nefarious hideouts of east Berlin & the music is similarly alternative with indie rock & metal ruling. Sunday is K4's gay night, transforming the grungy student venue into the 'Roza Klub'.

☆ **Latino Klub Cuba** Celovška 54; ☎ 01 434 3158. Latino beats, salsa music & free-flowing cocktails are all winning ingredients in this popular club at Casa del Papa outside the city centre.

☆ **Metelkova Mesto** Metelkova cesta; ☎ 01 432 3378; www.metelkova.org. This independent & unique cultural centre-cum-squat can easily keep open-minded visitors occupied on a night out. A predominantly young & alternative Slovene crowd is drawn to the clubs & bars that inject life into this former military barracks & squat. Venues include Klub Gromka with live music & international DJs, & Gala Hala, where the music on offer is nothing if not eclectic. The squat also has a gay nightlife scene – Klub Tiffany is a gay café-bar-cum-club & Klub Monkel is a lesbian nightclub that shares its premises with Tiffany's. All venues are at their best at weekends.

☆ **Tramontana** Narorjeva 6; m 041 767 447; www.tramontana.info; ⏰ 21.00–05.00 Wed–Sat. This central club also hosts small-scale concerts. If you are hankering after a school disco night this could be the place to go.

SHOPPING

Ljubljana is generally a good city for shopping despite some frustrating opening hours and prices for international brand names that are often not lower than those charged in London and Paris. Its compact size means that dedicated shoppers can cover the entire city centre on foot. Slovenska, which bisects the city centre, is one popular shopping boulevard with its big-name shops and the Nama department store. However, a far more pleasant experience is on offer in the Old Town squares of Stari trg, Mestni trg and Gornji trg, where medieval and Baroque buildings house eclectic boutiques selling everything from jewellery, perfume, shoes and clothes to traditional crafts and designer gear made in studios behind the stores. The right and left banks of the Ljubljanica River are also increasingly brimming with boutique stores and small art galleries. Gosposvetska cesta, near the Lev Hotel, also has some boutiques. BTC City on the outskirts of town opens seven days a week and is *the* place to head for some serious retail therapy.

ARTS AND CRAFTS

Dom Mestni trg 24; ✆ 01 241 8300. Large souvenir shop housed in a municipal building with wicker, wood, pottery & woollen crafts on sale, alongside alcohol & a wide range of Ljubljana-labelled souvenirs.

Kodre Zlatarstvo Cankarjevo nabrežje 27; ✆ 01 422 5110. Chunky rings & bracelets, dangling pendants & oversized looped earrings are just some

of the individual pieces by Slovene designers guaranteed to get you noticed.

Skrina Galerija Breg 8; ✆ 01 425 5161; www.skrina.si. Charming riverside gallery selling crafts from all over Slovenia including Idrija lace, Prekmurje pottery, Rogaška glass & beehive panels. It is cheaper to pay by cash than by credit card.

FOOD AND DRINK

Čajna Hiša Stari trg 3. Ljubljana's only dedicated teahouse also has a great shop selling speciality teas, mugs & tea paraphernalia. The city's supermarkets cannot even begin to match the myriad teas on sale in this charming oasis.

Mercator Kongresni trg 9; ✆ 01 241 4770. A central branch of this omnipresent supermarket chain that is open on Sun. Watch for the shady characters who often hang around begging outside; they are funnily enough at their most troublesome on Sun.

Mercator Stritarjeva 9; ✆ 01 241 4089. Another centrally located Mercator that is handy for supplies. Closed on Sun.

Plečnik Colonnades Adamič–Lundrovo nabrežje. The small shops selling bread, cheese, wine, ham &

fish are a great place to stock up on fresh Slovenian produce. This is also a good place to buy honey as a gift to take home.

Vino Boutique Slovenska 38; ✆ 01 425 6280. Small wine shop with knowledgeable staff. Check out the whole range of brands from around the country.

Vinoteka Enoteca Nazorjeva 12; m 041 796 000. This wine bar/wine shop is a good place for a relaxing drink, with plenty of bottles on hand if you find that must-have gift.

Vinoteka Movia Mestni trg 2; ✆ 01 425 5448; www.movia.si. Trendy wine bar & shop owned by the well-known Movia wine producer. Most of their wine is exported to the USA, so snap up a bottle while you can.

CLOTHING AND FOOTWEAR

Hugo Boss Slovenska 41; ✆ 01 252 7789. Good-sized shop selling men's designer clothing.

Katarina Silk Gornji trg 5; ✆ 01 425 0010. Stylish silk scarves & other items are handcrafted on the premises.

Max Mara Miklošičeva 6; ✆ 01 426 5880. Elegant designer clothing store for women located opposite the Grand Union Hotel.

Sisley Čopova 7. Decent-sized branch of this Italian designer-clothes retailer for men & women.

Transport Čopova 3. The New York City street map that adorns the façade makes this fashionable shoe shop easy to find.

Zara Cankarjeva 2; ✆ 01 421 4500. Large outlet for women's designer clothing.

DEPARTMENT STORES AND SHOPPING CENTRES

BTC City Šmartinska 152; ✆ 01 585 1100; www.btc-city.com; ⊕ 09.00–20.00 Mon–Sat, 09.00–13.00 Sun. Bus 17 direction Letališka to BTC Uprava stop. This enormous shopping mall boasts over 400 shops including Top Shop, Top Man, Miss Selfridge, Levi's, Marks & Spencer, H&M & Benetton. It also has myriad sports facilities including tennis, badminton, go-karting & a water park complex (Atlantis), plus restaurants, multiplex cinema & a comedy theatre. The kind of place that local families love to spend a day in; whether you will want to is another matter.

BTC Emporium Letališka 3; ✆ 01 585 4800; www.emporium.si. Bus 17 direction Letališka to BTC Emporium stop. This shopping centre is a haven for those who love buying clothes. High-street shops like Dorothy Perkins & Levi's sell their wares alongside Hugo Boss, Lacoste & Fred Perry.

Maximarket Trg Republike 1; www.maxi.si. Don't be put off by its grungy appearance, this city-centre department store is regarded by most of the Ljubljančani to be the most prestigious department store in town. In addition to your usual department store fare it also has a decent deli & a health store.

Nama Tomišičeva 1; ☏ 01 425 8300. The large United Colours of Benetton outlet on the ground floor is one of the department store's biggest attractions. This is something of a local landmark & worth popping into solely for that reason.

MARKETS
Flea Market Cankarjevo nabrežje. This Sun morning market lines the Ljubljanica between the Triple Bridge & the Cobbler's Bridge.

Ljubljana Monmarte Cankarjevo nabrežje. On Sat from Jun–Sep the banks of the Ljubljanica are once again transformed into a market. This time arts & crafts are on sale between 10.00 & 15.00. A highlight for younger visitors is the many creative workshops that are held as part of the market.

Tržnica (Central Market) Vodnikov trg & Pogačarjev trg. Open daily except Sun, this is a great place to pick up cheap produce, flowers, clothes & even a small selection of souvenirs including wooden crafts & honey. It is a great place to spend an entire morning, finishing it off with a picnic lunch culled from the market or at one of the surrounding restaurants.

BOOKS
Geonavtik Kongresni trg; ☏ 01 252 7027. Friendly bookstore-cum-café.

Knjigarna Novak Wolfova 8; ☏ 01 422 3410. This small, friendly & centrally located bookshop sells a selection of English & other foreign-language books.

Mladinska Knjiga Slovenska 29; ☏ 01 241 0651. Often referred to as 'Knjigarna Konzorcij'. The biggest of the Mladinska Knjiga stores, sells a selection of English-language books, at a price.

Mladinska Knjiga Nazorjeva 1; ☏ 01 241 4700. With English-language titles.

OTHER PRACTICALITIES

POST OFFICES
✉ Slovenska 32; ⏰07.00–20.00 Mon–Fri, 08.00–13.00 Sat

✉ Trg Osvobodilne fronte 5; ⏰07.00–midnight Mon–Fri, 07.00–18.00 Sat, 09.00–12.00 Sun

INTERNET CAFÉS
🖥 **Napotnic.com** Trg Ajdoušcina 1; ☏ 01 431 1016; www.napotnica.com. Access per hr.

🖥 **Café Galerija** Mestni trg 5; m 041 676 660. Offers free Wi-Fi to those with their own laptops.

🖥 **Cyber Café Xplorer** Petkovškovo nabrežje 23; ☏ 01 430 1991; www.sisky.com

🖥 **Čerin** Trubarjeva 52; ☏ 01 232 0990. Pizzeria (see *Where to eat*, page 60) with free internet.

🖥 **Drog Art** Kolodvorska 20; ☏ 01 439 7270

🖥 **Gostilna Nobile** Zarnikova 3; ☏ 01 439 7040. Suburban eatery with 2 terminals.

🖥 **Klub Fabrka** Poljanska 9. Sup Mexican beer while you enjoy free internet. Also offering cheap internet phone calls.

🖥 **Slovenian Tourist Information Centre** Krekov trg 10. €1 for 30 mins.

BANKS You won't have to walk far to find a bank or ATM in the centre of Ljubljana.

$ **Banka Koper** Nazorjeva 6

$ **Nova Ljubljanska Banka** Branches include Trg Republike 2, Beethovnova 7, Dalmatinova 4, Čopova 3 and Mestni trg 16

MEDICAL FACILITIES
✚ **Ljubljana Medical Centre (Klinični Centre Ljubljana)** Zaloška 2; ☏ 01 552 5050. There is also a dental clinic at the same location (☏ *01 431 3113*).

For non-emergency medical care, or to find one of the city's many **pharmacies** (*lekarna*), seek advice where you are staying or at a tourist information centre. Centrally located pharmacies are at Miklošičeva 24 and Prešernov trg 5.

THE UNMISSABLES Prešeren Square (Prešernov trg) is at the physical, historical and spiritual heart of the city. This is where Ljubljančani come to meet their friends, watch the world go by from pavement cafés and stroll by the river. The square boasts three river crossings, plus the landmark **Franciscan Church of the Annunciation** (Frančiškanska Cerkev Marijinega Oznanjenja – see *Churches and cathedrals*, page 79) and a **statue** of **France Prešeren**. Ivan Zajec and Maks Fabiani's dramatic monument to the man trumpeted as Slovenia's greatest bard dates from 1905. Despite his bravado and his swirling muse the tortured writer is forced to gaze across his namesake square at a bust of Julija Primic, the love of his life. Julija may be peering back at Prešeren, but in real life she never returned his love, and many see her presence as a cruel and constant reminder of this most tragic of tragic Romantic poets and his unrequited love. Julija aside, the steps of this giant statue make a great place to relax with an ice cream or to meet some new friends.

As well as being the most popular meeting spot in the city, Prešernov trg boasts some of Ljubljana's finest examples of Art Nouveau architecture. The large white building standing proudly behind Prešeren is the **oldest pharmacy in Ljubljana**, while the city's first department store – the Centromerkur – sits to its left. On the opposite side of the square is the Hauptman House, now also owned by Centromerkur. Look out for the bronze model of the city, which has been at the bottom of Čopova since June 1991 when Slovenian independence was declared.

Ljubljana's most vibrant square also sees the coming together of France Prešeren and another of Slovenia's most famous sons, Jože Plečnik, with the designs of the latter giving the square its modern-day appearance. One of Plečnik's most famous works, the **Triple Bridge** (Tromostovje), was completed in 1931 with the addition of two straddling walkways to the main 19th-century span. Plečnik wanted to mimic the bridges that traverse Venice's canals, incorporating ornate Renaissance balustrades and a string of street lamps into his flamboyant design.

Ljubljana Castle (*Ljubljanski Grad; Grajska planota 1;* ☏ *01 232 9994; www.festival-lj.si/virtualnimuzej; castle: free entry;* ⊕ *May–Sep 09.00–21.00 daily; Oct–Apr 10.00–18.00 daily; virtual museum and viewing tower: adult/concession/family* €3/€2/€4) The castle hangs omnipresent above the city, vaulting into view when you turn many a street corner. If you are feeling lazy, catch the funicular from Krekov trg or take the tourist train from Prešernov trg (see *Tourist information/local tour operators* earlier in this chapter, page 51). The best option, though, is to walk up the steep slopes and see the view start to unravel below. Recent excavations have shown signs of settlement as far back as the 12th century BC, but the castle was first

---

TOURIST DISCOUNTS

The Ljubljana Tourist Card gives free or reduced entrance to the city's museums, galleries and some special events. It also gives the holder free city-bus travel and discounts on guided tours and some souvenirs. Some of Ljubljana's hotels, restaurants, bars and clubs also give Tourist Card holders a discount, as do some taxi companies, car-rental firms and shops. Valid for 72 hours from the time of purchase, the Ljubljana Tourist Card is available for €12.53 at TICs and some hotels.

fortified by the Celts and the Illyrians. Later the Romans also capitalised on the highly strategic location, with sweeping vistas right out over the whole city and up towards the Julian and Kamniške Savinje Alps.

In many ways the medieval fortress is most impressive from the outside, as once inside the central courtyard the shamble of buildings date from different periods, with a truly hideous 1960s functional section that has already aged badly. The 15th-century remnants are more appealing and there is a flurry of things to keep you occupied including a café, a well-stocked gift shop with souvenirs from all over the country, a tower with a great view and a multi-media exhibit. The last runs visitors through a 3D history of the city, tracing its development vividly from its Roman days as Emona, right through its grand Baroque era to the 1980s. The 20-minute show is well timed to avoid boredom setting in. The castle is also home to a string of cultural and religious events, including Sunday masses in summer, Ljubljana Summer Festival events and New Year fireworks. From June to September the castle's history is brought to life by knowledgeable guides who lead visitors through various halls, the chapel and the dungeon.

Mestni trg, Stari trg and Gornji trg
These connecting squares, which hug the base of Castle Hill, ripple through the heart of the Old Town in a flurry of appealing Baroque and medieval buildings. Many of the city's most popular cafés, bars and restaurants are located in or around these long squares, which buzz with life. Even the advent of supermarket chains and out-of-town malls has failed to kill off the impressive array of boutique shops and small businesses that help keep the area alive.

Ljubljanica
The Ljubljanica may not be as impressive and grand as some of Europe's great rivers, but what is often little more than a sleepy stream can churn into quite a lively rush of water after heavy rain or snowmelt. Boat tours of the river leave just across from Prešernov trg on the Old Town side. Strolling along the riverbanks is equally rewarding with a constantly changing view of the city. If you follow the banks south from Prešernov trg you will reach the **Trnovo district** (see *Krakovo and Trnovo*, page 78). This is a great place to relax on a balmy summer's day or to work off the cobwebs on a crisp winter's afternoon. From here you can cross to the Prule district and meander back up the river to the Old Town on the tree-shrouded lanes.

As well as being central to the social lives of the Ljubljančani, the attractive banks of the Ljubljanica also harbour some of the city's most impressive sights. The concrete riverbanks themselves are the work of Ljubljana's most influential architect, with Jože Plečnik having altered the river's course to prevent flooding. The steep concrete banks that predominate in the heart of the city are brightened up with trees, flowers, well-planned street lighting and even temporary art exhibitions. Plečnik also constructed the **Cobbler's Bridge** (Čevljarski Most) – so named because it was the location where cobblers once sold their wares (avoiding city taxes and catching passing pedestrian traffic) – with its balustrades and tall lamp posts. The medieval and Baroque dwellings that line the river reveal ornate coving, wrought-iron balconies and arched doorways, as well as colourful though often faded façades. Heading east along the river beyond the market brings you to the **Dragon Bridge** (Zmajski Most – see *Other sites and monuments*, page 75).

MUSEUMS/GALLERIES
Gallery of Modern Art
(*Moderna galerija; Tomšičeva 14;* ✆ *01 241 6800;* 🖷 *01 251 4120;* e *info@mg-lj.si; www.mg-lj.si; adult/concession €3.50/€2.50, free entry Sat;*

⊕ *Jul/Aug 12.00–20.00 Tue–Sun; Sep–Jun 10.00–18.00 Tue–Sun*) This is one of Ljubljana's true joys, and lovers of avant-garde art should make a beeline for this gallery and allow plenty of time. Even if your tastes are more traditional it is well worth looking around for some interesting domestic artists and a variety of temporary exhibits and, as the Museum of Modern Art is only a stone's throw from the National Gallery, you can combine both in a contrasting visit.

Edvard Ravnikas's building, which was completed in 1939 as war erupted across Europe, looks quite foreboding from the outside, with definite Plečnik influences clearly discernible. Inside it is spacious and flexible with an exhibition space on the ground floor as well as additional galleries in the basement. The main focus of the permanent collection is on Slovenian art from the 20th century, but the temporary exhibits draw on both domestic and international talents. Other activities include art workshops, discussion groups and publications on Slovenian art. The gallery also owns the **Mala Galerija** (Small Gallery) and exhibition space at Metelkova 22.

National Museum of Slovenia (*Narodni muzej Slovenije; Prešernova 20;* ↘ *01 241 4404;* f *01 241 4422;* e *info@narmuz-lj.si; www.narmuz-lj.si; adult/concession €3/€2.50, free entry 1st Sun of month. Combination ticket with the Slovenian Museum of Natural History adult/concession €5/€4;* ⊕ *10.00–18.00 Tue/Wed/Fri–Sun, 10.00–20.00 Thu*)

The museum is housed in a stunning neo-Renaissance palace, and has an impressive façade, a striking vestibule with ornate frescoes and an attractive stone-and-marble staircase with banisters adorned with white statues. Considering the size of the building the museum exhibits are surprisingly small. The permanent collection on the ground floor is displayed in corridors around a central courtyard, and consists mainly of stone relics and reliefs from Slovenia's Roman period. Descriptions of the artefacts are in both Slovene and English. As you travel through the exhibits you will also encounter an attractive Roman mosaic and a handful of Egyptian artefacts including a mummy, reputedly the only one in Slovenia.

The remaining exhibits are upstairs – take the right branch of the staircase when it splits, a spot marked by a bust of Prešeren. The left staircase will take you to the Natural History Museum, which shares the same building (see following listing). When we last visited there were two galleries open, one of which had an engaging display of prehistoric glass and amber from different regions of Slovenia. Large and informative boards in both Slovene and English provide information about the objects, their origins and the regions where they were found. Although temporary the exhibition showed what could be made of this space.

Slovenian Museum of Natural History (*Prirodoslovni muzej Slovenije; Prešernova 20;* ↘ *01 241 0940;* f *01 241 0953;* e *uprava@pms-lj.si; www.pms-lj.si; adult/concession €3/€2.50, free entry 1st Sun of month. Combination ticket with National Museum of Slovenia adult/concession €5/€4;* ⊕ *10.00–18.00 Fri–Wed, 10.00–20.00 Thu*)

This is a taxidermist's dream, brimming with stuffed mammals and amphibians. It also has a large collection of skeletons and a visually striking photographic exhibition of Slovenia's fauna and flora. It may be old-fashioned, but children love it. Highlights for younger visitors include more than 300 different varieties of birds – including a griffon vulture, golden eagle and white-tailed eagle – huge bears, stags and a wild boar. There is also a sizeable display of stuffed fish, including a shark and an enormous salmon. Not all of the exhibits have been conserved by taxidermy, with poisonous snakes pickling in preservative jars. A gruesome display of bones, including a human skeleton, the skeleton of a dog and the skulls of a gorilla and an antelope, and the skeletal reconstruction of an enormous woolly mammoth, also fascinate children visiting the museum.

The stunning pictures of Triglav National Park, which form part of the display on Slovenia's natural environment, are a highlight for older visitors. In other galleries myriad varieties of rocks and minerals hint at the country's diverse geology.

City Museum of Ljubljana (*Mestni Muzej; Gosposka 15;* ✆ *01 252 2930;* e *info@ mm-lj.si; www.mm-lj.si; free entry;* ◷ *10.00–18.00 Tue–Sun*) Until it closed for renovation in 2000, the City Museum was one of Ljubljana's most popular museums. It reopened to much fanfare in 2004, followed by the permanent collection which returned in 2005. Visitors can also admire the sheer beauty of the building and its brilliant refurbishment, walk amongst Roman ruins including a section of old Roman road, and watch projections of the planned permanent exhibitions. In addition there are regular temporary shows, some of them delving into the history of the city as the museum did before the revamp. The Auersperg Palace, in which the City Museum is housed, is multi-functional with children's workshops, adult classes, a congress hall and a relaxed café. When the permanent collection is installed it will follow the evolution of the city, the Auersperg family and the Ljubljančani.

Slovenska Kinoteka (*Miklošičeva 28;* ✆ *01 434 2520;* f *01 434 2521;* e *kinoteka@ kinoteka.si; www.kinoteka.si*) Part cinema and part museum, the recently refurbished Kinoteka, when fully functioning, exhibits artefacts and documents from cinematic history and has a regular schedule of retro and art-house cinema from Slovenia and around the globe. It is also a venue for the Ljubljana Film Festival, the annual Lesbian and Gay Film Festival (see *Chapter 2, Public holidays and festivals,* page 34) and other events.

Architectural Museum Plečnik Collection (*Arhitekturni Muzej Plečnik; Karunova 4;* ✆ *01 280 1600;* e *pz@aml.si; www.arhmuz.com; adult/concession* €4.50/€2.25; ◷ *10.00–18.00 Tue/Thu, 09.00–15.00 Sat*) Plečnik devotees must make the pilgrimage to the architect's beloved home, which is located near the Church of St John the Baptist in Trnovo. The building, which Plečnik made his home for 40 years, now comes under the auspices of the Architectural Museum. Most of the house, including his bedroom, drawing room and studio, is open to visitors. The Winter Garden is currently used for Plečnik study groups.

Slovenian School Museum (*Slovenski Šolski Muzej; Plečnikov trg 1;* ✆ *01 251 3024;* e *solski.muzej@guest.arnes.si; www.ssolski-muzej.si; free entry;* ◷ *09.00–13.00 Mon–Fri*) Reopened in 2004 after a renovation, this museum is primarily of interest to Slovene speakers and education enthusiasts. This specialised collection essentially looks at the history of teaching in Slovenia, teaching methods and aids, the evolution of schools and classroom furniture. Photographs of Slovenian schools through the centuries are also part of the collection, as are over 55,000 educational titles, which are kept in the museum's library.

Brewery Museum (*Pivovarski Muzej; Pivovarniska 2;* ✆ *01 471 7340;* e *pivovarski.muzej@pivo-union.si; www.pivo-union.si; free entry;* ◷ *by appointment, 08.00–13.00 1st Tue of month*) If your interest in Union, Ljubljana's home-grown beer, is insatiable and you can round up a group then you will be able to go on an organised tour at the Union Brewery, where there is a small museum dedicated to the hallowed brew. If you want to visit the brewery call ahead.

Tobacco Museum (*Tobačna muzej; Tobačna 5;* ✆ *01 477 7344;* f *01 477 7155;* e *tobacna@tobacna.si; www.tobacna.si; free entry;* ◷ *1st Wed and 3rd Thu of the month*

10.00–18.00 or by appointment) Visual exhibits in this museum trace the history of tobacco production from the time the tobacco plant was first discovered in America through to its export to Europe and Slovenia. Even in the absence of English translations visitors can learn a surprising amount about the development of the Ljubljana Tobacco Company, where the museum is housed. Ornate snuffboxes, cigarette holders and pipes are also on display.

Slovenian Ethnographic Museum *(Slovenski Etnografski Muzej; Metelkova 2;* ✆ *01 300 8700;* e *etnomuz@etno-muzej.si; www.etno-muzej.si; adult/concession €4.50/€2.50, free entry last Sun of the month;* ⊕ *10.00–18.00 Tue–Sun)* This often ignored museum on the edge of the city centre offers an insight into traditional Slovenian life through folk art, artefacts from rural life, folk craft and displays based around trade, textiles, home furnishings and architecture. The museum also has a collection of artefacts from around the world, with a focus on North America and Africa.

National Museum of Contemporary History *(Muzej Novejše Zgodovine; Celovška 23;* ✆ *01 300 9610;* f *01 433 8244;* e *uprava@muzej-nz.si; www.muzej-nz.si; adult/concession €3.50/€2.50, some exhibits are free on the first Sun of the month;* ⊕ *10.00–18.00 daily)* A range of audio-visual effects, photographs and artefacts take you on a journey through Slovenia's modern history, from the beginning of World War I to the country's declaration of independence in 1991. The collection resides in the attractively restored 18th-century Cekin Mansion on the outskirts of Tivoli Park. The remains of a Yugoslav army helicopter shot down over the city vividly evoke the 1991 war. They also put on a range of temporary exhibitions.

Railway Museum *(Železniški Muzej; Parmova 35 and Kurilniška 3;* ✆ *01 291 2641; free entry;* ⊕ *10.00–18.00 Tue–Sun)* In a country whose railways have a fascinating history, rail buffs will not want to miss the Railway Museum. As well as old photos of the network, largely put together by the Austro-Hungarians when they governed Slovenia, there are also hulking great train engines and accompanying wagons. For such a small country and city the array of over 60 locomotives is pretty impressive. Note that the museum is spread across two sites which are within walking distance of each other.

Architectural Museum *(Arhitekturni Muzej; Fužine Castle, Pot na Fužine 2;* ✆ *01 540 9798;* e *aml@aml.si; www.arhmuz.com; adult/concession €2.50/€1.25;* ⊕ *09.00–15.00 Mon–Fri, 11.00–18.00 Sat, 11.00–14.00 Sun)* The main collection of the Architectural Museum is dramatically housed in a Renaissance mansion. Given the significant focus on Jože Plečnik it is tempting to think of this as a Plečnik museum, but in fact the work of many other modern Slovenian architects is covered including Ivo Spinčič, France Tomažič, Ivo Medved and Vinko Glanz. The various departments of the Architectural Museum encompass industrial design, visual and electronic media and photography, with explorations also into the history of Fužine Castle itself as well as regular temporary exhibitions. Town planners or architects wanting to spend an afternoon on a busman's holiday may wish to delve into the comprehensive library, though much of the material is in Slovene. The permanent Plečnik collection is an edited version of the large exhibition staged at the Pompidou Centre in Paris in 1986, which covers all his main periods from his days in Vienna and Prague, through to his seminal work in Slovenia. Some of the most interesting exhibits are plans by the prolific architect for further additions to his beloved Ljubljana.

National Gallery (*Narodna Galerija; Prešernova 24;* ☏ *01 241 5434;* f *01 241 5403;* e *info@ng-slo.si; www.ng-slo.si; adult/concession* €*4.20/*€*3.90;* ◷ *10.00–18.00 Tue–Sun*) Designed by the Czech Škrabout and constructed a year after the 1895 earthquake as the National House, Slovenia's biggest art gallery boasts an impressive collection of sculpture and paintings from the Middle Ages through to the late 19th century. It also has an interesting photographic collection that gives a pictorial history of Slovenia. The gallery has recently been expanded, and a new wing has added a collection of works by European masters to those of well-known Slovene artists like Jakopič, Kobilca and Metzinger.

City Gallery (*Mestna Galerija; free entry;* ◷ *Mestna 1 & 2 Sep–Jun 10.00–18.00 Tue–Fri & Sun, 10.00–13.00 Sat; Jul/Aug 10.00–14.00 & 17.00–20.00 Tue–Fri & Sun, 10.00–13.00 Sat. Bežigrad 1&2 Sep–Jun 10.00–18.00 Tue–Fri, 10.00–14.00 Sat; Jul/Aug 10.00–14.00 & 17.00–20.00 Tue–Fri, 10.00–14.00 Sat*) Not content with one location the City Gallery manages to spread its eclectic wings across four sites, two of them in the heart of the city and two in the suburb of Bežigrad. In the original three-level building **Mestna 1** (*Mestni trg 5;* ☏ *01 241 1770;* e *mestna.galerija-lj@siol.net; www.mestna-galerija.si*) is a gallery with around a dozen temporary exhibitions a year. Nearby is the gallery's permanent collection **Mestna 2** (*Cankarjevo nabrežje 11/I;* ☏ *01 241 1790; www.mestna-galerija.si*), which houses nearly 200 works of art by both Slovene and international artists. There are two further galleries in Bežigrad, each with its own temporary exhibitions. The first, **Bežigrad 1** (*Dunajska 31;* ☏ *01 436 6957; www.mestna-galerija.si*) was brought under the wing of the City Gallery in 1996 and like its patron holds around a dozen exhibitions a year. Many exhibits tend to focus on installations, 'concrete poetry' and other multimedia projects. Although founded in 1976, the second Bežigrad branch, **Bežigrad 2** (*Vodnova 3;* ☏ *01 436 4057; www.mestna-galerija.si*) also came on board in 1996 with a similar emphasis in its exhibitions. Some exhibitions at Mestna 1 have waiting lists so it is worth planning your visit in advance.

Other galleries

Tivoli Gallery/International Centre of Graphic Art Grad Tivoli, Pod turnom 3; ☏ 01 241 3800; www.mglc-lj.si; ◷ 11.00–18.00 Wed–Sun

Mala Galerija (Small Gallery) Slovenska 35; ☏ 01 251 6800; ◷ 10.00–18.00 Tue–Sat, 10.00–13.00 Sun

ŠKUC Galerija Stari trg 21; ☏/f 01 421 3140; e galerija.skuc@guest.arnes.si; www.galerija.skuc-drustvo.si; ◷ 10.00–20.00 Tue–Sun

DESSA Architectural Gallery Židovska steza 4; ☏ 01 251 6010; f 01 421 7975; e ljdessa1@guest.arnes.si; ◷ 10.00–15.00 Mon–Fri

Galerija Hest Židovska 8; ☏ 01 422 0000; www.galerijahest-sp.si; ◷ 10.00–14.00 & 15.30–20.00 Mon–Fri, 10.00–13.00 Sat

Galerija Hest 35 Novi trg 6; ☏ 01 426 2168; www.galerijahest-sp.si; ◷ 15.30–20.00 Mon–Fri, 10.00–13.00 Sat

OTHER SITES AND MONUMENTS

Skyscraper (Nebotičnik) Ljubljana's original skyscraper, located at Slovenska 37, was the tallest building in the region when it was constructed in 1933. A café once tempted at the top of the building offering stunning views of the city's skyline. For now visitors have to content themselves with a street-level exploration as a debate focused on ownership and responsibility for its upkeep has led to its closure and there is little to suggest it will reopen soon. If you head a little further south down Slovenska to the Nama department store at Tomšičeva 1, and take the lift to the Global Café and Nightclub on the fifth floor, you can get a similar view.

Miklošičeva and Miklošičev Park In the streets immediately north of Prešernov trg visitors will discover a profusion of historically and culturally significant buildings that were constructed after the earthquake that devastated the city in 1895. Josip Vancaš's great Art Nouveau structure, the **Grand Union Hotel Executive**, at Miklošičeva 1, was opened in 1905 after having taken just 18 months to complete. In addition to its striking exterior the hotel boasts etched-glass windowpanes and an elegant interior that retains many period features. Opposite the hotel at Miklošičeva 4 is the **People's Loan Bank** (Slovenska Zadružna Kmetijska Banka), with its intricate decorations, symbols, blue tiles and attractive figures, two of whom sit on the roof. The MaxMara clothing store (Miklošičeva 6) features intricate detail below the roof and understated tiles that frame its arched windows.

More immediately striking is the former **Commercial Co-operative Bank** (Nekdanja Zadružna Gospodarska Banka) created by Ivan Vurnik – which is located opposite the hotel at No 8. Vurnik's wife, Helen, gave him a helping hand and is credited with painting it from head to toe in a vibrant pink, with its doors and windows framed by elaborate rusty red, yellow, blue and white geometric patterns. Ljubljana's most colourful building is especially impressive on a bright sunny day. One question, though, continues to perplex those who come to admire it: just how do you fit the whole building into your camera viewfinder?

Other impressive buildings on this side are the **Bamberg House** (Bambergova Hiša) at Miklošičeva 16 – look out for the ceramic reliefs of some of Slovenia's most renowned painters – the **Krisper House** (Krisperjeva Hiša) at Miklošičeva 20 and **Regali House** (Regali Hiša) at Miklošičeva 18. The first two secessionist structures are the masterpieces of Maks Fabiani who was commissioned to rebuild the area around Miklošičev Park, or Slovenska trg as it was formerly known, in the early 20th century. Fran Berneker is the architect behind Regali House. The former workers' chamber – notable for the seven marble figures, sculpted by Lojze Dolinar, that adorn the roof – is at Miklošičeva 28, the present-day location of the Slovenska Kinoteka (see *Museums/galleries* above).

On the western side of Miklošičev Park you can see two more examples of Art Nouveau architecture. Sadly the green façade of the **Chuden House** (Čudnova Hiša) is looking slightly the worse for wear. Presiding over the park from Tavčarjeva 9 is Ljubljana's **court building**. Notable features of this expansive neo-Classical structure include the four columns that stand tall over the main entrance, its balconied windows and the intricate geometric brickwork. Look out for the clock on the right gatepost that still tells the correct time.

Immediately opposite the courthouse you will see a statue of Franc Miklošič himself. The story of how the Slovene professor of Slavic studies came to be there is perhaps more interesting than the somewhat incongruous statue. The statue's pedestal was originally home to the Austro-Hungarian Emperor Franz Josef, who was later replaced by figureheads from the Socialist Federal Republic of Yugoslavia. Tired of constantly replacing the heads of state that resided here, the city authorities decided that the effigy should be neutral.

Central Market (Tržnica) This is worth visiting for Plečnik's dramatic colonnades alone – the riverside arcade of columns built in 1939–40 which follow the gentle curve of the Ljubljanica. The best time to visit the market, which fills Vodnikov trg and the smaller Podgačarjev trg, is on Saturday, when it seems like the whole city has turned out and brightly coloured and strongly scented flowers abound. On Podgačarjev trg you will also find **St Nicholas's Cathedral** (Stolna Cerkev Sv Nikolaja – see *Churches and cathedrals*, page 79) and the **Bishop's Palace** (Škofijski Dvorec). Constructed in 1512, the latter is one of Ljubljana's oldest buildings. In the five centuries since its construction it has played host to eminent

Europeans, with Napoleon Bonaparte and the Russian Tsar Alexander I rumoured to be amongst them.

The square is also home to the **Seminary** (Semenišče) that dates from the beginning of the 18th century. Two hulking stone giants, carved by sculptor Angelo Pozzo, guard the seminary's south portal. The real beauty of this theological college, though, lies in its library – an impressive combination of Giulio Quaglio's breathtaking frescoes and its Baroque furnishings. Viewing of the library is by appointment only, as the academy is still used today; this can be arranged at the Ljubljana TIC.

Dragon Bridge (Zmajski Most) The first concrete and iron bridge to cross the Ljubljanica is located at the northern end of Plečnik's colonnades and was erected in 1888 to commemorate the 40th anniversary of Austro-Hungarian Emperor Franz Josef's accession to the throne. Designed in secessionist style by Juriji Zaninovič, a Croatian architect who studied at the Wagner School in Vienna, and constructed in 1900–01, the bridge's chief attraction is the four large green dragons that sit in each corner of the bridge and the smaller dragons that guard the bridge's lights. Local legend claims that the dragons will wag their tails when a virgin crosses the bridge; others have somewhat cruelly nicknamed this impressive structure the 'mother-in-law' due to its fiery nature.

Mestni trg Perhaps the smartest of Ljubljana's three Old Town squares, Mestni trg owes much of its contemporary appearance to the Baroque period of the late 17th and 18th centuries. Here amongst the beautiful façades and courtyards of ancient palaces and middle-class houses you will find the seat of the city council, a smattering of expensive shops and some of the city's most refined bars and restaurants. As you walk down the street remember to look up to really appreciate the intricacies of the square's ornate façades – particularly noteworthy is the **Souvan House** (Souvanova Hiša) at No 24.

Town Hall (*Rotovž; Mestni trg 1;* \ *01 306 3000; free entry; atrium* ⊕*09.00–19.00 Mon–Fri*) There have been buildings on this site as far back as the 15th century, but most of today's Baroque structure was conjured up by Gregor Maček in 1718. Although the town hall still functions as a seat of power, tourists can flit amongst some of its most interesting parts. Key features to look out for are the external balcony, pentagonal clocktower, interior courtyard, Gothic entrance hall, the patterned arches of the Baroque arcade, the auditorium and the Hercules and Narcissus Fountain, the work of Robba's workshop.

Robba's Fountain Another of Robba's attractive fountains – the **Fountain of the Three Carniolan Rivers** – stands resplendent outside the town hall. Having recently been brought back to its best with a comprehensive renovation, this impressive copy depicts the three great rivers of Carniola: the Krka, the Ljubljanica and the sweeping Sava. Each of the rivers has been personified by a mighty triton pouring out water from large jugs. A number of visitors have suggested that Robba got his idea for the 1751 masterpiece from Italian artist Gian Lorenzo Bernini, who created the Fountain of the Four Rivers in Rome's Piazza Navona. Plans have been mooted to relocate the fountain inside the protective arms of the National Gallery.

Ribji trg This compact square, linking Mestni trg to the Ljubljanica, is entered through a small arch and boasts some of the oldest dwellings in the city. According to the plaque on house No 2, now the Abecedarium Café (see *Cafés and bars*, page

63), the building was constructed in 1528. For many Slovenes the house is important not because of its age, but as the former home of Primož Trubar (see *History*, page 5) who is said to have resided there in the 16th century.

Stari trg The main attractions on Stari trg are its bountiful cafés, restaurants, bars and shops, but if you can drag yourself away there is a number of buildings worth exploring. Look out for the beautiful wrought-iron balcony, the bust of Slovene poet Lili Novy and the particularly impressive Baroque frontage on the **Schwieger House** (Schwieger Hiša) at No 11a.

Levstikov trg The focal point of this attractive square, which received a Plečnik makeover in the early 1930s, is the **Church of St James** (Cerkev Sv Jakob – see *Churches and cathedrals* below). Outside the church is the Shrine to Mary, which was placed here in 1681 as a thank-you to God when the Turks bypassed Ljubljana. Across traffic-clogged Karlovška is the **Gruber Palace** (Gruberjeva Palača), which is widely regarded as one of Ljubljana's most impressive examples of late Baroque architecture. Constructed by Gabriel Gruber between 1773 and 1781 the building boasts a dome-capped oval stucco staircase, and its own chapel complete with frescoes by Kremser Schmidt depicting scenes from the life of the Virgin Mary.

Gornji trg A raft of Baroque and medieval dwellings climb gently eastward away from Stari trg and Levstikov trg on what is arguably Ljubljana's most attractive street, Gornji trg. Only a few of the houses retain their original medieval style; these can be identified by three windows running across the width of each building, while those with more windows have been combined and given a later Baroque style. Walking up the street, immerse yourself in window shopping with myriad handmade gifts, antiques and ornate jewellery amongst the offerings. Just beyond the midway point the highlight is the **Church of St Florian** (Cerkev Sv Florijana – see *Churches and cathedrals* below).

Kongresni trg This grand square was constructed in 1821 to commemorate the formation of the Holy Alliance, although it was later restyled by Plečnik. Just one block back from the Ljubljanica, it is a place where locals gather for free concerts and special events, yet curiously it does not flourish with pavement cafés and definitely plays second fiddle to Prešernov trg. Its highlights include the views back towards the castle and the flurry of impressive buildings that crowd all around it, including the university headquarters, the **Slovene Philharmonic Hall** (Slovenska Filharmonija), the **Ursuline Church of the Holy Trinity** (Uršulinska Cerkev Sv Trojice – *see Churches and cathedrals* below) and the **Kazina** [Author: not on map] – a stunning Classical construction. In the centre is a network of paths which form a star shape, and myriad benches that make good venues for enjoying a slice of pizza from the Ljubljanksi Dvor take-away on the square's east side.

University of Ljubljana (Univerza v Ljubljani) Josip Hudetz's epic neo-Renaissance building dominates the southern corner of Kongresni trg, having benefited from a successful and sympathetic recent revamp. Complete with attractive Baroque towers this impressive mansion was built shortly after the devastating 1895 earthquake. Note the 15 gilded coats of arms, which represent the Carniolan state and Carniolan towns. The fountain in the front courtyard is called Europa and was commissioned to commemorate the EU's recognition of an independent Republic of Slovenia in 1992.

Slovene Philharmonic Hall (Slovenska Filharmonija) Slovenia proudly boasts one of the oldest philharmonic orchestras in the world, established in 1701 as the **Academia Philharmonicorum Labacensium** and becoming the Philharmonic Society in 1794. Today's hall (see *Music*, page 62) is the building's third incarnation, as it was destroyed first by fire in 1887 and then by the earthquake in 1895. This impressive structure is very different from the wooden construction that originally stood on the spot. Be sure to look at the wave-like shape of the rear of the hall, which backs onto the Ljubljanica. Stunning as it is from the outside the best way to really enjoy the Slovene Philharmonic Hall is to catch a performance by Slovenia's Philharmonic Orchestra or the Chamber Choir who are based in the same building.

Trg Republike Ljubljana's biggest square, the centre of socialist-era Slovenia, is dominated by two hulking towers and the Cankarjev Dom Cultural and Congress Centre (see *Theatre*, page 61), all imposing leftovers from the 1980s. The reliefs on the façade of the Slovenian **National Assembly** (Državni Zabor) on the north side of the square are worth looking at. Sculpted by Zdenko Kalin and Karel Putrih, they depict heroic socialist scenes. You can also seek out the small memorial in the adjacent park, the work of Edo Mihevc and Boris Kalin, a tribute to Slovenia's national heroes.

SNG Drama; Slovene National Theatre (Slovensko Narodno Gledališče Drama) Designed by Alexander Graf and completed in 1911, the SNG Drama (see *Theatre*, page 62) took two years to construct and has an impressive façade. As you pass, pop into the entrance hall where you will find the busts of four of the country's most famous classical actors – Počkaj, Linhart, Levstik and Župančič.

NUK; National and University Library (Narodna in Univerzitena Knjižnica) Jože Plečnik was the man behind this deeply impressive library, widely regarded as his finest work. The futuristic and textured red-brick-and-stone exterior is constructed entirely from local materials; even the beautifully sculpted doors are striking, but it is the interior that really stands out. Visitors are allowed to climb the grand and austere black marble staircase, flanked by 32 dark marble columns, which leads to the reading room. Unless you are a member or prospective member this is as far as your exploration can go. Much of the lighting, layout and many of the fixtures and fittings inside also originate from Plečnik's studio. The library was built on the site of an old palace that was destroyed in the 1895 earthquake, taking five years to reach completion in 1940 as war broke out across Europe. Local legend has it that Slovene-language literature was secretly tucked away in the depths of the library when the city was occupied from 1941 to 1945.

While you may not be able to delve into Plečnik's stunning reading rooms you can at least pop down to the basement café/canteen designed by the great artist himself. Neat lines, funky tables and top-class *bela kava* are the order of the day and this is a good option for those looking to laze around with local students leafing through a newspaper or trying to strike up a conversation with your guidebook on show.

Slovene Academy of Arts and Sciences (Slovenska Akademija Znanosti in Umetnosti) The **Lontovž Palace** (Lontovž Palača)– a stunning Baroque mansion – has been the institution's nerve centre for almost 70 years and is of major cultural significance to the Ljubljančani. For visitors the building's ornate façade, which was designed by Jožef Schemerl and completed between 1786 and 1790, the busts of the academy's former presidents in the entrance hall, and Neptune's

Fountain in the courtyard are all of interest. Looking across Novi trg to No 5 you will find another of the academy's imposing properties, complete with heavy wooden doors and elaborate decoration below the windows.

Trg Francoske Revolucije This square is home to the only statue of Napoleon outside France, known as the Illyrian Monument. It was yet another work of Jože Plečnik, though perhaps not one of his finest with a rather frightening, garland-shrouded bust of France's finest perched precariously above the square. Zdenko Kalin's outsized bust of Simon Gregorčič also stands in the square as a memorial to the Slovene poet.

Križanke This former monastic complex, which dates back to the 13th century, was transformed by Jože Plečnik in the 1950s. Today the Križanke (see *Theatre*, page 61) is regarded as one of the city's premier performance venues. Even when there is no show on it is possible to visit the modest Church of St Mary and the Baroque Knights Hall, or admire the ornate arcades, busts and sculptures in the grounds; you will find an incarnation of Plečnik himself in the atrium. During the warmer months the Križanke courtyard is a great place to enjoy a coffee from the theatre's small café.

Krakovo and Trnovo Just a short stroll south along the left bank of the Ljubljanica will take you to the twin suburbs of Krakovo and Trnovo, commonly regarded as the oldest and most historic part of the city.

Krakovo is notable for its compact medieval housing, the produce grown in its allotments or market garden and sold at the daily market on Vodnikov trg, and the visible remains of the city's Roman era. On Mirje you find the city's best-preserved stretch of **Roman wall**, complete with Plečnik modifications. According to locals the Emperor Augustus laid the first stone of the wall in AD14. The slightly incongruous pyramid at the eastern end of the wall stands 6m tall and shows you the minimum height that the Roman wall would have been originally. Other remnants of Emona are part of an open-air archaeological museum at Mirje 4 where you can see the ruins of an old Roman house. The building's second claim to fame arises from the fact that it was once home to the Slovene painter Rihard Jakopič.

The lively suburb of Trnovo, separated from Krakovo by the Gradaščica Canal, boasts a string of waterfront bars, cafés and restaurants on Eipprova ulica, as well as the **Church of St John the Baptist** (Cerkev Sv Janeza Krstnika– see *Churches and cathedrals* below), and the former home of Jože Plečnik at Karunova 4. Today the architect's house forms part of the **Architectural Museum** (Arhitekturni Muzej – see *Museums/galleries* above). Plečnik invested a lot of time and energy in landscaping his beloved Trnovo and Krakovo, and his influence can be seen in the gentle sloping embankment of the canal, tree-lined promenades, the **Trnovo Pier** (Trnovski Pristan) and the **Trnovo Bridge** (Trnovski Most) which traverses the Gradaščica. The bridge is made of iron and concrete and incorporates a distinctive pyramid at each corner, and an obelisk.

SNG Opera; Slovenian National Opera and Ballet Theatre (Slovensko Narodno Gledališče Opera in Balet) The Opera and Ballet Theatre (see *Music*, page 62), one of Ljubljana's most attractive buildings, sits proudly in the centre of a square brimming with impressive architecture. The ornate neo-Renaissance design was the brainchild of Czech architects J V Hráskey and A J Hrubey, and came into being in 1882. The ornate figures that shelter in niches and adorn the tympanum above the main entrance are the work of sculptor Alojz Grand.

Žale Ljubljana's main burial place (bus 2 direction Zelena jama) takes its name from the old Slavic word for cemetery. Opened in 1906 and still used today, Žale is laced with grand architecture and layers of history. Graves include those of both Italian and Slovene soldiers killed in World War I. The tombs and headstones of Slovenia's famous personalities are intricate works by some of the country's most reputable artists. Legendary Slovenian architect Jože Plečnik has also stamped his distinctive mark on the cemetery, including its dramatic colonnaded entrance (1938–40), the Farewell Park, a small chapel and the *Tomb of Blumauer* (1942). Other notable features include Zdenko Kalin's *Fountain of Life*, a hexagonal pond flanked by six frolicking figures, Kralj's *Tomb of the Menardi Family* (1930), Dolina's tombstone of J E Krek (1920) and an ossuary containing the bones of Slovene soldiers who died in World War I and, in the new part of the cemetery, a memorial commemorating the victims of the ten-day war for independence in 1991.

CHURCHES AND CATHEDRALS

Cathedral of St Nicholas (*Stolna Cerkev Sv Nikolaja; Dolničarjeva 1;* ➘ *01 231 0684*) The dedication to the patron saint of fishermen and sailors is fitting for this cathedral located near the Ljubljanica. The original probably stood on the site as far back as the 13th century, but most of today's incarnation is the result of work carried out at the beginning of the 18th century, with the main architect, the Italian Andrea Pozzo, completing work on the city's most important spiritual building in 1706. The cupola was added by Gregor Maček, who took over the construction of the cathedral in the later years. The Cathedral of St Nicholas has two entrances and it is worth exploring both. The weighty bronze portal on the south side of the church is known locally as the City Door and is composed of the busts of various bishops of the city, the work of local sculptor Mirsad Begič. Another local artist, Tone Demšar, added an impressive relief to the main, or Slovenian, door in preparation for the Pope's triumphal 1996 visit. The image that now adorns this western portal depicts 1,250 years of Christianity.

Equally noteworthy are the frescoes that adorn both the exterior and the interior. On the southern façade you can see Giulio Quaglio's depiction of the Annunciation, while his image of Jesus Christ in Jordan can be found on the northern wall. Quaglio was also the master behind the ceiling frescoes in the nave. Janez Wolf's painting *The Angel's Proclamation of Zahriah Wolf* on the cathedral's eastern façade, Langus's altar painting, Plečnik's bishop's throne and Robba's cherubs, which adorn the Altar of Corpus Christi, are also worth seeking out.

Franciscan Church of the Annunciation (*Frančiškanska Cerkev Marijinega Oznanjenja; Prešernov trg;* ➘ *01 425 3007*) Franciscan monks commissioned this attractive pink-coloured church, one of the symbols of the city, in the middle of the 17th century. Numerous renovations have seen the building alter considerably over time and today's church dates largely from the 18th century. The inspiration for the structure's attractive façade came from a late-Renaissance church in Florence, Santa Maria Novella. Internally, the oldest building on the square (it survived the 1895 earthquake) is less impressive with the most distinguished feature being an altar designed by Francesco Robba. Also look out for Matevž Langus's frescoes near the windows, and those added to the nave by Matej Sternen in 1935–36. The adjoining monastery didn't fare so well in the earthquake, with the majority of it needing to be rebuilt. Today it boasts a library housing more than 10,000 books and manuscripts.

Church of St John the Baptist (*Cerkev Sv Janeza Krstnika; Kolezijska 1;* ➘ *01 283 5060*) Fabled as the place where the Romantic Slovene poet France Prešeren first spotted Julija Primic – his great unrequited love – the church is usually referred to as the Trnovo Church. The church was originally constructed in the middle of the 18th century and underwent various renovations and reconstructions that altered its appearance. Today's neo-Romanesque incarnation dates from the early 20th century when it was rebuilt after the 1895 earthquake that devastated much of Ljubljana. Internally the church's most noteworthy aspects are Metzinger's Baroque masterpiece – a stunning altar painting of the church's patron St John the Baptist – the frescoes designed by Sternen and Goršič and a mid-19th-century organ.

Church of St Florian (*Cerkev Sv Florijana; Gornji trg 18;* ☏ *01 252 1727*) This Old Town church was built in 1672 after a devastating fire engulfed this part of the city. Seventeenth-century locals hoped that dedicating the church to the patron saint of fires and firemen, St Florian, would protect it against any future blazes. Plečnik stamped his indelible mark on the church in the 1930s when he moved the main portal, bricking up the original and placing Robba's statue of St John Nepomuk in front of it. Another of Robba's works, a dramatic depiction of St John being tossed into Prague's Vlatva River from the Czech capital's Charles Bridge, is also located inside. The church is at its most atmospheric during services and regular classical concerts.

Church of St James (*Cerkev Sv Jakob; Gornji trg 18;* ☏ *01 252 1727*) Built by Jesuits in 1613 to complement their monastery, this imposing Old Town church boasts the highest belltower in the city, an attractive Baroque interior and a Jesuit chapel with intricate stucco work and an unusual octagonal shape. Before the 1895 earthquake the church actually had two belltowers. The sacristy was also added after the earthquake. Francesco Robba, who lived on Levstikov Square, designed the church's high altar, which was added in 1732. When Plečnik was commissioned to redesign the square in 1933–34 some say he planted a row of poplar trees to hide the church's façade, which he disliked intensely.

Ursuline Church of the Holy Trinity (*Uršulinska Cerkev Sv Trojice; Slovenska 21;* ☏ *01 252 4862*) Located on the western side of regal Kongresni trg, this central church boasts an attractive Baroque façade and conceals an enormous multi-coloured altar constructed with African marble, and altar paintings by Valentin Metzinger. Built in 1726 in Venetian style, the church's most striking external features are the six columns that flank its entrance and a balustrade staircase designed by Jože Plečnik.

A copy of the Column of the Holy Trinity stands outside. The original – widely believed to be the work of Mislej and Robba and erected back in 1693 as the Ljubljančani gave thanks for those who survived the plague – is in the safe hands of the City Museum.

Church of St Peter (*Cerkev Šempetrska; Trubarjeva 80;* ☏ *01 231 7965*) Designed by Italian artist Giovanni Fusconi, the church was constructed between 1729 and 1733. Its somewhat bland exterior is brightened up by Ivan and Helen Vurnik's (of the Co-operative Bank fame, see *Miklošičeva and Miklošičev Park*, page 73) attractive mosaics. St Peter sits proudly above the main entrance. The interior is also adorned with stunning frescoes painted by Franc Jelovšek, a local Slovene artist.

Serbian Orthodox Church (*Srbska Pravoslavna Cerkev;* ☏ *01 252 4002*) Partially hidden behind trees on Prešernova the church has an attractive façade and a brightly decorated Orthodox interior. With a statue of Primož Trubar standing outside this is a place for Ljubljana's other faiths, Protestant and Orthodox Christians, in a country dominated by Roman Catholicism.

Church of St Francis of Assisi (*Cerkev Sv Frančiška Asiškega; Černetova 20;* ✆ *01 583 7270*) One of Plečnik's most striking and unique churches can be found in the suburb of Šišak (bus 22 direction Kamna Gorica to Drenikova stop). The Church of St Francis of Assisi features a square ground plan, 20 magnificent internal pillars and a futuristic belltower. Internally the church takes the shape of a covered square complete with colonnades, a flat wooden ceiling and highly individual altars and furnishings.

Church of St Michael (*Cerkev Sv Mihaela; Črna vas 48, Barje;* ✆ *01 427 2218*) Another of Plečnik's creations, the Church of St Michael (bus 19 direction Barje) at the heart of the Ljubljansko Barje (Ljubljana Marshes), was built in the periods 1920–28 and 1937–40 around ten pillars. This fortress-like wooden church was constructed on a very tight budget and innovative ways of cutting costs reputedly included using sewage pipes rather than concrete for the pillars.

PARKS AND ESCAPES
Tivoli Garden Just a small part of Ljubljana's green lung, this immaculately landscaped garden hangs tantalisingly on the edge of the city centre. Its walkways, trees, fountains and benches are the perfect venue for relaxing away from what big-city bustle Ljubljana can muster. This garden also boasts a children's playground, cafés and a recreation centre with a pool, roller skating, tennis and bowling. There is also a large glass greenhouse near the southern entrance to the park.

Krajinski Park Tivoli Tivolski Vrh, Šišenski, Debeli and Rožnik hills, Rkovnik and Mostec collectively make up the largest part of Ljubljana's green lung. The most visited area is Rožnik Hill where visitors find the charming Church of St Mary, the Ivan Cankar Memorial Room and restaurants that feel more like countryside inns. Myriad walking, running and mountain-biking trails weave their way through the park's densely forested hills. Maps and waymarks help keep walkers on the right track, although vandals have damaged some of the signposts. If you are feeling really energetic you can flex your muscles and test your aerobic stamina on a variety of fitness tracks that offer alfresco circuit training.

Ljubljana Zoo (*Živalski Vrt; Večna pot 70;* ✆ *01 244 2188;* e *info@zoo-ljubljana.si; www.zoo-ljubljana.si; adult/child €6/€4.50;* ⊕ *Apr & Sep 09.00–18.00 daily, Mar & Oct 09.00–17.00 daily, Nov–Feb 09.00–16.00 daily*) The city's zoo has an agreeable forest location, and is home to over 500 animal species. Younger visitors coo over the farm animals, beavers, deer and mouflon sheep, while older visitors are more appreciative of the zoo's Siberian tiger, giraffes, zebras and leopards. A café, hands-on activities, children's playground and archaeological collection help keep everyone happy.

Ljubljana Marshes (Ljubljansko Barje) This peaty marshland 3km from the centre of town (bus 19 direction Barje) is a real throwback to life in Ljubljana when marsh dwellers lived in houses built on stilts in 2000BC. Today the houses have gone but this boggy land, which is believed to be around two million years old, is still home to around 70 animal species and is visited by more than 250 species of birds each year, making it something of an ornithologist's paradise. Tourist offices in the city can now organise birding guides for avid twitchers. Plečnik's **Church of St Michael** (Cerkev Sv Mihaela – see *Churches and cathedrals* above) is also here. It is also possible to take a hot-air balloon trip over the marshes (see *Tourist information/local tour operators*, page 51), the best way to get a real feel for the landscape.

Šmarna Gora There is no doubting the city's most popular hill. Šmarna Gora, 10km northwest of the city centre (bus 8 direction Brod), is awash at weekends with Ljubljančani fleeing the city. Once a fortress against the Ottomans, today the 669m-high hill is invaded by day trippers seeking a bit of exercise and sweeping views back towards the city. For any reasonably fit adult the trip to the top can be tackled in under an hour. Look out also for the Church of the Holy Mother, with its frescoes by Matevž Langus. You will see Šmarna Gora from many spots in the city and on your way in from the airport, so don't be lazy and have a go if you are fit enough.

Trnovo Golf Course (m *051 366 690; www.golgtrnovo.com;* ⊕*07.30–21.00 daily*) Slovenia's first public course opened to the south of the city in June 2006. It is suitable for both beginners and more advanced golfers, with different teeing-off positions. The nine-hole course is a par 34. If you just want to hone your skills there is also a driving range, five practice greens and a putting green.

Gorenjska

If it is mountains you have come to Slovenia to see then this is the region for you. Everywhere you look in Gorenjska voluminous peaks rise improbably from sweeping river valleys and the skyline dances with ridges and skyscraping peaks, many of which retain a liberal dusting of snow for much of the year. Quite simply Gorenjska boasts some of the finest mountain scenery anywhere in the world. In the famous resort at Lake Bled they are well aware of this gift and tourism these days is an increasingly slick affair, though there is always somewhere to escape the crowds even at the height of summer. Then there is the lake at Bohinj, much larger and if anything even more impressive and with far fewer tourists. If the weather is good and you have time the best plan is to just get out into the hills for a gentle hike on the lower slopes or for a serious climb, if you have the gear and experience, up the likes of Mount Triglav, a peak with mythical status for many Slovenes. After a hard day in the outdoors cosy *gostilnas* await with sublime Bohinj trout a speciality, with perhaps a wickedly creamy *kremna rezina*, another Gorenjska speciality, for dessert.

KAMNIK

Just a half-hour drive north of Ljubljana is the pretty medieval town of Kamnik, a quiet and relaxed place that is perfect for a minimum-effort day trip or a stopover *en route* to Logarska Dolina even further north (see *Chapter 9, Štajerska*, page 205). The spectacular Kamniške Savinje Alps loom behind the compact old centre, though there is not too much to do bar floating around the sprinkling of cafés, bars and churches and admiring the view. Kamnik is not a big place so the best plan is just to stroll down the main street, Glavni trg, and onto old-world Šutna, taking in the town's attractions as you go.

GETTING THERE Frequent buses and trains leave Ljubljana for Kamnik. The bus is generally a little quicker and takes 25–30 minutes, although some services take almost an hour, while the trains take around 50 minutes.

Bus station Perovo 30; ☏ 01 830 9415; www.kam-bus.si

Railway station Kranjska 4; ☏ 01 839 4090

GETTING AROUND Kamnik is easily navigable by foot. Taxis are available locally.

TOURIST INFORMATION/LOCAL TOUR OPERATORS

🆔 **Tourist Information Centre** Glavni trg 3; ☏ 01 831 8250; f 01 831 8192; e tic@kamnik-tourism.si; www.kamnik-tourism.si; ⊕ Nov–Mar

10.00–18.00 Mon–Fri, 10.00–14.00 Sat; May/Jun & Sep/Oct 10.00–18.00 Mon–Sat; Jul/Aug 09.00–20.00 Mon–Sat

AUSTRIA

Kamniške Savinje Alps

Kamnik

LJUBLJANA

Kranj

Crngrob

Suha

Škofja Loka

✚ Hospital

Cerkno

Spodnji Idrija

Idrija

Begunje

Brezje

Kropa

Radovljica

...ba

Bled

Vintgar Gorge

Studor

Bohinjska Bistrica
Mt Koblo
▲ 1227 m

Stara Fužina

Ribčev Laz

Lake Bohinj

Savica Falls

Mt Triglav
▲ 286 m

Triglav National Park

Kranjska Gora

Vršič Pass

Mt Vogel
1922 m ▲

Tolmin

▲ 2208 m

Bovec

Kobarid

ITALY

ITALY

Šmartno

N

Bradt

15km

15 miles

0

0

Dolina Adrenalina Cankarjeva 15; m 041 556 100; e info@dolinaadrenalina.com; www.dolinaadrenalina.com. Adventure tour operator

organising canyoning, mountain biking, mountain guiding & paragliding.

WHERE TO STAY

⌂ **Pension Kamrica** (5 rooms) Trg Svobode 2; ✎ 01 831 7707. Located on a quiet street just behind Šutna this small pension has good-sized rooms & private parking. $$$

⌂ **Prenočišča Špenko** (12 rooms) Prešernova 14c; ✎ 01 831 7330. Less appealing than Kamnik's

other centrally located pensions the rooms here are still an option. $$

⌂ **Pri Cesarju** (10 rooms) Tunjiška 1; ✎ 01 839 2917. This pension just north of Glavni trg has decent rooms & some trpls. $$

Camping

Ⰰ **Kamp Resnik** Nevlje 1a; ✎ 01 831 7314; f 01 831 8192. A 1ha campsite on the banks of the

Nevljica River with 100 pitches, washing machine & 2 bungalows to rent. Bungalow $$$, camping $

WHERE TO EAT

✗ **Kavarna Veronika** Glavni trg 6; ✎ 01 839 1143; ⊕08.00–01.00 daily. Pleasant café with terrace located beneath the castle, serving cakes, sandwiches & ice cream. $$

✗ **Okrepčevalnica de Cecco** Šutna 68; ✎ 01 831 7447; ⊕10.00–midnight Mon–Thu, 10.00–01.00 Fri/Sat. Busy spaghetteria at the end of Šutna with

decent pasta options & Swiss specialities like fondue. $$

✗ **Picerija Napoli** Sadnikarjeva 5; ✎ 01 839 2744; ⊕11.00–23.00 Mon–Sat, 12.00–22.00 Sun. This centrally located pizzeria is Kamnik's best centrally located eating option. Dine on the terrace during the summer months. $$

OTHER PRACTICALITIES

✉ **Post office** Glavni trg 27; ⊕08.00–19.00 Mon–Fri, 08.00–12.00 Sat

$ **Ljubljanska Banka** Glavni trg 10; ⊕08.00–12.00 & 15.00–17.00 Mon–Fri

$ **SKB Banka** Glavni trg 13; ⊕08.00–12.00 & 15.00–17.00 Mon–Fri

✚ **Medical centre** Novi trg 26; ✎ 01 830 8600

WHAT TO SEE

Church of St Jacob (Cerkev Sv Jakoba) Ljubljana's main man Jože Plečnik ventured north to give the town one of his trademark designs with his impressive altar, though most of the rest of the church, on Frančiškanski trg, is Baroque.

Franciscan Monastery (*Frančiškanski Samostan; Frančiškanski trg;* ✎ *01 831 8030;* ⊕*by appointment*) This 15th-century monastery is nothing special, but its claim to fame is that it holds the first translation of the Bible into the Slovene language, written in the 15th century by Jurij Dalmatin, a Protestant minister.

Miha Maleš Gallery (*Galerija Miha Maleš; Glavni trg 2;* ✎ *01 839 1616; adult/concession €2.50/€1.50;* ⊕*09.00–13.00 & 16.00–19.00 Tue–Sat*) This gallery celebrates the life and work of local boy-made-good Miha Maleš, who was born in the town at the start of the 20th century. Today the collection has expanded to include an ever-changing range of temporary exhibits.

Terme Snovik (*Molkova pot 5;* ✎ *01 830 8631;* f *01 830 8620;* e *terme.snovik@ zarja-kovis.si; www.terme-snovik.si; adult/concession/child from €7/€6/€5;* ⊕*09.00–20.00 daily*) This spa complex has thermal pools with temperatures of up to 31°C, whirlpools, massage and sports facilities, an enormous indoor pool and a modern sauna centre with a range of wet- and dry-heat treatments.

Sunta This old quarter is the most charming part of Kamnik. Its attractions include the Church of the Annunciation, with its frescoes by Matija Kozelj, and the Sadnikar Collection, with its eclectic collection of antique furniture, weapons and art. The Zaprice Castle is also worth popping into, a Baroque mansion that is home to the Kamnik Museum, which does its best to fill you in on the history of this sleepy town.

LJUBLJANA TO BLED – OFF THE TOURIST HIGHWAY

Many time-starved visitors rush straight through on the fast road to Bled from Ljubljana, but if you follow suit you will miss out on a flurry of historical towns and villages. If you really are desperate to get to Bled then consider staying by the lake and making a couple of trips back to these gems.

ŠKOFJA LOKA

On a balmy summer night with Loka Castle twinkling floodlit above and the Old Town rambling down the hillside below, Škofja Loka, perhaps our favourite town in Slovenia, casts an alluring spell. It may be blighted by a handful of apartment blocks on its outskirts and a faceless New Town, but the surrounding countryside offers plenty of hiking and cycling opportunities, as well as a brace of remarkable churches. Much of the protected Old Town may need more than a lick of paint, but the local authorities have invested in English-language information plaques on buildings and have made a real effort in revamping the castle's museum.

HISTORY Škofja Loka (Bishop's Meadow) is swathed in tales of German emperors and Freising bishops dating back more than 1,000 years. It also enjoyed a golden age as a trading hub on the route from Bavaria to the Adriatic, though this trade was decimated in the 15th century when the natural disaster of an earthquake combined with sacking at the hands of both the Ottomans and the Counts of Celje. Fortunately most of the destroyed Old Town buildings were reconstructed centuries ago and prosperity returned to the town under the Austro–Hungarians. These days the sprinkling of industry in the suburbs is in decline and tourism is emerging as Škofja Loka's welcome new breadwinner.

GETTING THERE Škofja Loka is a 30-minute drive from Ljubljana. Regular buses from Kranj (20 minutes), Ljubljana (40 minutes) and Cerkno (45 minutes) also stop here, as do trains from Kranj (10 minutes), Ljubljana (25 minutes), Radovljica (30 minutes) and Lesce-Bled (35 minutes).

Bus station Kapucinski trg 13; ☎ 04 517 0300; www.alpetour.si

Railway station Kidričeva cesta 61; ☎ 04 294 4174. The station is 3km from town with an hourly bus link on Mon–Sat.

GETTING AROUND Škofja Loka's historic core can easily be explored on foot. Bicycle hire will also let you really discover the town's beautiful setting and explore the verdant Poljanska Valley. More serious cyclists can pick up information from the tourist information centre or the Blegoš tourist office (see *Tourist information* below) about 12 cycle routes covering 300km (including a 50km ride around Škofja Loka) in the Loka area. Both offices also stock information leaflets about hiking in the Škofja Loka hills, including 22 themed trails. Taxis are available locally.

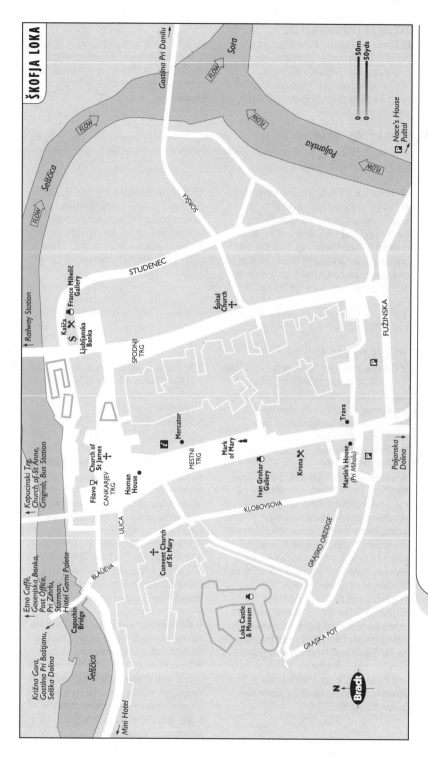

ŠKOFJA LOKA

Selščica

FLOW

Selščica

FLOW

Sora

FLOW

Gostilna Pri Danilu

FLOW

FLOW

Poljanska

FLOW

P Nace's House
Puštal

0 ____ 50m
0 ____ 50yds

↑ Railway Station

↑ Kapucinski Trg,
Church of St Anne,
Crngrob, Bus Station

↑ Etno Caffè,
Gosenjska Banka,
Post Office,
Pri Zihrlu,
Starman,
Hotel Garni Paleta

Križna Gora,
Gostilna Pri Boštjanu,
Selška Dolina

Mini Hotel

Capuchin
Bridge

BLAČEVA

ULICA

CANKARJEV
TRG

Filavo Ⓡ
Homan
House

Church of
St James ✝

Convent Church
of St Mary ✝

Loka Castle
& Museum

GRAJSKA POT

GRAJSKO OBZIDJE

KLOBOVSOVA

Ivan Grohar
Gallery

MESTNI
TRG

Mark
of Mary

Krona ✖

Martin's House
(Pri Miholu)

Trava

P

Poljanska
Dolina ↓

FUŽINSKA

P

Mercator

ℹ

Kašča $ ✖ France Mihelič
Gallery

Ljubljanska
Banka

SPODNJI
TRG

STUDENEC

SORŠKA

Špital
Church ✝

N Bradt

TOURIST INFORMATION

■ Tourist Information Centre Mestni trg 7; \f 04 512 0268; e td-skofja.loka@siol.net; www.skofjaloka.si; ⊕08.30–19.00 Mon–Fri, 10.00–17.00 Sat/Sun. Friendly staff dish out leaflets & advice. A fairly big choice of traditional Slovenian souvenirs is also on sale.

Blegoš Kidričeva 1a; \ 04 517 0600; f 04 517 0605; e info@lto-blegos.si; www.lto-blegos.si. The large local tourist office is less conveniently located at the top of the busy junction to the east of Kapucinski trg.

WHERE TO STAY
The closure of the Hotel Transturist means that accommodation in the centre of Škofja Loka is in short supply. If you don't want to be disappointed book ahead.

⌂ Hotel Garni Paleta (4 rooms) Kapucinski trg 17; \ 04 512 6400 or m 041 874 427; e paleta.art@siol.net; www.paleta-skofjaloka.si. Rooms at this small family-run hotel are clean & comfortable. The 2 4-bed rooms, which have a dbl bed & a bunk bed, are ideal for families. For singles & couples there are 2 dbl rooms. Room 3 has views over the Selščica River to the Old Town. $$$

⌂ Mini Hotel (8 rooms) Vincarje 47; \ 04 515 0540; f 04 515 0542; e metka@minihotel.si; www.minihotel.si. This well-equipped hotel 2km from the Old Town also has a sports centre with an outdoor pool, games courts, sauna & fitness studio. Rooms also have great views of the Alps. $$$

The tourist office can also book apartments or tourist farms in and around Škofja Loka ($$–$$$).

✗ WHERE TO EAT AND DRINK

✗ Gostilna Pri Danilu Reteče 48; \ 04 515 3444; ⊕12.00–22.00 Tue–Sat, 12.00–16.00 Sun. This restaurant serving traditional Slovenian dishes with flair is located 6km from Škofja Loka. Rich game, Carniolan sausage & smoked trout are all recommended. $$$$

✗ Gostilna Pri Boštjanu Križna Gora 8a; \ 04 510 3320; f 04 514 1444; e restaurantpribostjanu@email.si; ⊕10.00–22.00 Wed/Thu & Sun, 10.00–midnight Fri/Sat. Bawdy & raucous at weekends & public holidays, this large restaurant boasts an outdoor terrace with stunning mountain views as well as a cosier space inside with lots of timber & traditional ovens. If you are feeling hungry call ahead & arrange a whole leg of veal or pork served with various garnishes. Well worth the 5km journey out of town. $$$

✗ Kašča Spodnji trg 2; \ 04 512 4300; ⊕12.00–23.00 Mon–Sat. This basement restaurant serving hearty Slovenian food & pizzas beneath the Galerija Franceta Miheliča is the best dining option in the Old Town. If you'd rather stay above ground there is a small terrace, but you will have to put up with the constant stream of traffic passing by. More adventurous diners can sample the likes of tripe goulash & horse fillet. $$$

✗ Krona Mestni trg 32; \ 04 512 7910; ⊕11.00–13.00 Mon–Sat. More salubrious than it looks from the outside, this restaurant serves homemade Slovenian dishes. $$$

✗ Starman Stara Loka 22; \ 04 512 6490; f 04 512 6491; e starman22@siol.net; ⊕07.00–22.00 Mon–Thu, 07.00–midnight Fri/Sat. This traditional eatery dishes up hearty meat dishes, grilled fish & national specialities like buckwheat porridge with boletus mushrooms, the lashings of cream served with the latter make it similar in taste to stroganoff. When we visited even the starter portions were huge. $$$

✗ Homan Mestni trg 2; \ 04 512 3047; ⊕08.00–23.00 Mon–Thu & Sun, 08.00–02.00 Fri/Sat. Café, pizzeria & restaurant rolled into one in a historic building right at the heart of the Old Town. Locals flock to Homan for its tasty cakes & pastries. $

⊞ Mercator Mestni trg 9. Blink & you could miss this small & centrally located grocery store. Look out for the display of groceries in the window.

⊞ Trava Mestni trg 24/23. This independent grocery store (a rarity in Slovenia these days) is located at the southern entrance of the Old Town. More remarkable because it is located in one of the houses designated as one of Škofja Loka's cultural monument, the Brlcova Hiša.

above **Otočec Castle, Dolenjska** (RM) page 179

below **Celje Castle** (RM) page 201

above **Škocjan Caves entrance**
(RM) page 141

left **Postojna Caves**
(RM) page 163

top   **Kranjska Gora, Gorenjska** (RM) page 117
above left   **Lake Bled** (STB) page 101
above right   **Soča River near Bovec** (RM) page 123
below   **Lake Bohinj** (STB) page 107

top   **White-water rafting,
Soča River** (STB) page 128

above   **Skiing, Triglav Lakes**
(STB) page 115

left   **Walking a ridge,
Julian Alps** (RM) page 114

above left **Cycling, Logarska Dolina, Štajerska** (RM) page 206

above right **Walking sign in the Julian Alps** (RM) page 114

below **Mountain huts, Julian Alps** (RM) page 16

top **Typical Štajerska church** (RM) page 189

above **Farmstay, Gorenjska** (RM) page 83

left **Typical Štajerska /Prekmurje meal** (RM) page 189

above **Ptuj** (AG) page 206

below **Glavni trg, Maribor, Štajerska** (RM) page 194

Piran (RM) page 153

ENTERTAINMENT AND NIGHTLIFE

♀ **Etno Caffé** Kapucinski trg 15. The bar's large windows offer views of the Selščica River & the Old Town.

♀ **Filavo** Cankarjeva trg 2. Pull up a chair on the outside terrace & take in the faded beauty of one of Škofja Loka's most attractive squares.

♀ **Homan** (see *Where to eat above*) With a 02.00 closing on Fri & Sat, the Homan bar & café can be lively on summer evenings.

♀ **Pri Miholu** Mestni trg 24. Bar with a compact, but pleasant, outdoor terrace forming part of the Old Town walls.

⏏ **Pri Zihrlu** Kapucinski trg 22. The covered terrace, which looks over the Selščica River to the walled Old Town, makes this café, located just below the Capuchin Bridge, the hottest spot in Škofja Loka. Listen to the water ripple by & gaze up at the castle as you enjoy a huge milky coffee (*bela kava*).

OTHER PRACTICALITIES

$ **Ljubljanska Banka** Spodnji trg 1; ⏰08.00–18.00 Mon–Fri, 08.00–12.00 Sat

$ **Gorenjska Banka** Kapucinski trg 8; ⏰08.00–18.00 Mon–Fri, 08.00–12.00 Sat

✉ **Post office** Kapucinski trg 9; ⏰07.00–19.00 Mon–Fri, 07.00–12.00 Sat

✚ **Medical centre** Stara 10; ✆ 04 502 0000

WHAT TO SEE

A walking tour The best way to discover one of Slovenia's best-preserved medieval Old Towns is on foot, and the logical place to begin a walking tour of Škofja Loka's historic core is at **Loka Castle** (*Loka Grad; Grajska pot 13;* ✆ *04 517 0400;* €*2.50;* ⏰ *10.00–18.00 Tue–Sun*). Follow the path that runs up the hill adjacent to the town's medieval walls. In the castle's courtyard you will notice the coats of arms adorning the walls, all of which feature a black king. Local legend puts this down to bygone days when the black servant of a wealthy landlord saved him from a bear, and the king promised that his heroic deed would be remembered for ever.

A lot of effort went into the renovation of the **castle museum** and now there is a welcome English-language leaflet as well as information notes for many of the artefacts. Some of the more interesting exhibits are a scale model of the castle showing the original 25m-high central tower, a relief map of the town and a slightly fusty but illuminating natural history section with wildlife from the surrounding countryside. Unfortunately one of the most interesting sections, about the German occupation of the region and subsequent partisan resistance, is in Slovene only, though many of the graphic photographs speak for themselves.

Back down the hill **Martin's House** (*Martinova Hiša*), part of a 14th-century defensive extension of the city walls and home to the Pri Miholu bar (see *Entertainment and nightlife* above), stands beside the **Poljanska Dolina gate**, which leads to Mestni trg. This is the last house in Škofja Loka that dates from this time. Elegant houses dating from the 16th and 17th centuries, which have since been converted into shops, cafés and restaurants, flank this long pedestrianised square (throughout the Old Town you will find buildings marked with a blue and white shield; this shows that they are considered cultural monuments. The brief accompanying descriptions are in both Slovene and English). You can visit the **Ivan Grohar Gallery** (*Galerija Ivana Groharja; Mestni trg 37;* ✆ *04 512 2692*), named after the craftsman whose work is on display in the castle museum. To your right notice the column with three statues, the **Mark of Mary** erected in 1751 to give thanks for protection against fire and the plague, and the 19th-century fountain displaying Škofja Loka's coat of arms. The Renaissance **Homan House** (*Homanova Hiša*) at No 2, with its ornate frescoes of St Christopher and a medieval soldier, is another highlight. Continue on to the late Gothic **Church of St James** (Cerkev Sv Jakob), which dates back to 1471, with an interior restyled by Jože Plečnik; it is on Cankarjev trg at the end of

Mestni trg. The dark hardwood pews contrast dramatically with the brightly coloured stained-glass windows and the frescoed vaulted ceiling. Mestni trg is also home to the **former town hall**; restored in 1972 this 16th-century building boasts Baroque frescoes and an attractive Gothic portal.

At the end of the street cross the Selščica River, a branch of the Sora, pass the bus station and turn left once you have passed the post office, and you will come to the small **Church of St Anne** (Cerkev Sv Ane) that is worth popping into. From here cross back over the river on the 14th-century **Capuchin Bridge** (Kapucinski Most). Ironically it was commissioned by Bishop Leopold, who met his fate when he tumbled from his horse and fell to his death in the waters below. The statue in the middle is of St John of Nepomuk.

Back across the river you will soon come to the Nun's Church or the **Convent Church of St Mary** (Nunska Cerkev) on Blaževa. Its current Baroque design was the result of a 17th-century fire. From here walk behind the Church of St James and follow Cankarjeva under the old **school** (*šcola*) at Cankarjeva trg 10 – another cultural monument – down to Spodnji trg, the aptly named lower square. Marred by fast-moving traffic, Spodnji trg does have a handful of interesting buildings, including several cultural monuments; be careful when you are walking around this part of Škofja Loka because there are no pavements. The most interesting building on the square is the **France Mihelič Gallery** (*Galerija Franceta Mihelíča; Spodnji trg 1;* ☏ *04 517 0400;* €2; ⊕*12.00–17.00 Tue–Sun*), where paintings by the Slovene artist France Mihelič, who died in 1998, are exhibited in an impressively refurbished old granary. Heading further along Spodnji trg brings you to the **Špital Church** (Spodni trg 9), which began life in the mid 16th century as a poorhouse. After being decimated by fire in 1720 the building reopened as a church.

Stara Loka Equally appealing at the Old Town itself, the suburb of Stara Loka, located just north of the Selščica River, rewards those who make the time to walk around it with a clutch of historic houses (the settlement dates from the late 10th century), **Old Loka Castle** (Stara Loški Grad) and the **Church of St George** (Cerkev sv Jurija). The castle houses the small **Post and Telecommunications Museum** (*Muzej Pošte In Telekomunikacij;* €2; ⊕*09.00–13.00 Tue/Thu, 10.30–17.00 Sat/Sun*), but the real reason to make the 1km walk from the Capuchin Bridge is to dine at **Starman** (see *Where to eat and drink* above).

Nace's House (*Nacetova Hiša; Pruštal 74;* ☏ *04 029 5916;* €2; ⊕*Sat only by appointment – ask at the TIC or call ahead*) Located in the suburb of Pruštal on the right bank of the River Sora, this stone and timber house, which once served as an inn, offers a real insight into local living down the ages, through both its original 16th-century elements and sections that were added in the 18th century. Highlights include the black kitchen (so-called because it is thick with the soot that did not have a chimney to escape through), a workshop brimming with old tools and a room where aggressive or drunk guests were locked away until they calmed down. Call ahead and the granddaughter of the last resident who lived here until 1977, opera singer Polde Polenec, may even show you around herself. From the expansive garden there are good views back across the river towards the castle and Old Town so bring your camera.

AROUND ŠKOFJA LOKA

CRNGROB If you have your own wheels or fancy getting your walking shoes on, head for two fascinating churches outside Škofja Loka. The village of

Crngrob, which translates ominously as 'black grave', is accessible on the ramshackle road from town, but a better option is to take the main road north towards Kranj and turn down the sealed road from there. The **Church of the Annunciation** (Cerkev Marijino Oznanjenje), which dominates from a grassy redoubt, is massively out of proportion with the small hamlet below, but it has always been a church of pilgrimage rather than just serving the local parishioners. Today's structure evolved over more than four centuries, with the original single-nave church constructed in the 17th century. By 1853 it had three naves, a beautiful rib-vaulted ceiling, presbytery, belfry and neo-Gothic portico.

Make sure you have a good look at the large fresco outside of **St Christopher** – local folklore has it that you will not die on the same day that you see it, though the locals we asked were unclear whether taking a photo would work, and having a peek at it every day would grant one immortality. Venture beneath the portico and you will come across frescoes on either side of another door. To the left is *The Passion of Christ*, while to the right are warnings on activities banned on the Lord's Day, with a vivid depiction of what happens if you disobey – a dragon awaits to snatch sinners to a fiery new home in hell.

Highlights inside the church include the largest gilt altar in Gorenjska, dating from 1652, ornate frescoes, and ceiling joints above the altar which are actually the coats of arms of various donors including Bavarian families – a legacy of the region's past. More intriguing is the large rib that hangs from a timber beam. This commemorates a local legend about a girl who was so big that she could stand with one foot on the hill of Šmarjetna Gora, near Kranj, and the other foot on Šmarna Gora, near Ljubljana. As she stood astride the valley the giant girl gathered from the River Sava the stones used to construct the church.

If you are feeling brave head through the door to the right of the altar where you can ascend to the choir stalls and then head up what has to be Slovenia's narrowest stone staircase to the rafters, where the wooden construction of the roof reveals itself – not for the faint-hearted or less than sure-footed. There is a daily mass at 16.00; when it is closed pick up the key at house No 10.

⌂ Where to stay

⌂ **Pri Marku** (10 rooms) Crngrob 5; ☎ 04 513 1626; f 04 513 9790; e info@pri.marku-porenta.si; www.pri-marku-porenta.si. This pleasant farm accommodation is cosy & homely, with wonderful home-baked rolls for b/kfast. $$

✖ Where to eat

✖ **Gostišče Crngrob** Crngrob 13; ☎ 04 513 1601; ⏰ 10.00–22.00 Thu–Tue. Offers hearty Slovenian meat dishes & views of the valley and mountains. $$

SUHA

The roadside **Church of St John the Baptist** (Cerkev Sv Janez Krstnik) in Suha, 2.5km from Škofja Loka, may not be as immediately striking as those in Crngrob, but its interior frescoes are perhaps more impressive and cover the entire rib-vaulted ceiling of the presbytery. Vivid images include the *Last Judgement*, scenes from Christ's life and illustrations of disciples and angels. The **Špan's Home** (Španova domačija), with its external Baroque frescoes and 18th-century shrine, is also worth visiting. If you don't make it to Suha the museum in Škofja Loka's castle has a scale model of the house and copies of the church frescoes. You can usually get the key from No 32 near the church.

ŠKOFJA LOKA TO KROPA

An enjoyable amble through the **Selca Valley** (Selška Dolina) awaits those with their own transport. The road drifts northwest of Stara Loka towards higher ground through a phalanx of forests and tiny villages. Worthwhile stop-offs include Selca itself, with its striking **Church of St Peter** (Cerkev Sv Petra) just left of the main road, and Jamnik, where the **Church of St Primoz** (Cerkev Sv Primoz) enjoys one of the most impressive settings of any ecclesiastical building in Slovenia. A small track leads right to the church, but you may want to walk from the surfaced road. Get your camera ready for great shots of the church dwarfed by a sweep of mountains and the settlements of Radovljica and Lesce lying far below. This was serious partisan country during World War II with local volunteers clashing repeatedly with the occupying Axis forces. A memorial in neighbouring Drugosce marks the brutal German reprisal killings that saw much of the village population wiped out.

RADOVLJICA

Radovljica enjoys an enviable location just east of the confluence of the two main forks of the Sava River, with its Old Town perched on what was once the terminal moraine for the Bohinj Glacier and the Julian Alps rising dramatically to the west on a clear day. Written mentions of Radovljica can be traced as far back as the 11th century and its golden age came before the arrival of the Austro-Hungarians, when it flourished as a major market town and trading hub in the 15th and 16th centuries. The late medieval Old Town is the most interesting district, basically consisting of one main square with a liberal sprinkling of fine Baroque, Gothic and Renaissance architecture. If you are *en route* to Bled, Radovljica is worth popping into.

GETTING THERE Radovljica railway station can be reached by train from Lesce-Bled (5 minutes), Kranj (20 minutes), Škofja Loka (35 minutes) and Ljubljana (55 minutes). Buses run from Bled (15 minutes), Kropa (20 minutes), Ljubljana (1½ hours), Kranjska Gora (1 hour 25 minutes), Ribčev Laz for Lake Bohinj (45 minutes).

Railway station Cesta Svobode (just south of the town centre)

Bus station Kranjska cesta

GETTING AROUND Radovljica's compact Old Town centre is easily navigable on foot.

🚕 **Taxi Orel** Gradnikova 72; m 041 710 747; www.bled-taxi.si

TOURIST INFORMATION
🛈 **Tourist Information Centre** Gorenjska 1;
☏ 04 531 5300; e tdradovljica@siol.net;
🕐 09.00–18.00 Mon–Fri, 08.00–13.00 Sat

WHERE TO STAY
🏠 **Gostilna Kunstelj** (10 rooms) Gorenjska 9;
☏ 04 531 5178; f 04 530 4151;
e kunstelj@siol.net; www.kunstelj.com. Friendly &

welcoming *gostilna* on the edge of the Old Town with decent food options, 9 comfortable dbl rooms & an apt. $$$

Radovljica's most famous son Anton Tomaž Linhart was born in the town on 11 December 1756. Educated in Ljubljana and Vienna Linhart began his working life as an archivist, after which he became a school inspector and schools commissioner. In the latter post he was responsible for the opening of 18 rural schools around the capital. His other services to education include the opening of a central public library in Ljubljana. Linhart's great loves though were history and the theatre, with his accomplishments in these fields including a written *History of Carniola and Other Lands of the South Slavs of Austria*, a translation and adaptation into Slovene of a German comedy *Daughter of a Mayor (Micka)* and his own comedy *The Happy Days*, also known as *Matiček Gets Married*. Anton Tomaž Linhart died in Ljubljana at the age of 38. Today Slovenes remember Linhart for his role in promoting a Slovene national conscience and the use of the Slovene language as part of the country's Enlightenment.

🏠 **Grad Podvin** (24 rooms) Mošnje 1; ☎ 04 532 5200; f 04 532 5250; www.robas.si/grad-podvin. The castle, 4km from Radovljica, offers compact & functional rather than luxurious rooms. It also has indoor & outdoor tennis courts & an open-air swimming pool. $$$

🏠 **Hotel Grajski Dvor** Krajska 2; ☎ 04 531 5585; f 04 531 5878; e info@hotel-grajski-dvor.si; www.hotel-grajski-dvor.si. Simple but adequate accommodation. $$$

Camping
⛺ **Camping Radovljica** Kopališka 9; ☎/f 04 531 5770; e pkrad@plavalniklub-radovljica.si; www.plavalniklub-radovljica.si. This small campsite enjoys a pleasant forest location & guests can use the adjacent 50m outdoor swimming pool. €8 pp.
⛺ **Camping Šobec** (see *Bled, Where to stay*, page 105)

✖ WHERE TO EAT AND DRINK
✖ **Gostilna Avgustin** Linhartov trg 15; ☎ 04 531 4163; ⏱11.00–23.00 daily. Serving good-value & hearty Slovenian food. Make sure you go through to the restaurant or terrace at the back with its views over the gorge. On a lovely summer's day table 35, located on its own separate balcony, is ideal for a romantic meal for 2. $$$
Gostilna Kunstelj (see *Where to stay* above) ⏱11.00–23.00 daily. $$$
✖ **Gostilna Lectar** Linhartov trg 2; ☎ 04 537 4800; www.lectar.com; ⏱11.00–23.00 daily. At the heart of the Old Town but without the spectacular views of Avgustin. A local favourite. $$$

✖ **Grajska Gostilnica** Kranjska 2; ☎ 04 531 4445; ⏱11.00–23.00 daily. The tempting menu at the Hotel Grajski Dvor's stylish new restaurant fuses Italian & Slovenian cuisine. $$$
♀ **Linhartov Hram** Linhartov trg 26. In the summer this café-bar spills out onto the main square. A perfect place to quaff Union beer on draught or sample Teran wine.
♀ **Vinoteka Sodček** Linhartov trg 8; ☎ 04 531 5071; ⏱08.00–21.00 daily. Wine bar-cum-wine shop selling a wide selection of Slovenian wines, *pršut* & cheese. You can also buy wine on tap.

SHOPPING
Kulturnica Blaž Kumerdej Linhartov trg 3; ☎ 04 531 5100. Sells Slovenian wines, spirits, liqueurs – including the famous pear brandy produced by monks at the Pleterje Monastery – vinegars, honey & cheese.

OTHER PRACTICALITIES
✉ **Post office** Kranjska 1; ⏱08.00–19.00 Mon–Fri, 08.00–12.00 Sat

$ **SKB Banka** Gorenjska 10; ⏱08.00–18.00 Mon–Fri

WHAT TO SEE With everyone now more or less adhering to the parking ban in the rectangular Linhartov trg, named after Radovljica's greatest son (18th-century Slovene dramatist Anton Tomaž Linhart), the appeal of one of the most attractive historic quarters in Slovenia has been greatly enhanced. On the right-hand side of the square is the **Šivec House** (*Šivčeva Hiša; Linhartov trg 22;* €*2;* ⊕*only when exhibitions are being held; Jan–May and Oct–Dec 10.00–12.00 & 16.00–18.00 Tue–Sun; Jun/Sep 10.00–12.00 & 17.00–19.00 Tue–Sun; Jul/Aug 10.00–12.00 & 18.00–20.00 Tue–Sun*), a burgher dwelling dating from the mid 16th century. Notice the 17th-century mural on the façade and the late Gothic entrance hall and vaulted ceiling – all features that were typical of Gorenjska at this time. Šivec these days has been given a new lease of life as a gallery, which is home to an eclectic range of temporary exhibitions. Other notable buildings include the **Vidič House** (*Vidičeva Hiša*), also with a mural façade and this time with a fountain as well, and the **Linhart House** (Linhartov Hiša), with a plaque noting that this was the writer's birthplace. At the furthest end of Linhartov trg is the rather shabby (we were assured that it was going to be renovated towards the end of 2007) **Church of St Peter** (Cerkev Sv Petra), which was originally Romanesque though it was given a late-Gothic makeover. The sculptures by Angelo Pozzo on the Baroque high altar and the fresco of St Christopher are also worth popping inside for.

Back around the corner on Linhartov trg, to the right is Radovljica's main tourist attraction, the **Museum of Apiculture** (*Čebelarski Muzej; Linhartov trg 1;* ␆ *04 532 0520; www.muzeji-radovljica.si;* €*2.50;* ⊕*Mar/Apr & Nov/Dec 10.00–12.00 & 15.00–17.00 Tue–Sun; May–Oct 10.00–13.00 & 15.00–18.00 Tue–Sun*), which is housed on the first floor of a Baroque manor house. While spending an hour or so studying bees may not seem too alluring this museum is interesting simply by the fact that it exists. Although you can learn everything you never knew you wanted to know about bees and their lives, especially the local Carniolan grey bee, perhaps the most interesting sections are those displaying the traditional painted beehives, mainly from the golden age of bee-keeping in the 18th and 19th centuries, which are artworks in themselves. Handily, most exhibits are labelled in English. The adjacent **Linhart Room** (⊕*Mar/Apr & Nov/Dec 10.00–12.00 & 15.00–17.00 Wed/Sat/Sun; May–Oct 10.00–13.00 & 15.00–18.00 Tue–Sun*) is given over to a collection of artefacts that belonged to Anton Tomaž Linhart.

KROPA

From the 14th to the 20th century this picturesque village, whose name translates as 'boiling water', was awake with the sound of clanging and hammering as one of Slovenia's leading iron-forging centres. Furnaces blazed day and night as the River Koprarca was diverted to power no fewer than 50 waterwheels and the local forests harvested to fire the smelters. Kropa's fame extended beyond Slovenia and its 100-plus varieties of nails and myriad other items were in demand all over Europe. By the mid 18th century, Kropa's only real industry was firmly in decline as domestic iron-ore deposits dried up and increasing competition put the remote village out of touch. The Plamen factory, which you can still see in the village today, staggered on until 1997 when it switched to the production of car parts. Today Kropa's new industry is tourism, which has helped keep some of the craftsmen in employment and ensured that Kropa's heritage is not forgotten altogether.

GETTING THERE Kropa is just 10km from Radovljica on a winding, tree-lined narrow road – head in the direction of Lesce and then turn left at the sign and you will come to it after a ramble of countryside. Reasonably regular buses also run from Radovljica (20 minutes), Kranj and Lesce, although there are no services on Saturdays or Sundays.

⌂ WHERE TO STAY

⌂ **Gostilna Pr' Kovač** (4 rooms) Kropa 30; ☎ 04 533 6320 or 📱 041 414 046. Accommodation comes in the form of 3 apts & 1 dbl room. Guests also have access to a sauna. $$

✗ WHERE TO EAT

✗ **Gostilna Pr' Kovač** ⏰ 10.00–23.00 daily. Although we didn't eat on our last visit the charming owner assured us that he had 'everything to eat'. $$

✗ **Gostilna Pri Jarmu** Kropa 2; ☎ 04 533 6750; ⏰ 10.00–23.00 Fri–Tue – also ⏰ mid May–Aug Thu. This simple *gostilna* is Kropa's other dining option. $$

🛒 **Mercator** 3a Kropa. Handy local mini-market.

OTHER PRACTICALITIES

✉ **Post office** 3b Kropa; ⏰ 08.00–09.30 & 10.00–17.00 Mon–Fri, 09.00–12.00 Sat

WHAT TO SEE The main square, the Plac, is a good place to start exploring and there is space to park just downhill. If you are really keen to delve into Kropa's forging history make the effort to head up the hillside to the **Slovenian Smelting Furnace**, which dates back to the 14th century when it was capable of producing 100kg of iron for forging in ten hours with the help of 800kg of charcoal. You can see iron wherever you look in Kropa – look out in particular for the trademark dragons, which were said to ward off evil spirits outside many of the village's houses.

From here cross the bridge by the waterfall slightly upstream and descend to **Gostilna Pr' Kovač**, a good place to stop for a drink and try to conjure up Kropa's old days – most of the clanging may be gone, but the rushing waters of the river and its diverted channels still echo all around. From here you can also see two distant hillside churches nestled amongst the trees. As you pass the Plac you will see the sturdy Resistance Monument, which was forged in the village in 1965 as a tribute to the local people who were heavily involved in fighting Axis forces in World War II. Stick to the right bank of the river as you head down the hillside and watch out for traffic whose sound the water tends to drown out. After decades of decline many of Kropa's charming houses, brightened by pretty window boxes, are now being touched up and returned to their original bright selves with strong Renaissance and Baroque touches. A number, though, are still in desperate need of renovation.

Soon you will come across the small **Iron Forging Museum** (*Kovaški Muzej; Kropa 10; ☎ 04 533 6717; adult/concession €2.50/€2; ⏰ Mar/Apr & Nov/Dec 10.00–12.00 & 15.00–17.00 Tue–Sun; May–Oct 10.00–13.00 & 15.00–18.00 Tue–Sun*) on the right, which is housed in the attractive **Klinar House** (Klinar Hiša). Inside are iron-working artefacts dating from the 15th to 19th century, models of a working forge as well as a scale model of Kropa in the early 19th century. The museum gives an idea of the scope of the village's production – everything from tiny tacks for snow boots right through to hulking industrial spikes for hammering sections of concrete together. The highlights of the exhibition are works by Joža Bertoncelj, one of Kropa's most renowned iron sculptors. Guided tours of the museum can be organised in advance and if you call ahead they may even consider opening the museum especially for you.

Across the road is the **UKO Forger's Workshop** (*Umetniško Kovaštvo; Kropa 7b and 7a; ☎ 04 533 7300; ⏰ Sep–Jun 07.00–15.00 Mon–Fri, 09.00–12.00 Sat; Jul/Aug 07.00–18.00 Mon–Fri, 09.00–12.00 Sat*) and a store where today's craftsmen sell their work. In the visitors' book are some complaints about the expense, but prices for those unique souvenirs are reasonable when you consider that this is niche not mass production and you are buying a piece of history. Similar souvenirs on sale elsewhere in Slovenia generally cost 30–50% more.

KRANJ

Only 10km from Škofja Loka on the main road, Slovenia's fourth-largest city may be blighted by a swathe of factories on its outskirts, but its ethnically diverse citizens – thanks to workers brought in from other parts of Yugoslavia in the 1970s and 1980s – are justifiably proud of a charming Baroque Old Town that rests spectacularly on a rocky bluff surrounded by the Sava and Kokra rivers, with the lofty peaks of the Kamniške Savinje Alps framing the background. With a sprinkling of accommodation options, numerous bars and a choice of restaurants Kranj invites an overnight stay and is a good base for exploring the rest of this part of Gorenjska. Kranj is an essential stop for fans of the great Slovene writer France Prešeren as he lived here for the final years of his life and died in the Old Town in a house that is now a dedicated museum.

HISTORY Archaeological finds in the area date back as far as the 8th century BC, although Kranj didn't really rise to the fore until the 13th century when it became a city and important trading centre. In the 19th century Kranj was very much at the heart of industrial development, with factories springing up on the banks of the Sava. Kranj has also enjoyed brief periods as the informal capital of the Slovenian lands, surpassing the importance of Ljubljana prior to the construction of the Vienna–Trieste railway (which elevated the status of the present-day capital) in the 1850s. Kranj also flourished in the late 19th and early 20th centuries, at a time when Ljubljana was suffering from the effects of the devastating 1895 earthquake. Today tourism is rapidly becoming the city's main industry as its traditional manufacturing industries wane and its role as a convention and fair venue evaporates, with a shopping mall now occupying the island that used to be the main venue.

GETTING THERE Just 10km from Škofja Loka, Kranj is within easy cycling and driving distance. If you arrive by car there is a pay-and-display car park on Slovenski trg, just north of the Old Town. Regular buses run from Škofja Loka (20 minutes), Radovljica (30 minutes), Bled (40 minutes) and Ljubljana (40 minutes). Kranj is served by trains from Škofja Loka (10 minutes), Radovljica (20 minutes), Lesce-Bled (25 minutes) and Ljubljana (35 minutes).

A word of warning: the city was known locally as 'Kranjsterdam' in the 1990s as it had a serious hard-drug problem. This seems to have eased in recent years, but exercise caution especially around the bus and railway stations after dark. By no means is this London or New York, but be just a touch more careful than you would be elsewhere in Slovenia.

Bus station Stošičeva; ☎ 04 201 3210

Railway station Koldovorska 11; ☎ 04 294 4133 (10 mins' walk from the Old Town)

GETTING AROUND Kranj's Old Town is largely pedestrianised. Local buses and taxis (☎ *04 206 1678*) are available for longer journeys.

TOURIST INFORMATION/LOCAL TOUR OPERATORS

🖸 **Tourist Information Centre** Glavni trg 2; ☎ 04 238 0450; www.tourism-kranj.si; ⏱08.00–18.00 Mon–Fri

🖸 **Tourist Information Centre** Koroška 29; ☎ 04 236 3030; f 04 236 3031; e www.tourism-kranj.si; ⏱08.00–14.00 Mon–Fri. Now Kranj's secondary

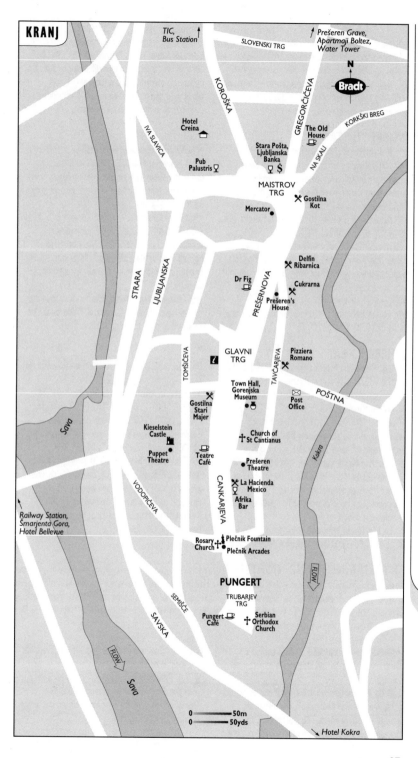

KRANJ

TIC,
Bus Station

SLOVENSKI TRG

Prešeren Grave,
Apartmaji Boltez,
Water Tower

N

KOROŠKA

GREGORČIČEVA

Bradt

IVA SLAVICA

Hotel
Creina

KORKŠKI BREG

The Old
House

Stara Pošta,
Ljubljanska
Banka

NA SKALI

Pub
Palustris

$

MAISTROV
TRG

Gostilna
Kot

Mercator

STRARA

LJUBLJANSKA

Delfin
Ribarnica

Dr Fig

PREŠERNOVA

Cukrarna

Prešeren's
House

GLAVNI
TRG

TAVČARJEVA

Pizziera
Romano

TOMSIČEVA

POŠTNA

Town Hall,
Gorenjska
Museum

Post
Office

Sava

Gostilna
Stari
Majer

Kieselstein
Castle

Church of
St Cantianus

Puppet
Theatre

Teatre
Café

Preseren
Theatre

VODOPIČEVA

CANKARJEVA

La Hacienda
Mexico

Kokra

Afrika
Bar

Railway Station,
Šmarjenta Gora,
Hotel Bellevue

FLOW

Rosary
Church

Plečnik Fountain

Plečnik Arcades

PUNGERT

SEMIŠČE

TRUBARJEV
TRG

SAVSKA

Pungert
Café

Serbian
Orthodox
Church

FLOW

Sava

0 ——50m
0 ——50yds

Hotel Kokra

97

tourist office the branch is officially open on weekday mornings. When we turned up, however, the information officer had popped over to the new Glavni trg office for a chat with her colleague. When we finally tracked them down the tourist information staff were keen to hurry us out of the door & continue their discussion.

Kompas Koroška 5; ☎ 04 201 4261; e creina@kompas.si; www.kompas.si
Lifetrek Adventures Partizanska 18; ☎ 04 201 4875; e info@lifetrek.si; www.lifetrek-slovenia.com. Organising everything from canyoning & rock climbing to scuba diving, via ferrata & rafting from their offices in Bled, Kranj & Ljubljana.

🏠 WHERE TO STAY

🏠 **Kokra Hotel** (78 rooms) Brdo Estate; ☎ 04 260 1000; www.brdo.com. Located on the Brdo estate near to Kokra Castle (around 3km from Kranj), rooms are decent but not as grand as you might expect. $$$$

🏠 **Apartmaji Boltez** (10 rooms) Oldhamska 10a; ☎ 04 201 4070; f 04 201 4071; e apartmaji@boltez.si; www.boltez.si/apartmaji. Modern apts next to the water tower, catering to a business crowd, with refrigerators & free broadband internet access in all rooms & apts. Sgl $$$, dbl $$$–$$$$, trpl $$$$, quads $$$$

🏠 **Hotel Bellevue** (18 rooms) Šmarjetna Gora 6; ☎ 04 270 0000; f 04 270 0020;

e bellevue@bellevue.si; www.bellevue.si. Hilltop hotel 2km from Kranj's Old Town with stunning panoramic views. The most expensive rooms have water beds. All rooms have wireless internet access. Sgl $$–$$$, dbl $$$

🏠 **Hotel Creina** (89 rooms) Koroška 5; ☎ 04 202 4550; f 04 202 2483; e info@hotel-creina.si; www.hotel-creina.si. Kranj's only central hotel is housed in an ugly socialist-era building with equally uninspiring rooms, & caters largely for a business clientele. $$$

🏠 **Tourist farms** Private accommodation in the rural villages of Naklo, Jezersko & Preddvor can be arranged through the tourist office. $–$$

✗ WHERE TO EAT

✗ **Gostilna Stari Majer** Glavni trg; ☎ 04 236 4550; ⊕ 09.00–22.00 daily. This centrally located restaurant serves bog-standard Slovenian dishes. $$$

✗ **Delfin Ribarnica** Tavčarjeva 1; ☎ 04 202 2909; ⊕ 08.00–14.00 Mon–Sat. Fishmonger & lunch restaurant serving good-quality fresh fish. We recommend the tasty brodet (fish stew). $$

✗ **Gostilna Kot** Maistrov trg 4; ☎ 04 202 6105; ⊕ 07.00–23.00 Mon–Fri, 07.00–18.00 Sat. Serving decent Slovenian food at rock-bottom prices, this busy eatery is justifiably popular. The daily specials are always a good bet. $$

✗ **La Hacienda Mexico** Cankarjeva 1; ☎ 04 236 8224; ⊕ 12.00–23.00 daily. Making a decent stab at

Mexican cooking the Old Town's newest restaurant serves up fajitas, burritos & the like. $$

✗ **Pizzeria Romano** Tavčarjeva 31; ☎ 04 236 3900; ⊕ 07.00–23.00 Mon–Thu, 07.00–midnight Fri/Sat, 16.00–23.00 Sun. Cheap pizzeria with an outdoor terrace with great mountain views. $$

✗ **Cukrarna** Tavčarjeva 9; ☎ 04 281 8290; ⊕ 08.00–23.00 Mon–Thu, 08.00–midnight Fri/Sat, 08.00–22.00 Sun. Bright & hip café with a children's area & terrace with mountain views to the rear. It also sells mouth-watering cakes & ice creams. $

🏪 **Mercator** Maistrov trg 11. Supermarket in the heart of the Old Town.

ENTERTAINMENT AND NIGHTLIFE Kranj has a large number of bars, which the locals claim date back to the days when there was no running water so everyone drank wine instead – it seems that a taste for alcohol persists. You can drink anywhere in the Old Town without worrying about the handful of drunks who loiter around the bus station.

♀ **Afrika Bar** Cankarjeva 5. Hidden behind a hairdressers, with African artefacts & a small inner courtyard.
🖥 **Dr Fig** Prešernova 4. It only seems fitting to drink in a café-bar dedicated to Kranj's most famous former resident. The poet earned the nickname Dr Fig because he used to dish out the

dried figs that he always carried in his pockets for the local children.
♀ **Pub Palustris** Reginčeva 4. A cross between an Irish pub & an Australian bar, with Kilkenny & Guinness on draught, a crocodile skin on the ceiling & raised outdoor terrace.

No-one more vividly and emotively captures the emotions of the Slovenes than national bard France Prešeren. It is fitting that Prešeren's verse, 'Zdravljica' ('A Toast'), is used today as the national anthem and that it is his figure that stands grandly overlooking the square dedicated to him in central Ljubljana. Prešeren was born in 1800 in Vrba, a village near the capital, but the most romantic and tragic phase of his life began at a service in the **Church of St John the Baptist** (Cerkev Sv Janeza Krstnika) in Trnovo where he fell madly in love with the teenage Julija Primic. She was from a wealthy family and her parents were less than impressed with the poet-lawyer's prospects. The two were destined never to be together. A lonely and heartbroken Prešeren died prematurely in 1849 in Kranj, and much of his best verse was inspired by his feelings for Primic. Many visitors take the semi-naked muse (the subject of much controversy when it was revealed in 1905) above his figure in Prešernov trg in Ljubljana to be Julija, but the young woman is actually depicted in a bust on the front of a building on adjacent Wolfova, with some locals rather unkindly suggesting she is there to eternally mock him.

Pungert Café Pungert 6. A welcome addition to this part of town, the walls of this colourful café are adorned by photography exhibits that change every 3 weeks. Drop by during the summer & you might even catch live music on the outdoor terrace.
Stara Pošta Koroška 2; 04 202 6075. Trendy 4th-floor bar with good views from its small outdoor terrace.

Teatre Café Glavni trg 8. Cosy up in the funky interior with its selection of curios & vaulted ceiling, or take to the terrace & watch local life bustle buy on the Old Town's main square.
The Old House Na Skali 5. Café-bar with a lively outdoor terrace.

OTHER PRACTICALITIES
Post office Poštna 4; 07.00–15.00 Mon–Fri
$ Banks There is a cluster of banks on Koroška near the entrance to the Old Town including Ljubljanska Banka at No 2.

Medical centre Gosposvetska 10; 04 208 2020
Dentist Gosposvetska 8a; 04 208 2418

WHAT TO SEE
A walking tour The compact Old Town is the place to base all your sightseeing, though consider starting your exploration at the imposing early 20th-century **Water Tower**. Located at the junction of Oldhamska, Kokrskega odreda and Partizanska, the tower stands 34m high, from where the short walk south to the Old Town takes you through a green and appealing residential district. Keeping the Kokra River on your left you will come across France Prešeren's last resting place, **Prešeren Grave** (Prešernov Gaj) in a small cemetery. His tomb was paid for with local donations and it is the most impressive in the cemetery, which also features the graves of rich local families and various Kranj luminaries.

Continue south down Gregoričiceva and after five minutes you will come to **Maistrov trg**, the divide between Kranj's dodgy socialist-era architecture and its more appealing Old Town. You are now on the promontory that proved a successful natural protective ring for the city for centuries, with the Kokra River running to your left and the Sava to your right. The confluence of the rivers marks the furthest extremity of the Old Town, and is just a short walk south at Pungert.

Prešeren's House (*Prešernova Hiša; Prešernov 7;* 04 201 3950; *adult/concession* €2/€1.30; 10.00–18.00 *Tue–Sun*) In 2002, the bard's former residence reopened after a much-needed revamp and now it has English-language information boards to help guide visitors through. This is no fusty old museum and the ground level and late-Gothic cellar are given over to temporary exhibitions by innovative domestic artists. The exhibits dedicated to Prešeren himself are on the first floor and spread through various rooms occupied by the poet during his tenure here from late 1846 to February 1849, when he served as the city's first independent lawyer.

The museum's text – displayed on boards that are not attached to the walls due to a preservation order that bans any changes to the house – chronicles Prešeren's life, from his school years through to his death and also, of course, his infatuation with Julija Primic. Slightly unnerving sounds of hollering and coughing, which are supposed to convey the writer's anguish, add to the atmosphere. Exhibits include Prešeren's bed, desk, diaries and even the original entry of his birth in the city's register. The museum staff hope to open up the attic as an extra display area, but they say their hands are tied by a legal wrangle over rights to what is currently a defunct space.

Continue south and you will soon come to **Glavni trg** (which like so many of Slovenia's historic squares is blighted by parked cars) with its jumble of Gothic and Renaissance buildings. The standout is perhaps the **Town Hall/Gorenjska Museum** (*Mestna Hiša/Gorenjski Muzej; Glavni trg 4; ✆ 04 201 3950; adult/concession €2/€1.30; ⊕ 10.00–18.00 Tue–Sun*) which, like Prešeren's house, was originally two buildings and now performs twin functions as a civic space for weddings and other events and as the **Gorenjska Museum**. There are two floors of exhibition space with a rather dated series of displays on the evolution of man in the Kranj area (though it does have some interesting artefacts), as well as an exhibit on iron production in the region. The small room used for weddings has a stunning Baroque wooden ceiling and two Renaissance porches. Look out also for the early Slavic graves that are visible through transparent panels in the floor of the vestibule and which date back as far as the 9th century.

The next building of note is the **Church of St Cantianus** (Cerkev Sv Kancijan) just a short distance further along Glavni trg. The first church on the site dates back to the 6th century, but today's incarnation is based upon a Gothic model that has been added to down the centuries. The central design, with its nave and aisles of equal height, was taken up as a template in Cerknica, Radovljica and Škofja Loka. Also look out for 15th-century frescoes depicting angelic musicians, and an organ whose chest dates back to the mid 19th century. If your visit to the town hall did not satiate your interest in Slavic bones then below the northern flank of the church is an ossuary. It is officially closed, but if you ask nicely at the town hall or tourist office they may be able to arrange a brief visit. Plans have been mooted to reopen the small ossuary with a more modern display, but nothing definite has been agreed upon.

Take a minute to look at the two statues on the south side of the church. Beside the church itself you will see a priest being dragged into the Sava by an octopus as a distraught woman stands at the side. The towering Tito-like figure that looms outside the **Prešeren Theatre** (whose façade was designed by Jože Plečnik) is supposed to be Prešeren himself.

There is also a story behind the fountain that marks the beginning of Glavni trg. Erected in 1998 to replace a fountain that had been standing on the spot since 1836, today's incarnation is the work of local designer and eccentric Marko Pogacnik. According to Pogacnik the fountain stands on a spot where supernatural powers infuse Kranj with positive energy, and the artist believed that this energy had the power to 'heal the earth'. This seems to raise a wry smile from the locals, who evidently don't share Pogacnik's off-the-wall optimism. The two streams of water spurting from the fountain represent the Kokra and Sava rivers.

As you continue down the street it becomes pretty Cankarjeva, where many of the buildings have benefited from renovation, and then merges with Tavčarjeva where the Old Town comes to an abrupt end at Pungert. Here there is a small park and a viewing platform that looks out onto the Kokra River. The round **Pungert** itself, the last remaining of the city's three medieval defence towers, Kranj's Old Town wall and the newly refurbished **Serbian Orthodox Church** (Srbska Pravoslavna Cerkev) are also located in this part of town. The building, which is dedicated to the saints Sebastian, Fabian and Rok, dates back to the 15th century, although it didn't become a centre of the Serbian faith until the 20th century when the Serbian Orthodox Church was established. Immediately south of the church you will find the **Pungert** itself. The town's old defensive tower may still be marred by graffiti (see *Entertainment and nightlife* above), but it now houses a friendly café brightened up by a string of rotating photography exhibitions.

Retracing your steps bear left at the **Plečnik Fountain** onto Tomšičeva. Combined, the fountain, **Plečnik's Arcades** (Plečnik's bid to create a grand entrance to the city) and the **Rosary Church** are arguably the Old Town's most attractive sights. To the left, behind a wrought-iron gate, you will find the **Kieselstein Castle** (Kieselstein Grad). More a manor house than a castle, it is one of the oldest buildings in Kranj and dates from the mid 13th century. Sections of the Old Town wall can be found in Kieselstein's courtyard and it is a venue for many of the city's cultural events as well as the permanent home of Kranj's **Puppet Theatre**. There are also outdoor cultural events here in the summer months.

BREZJE

The hamlet of Brezje, whose population is only around 500, has been dubbed the 'National Shrine of Slovenia' or Slovenia's spiritual heart. It is worth visiting principally to see the **Basilica of the Virgin Mary** (Marija Pomagaj). Today's church has been evolving since the 15th century, with the latest and most significant addition being the Chapel of the Virgin Mary in 1880. Inside the chapel you will find Layer's *Madonna and Child*, which Slovenes believe has miraculous powers, making this one of the country's biggest places of pilgrimage for over 100 years.

GETTING THERE Brezje can be reached by bus from Bled. There are four buses a day, taking approximately 20 minutes.

TOURIST INFORMATION
⚹ **Tourist Association Brezje** ☏ 04 530 9330; www.brezje.si. Can provide further information about the basilica & tourist farms in the vicinity of the village.

BLED

Despite the best efforts of the gaggle of socialist-era hotels that litter its banks there is no denying the ethereal beauty of Lake Bled, which national Slovene bard France Prešeren once eulogised as 'this second Eden, full of charm and grace'. Early in the morning as the mists clear and the bells ring out from the famous island church in the middle of the lake there are few better places to be in Europe, with hulking alpine peaks rising all around (you can even see epic Triglav on a clear day) and birds joining in the celebration of the new day. Throughout the day *pletna* (gondolas) ferry tourists to the church while Bled's wash of restaurants and

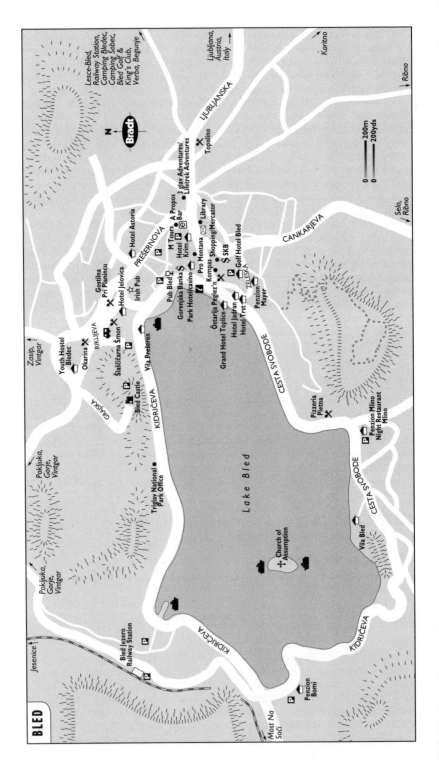

BLED

Lesce-Bled,
Railway Station,
Camping Bledec,
Camping Šobec,
Bled Golf &
King's Club,
Verba, Begunje

Ljubljana,
Austria,
Italy →

Kortno →

LJUBLJANSKA

Topolino

3 glav Adventures/
Lifetrek Adventures

A Propos
Bar

Library

M Tours
Hotel
Krim

Shopping/Mercator

SKB

CANKARJEVA

Ribno →

Selo,
Ribno →

PREŠERNOVA

Hotel Astoria

Gostilna
Pri Planincu

Hotel Jelovica

Irish Pub

Pro Montana

Kompas

Golf Hotel Bled

Pub Bled

Gorenjska Banka

Park Hotel/casino

Ostarija Peglez'n

ŽELEŠKA

Penzion
Mayer

Hotel Jadran

Hotel Trst

Grand Hotel Toplice

Zasip,
Vintgar →

Youth Hostel
Bledec

RIKLJEVA

Okarina

Šta čilarna Šmon

Vila Prešeren

Pizzeria
Pletna

Penzion Mlino
Night Restaurant
Mlino

Bled Castle

GRAJSKA

CESTA SVOBODE

KIDRIČEVA

Pokljuka,
Gorje,
Vintgar →

Triglav National
Park Office

Lake Bled

Pokljuka,
Gorje,
Vintgar →

Vila Bled

CESTA SVOBODE

KIDRIČEVA

Church of
Assumption

KIDRIČEVA

Jesenice →

Bled Jezero
Railway Station

Penzion Bomi

Most Na
Soči →

N

Bradt

0   200m
0   200yds

102

THE BAPTISM ON THE SAVICA

The action in France Prešeren's masterpiece *The Baptism on the Savica* takes place in Bohinj and Bled. The poem vividly depicts the battle between the Germanic-Christian army and an early Slovene pagan army at a fortress where Bled Castle stands today. After the fighting comes the baptism at the Slap Savica (Savica Waterfalls) in Bohinj. The subtext of the writing is the notion that while the Slovenes accepted the Christian faith they rejected Germanic rule. When Prešeren wrote this, Slovenia was under Habsburg rule, therefore this clearly had political connotations at the time. At various places within the poem the reader's attention is also drawn to the beauty of Lake Bled, which Prešeren refers to as 'paradise serene'.

bars switch on to the needs of the increasing number of foreign visitors. Somehow Bled is never spoiled and there is always an escape, whether it be setting off for a stroll around the lake, finding a quiet spot to lean against a tree and listen to the lapping of the water, or taking a rowing boat out on Slovenia's most famous stretch of water and one of Europe's most picturesque lakes. On a warm summer's day you can even join the locals as they slip into the cool waters for a swim.

HISTORY In 2004, Bled celebrated its millennium – the first written mention of the settlement came in 1004 when it was awarded to the Bishop of Brixen. Over the following centuries pilgrims flocked to Bled, ensuring that the town had a constant stream of income. In the late 19th and early 20th centuries Bled re-emerged as a popular spa resort: the moneyed classes of the Austro-Hungarian Empire were attracted by its climate and the lake's waters, which are said to have curative and restorative properties. The success was largely due to new railways from Italy and Austria and the efforts of one Dr Arnold Rikli, who built a bathing area here and spent the best part of half a century extolling the virtues of Bled. After World War II the new regime in the region held Bled in such high esteem that Tito chose it as the site of his summer retreat, a place to relax and the perfect venue for entertaining his illustrious guests. These days Bled owes much of its continued success to the fact that it is an easy drive from Ljubljana and the Italian and Austrian borders. Bled has been part of the Triglav National Park since the latter's inception in 1906 and further development in the area is now carefully controlled.

GETTING THERE Regular buses serve Bled from Ljubljana (1½ hours), Ribčev Laz/Lake Bohinj (40 minutes) and Radovljica (15 minutes). Trains from Ljubljana (45 minutes–1 hour), which go via Škofja Loka (35 minutes), Kranj (25 minutes) and Radovljica (5 minutes) also stop at Lesce-Bled. Lesce-Bled station is around 4km from the centre of Bled; buses that connect the two run every 30 minutes and take ten–15 minutes. The closest railway station to the centre of Bled is Bled Jezero (1.5km out of town), which is served by trains from Bohinj (20 minutes).

Lesce-Bled train station Zelezniska 12, Lesce;
📞 04 531 8384
Bus station Cesta Svobode 4; 📞 04 574 1114

Bled Jezero train station Koldovorska 50; 📞 04 294 2363

GETTING AROUND

🚖 **Taxi** m 031 205 6111
🚖 **Taxi Orel** Gradnikova 72; m 041 710 747;
www.bled-taxi.si

Tourist train Tacky & not cheap, this train circles around Lake Bled on a 45-min trip during the tourist season. Running from 09.00 until almost 21.00, it does provide access to the restaurants & bars around town if you are staying somewhere more remote. Fare €2.50.

Horse and cart Pick-up by the Festival Hall. For a trip around the lake bank on parting with around €30.

TOURIST INFORMATION/LOCAL TOUR OPERATORS

⬛ Tourist Information Centre Cesta Svobode 10; ✆ 04 574 1122; e tdbled@telemach.net; www.bled.si; ⏱ Jul/Aug 08.00–21.00 Mon–Sat, 10.00–18.00 Sun; Mar–Jun 08.00–19.00 Mon–Sat, 11.00–17.00 Sun; Nov–Feb 09.00–18.00 Mon–Sat, 12.00–16.00 Sun
ProMontana Ljubljanska 1; ✆ 04 578 0662; f 04 578 0661; e bled@promontana.si; www.promontana.si. Outdoor specialist offering hiking, mountaineering, climbing, caving, canyoning, kayaking, paragliding, rafting, snowshoeing, ice climbing, ski mountaineering & mountain biking from Bled & Bohinj. They can also arrange overnight stays in cabins (sleeping 4–12) in Triglav National Park & hire out various pieces of equipment.
Kompas Bled Ljubljanska 4; ✆ 04 574 1515; f 04 574 1518; e info@kompas-bled.si; www.kompas-bled.si. Accommodation & excursions.

M Tours Prešernova 3; ✆ 04 575 3300; f 04 575 3311; e mtours@mtours.net. Full tourist service.
Triglav National Park Kidričeva 2; ✆ 04 574 1188; f 04 574 3568; e triglavski-narodni-park@tnp.gov.si; www.sigov.si/tnp. Day trips & overnight guided tours.
3glav Adventures Ljubljanska 1; m 041 683 184; www.3glav-adventures.com. This adventure company specialises in extreme sports like paragliding, canyoning, rafting & skydiving. Horseriding, kayaking, mountain biking & hiking are just some of the other activities on offer.
Lifetrek Adventures Ljubljanska 1; ✆ 04 578 0662; e ziva@lifetrek.si; www.lifetrek-slovenia.com. Organising everything from canyoning & rock climbing to scuba diving, via ferrata & rafting from their offices in Bled, Kranj & Ljubljana.

⌂ WHERE TO STAY

⌂ **Vila Bled** (30 rooms) Cesta Svobode 26; ✆ 04 579 1500; f 04 574 1320; e hotel@vila-bled.com; www.vila-bled.com. Our favourite place to stay in Bled. Tito's ghost still haunts this palatial lakeside villa, which was once his favourite retreat. You can even send emails from his old desk. The hotel was impressively refurbished in 2004 with the addition of the health spa in the basement. Located on a quiet stretch of Lake Bled this really is an unforgettable place to stay. $$$$$
⌂ **Grand Hotel Toplice** (87 rooms) Cesta Svobode 12; ✆ 04 579 1000; f 04 574 1841; e info@hotel-toplice.com; www.hotel-toplice.com. This impressive 5-star hotel, with a thermal pool, sauna, steam room & Turkish bath, is surprisingly good value for money. Make sure you book a lake-view room. Even if you are not staying come to the lounge for a coffee & a slice of *kremna rezina* & just take in the view. $$$$–$$$$$
⌂ **Golf Hotel** (150 rooms) Cankarjeva 4; ✆ 04 579 1700; f 04 579 1701; e reservations.golf@gp-hoteli-bled.si; www.hotel-golf-bled.com. This plush hotel has large guest rooms with balconies. It also has thermal pools, a sauna & a golf course. $$$$–$$$$$
⌂ **Hotel Astoria** (72 rooms) Prešernova 44; ✆ 04 579 4400; f 04 579 4401; e Astoria@vgs-bled.si; www.hotelastoria-bled.com. Handily located for the bus station & just back from the lake itself.

Just over two-thirds of the rooms at this hotel have been recently upgraded to 4-stars, so make sure you book one of these. $$$$
⌂ **Park Hotel** (217 rooms) Cesta Svobode 15; ✆ 04 579 1800; f 04 574 1801; e reservations.park@gp-hoteli-bled.si; www.hotel-park-bled.com. Enormous hotel with a thermal pool, small fitness centre, sauna & solarium. Recently renovated rooms are modern & comfortable & many have views of the lake. $$$$
⌂ **Hotel Jadran** (45 rooms) Cesta Svobode 12; ✆ 04 579 1365; f 04 574 1661; e info@hotel-toplice.com; www.hotel-jadran-bled.com. Pleasant 3-star hotel in the centre of town with balconied rooms. $$$
⌂ **Hotel Trst** (32 rooms) Cesta Svobode 19; ✆ 04 579 1000; f 04 574 1841; e info@hotel-toplice.com; www.hotel-trst.com. Ask for a lake-view room with a balcony. $$$
⌂ **King's Club House** (9 rooms) Kidričeva 10C; ✆ 04 537 7711; e clubhouse@golf.bled.si; www.golf.bled.si. This luxurious clubhouse has well-equipped rooms. $$$
⌂ **Penzion Mayer** Želeška 7; ✆ 04 576 5740; f 04 576 5741; e penzion@mayer-sp.si; www.mayer-sp.si. A 4-star pension with pleasant en-suite rooms. $$$
⌂ **Hotel Jelovica** (100 rooms) Cesta Svobode 8; ✆ 04 579 6000; f 04 574 1550; e jelovica@hotel-

jelovica.si; www.hotel-jelovica.si. Separated from the lake by a park the hotel has decent rooms & good facilities including a health centre with swimming pool, a bar & a restaurant. $$–$$$$

⌂ **Vila Prešeren** Kidričeva 1; ☎ 04 578 0800; f 04 578 0810; e vila.preseren@siol.net; www.vila.preseren.s5.net. Upmarket guesthouse with lakeside location & a good fish restaurant. The 2 suites are a real step above the rest of the rooms with whirlpool baths & private balconies overlooking Lake Bled. Dbl $$–$$$, suite $$$$

⌂ **Hotel Krim** (115 rooms) Ljubljanska 7; ☎ 04 579 7000; f 04 574 3729; e hotelkrim@ hotel-krim.si; www.hotel-krim.si. Catering largely to package-holiday groups, this hotel located 100m from the lake has light & pleasant enough rooms. Rates are also very reasonable. $$–$$$

Camping

⚐ **Camping Bledec** Kidričeva 10c; ☎ 04 575 2000; f 04 575 2020; e info@camping.bled.si; www.camping.bled.si. Set back from the side of Lake Bled, this campsite located 2km from the centre of Bled has 290 pitches spread over 6ha. Facilities include a laundry & internet access. A restaurant & grocery store are located nearby. Tents & static caravans are available to rent. Bungalow rental $$, camping $

⚐ **Camping Šobec** Šobečeva 25; ☎ 04 535 3700; f 04 535 3701; e sobec@siol.net; www.sobec.si. Slovenia's largest campsite reclines in an enviable location nestled amongst the forest that lines a

curve in the Sava River, & overlooked protectively by the towering Julian Alps. Spread out over 15ha the site rarely feels crowded & you can often bag a prime riverside pitch. Children's playgrounds, a boating & fishing lake, minigolf & tennis courts help keep everyone happy. Not to mention rafting trips from the camp (many campers also bring their own rafts & kayaks), walking trails that lead off from the site & guided mountain treks in the capable hands of owner Rado Urvec. With tents & good-value wooden bungalows that sleep 6 for rent you don't even need your own tent or caravan. Bungalow rental $$$–$$$$$, camping $

⌂ **Penzion Mlino** (29 rooms) Cesta Svobode 45; ☎ 04 574 1404; f 04 574 1506; e mlino@mlino.si; www.mlino.si. Guesthouse in a more secluded location close to Vila Bled with good food & simple rooms. $$

⌂ **Penzion Bomi** (7 rooms) Kidriceva 12; ☎ 04 574 3594; e bomi@siol.net. Pleasant alpine-style guesthouse in an elevated position at the southwestern extremity of Lake Bled. All rooms have their own balconies & 3 have lake views. $$

⌂ **Youth Hostel Bledec** (13 rooms) Grajska 17; ☎ 04 574 5250; f 04 574 5251; e bledec@mlino.si; www.mlino.si. Light & clean accommodation in mainly 3- or 4-bed rooms, with dbls/twins & bunks. A great location, its own restaurant, bar & internet access led one traveller to eulogise in the guestbook: 'This is the best hostel I have ever stayed at.' Rates are pp. $

✗ WHERE TO EAT

✗ **Kings Club House** Kidričeva 10c; ☎ 04 537 7711; e clubhouse@golf.bled.si; www.golf.bled.si; ⌚ 11.00–23.00 daily. Elegant restaurant with a terrace overlooking the golf course. A Mediterranean-influenced menu with generous & tasty portions. There are also 9 luxurious rooms & suites. $$$$$

✗ **Topolino** Ljubljanska 26; ☎ 04 574 1781; www.topolion-slo.com; ⌚ 12.00–23.00 Wed–Mon. Highly recommended by the locals, serving a good-quality mix of Hungarian- & Italian-influenced Slovenian food. $$$$$

✗ **Park Hotel** (see *Where to stay*) ⌚ 11.11–23.00 daily. The menu at the hotel's funky new restaurant fuses Slovene & Mediterranean flavours with starters like rocket with beef fillet & seafood risotto. Fresh-fish dishes & grilled meat comprise the mains & the *kremna rezina* is divine. $$$$

✗ **Vila Prešeren** (see *Where to stay*) ⌚ 12.00–23.00 daily. On warm summer evenings this

is *the* place to come for romantic views of the lake. Dining inside is not nearly as pleasant, as the service can be a bit hit & miss. Trout with garlic & herb sauce is a good bet. $$$$

✗ **Gostilna Pri Planincu** Grajska 8; ☎ 04 574 1613; ⌚ 12.00–22.00 daily. Homely pub-style set-up with more tables through the back & an outdoor terrace. Although it has no views this eatery, serving hearty local food, is popular with locals & tourists. $$$

✗ **Night Restaurant Mlino** Cesta Svobode 45; ☎ 04 574 1404; ⌚ 12.00–01.00 daily. Late-night eatery serving tasty traditional food. $$$

✗ **Okarina** Ljubljanska 8; ☎ 04 574 1458; ⌚ 12.00–midnight daily. Serving a mixture of Indian & Slovenian dishes in pleasant surrounds & with separate dining rooms for smokers & non-smokers, & a candlelit terrace to the rear. Fresh chilli sauces add extra spice to tikka & masala dishes cooked for Slovenian palates. $$$

✗ **Penzion Mayer** (see *Where to stay*) ⊕17.00–midnight Tue–Fri, 12.00–midnight Sat–Sun. Platters of Slovenian cheese & *pršut* & excellent boiled trout have helped this restaurant earn its well-deserved reputation for good food.
✗**Ostarija Peglez'n** Cesta Svobode 19a; ☎ 04 574 4218; ⊕11.00–midnight daily. Located opposite Hotel Toplice some of the outside tables have views of the lake, albeit across the busy main road. A reasonably extensive menu features tasty meat & fish grills & tempting desserts. $$$

✗ **Pizzeria Pletna** Cesta Svobode 37; ☎ 04 576 7211; ⊕12.00–23.00 daily. Good-value *pizzeria* in Mlino serving pizzas. $$
✗ **Šlaščičarna Šmon** Grajska 3; ☎ 04 574 1616; ⊕07.30–21.00 daily. Many Slovenes will tell you that this pastry shop sells the best *kremna rezina* in the country. $
⚏ **Mercator** Ljubljanska 4. Supermarket in the shopping centre.

ENTERTAINMENT AND NIGHTLIFE

♀ **Gostilna Pri Planincu** (see *Where to eat*) Old Worldy pub with bags of atmosphere, especially popular with backpackers.
⯅ **Grand Hotel Toplice Café** Cesta Svobode 12a; ☎ 04 579 1000. Great views of the lake & a refined atmosphere, all very regal. Great place for a *kremna rezina* cream cake.
Bled Shopping Centre Unsightly shopping complex opposite the Park Hotel with a few rowdy bars & nightclubs.

☆ **Casino Bled** Cesta Svobode 15; ☎ 04 574 1811; www.casino-bled.si; ⊕15.00–05.00 daily. This is the place to come if you're feeling lucky or fancy a big night out.
♀ **Pub Bled** Cesta Svobode 19a; ☎ 04 574 2622. Popular pub with live music, DJs, cocktails & friendly staff.
♀ **Irish Pub** Cesta Svobode 8a; m 041 672 069. Irish theme bar with an obvious appeal adjacent to the Hotel Jelovica.

OTHER PRACTICALITIES

✉ **Post office** Ljubljanska 10; ⊕07.00–19.00 Mon–Fri, 07.00–12.00 Sat
▣ **Internet access** is available at **Bled Library** (*Ljubljanska 10*) & the **A Propos Bar** in Bled shopping centre (*Ljubljanska 4*).

$ **Gorenjska Banka** Cesta Svobode 15 (In Park Hotel shopping arcade) ⊕09.00–11.30 & 14.00–17.00 Mon–Fri, 08.00–11.00 Sat
$ **SKB Banka** Ljubljanska 4 (Bled shopping centre) ⊕08.30–12.00 & 14.00–17.00 Mon–Fri

WHAT TO SEE

Church of the Assumption (Cerkev Marijinega Vnebovzetja) The tiny Church of the Assumption, set adrift on the small island in the middle of the lake, is perhaps Bled's best-known and most alluring sight. Today's structure dates back to the late 17th century, but evidence suggests that there has been a church on Bled Island since the 9th century, and that before this the picture-postcard island was a Stone Age burial ground. Look out for the remnants of the 15th-century frescoes and a wooden statue of the Madonna dating from the same period.

To reach the church take a gondola from below the tourist office, Mlino or from the jetties near the Grand Hotel Toplice on the eastern shore. From the quay on the island you then have to climb the 99 steps to the top. If you are staying at Vila Bled a more romantic way to visit the island is to get up early and row over to the island yourself, using one of the hotel's own boats. Boats can also be rented from Mlino, on the southwestern shore of the lake and the Castle Baths. An early-morning visit will also save you from the clamour to ring the bell in the 15th-century belfry, which is supposed to help your wishes come true. The church is a favourite wedding spot for foreigners as well as Slovenians (*contact Bled Catholic Parish for details; Riklijeva 26;* ☎ *04 574 4046*).

Bled Castle (*Blejski Grad; Grajska 25;* ☎ *04 578 0525; adult/concession €3.50/€2.50;* ⊕*Mar–Oct 08.00–19.00 daily; Nov–Feb 09.00–16.00 daily*) Presiding majestically from a rocky outcrop 139m above the lake is one of

Slovenia's most impressive castles. There are tourist trains up here in summer as well as car-parking space, but if you are feeling energetic, take on the heart-pumping trek. Even before the Bishop of Brixen arrived in the area there was already said to have been a fortification on the strategically important site, though today's incarnation is largely the result of a 20th-century revamp. Romanesque elements can still be found in the walls, and late Gothic in the chapel. The **museum** illuminates the eclectic history of both the castle and the Bled region in general, while visitors can pick up a hand-pressed certificate to say they have been to Bled Castle. On a sunny day relaxing in the café with the mountains and lake spreading out into the distance is the real pleasure. Classical music concerts are also held at the castle on summer nights.

Walk around the lake There is no better way to appreciate Lake Bled than to stroll along the easy path that hugs its banks. A good place to start is at the Grand Hotel Toplice (no muddy boots or beachwear allowed) so that in moments of tiredness you can dream of returning here at the end for coffee and a *kremna rezina*, the delicious vanilla-and-fresh-cream cake that they serve in their opulent waterfront café. As you head west you spend a short section by the main road, which is not too pleasant with tour buses rattling by in summer, but as you pass the hamlet of Mlino the path heads back down to the lake and then on to the grounds of the recently refurbished Vila Bled, Tito's old summer home. Soon after the Vila the path becomes a wooden walkway with the lake lapping against it and beech and chestnut trees overhanging the water. Looking back east is the church on the island – this is a good place for photographs as sunset approaches.

Continuing clockwise the path passes a small watersports centre and campground before coming across Slovenia's only rowing club at Zaka (*www.vesl-klub-bled.si*), which was the base for Slovenia's two gold-medal rowers at the Sydney 2000 Olympics. As you circle back round, the view changes again and Bled Town starts to get lost behind the trees as the path meanders past the grand holiday homes of Slovenia's rich and famous. In summer the final approach to Bled Town is awash with the clamour from the bathing area below the path – if you want to escape take the path to the right that is signposted 'Grad 1' and which leads up in a steep ascent to the castle. Coming back into town the hustle and bustle of the resort soon engulfs you before the respite of a neatly laid-out park by the eastern shores of the lake. Take a pew here to appreciate the effort of the serious rowers who hammer up and down the marker lanes in the centre of the lake. By now you should have worked up enough of an appetite to fully appreciate a sugary treat as you admire the views.

Vintgar Gorge (*Blejski Vintgar; adult/concession €2.50/€1.25; ⊕mid Apr–Mar 08.00–19.00 daily*) The trek to Vintgar Gorge, located just 4km from Bled, is an easy and rewarding one. If you are stuck for time, however, you might want to drive to the car park, or time your visit to coincide with one of the local buses. The gorge runs for over 1.5km and cuts deep into the rock. It is, of course, at its best after heavy rain, though it can be slippery at these times and extra care should be taken. A series of walkways guide visitors and the path is easy to follow. There are snack bars on hand too if you are hungry.

BOHINJ

A pleasant 26km drive south of Lake Bled, following the path of the Sava Bohinjska River, is glacial Lake Bohinj. Slovenia's largest lake (1km wide by 4.2km long) is if anything even more dramatic than Lake Bled: a wider, longer

4

BOHINJ

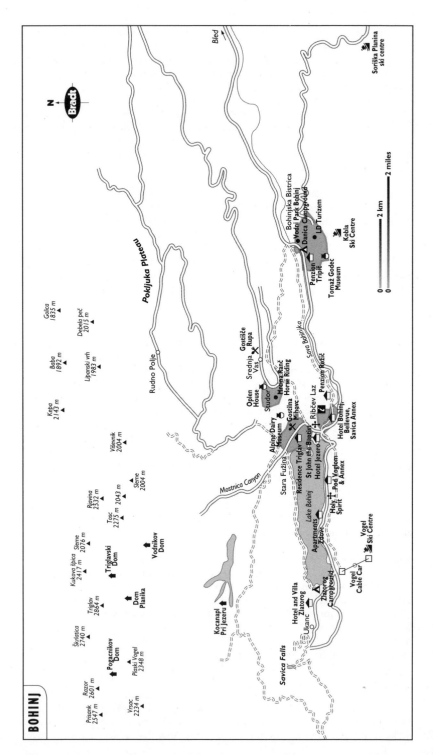

Prisank 2547 m ▲

Razor 2601 m ▲

Vrsac 2234 m ▲

Škrlatica 2740 m ▲

Pogačnikov Dom ▲

Plaski Vogel 2348 m ▲

Triglav 2864 m ▲

Kukova Špica 2417 m ▲

Sleme 2076 m ▲

Dom Planika ▲

Triglavski Dom ▲

Vodnikov Dom ▲

Kanjavec 2568 m

Kocanapl Pri Jezeru ▲

Rjavina 2532 m ▲

Tosc 2275 m 2043 m ▲

Sleme 2004 m ▲

Viš,evnik 2004 m ▲

Kepa 2143 m ▲

Baba 1892 m ▲

Lipanski vrh 1983 m ▲

Golica 1835 m ▲

Debela peč 2015 m ▲

Pokljuka Plateau

Rudno Polje ○

N
Bradt

Bled

Soriška Planina ski centre ▲

Bohinjska Bistrica
Vodni Park Bohinj ●
Danica Campground △
LD Turizem ☐
Kobla Ski Centre ▲

Penzion Tripič ☐
Tomaž Godec Museum ●

0 ——— 2 km
0 ——— 2 miles

Gostišče Rupa ✕

Srednja Vas ○

Oplen House ●
Studor ▲

Mrcina Ranč Horse Riding ▲

Sava Bohinjka

Penzion Rožič ☐

Alpine Dairy Museum ●
Gostilna Mihovc ✕

Ribčev Laz †
St John the Baptist †

Hotel Bohinj, Bellevue, Savica Annex ☐

Residence Triglav ☐
Hotel Jezero ☐

Stara Fužina

Mostnica Canyon

Pod Voglom & Annex ☐
Holy Spirit †

Lake Bohinj

Apartments Zlatok ☐

Vogel Ski Centre ▲

Hotel and Villa Zlatorog ☐

Ukanc ○

Zlatorog Campground △

Vogel Cable Car ☐

Savica Falls

and wilder expanse of alpine water that snakes away towards the looming hulk of Triglav. While the most accessible end of Lake Bohinj has a straggle of tourist developments and is plied by lake cruises, development is on a much less obvious scale and this is the place to come for a get-away-from-it-all break, without all the frills of Bled.

HISTORY The area around the lake, encompassing half a dozen small villages and the tourist base of Ribčev Laz, is known as Bohinj. Human habitation here can be traced as far back as the Iron Age. The first written mention of Bohinj came later than Bled in 1070 when Germanic settlers arrived. The prevalence of iron ore had boosted the local economy by the 16th century and when it started to wane in the 19th century tourism was already emerging in an embryonic form with Viennese tourists visiting here from health retreats in Bled. Today it is emerging as something of an adventure-sports centre.

GETTING THERE Lake Bohinj is 26km from Bled and the lake and nearby villages are an easy 20-minute drive away. Buses connect Ribčev Laz to Stara Fužina (10 minutes), Studor (10 minutes), Bohinjska Bistrica (15 minutes), Bled (40 minutes) and Ljubljana (1¹/₂ hours). Trains from Bled Jezero (20 minutes) and Nova Gorica (1 hour 20 minutes) stop at Bohinjska Bistrica. There is also a car-train service (m *041 320 973*) between Bohinjska Bistrica and Most na Soči, via Podbrdo, which cuts through the mountains between the Gorenjska and Primorska regions.

GETTING AROUND During high season (June–September) **buses** run from Bohinjska Bistrica to the Savica Waterfall, picking up at the Hotel Jezero in Ribčev Laz on the way. A bus service also runs from Stara Fužina to the falls via the Hotel Jezero.

🚖 **Taxi Orel** Gradnikova 72; m 041 710 747; www.bled-taxi.si

Various tour operators in Bohinj rent out **bicycles** and mountain bikes.

TOURIST INFORMATION/LOCAL TOUR OPERATORS

🛈 **Tourist Information Centre** Ribčev Laz 48; ☎ 04 574 6010; f 04 572 3330; e info@bohinj-info.com; www.bohinj.si. The TIC provides information & souvenirs. Staff can arrange accommodation & there is also a currency exchange. It also sells the Bohinj Guest Card which gives discounts on accommodation, parking, restaurants, activities & entrance to museums.
LD Turizem Mencingerjeva 10, Bohinjska Bistrica; ☎ 04 574 7600; f 04 574 7601; e info@ld-turizem.si; www.ld-turizem.si. Tourist agency providing information, private accommodation, bicycle rental & outdoor activities.
Alpinum Ribčev Laz 50; ☎ 04 577 8000; f 04 572 3446; e info@alpinum.net; www.alpinum.net. Tourist

agency offering camping & hotel accommodation alongside an extensive list of summer & winter sports, including mountain biking, paragliding, hiking, skiing & ice climbing.
Pac Sports Ribčev Laz 50; m 041 698 523; e info@pac-sports.com; www.pac-sports.com. Offering paragliding, rafting, canyoning, hydrospeed, mountain biking & kayaking amongst other sports. They also rent out mountain bikes, kayaks, canoes & rafts.
Alpinsport Ribčev Laz 53; ☎/f 04 572 3468; e alpinsport@siol.net; www.alpinsport.si. Organising accommodation & a wide range of winter & summer sports.

🏠 **WHERE TO STAY** The tourist information centre in Ribčev Laz (see above) can arrange private accommodation for around €15 per person. A surcharge is generally applied for stays of less than three days, for single occupancy and for breakfast, although the last charge is often nominal.

🏠 **Hotel Bohinj** (20 rooms) Ribčev Laz 45; ☎ 04 572 6000; f 04 572 3446; www.alpinum.net. Alpine-style hotel located opposite the tourist information centre. Some of the modern rooms have their own balconies or terraces. The hotel also has a fitness centre & tennis courts, & offers bike hire to guests. $$$–$$$$

🏠 **Hotel Jezero** (63 rooms) Ribčev Laz 51; ☎ 04 572 3375; e hotel.jezero@cc-line.si; www.bohinj.com/alpinum/jezero/hotel_jezero_en.htm l. Modern lakeside hotel with an indoor pool, sauna, solarium, fitness centre & restaurant. Ask for a room with a balcony. $$$–$$$$

🏠 **Hotel Bellevue & Savica Annex** (57 rooms) Ribčev Laz 65; ☎ 04 572 3331; f 04 572 3684; www.alpinum.net. Located on a hill above the lake with a restaurant & tennis courts. Balconied rooms are worth the extra cost. $$$–$$$$

🏠 **Hotel & Villa Zlatarog** (72 rooms) Ukanc 65; ☎ 04 572 3381; f 04 572 3384; www.alpinum.net/eng_ok/html/hotel_zlatorog.html. Around 5km out of Ribčev Laz this hotel enjoys a peaceful lakeside location. Dining in the hotel's organic restaurant is also well worthwhile. $$$–$$$$

🏠 **Penzion Rožič** (30 beds) Ribčev Laz 42; ☎ 04 572 3393; f 04 574 6111; e rozic@siol.net; www.penzion-rozic.com. The pension has decent en-suite rooms & offers bicycle & boat rental. $$–$$$

🏠 **Residence Triglav** (27 apts) Stara Fužina 23; ☎ 04 572 9700; www.residencetriglav.si. Geared towards the backpacker market, dormitory-style accommodation is provided in apts with balconies sleeping 2–5 people. They can organise canyoning (€38 pp), mini rafting (€18) & bicycle rental (€13). If you don't have your own transport free pick-ups at the bus & railways stations can also be arranged. Rates are pp. $

🏠 **Hotel Pod Voglom & Annex** (27 rooms) Ribčev Laz 60; ☎ 04 572 3461; f 04 572 3073; www.alpinum.net. Good-value 2-star hotel on the shores of Lake Bohinj. Some rooms have shared bathrooms. Bike hire is available to guests. $$

🏠 **Apartments Zdovc** (10 apts) Ribčev Laz 138; ☎ 04 572 3594; f 04 574 6420; e zdovc@asf-bohinj.eu; www.bohinj.si/zdovc. Apts sleeping 4–6 people, with private kitchens on the outskirts of the village. Guests can use a shared hot tub, sauna & small fitness centre. Supplements are charged for stays of less than 3 days, for b/fast & for use of leisure facilities. $$

🏠 **Pension Tripič** (13 rooms) Triglavska 13, Bohinjska Bistrica; ☎/f 04 572 1282; e pension.tripic@bohinj.si; www.bohinj.si/tripic. Good-sized rooms sleeping 2–5 people. The pension, in the centre of town, also has a meeting room, restaurant, sauna & solarium. $$

Camping

⚡ **Zlatorog Campground** Ukanc 2; ☎ 04 572 3482; f 04 572 3446; e info@aaturizem.com; www.alpinum.net. Well-equipped campsite nestled on the shore of Lake Bohinj, with space for 150 tents, campers & caravans. Bicycle hire is available & campers have access to an indoor pool & tennis courts located 200m from the site. $

⚡ **Danica Campground** Ribčev Laz 48, Bohinjska Bistrica; ☎ 04 572 3370; f 04 572 3330; e tdbohinj@bohinh.si; www.bohinj.si/camping-danica. This spacious campsite has 165 pitches, laundry, internet access & a range of sports facilities. The majestic mountain views are the real winner though. Rates are pp. $

🍴 **WHERE TO EAT** Many accommodation establishments in Bohinj offer half- and full-board options.

🍴 **Gostišče Rupa** Srednja Vas 87; ☎ 04 572 3401; ⏲ Jul/Aug 10.00–midnight daily; Sep–Jun 10.00–midnight Tue–Sun. Restaurant in the shadow of the Julian Alps with an outdoor terrace, home cooking, first-rate trout & staff wearing traditional folk costumes. $$$

🍴 **Penzion Rožič** (see Where to stay) ⏲ 12.00–22.00 daily. Serving good Slovenian food in a homely restaurant or on a covered outdoor terrace. $$$

🍴 **Gostilna Mihovc** Stara Fužina; ☎ 04 572 3390; ⏲ 10.00–midnight daily. With hearty Slovenian cooking & homemade brandy. $$

🍴 **MK Pizzeria** Ribčev Laz 48; ⏲ 11.00–23.00 daily. Decent pizzas & grills in a central location by the tourist information centre. $$

🛒 **Mercator** Ribčev Laz 49. Handily located supermarket next to the tourist information centre.

OTHER PRACTICALITIES
✉ **Post office** Ribčev Laz 47; ⊕08.00–09.30,
10.00–15.30 & 16.00–18.00 Mon–Fri, 08.00–12.00
Sat. Also has a handily located ATM.

WHAT TO SEE
Lake Bohinj In high season there are myriad ways to explore the lake's relatively balmy waters with tourist craft, rowing boats and canoes to choose from. Another option is simply to follow the trail around the lake, but note that this takes at least three hours at a brisk pace and it can be miserable if you get caught in a downpour and have to trudge around soaked. Some readers have bemoaned the trees that block the lake views on the walk – we think they are all part of the charm. An easier choice is to take a bus from Ribčev Lav to the Hotel Zlatorog and then walk back from there. From May to October you can join one of six daily cruises on the lake (m *041 434 986*) with departure points at Ribčev Laz and Camp Zlatorog. Out-of-season trips run subject to demand and weather. You can swim in Lake Bohinj but watch out for areas reserved for naturists.

Mt Vogel Cable Car (*Ukanc 6;* ☎ *04 572 9712; www.vogel.si; adult/concession €10/€7 return, €7/€5 single;* ⊕*07.00–18.00 daily*) The cable car up Mt Vogel provides spectacular views over the lake and Julian Alps in both summer and winter. On a clear day you can even see Triglav. The station at the Ski Hotel is at a lofty 1,535m. If you are feeling energetic, two hiking routes – one from Ribčev Laz and one from Ukanc – also take you to the top.

Savica Falls (Slap Savica) Continue around the banks of Lake Bohinj away from Ribčev Laz and the road delves into verdant alpine forests which hide a couple of hotels and the access to the cable car up the slopes of Mt Vogel (see above). Further on, the old gravel track has thankfully been sealed and driving up to the Savica Falls, perhaps the most dramatic waterfall in Slovenia, is no longer a struggle except when there are tour buses vying for road space in the summer. The best time to appreciate Savica is in spring when the snow is melting and the water thumps its way 78m down from the rocky heights above and smacks into the pool below. The steep path (*access to the Savica path; adult/concession €2/€1*) is well marked, although it can be slippery, but it is no longer possible to get right up to the base of the waterfall as a padlocked gate now blocks access. There is, however, a small gazebo which provides a good vantage point and also gives a bit of cover when alpine rains move in for the day. Look for the plaque that commemorates the 19th-century visit of Archduke Johann of Austria. There is supposed to be a charge for parking, though this is not always applied.

Churches
Church of St John the Baptist (*Cerkev Sv Janez Krstnik; €1;* ⊕*Jul/Aug 09.00–12.00 & 17.00–20.00 daily; out of season ask at the TIC*) Located opposite the small stone bridge in Ribčev Laz, The Church of St John the Baptist offers stunning views of Lake Bohinj. This church, which has its origins in the 13th century, is the most interesting building around Bohinj. It has undergone various revamps throughout its history and now features a Baroque belltower as well as 17th-century altars, but it still boasts a wealth of preserved 14th-century frescoes and its façade is decorated, typically for Gorenjska, with a depiction of St Christopher.

Church of the Holy Spirit (Cerkev Sv Duh) The highlight of this Baroque church is Matija Koželj's fresco of St Christopher.

Museums

Tomaž Godec Museum (*Muzej Tomaž Godca; Zoisova 15, Bohinjska Bistrica;* ☎ *04 572 1763; adult/concession €1.70/€1.25;* ⊕ *Jan–Apr 10.00–12.00 & 16.00–18.00 Wed & Sat/Sun; May–Oct 10.00–12.00 & 16.00–18.00 Tue–Sun*) Quite bizarrely every 10th entrance ticket to this museum, dedicated to a communist Slovene war hero, is free. Renowned as a championship skier before the outbreak of fighting, Godec was instrumental in the 1941 uprising against the Germans, though he paid the ultimate price for his heroics when he was captured and executed by the Germans a year later. The building was the venue for the setting up of the Central Committee of the Yugoslav Communist Party in 1939, a meeting where Tito himself was present.

Alpine Dairy Museum (*Planšarksi Muzej; Stara Fužina 181;* ☎ *04 572 3095; adult/concession €1.70/€1.25;* ⊕ *Jan–Jun & Sep/Oct 10.00–12.00 & 16.00–18.00 Tue–Sun; Jul/Aug 11.00–19.00 Tue–Sun*) This museum steps back to the time when Bohinj was at the centre of alpine dairy farming in Slovenia, an industry that was gradually 'killed off' by modern methods and by the opening of a new dairy in Srednja Vas in 1971. Reconstructed alpine huts and dairy exhibits form the crux of the collection.

Oplen House (*Oplenova Hiša; Studor 16, Srednja Vas;* ☎ *04 572 3522; adult/concession €1.70/€1.25; Jan–Jun & Sep/Oct 10.00–12.00 & 16.00–18.00 Tue–Sun; Jul/Aug 11.00–19.00 Tue–Sun*) Oplen House is a traditional farmhouse constructed in the 19th century from stone and wood, in a longhouse style that combines living and farming space. Today visitors can explore the preserved living room, bedroom, attic, cellar and black kitchen. In the barn there is a display of traditional farming tools. If the museum is closed when you arrive the caretaker, Gregor Resan, lives next door at No 14a.

ACTIVITIES AROUND BLED AND BOHINJ

There is a seemingly endless swathe of activities on offer in and around Bled and Bohinj, with operators providing a pick-up service from both resorts. Summer pursuits include mountain biking, hiking and fishing, while adrenaline junkies can try their hand at climbing, tandem paragliding, canyoning, kayaking, rafting, canoeing or hydrospeed. When the mercury drops these are replaced by downhill and cross-country skiing, ski tours and ice skating. In the depths of winter it is also possible to climb both the Julian Alps and frozen waterfalls. Alpinum, Pac Sports, Alpinsport and ProMontana all organise sporting activates (see *Tourist information/local tour operators* under *Bled* and *Bohinj*, pages 104 and 109).

VODNI PARK BOHINJ (*Triglavska 17;* ☎ *04 577 0210;* e *bohinj.vodnipark@siol.net; www.vodni-park-bohinj.si;* ⊕ *09.00–21.00 daily*) This aquatic playground has all the things that you would expect from a water park, including hot tubs, swimming pools, water slides, a wellness centre, indoor swimming pool and saunas. For those who would rather stay dry it also has a couple of climbing walls and a small fitness centre.

KAYAKING AND CANOEING Canoeing and kayaking are possible on lakes Bled and Bohinj, while kayaking also takes place on the upper Sava Bohinjka River. In addition tour operators organise excursions to the more challenging waters of the lower Sava Bohinjka, Radovna and Soča. Week-long kayaking courses (5–10 hours of tuition €55–100) and guided kayak expeditions are also available.

Serious mountain bikers can pick up the *Cycling Tour Around the Julian Alps* map from tourist information centres in Kranjska Gora, Bled, Bohinj, Tolmin and Bovec, as well as from information centres/points in some campsites and other towns. This 232km circular trail is split into five stages. The first from Kranjska Gora to Bled covers 49km and climbs to 366m at its highest point. The Bled–Bohinj leg extends just over 31km and climbs to 780m (a shorter and easier option is to cycle 28km and rising just 155m). Following the trail between Bohinj and Tolmin covers 62km, ascends Soriška planina (a 12km ascent covering 765m); for a more gentle alternative bypass Soriška planina by tunnelling through the mountain on the train between Bohinjska Bistrica and Podbrdo. The 39km between Tolmin and Bovec ascends 260m. The final Bovec–Kranjska Gora leg is a real killer, covering 50km and climbing to 1,211km, but it rewards cyclists with stunning vistas from the Vršič Pass (beware this road can be very busy during the summer and can be impassable because of snow right through to the end of May).

CANYONING Canyoning is the navigation of riverbeds and waterfalls by jumping, swimming and using climbing ropes and can be done at a variety of levels from beginner to advanced (€35–60 for a single trip). It centres on the Mostnica Canyon between Stara Fužina and the Voje Valley.

PARAGLIDING AND TANDEM PARAGLIDING Paragliding is a great way to experience the Julian Alps. You can take a tandem flight with an experienced instructor-pilot, take beginner's lessons or join a five-day certificate course. Flights typically take off from Vogar or Vogel. Trial flights cost €55–80, tandem flights from €65, courses €250–350.

GOLF The 18-hole **King's Course** near Bled (*Kidričeva 10c;* \ *04 537 7711;* f *04 537 7722;* e *info@golf.bled.si; www.golf.bled.si*) is probably the finest golf course in the country and enjoys a stunning setting that gives many courses elsewhere in Europe a run for their money. The set-up here is getting increasingly slick with a resident professional and a revamp of the clubhouse to include a posh restaurant and some luxurious rooms. Golfers can also play the nine-hole Lake Golf Course.

RAFTING Navigating white water in a six-to-eight-person rubber raft is an exhilarating experience. Rafting (€20–30 for a single trip) generally takes place on the Sava Bohinjka and the Sava Dolinka, with rapids from grade one (gentle) to four (quite ferocious). Water levels on the Sava Bohinjka are often too low to raft in July and August.

FISHING Anglers can try their luck on Lake Bohinj (March–September) and on the Sava Bohinjka River (April–October). Fishing is by permit only and these are issued for one to seven days.

WALKING There are myriad choices in the natural oasis of the Triglav National Park. The best option is to pick up a map at the tourist office in Bled or Bohinj and then set out. Many low-level trails are suitable for all, but be sure to take local advice on more tricky options as the weather can close in very quickly in these parts.

Climbing Triglav is something that every Slovene is meant to do at least once in their life. Corner a handful of Slovenes, though, and you will be lucky if half have been to the summit of this 2,864m monster, and this is not just through apathy. Climbing Triglav is no picnic as it is more than twice the height of Ben Nevis (1,344m), the UK's highest peak, although none of the ascents starts at sea level. Any fit adult should be able to manage the climb, but before attempting an ascent it is essential to prepare yourself properly and to carry the right gear. A good head for heights is also an advantage, as the sinewy ridges on the approach to the summit are not for the faint-hearted. The reward for careful preparation and physical exertion, though, is the bounty of sweeping views of the Julian Alps and Italy on one side and the Karavanke and Austria on the other, while Slovenia unfurls all around.

Slovenia's highest peak has inspired a sense of awe for centuries, with early Slav settlers believing that the imposing limestone mountain was home to a powerful three-headed deity. Today the mountain, which has been protected as a national park since 1981, is revered for its beauty (not the supernatural power that inhabits it) and takes pride of place on the Slovenian flag.

Most people take two days to tackle the summit – to which there are around two dozen routes – and stay overnight in one of many mountain huts. Most huts open from June–September and offer basic and hearty Slovenian food, with accommodation costing €10–15 per person.

Dramatic and forbidding, the northern approaches involve an ascent of the mountain's steep 1,200m north face and are definitely not for beginners. The southern approaches offer somewhat gentler routes, with those tackling Triglav for the first time frequently starting near Bohinj.

The quickest route to the summit is from the Sport Hotel in Rudno Polje (1,345m above sea level), 18km southwest of Lake Bled. Rudno Polje can be reached

CYCLING AND MOUNTAIN BIKING Bikes can be rented from tour operators in either Bohinj or Bled and at many hotels. Lakeside cycling is an easy and fun way of getting around, but conditions in the surrounding mountains and hills are much more challenging. More experienced mountain bikers can check out the forested paths that weave their way through the valley and upwards towards the mountain summits. Bicycle rental and guided trips (one day €10–40) are both available.

MOUNTAIN HIKING AND CLIMBING Mountain hiking is one of the biggest draw-cards for visitors to Bled and Bohinj, many of whom want to scale the lofty heights of Triglav. Not for novice climbers, the ascent and descent of Triglav are tricky and hiring the services of a local and experienced guide is recommended (ask at the TIC or check with a local tour operator). You should not hike in or climb any of Slovenia's mountains alone or without the proper equipment and safety gear.

The best-known climbing sites in Bohinj are just below the Bellevue Hotel in Ribčev Laz and at Pod Skalco, Bitnje and Bohinjska Bela. The Julian Alps provide a myriad climbing opportunities, with over 200 routes catering to everyone from the beginner to the more experienced climber. The Pod Skalco and Bellevue sites are popular with beginners and a range of courses take place here. There is also a climbing wall at the Pod Voglom Hotel for you to hone your skills. Again it is sensible to engage the services of a local guide for tougher ascents.

Other popular summer routes leave from the Mount Vogel cable-car station; again the majority of these are suitable only for experienced mountaineers.

by car, or by a daily bus that departs Bled at 08.25. From Rudno Polje the summit lies at the very least six hours away, with many climbers opting to stay in the 53-bed Vodnikov Dom na Velem Polju mountain hut (approximately three hours away) or the 62-bed Dom Planika pod Triglavom (around five hours away). Slovene teenagers like to try to complete the ascent and descent from Rudno Polje to the summit in a single day, but this is a difficult feat for even the fittest person and is definitely not recommended for the inexperienced.

A more popular route takes you from the Zlatorog Hotel in Bohinj to the summit via Slap Savica (Savica Falls), Komarča Crag, Črno Jezero (Black Lake), Veliko Triglavsko Jezero (Great Lake), Zeleno Jezero (Yellow Lake), the Hribarice Plateau (2,358m) and the Dolič Saddle (2,164m). From Bohinj the summit is at least seven hours away, with the last hour or so traversing some fairly challenging terrain including rocks and a cliff face – where steel pegs acting as footholds and fixed cables assist with the final push to the top – and, quite often, snow.

There are three mountain huts on the way – the Dom Planika pod Triglavom, the 104-bed Koča pri Triglavskih Jezerih (four hours from Bohinj) and the 60-bed Tržaška Koča na Doliču (five hours from Bohinj). An alternative and longer route takes hikers from the village of Stara Fužina through the Planica Viševnik meadows to the Koča pri Triglavskih Jezerih hut.

The information given in this box is not a comprehensive guide to climbing Triglav. Before any summit attempt it is important to get local advice or to seek the services of a guide (highly recommended). It is also essential to purchase a detailed map and a good idea to buy one of the books written about hiking in the Julian Alps (see *Appendix 2, Further Information*). The Mountain Club P D Ljubljana–Matica (*Miklošičeva 17;* \ *01 231 2645;* e *info.pdljmatica@siol.net; www.planinskodrustvo-ljmatica.si*) can provide information about guides and mountain huts.

HYDROSPEED This is basically body boarding on the Sava, but with a wetsuit to keep you warm and help protect against the bumps (from € 25).

HORSERIDING The **Mrcina Ranč Horseriding Centre** (*Studor;* m *041 790 297;* e *info@ranc-mrcina.com; www.ranc-mrcina.com; around € 20 for a 1hr trip*) offers a variety of courses which allow visitors to ride their Icelandic horses, from an oval riding track for beginners to country riding, riding camps and even horse sledding in the winter. One-hour excursions take you to the Devil's Bridge in Stara Fužina, while three-day trips explore the Pokljuka Plateau. They also operate a riding school. More unusual are their 'adrenaline tours', which combine riding with either canyoning or tandem paragliding.

Namesh (*Gorje;* m *041 558 761;* e *stella@namesh.org*) also offer a variety of horseriding excursions from their farm in Gorje. Trips include a short jaunt along the Radovna River, an ascent to the top of the Mežakla Plateau and a longer route that takes in alpine meadows, woods and valleys. If you don't have your own wheels they'll also arrange transfers to and from Bled.

ALPINE SKIING There is a simple and short ski run at **Straža Bled** (*Rečiška 2;* \ *04 578 0534*) on the southwest flank of Lake Bled. It operates during the day and evening when there is enough snow (often until early April). A ski lift ferries you up, but blink and you will miss the descent. There are nice views here and if you are a beginner or are just short of time it is not a bad option. There is a number of ski resorts around the Bohinj Valley including **Kobla** (*Cesta na Ravne*

7, Bohinjska Bistrica; ℡ 04 574 7100; e kobla@siol.net; www.bohinj.si/kobla), with 23km of slopes and cross-country runs; **Vogel** (Ukanc 6; ℡ 04 572 9712; www.vogel.si), Bohinj's main resort, with 38km of pistes and a long season; and **Soriška Planina** (Selca 86, Selca; ℡ 04 511 7835; e alpmetal@krajnik.net), which has much more impressive facilities and a number of decent runs. The ski slopes in the Bohinj area cater to everyone from the beginner to the advanced skier. Instruction is also available in snowboarding, carving and telemark skiing.

CROSS-COUNTRY SKIING Myriad trails in Vogel, the Pokljuka Plateau and Rudno Polje host the Cross-Country Skiing World Cup each year, and over 60km of well-maintained trails are open to visitors. One popular trail links Bohinjska Bistrica to Ribčev Laz.

ICE SKATING In winter part of Lake Bohinj near Pod Skalco is given over to an artificial ice rink. Skate hire is available.

SUMMER TOBOGGANING A summer toboggan run operates in Straža running 520m and descending 131m at a maximum speed of 40km/h. The run operates at various times from early April through to early November, with daily opening from mid June to early September and at the tail end of October and early November (one ride €5, concessions €3).

FLYING Get a panoramic view of the alpine scenery without making any effort with a panoramic flight (April–October) from the **Lesce Alpine Flying Centre** (Begunjska 10, Lesce; ℡ 04 532 0100; e info@alc-lesce.si; www.alc-lesce.si). Short jaunts start at €70 stretching to €200 for one hour (maximum three passengers).

OLD-TIMER TRAIN This vintage steam train stops at both Bled Jezero and Bohinjska Bistrica on its summer run (May–October) between Jesenice and Most na Soči. It tends to make just one or two public outings monthly. Tickets must be booked in advance, which can be done through the tourist information centres in Bled or Bohinj.

DAY TRIPS AROUND BLED AND BOHINJ

BEGUNJE The alpine village of Begunje, which lies just northeast of Bled and Radovljica, stakes various claims to fame including its Elan sports factory and one of Slovenia's most influential and popular folk groups, the **Avsenik Brothers** (www.avsenik-sp.si). It has also had a voluntary fire department for more than 100 years and was the birthplace of Anton Bonaventura Jeglič, who was the Bishop of Ljubljana from 1898 to 1930 and is still remembered by Slovenes as a man who championed the national cause.

It is Begunje's sights that draw non-Slovenes to the town. These include the ruins of the medieval **Kamen Castle** (Kamen Grad), which dates from the 12th century. Limited funding has reined in dreams of restoring the castle to its former state, although the Roman Tower has been renovated and the castle remains an impressive sight against the backdrop of the Julian Alps. On 25 June each year the castle comes alive with medieval re-enactments, archery tournaments and a large bonfire, as the residents of Begunje celebrate National Day.

The 16th-century **Katzenstein Castle**, which was reconstructed in the 17th century and served as a Gestapo prison during World War II, is another notable sight and some of the former cells have been opened as the **Museum of Hostages** (Muzej Taclev; Begunje 55; ℡ 04 533 3790; €2; ⊕ Mar/Apr & Nov/Dec

09.00–13.00 Wed/Sat, 14.00–17.00 Sun; May/Jun & Sep/Oct 09.00–14.00 Tue–Fri, 13.00–17.00 Sat/Sun; Jul/Aug 13.00–17.00 Tue–Sun). In the castle gardens you can find two of Jože Plečnik's structures – the Murka and Jožamurka sheds. Others are the **Church of St Urh** (constructed and modified from the 15th to 18th century) and the simple, white **Church of St Peter** (Cerkev Sv Petra), where many believe that a healing breeze is blown from a nearby hole.

VRBA Fans of France Prešeren can make the pilgrimage to the village of Vrba, a short drive northeast of Bled. The house where he was born was converted into a museum just before the onset of World War II. It is not as illuminating as the Prešeren House in Kranj; in many ways it is more interesting as an example of 19th-century Gorenjska architecture and furnishings than as a testament to the great man.

KRANJSKA GORA

It is easy to see why the playground of Kranjska Gora, perched on the border between three countries in a stunning location at the foot of the Julian Alps, has become so popular. In winter it is a fully fledged winter-sports resort – Slovenia's largest – offering skiing, ski jumping, tobogganing, cross-country skiing, snowboarding and a base for exploring the Julian Alps. Compared with the resorts in France and Austria, Kranjska Gora offers great value. When the snow finally melts the sweeping slopes and sky-crunching peaks are the perfect oasis for walking, hiking and climbing. The Old World charm of this small village has definitely been lost in a scramble of hotels, restaurants, bars and even casinos, as well as, of course, the web of ski slopes and lifts, but if it all gets too much just turn your eyes skywards and the epic beauty of the mountains soon helps you forget the rest.

The first written mentions of Kranjska Gora go back to the 14th century, but it was never really a major population centre due to the difficult terrain and the harsh winters. During World War I Russian prisoners of war were brought into the region to help forge a track through the untamed mountains (see *Over the Vršič Pass to Primorska*, page 120), but even today this elevated through-road can be shut by snow and avalanche threats as late as mid May. There seems to be no stopping Kranjska Gora's rise and rise today, with new and revamped hotels, better snow machines and improved lifts. A round of the Ski Jumping World Cup is also held every year at nearby Planica, a long wild weekend of high-quality sport and wanton socialising excess that has taken a hallowed place on the calendar for many Slovenes.

GETTING THERE Motorists travelling to Kranjska Gora from Primorska should be aware that the Vršič Pass can be closed from the first heavy snowfalls until late May.

Regular buses run to Kranjska Gora from Bled (1 hour 25 minutes), Radovljica (1 hour 25 minutes) and Ljubljana (2½ hours). In July and August buses also link the resort to Bovec (1½ hours).

GETTING AROUND
🚕 **Taxi Merteli** ☎ 04 588 1655

TOURIST INFORMATION/LOCAL TOUR OPERATORS
ℹ️ **Tourist Information Centre** Tičarjeva 2; ☎ 04 580 9440; f 04 580 9441; e tic@krnajska-gora.si; www.kranjska-gora.si

Globtour Borovška 95; ☎ 04 582 0200; f 04 588 1979; e globtour.kranjskagora@globtour.si; www.globtour.si

Julijana Podkoren 5; ✆ 04 588 1325; e julijana@siol.net; www.sednjek.si

Skipass Travel Borovška 95; ✆ 04 582 1000; f 04 582 1014; e info@skipasstravel.si; www.skipasstravel.si

🏠 **WHERE TO STAY** Staff at Kranjska Gora's tourist offices and tour operators will help you find private accommodation. Rooms cost €10–25 per person depending on the season and the grading of the property. Apartments sleeping two people start at €35.

🏠 **Hotel Kompas** (149 rooms) Borovška 100; ✆ 04 589 2100; f 04 588 4479; e info@hitholidays-kg.si; www.hitholidays-kg.si. This recently renovated hotel offers pleasant enough rooms, a sauna, steam room, pool & spa treatments. Book a mountain-facing room & enjoy the spectacular views from your balcony. $$$–$$$$

🏠 **Grand Hotel Prisank** (110 rooms) Borovška 93; ✆ 04 588 4477; f 04 588 4479; e info@hitholidays-kg.si; www.hitholidays-kg.si. Kranjska Gora's pinkest hotel has modern rooms & a pleasant resort-hotel ambience. $$$–$$$$

🏠 **Hotel Larix** (120 rooms) Borovška 99; ✆ 04 588 4100; f 04 588 4479; e info@hitholidays-kg.si; www.hitholidays-kg.si. Guestrooms are bright & clean. The wellness centre has a sauna, pool, steam room, solarium & a variety of spa treatments. $$$–$$$$

🏠 **Hotel Kotnik** (15 rooms) Borovška 75; ✆ 04 588 1564; f 04 588 1859; www.hotel-kotnik.si. Pleasant, small & bright yellow hotel at the heart of town. Good-sized rooms are light & comfortable. $$$–$$$$

🏠 **Hotel Lek** (69 rooms) Vršiška 38; ✆ 04 588 1520; f 04 588 1343; e recepcija@hotel-lek.si; www.hotel-lek.si. Modern hotel with pool, sauna, hot tub, tennis courts & stylish rooms. $$$–$$$$$

🏠 **Hotel Alpina** (105 rooms) Vitranška 12; ✆ 04 589 3100; f 04 589 3051; e info@hitholidays-kg.si; www.hitholidays-kg.si. Reasonably priced hotel with a sauna & steam room. $$$

🏠 **Vila Triglav** (8 rooms) Ivana Krivca 6; ✆ 04 588 1478; e info@rozle.si; www.rozle.si. 2km out of town near Jasna Lake, with sauna, jacuzzi, pool & fitness room. Rooms & apts sleep 2–4 people. $$$–$$$$

🏠 **Hostel Nika** (66 beds) Čičare 2; ✆ 04 588 1000; e Zvone.oreskovic@s5.net. Located just north of the centre this hostel offers clean & functional accommodation in sgl, dbl, twin & dormitory rooms. Rates are pp. $

Camping

⛺ **Camping Špik** Jezerci 21, Gozd Martuljek; ✆ 04 588 4477; f 04 588 4480; e recepcija.spik@ hitholidays-kg.si. 4km east of Kranjska Gora, the campsite has an outdoor pool, children's playground, artificial climbing wall & courts for beach volleyball & tennis. Rates are pp. $

🍴 **WHERE TO EAT**

🍴 **Gostilna Pri Martinu** Borovška 61; ✆ 04 582 0300; ⏰ 10.00–23.00 daily. The modern conservatory & terrace to the rear with views of the mountains compensate for the decidedly average food & brusque service. Soups are a good option as are the specials on the first page of the menu. This *gostilna* also has rooms. $$$

🍴 **Hotel Kotnik** (see *Where to stay*) ⏰ 11.00–22.00 daily. The hotel has 2 good restaurants, one serving pizza & the other grilled meat dishes. $$$

🍴 **Sang Hai** Naselje Slavka Cerneta 34; ✆ 04 588 1346; www.sanghai-restavracija.com; ⏰ 12.00–midnight daily. You may not get the most authentic Chinese meal, but it makes a change from the hearty Slovenian dishes being served up elsewhere. $$$

ENTERTAINMENT AND NIGHTLIFE

🍸 **Cocktail Club Manhattan** Grand Hotel Prisnak, Borovška 93; ✆ 04 588 4820. Lounge bar meets Texan desert, with oversized fossils as décor; truly bizarre. This basement bar also has 2 pool tables, cocktails & a Wurlitzer jukebox playing wonderfully misnamed tunes like 'Even better than the real thin', & 'Number of the best'.

🍸 **Papa Joe Razor** Borovška 83; ✆ 04 588 1526. Good food & 05.00 closing make this late-night bar-restaurant a big hit.

☆ **HIT Casino** Vršiška 23; ✆ 04 458 8200; www.hit.si. South of the town centre & just across the Pišnica River, the casino is open 24 hrs. If gambling isn't your thing then the bars & cabaret offer alternative entertainment. Strictly over 18s, with passport or national identity required for entry.

A monthly guide to events at the Casino can be picked up around town.
☆ **Casino Larix** Borovška 99; ✆ 04 588 4700; www.casino-larix.com. Smaller & centrally located casino attached to the Hotel Larix.

OTHER PRACTICALITIES You can find banks, ATMs, shops, supermarkets, post office, bars and cafés on Borovška.

✉ **Post office** Borovška 92; ⊕ 08.00–18.00 Mon–Fri, 08.00–12.00 Sat.

WHAT TO SEE

Liznjek House (*Liznjekova Hiša; Borovška 63;* ✆ *04 588 1999; adult/concession €2.30/€1.70;* ⊕ *Jan–Mar, May–Oct & Dec 10.00–17.00 Tue–Fri, 10.00–16.00 Sat/Sun*) This 18th-century house in the preserved old quarter of town provides an insight into life before Kranjska Gora emerged as a major tourist resort. It may have been the home of a wealthy local landowner but the chimney-less black kitchen and some other period features are typical of Gorenjska, and the museum is a decent wet-weather option.

Church of the Assumption (Cerkev Marijinega Vnebovzetja) Like many of the other churches in the Gorenjska region, the parish church, at Borovška 78, has evolved over time, with different aspects added through the centuries. Local literature claims that there has been a church in the town since the 14th century, although the building that stands today started life in 1510. The addition of St Joseph's Chapel in 1758 expanded the northern end of the church, while the construction of the choir in 1837 united the church and its tower. The last renovation also brought a further chapel and Gothic windows. Towards the end of the 19th century the church acquired neo-Gothic altars and the ceiling frescoes were repainted.

A recent restoration programme has seen the church returned to its 19th-century splendour. The vaulted ceiling of the nave, part of the original 16th-century structure, is one of the most impressive in Gorenjska and it is well worth tearing yourself away from the mountains to have a good look. The church is also home to two Gothic sculptures that many locals date back to the late 15th century.

ACTIVITIES

Skiing and snowboarding The massif around Kranjska Gora, with around 30km of pistes and 40km of cross-country courses, is one big winter-sports playground during the months when snow conditions are good, usually from December to early March, though the season can last a bit longer depending on the weather. Facilities are improving every year, with new ski lifts and floodlights for night skiing recently added. There are myriad ski slopes in and around Kranjska Gora with plenty of choices for everyone from tentative beginners looking to learn the ropes with the help of the numerous instructors in the resort, right through to experienced skiers seeking an adrenaline-pumping challenge on the Ruteč and Zelenci. The slopes include both downhill and slalom options. Snowboarding has also come of age in Kranjska Gora over the last few years.

Kranjska Gora Ski Centre Borovška 103; ✆ 04 588 1414; f 04 588 1181; www.rtc-zicnice- kranjskagora.si. The ski centre sells ski passes valid from 2 hrs to 10 days, which cost from €60.

Discounts are available on passes for children & those over 55.

Intersport Bernik Borovška 88a; ✆ 04 588 1470; www.intersport-bernik.com. This jack of all trades offers everything from bike hire, quad biking, walking & paintballing to skiing & ski-equipment hire. They also have a ski school & a winter ice-skating rink, & let apts.

ASK Kranjska Gora Ski School Borovška 99a; ✆ 04 588 5302; e sola@ask-kg.com; www.ask-kg.com. Tuition for cross-country skiing, alpine skiing & snowboarding is given on a group or individual basis. Adult courses with 2 hrs of lessons each day cost €28–76 for 1–6 days. Private lessons cost €25.40 per hr for 1 or 2 people. Discounts for children.

Sport Point Borovška 93a; ✆ 04 588 4883; www.sport-point.si. Great shop renting skis, sledges, ski boots, ice skates & mountain bikes. It also has a good coffee shop.

Walking The walking options around Kranjska Gora are almost endless, from one-hour low-level walks around the fringes of the resort, through to epic adventures over precipitous ridges to the lakes of Bohinj and Bled or serious ascents of the voluminous peaks that shoot like rockets above. Mike Newbury's book *A Guide to Walks & Scrambles in the Julian Alps Based on Kranjska Gora* (see *Appendix 2, Further Information*) features a number of routes. On a clear day the easy stroll to Jasna Lake, 2km to the south of Kranjska Gora, is unforgettable as this impossibly blue lake shimmers with the Julian Alps as a dramatic backdrop. A statue of Zlatorog is on hand to provide perfect tourist photo opportunities.

Climbing The local men have held a reputation for centuries as first-class walking guides and the art is still very much in evidence in the resort today. There is a tempting range of testing peaks to choose from including Jalovec (2,645m), Prisank (2,547m), Razor (2,601m) and Škrlatica (2,740m). You can also reach the summit of Triglav from Mojstrana, 13km west of Kranjska Gora, though it is certainly not the fastest or easiest ascent.

Spas and swimming pools When the weather conspires against outdoor activities, or if you just feel like it after a limb-bursting day on the slopes, a number of hotels including the Larix, Kompas, Lek and Alpina offer heated indoor swimming pools and more specialised spa services. Non-residents can generally pay to use the facilities.

SPECIAL EVENTS

Ski Jumping World Championships Planica, a village close to Kranjska Gora, lays claim to be the home of ski jumping and the sport has come home to roost with a round of the World Championships now held in February or March every year on the site of the first-ever World Championships in 1972. Fittingly the 100m barrier was conquered here in 1936 and the 200m barrier was smashed in 1994 by the Slovenian teenager Primož Peterka on the giant ski jump that was built in the 1960s. The World Championships are a major sporting event and many Slovenes also use this as the perfect excuse to spend a few days immersed in the restaurants and bars of the packed resort of Kranjska Gora.

OVER THE VRŠIČ PASS TO PRIMORSKA

The vertiginous route up from Kranjska Gora over the Vršič Pass to Primorska is one of the most dramatic mountain passes, and certainly the highest in Slovenia, a stunning experience whether you are walking, cycling (poor you) or driving. The route sweeps up in a flurry of winding turns and improbable ascents, rushing onwards through the harsh rock and ice. Hundreds of Russian prisoners of war died to forge this road and even today the extremities of this landscape are demonstrated as it is often closed for much of the winter, not reopening until late spring. The route is easy to follow and each turn is numbered with a marker.

Many people do not set aside enough time for exploring the Vršič Pass properly, choosing instead to use it as a scenic route down into Primorska and on to the coast, though if you do this you are missing out on a lot so try to squeeze in at least a long day with your own transport (local buses are very limited). **Lake Jasna** (Jasna Jezero) is just beyond Kranjska Gora and worth visiting before you push on to the **Russian Chapel** (Ruska Kapelica, turn No 8) dedicated to the fallen Russian soldiers of World War I, most of whom perished as a result of landslides. Further up the road is a cemetery for some of them (turn No 21), before you continue on to Vršič and the highest point on the road at 1,611m, where you have to pay to park.

From Vršič the road starts to curl south in search of the Adriatic, but if you have time you can take a while and tackle some of the hiking trails that lead off from here (there is a mountain hut on Vršič itself). At turn No 49 you can stop and follow a path to the source of the mighty Soča River, with which you will become very well acquainted if you are planning to spend any time in Primorska. The river lies around 2km from the road. Now you are in Primorska proper. The descent is through the Trenta Valley with the adventure-sports oasis of Bovec and the culinary centre of Kobarid awaiting to the south.

SLOVENIA
SKIING

I FEEL
SLOVENIA

www.slovenia.info

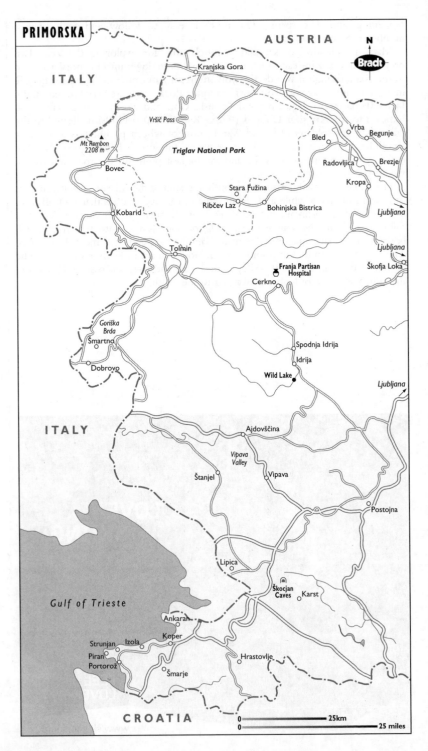

5

Primorska

If Slovenia really is, to borrow the cliché, 'Europe in Miniature', then Primorska is surely Slovenia in miniature. The smorgasbord of scenery ranges from the sweeping mountains of its northern Julian Alps fringes, right down the verdant Soča (pronounced 'socha') Valley to the harsh Karst and finally to the Adriatic Sea. This is Slovenia's only region with a coastline, although in this book we have given its coastal strip a chapter of its own (*Chapter 6, The Slovenian Adriatic*). After a morning skiing or climbing in the Alps you can be savouring a fresh seafood lunch by the Adriatic within a couple of hours and this makes Primorska a popular destination for visitors, from those looking to ski or fling themselves off a bridge on a bungee jump to those just wanting to relax with a glass of wine in the bucolic escape of Goriška Brda. The food here is a joy as the climate is perfect for growing various varieties of fruit and vegetables, with plump olives, sturdy red wines and flavoursome tomatoes, the last something of a rarity in many European supermarkets these days.

BOVEC

In the northern corner of Primorska is a town that was profiting from rural package tourism until the implosion of Yugoslavia in 1991. There followed a disastrous earthquake in 1998 that destroyed many of its buildings, though thankfully it did not take the life of any of its inhabitants. In 2004, the region was hit once again by a serious earthquake. Rather than succumbing to these blows, Bovec has picked itself up and engineered a remarkable re-emergence as a world-class adventure-sports playground and today the outlook is looking rosier. Bovec enjoys a stunning location set just to the south of the Julian Alps in the upper Soča Valley near the eponymous river renowned for its vivid emerald colour. This world of craggy peaks, wild waters and equally wild weather may today be an oasis for adrenaline junkies, but in World War I it was a living and dying hell for a million soldiers who perished on the Soča Front. On a wet day when incessant cold rain and high winds hamper many activities Bovec can be a pretty miserable place, but as soon as there is a gap in the clouds out come the rafts, canoes, skis and mountain bikes.

GETTING THERE Bovec is accessible by bus from Ljubljana (3½ hours), Nova Gorica (1½ hours), Tolmin (50 minutes), Kobarid (30 minutes) and, in July and August, Kranjska Gora (1½ hours). Buses stop near the Letni Vrt Restaurant on Trg Golobarskih Žrtev.

GETTING AROUND Most of the activity specialists in Bovec offer bicycle hire with half-day rental starting at around €10, up to five-day rentals from €50 (see *Extreme-sports operators*, page 128).

🚖 **Taxi** ↘ 05 388 6128

TOURIST INFORMATION/LOCAL TOUR OPERATORS

⛏ Tourist Information Centre Trg Golobarskih Žrtev 8; ☎ 05 389 6444; f 05 389 6445; e info@bovec.si; www.bovec.si; ⏰ Jul/Aug 09.00–20.00 daily; Jan–Sep 09.00–17.00 Mon–Fri; Sep–Dec 09.00–12.00 & 16.00–18.00 Sat, 09.00–12.00 Sun

Gotour Bovec Trg Golobarskih Žrtev 50; ☎ 05 389 6366; f 05 389 6368; e gotour.bovec@siol.net; www.gotour.bovec.com. Arranges private accommodation.

⌂ WHERE TO STAY

Private rooms are generally easy to find; simply look for the *sobe* or *zimmer frei* signs in the quiet Brdo area of town and on Rupa, which runs past Bovec's hotels. Alternatively the tourist office and the tour operator listed above will help you book a room.

⌂ Hotel Dobra Vila (10 rooms) Mala Vas 112; ☎ 05 389 6400; www.dobra-vila-bovec.com. Our favourite place to stay in Bovec is an attractive boutique hotel housed in an early 20th-century building. The hotel is peppered with unique design touches. $$$–$$$$

⌂ Hotel Kanin (125 rooms) Ledina 6; ☎ 05 388 6022; f 05 388 6081; e hoteli.bovec@siol.net; www.hotel-kanin.com. Feels like an American motel, but with stunning views from the private balconies. There is also a good-sized swimming pool, a sauna & a small fitness room. Beware the hordes of marauding children in the corridors. $$$

⌂ Alp Hotel (103 rooms) Trg Golobarskih Žrtev 48; ☎ 05 388 4000; f 05 388 4002; e hotelalp1@siol.net; www.alp-chandler.si. British-owned & run 3-star hotel with friendly service & good-sized rooms. $$–$$$

⌂ Apartments Kaninska Vas (395 apts) Kaninska Vas 7; ☎ 05 388 6811; f 05 389 5588; e tusi@siol.net; www.tusi.si. The apts are in 23 houses just 400m from the centre of town & sleeping 2–6 people. All with private kitchens, bathrooms & satellite TV. Some with balconies. $$–$$$

Camping

⚲ Kajak Kamp Toni Vodenca 1; ☎ 05 389 6454; e info@kajakkamptoni.com; www.kayakkamptoni.com. Located at the confluence of the Soča & Koritnica rivers, with space for 50 tents & 20 caravans. Kamp Toni is on the spot where the Germans launched their gas bombs in their Front-busting assault during World War I. Rates are pp. $

⚲ Camp Liza Vodenca 4; ☎ 05 389 6370; e info@camp-liza.com; www.camp-liza.com. Also near the confluence of the Soča & Koritnica, with space for 45 tents. Rates are pp. $

⚲ Kamp Polovnik Ledina 8; ☎ 05 388 6007; e kamp.plovnik@siol.net; www.kamp-plovnik.com. Small campsite with just 70 pitches located 500m from the centre of town. Rates are pp. $

⚲ Camping Trenta Trenta 60A, Trenta; m 041 615 966; www.campingtrenta.of.com. 45 pitches. Rates are pp. $

✗ WHERE TO EAT

✗ Gostišče Martinov Hram Trg Golobarskih Žrtev 27; ☎ 05 388 6214; ⏰ 10.00–22.00 Wed–Mon. Decent restaurant with a pleasant outdoor terrace. Soups, salads & pastas are perfect for a light meal. Fish, grilled meats & Balkan specialities also feature on the extensive menu. $$$

✗ Gostilna Sovdat Trg Golobarskih Žrtev 24; ☎ 05 388 6027; ⏰ 11.00–22.00 Mon–Sat. Slovenian dishes in more intimate surrounds. $$$

✗ Gostišče Stari Kovač Rupa 3; ☎ 05 388 669; e stari_kovac@hotmail.com; www.starikovac.com; ⏰ 12.00–23.00 Tue–Sun. Small inn serving delicious wood-fired pizza in its restaurant, terrace or summer garden. They also have 3 well-equipped apts sleeping 2–8 people. $$$

✗ Letni Vrt Trg Golobarskih Žrtev 12; ☎ 05 389 6384; ⏰ 11.00–22.00 Wed–Mon. Centrally located restaurant serving pizzas, fresh trout & grills. The restaurant is more atmospheric in the summer when its ornate garden is open. $$$

ENTERTAINMENT AND NIGHTLIFE

⛁ Plec Café Trg Golobarskih Žrtev 18; ⏰ until 01.00 daily. This café-bar has pool tables & a garden.

⚲ Pink Panther Bar Kaninska Vas 7; m 031 588 854; ⏰ until 01.00 daily. Lively bar close to the Kaninska Vas Apts.

OTHER PRACTICALITIES You will find supermarkets, outdoor-clothing shops, banks and a pharmacy on Trg Golobarskih Žrtev.

✉ **Post office** Trg Golobarskih Žrtev 9;
🕓 08.00–18.00 Mon–Fri, 08.00–12.00 Sat

WHAT TO SEE

War museums While Kobarid's first-rate war museum is rightly regarded as giving the most comprehensive insight into the fighting on the Soča Front, there are three small private museums in Bovec that are, if anything, even more poignant as they have been put together by locals in their own homes. All three are worth visiting and are truly unique.

The **Museum of the 4th Bosnia Herzegovina Regiment** (*Brdo 53;* ✆ *05 388 6577; http://prohereditate.com/sl/museum/C0004; Miloš Domevšček,* 🕓 *by arrangement*) was compiled by the grandson of a Bosnian soldier who fought for the Austro-Hungarians. He started collecting artefacts from the battlefields surrounding Bovec in 1997 after taking an interest in the old sepia image of his grandfather that hung in the family home, and by 2001 he had gathered enough to open a modest collection. Today the two-room museum is awash with old rifles, grenades and pieces of kit, with some unusual items such as an STD medicine pack with instructions in nine languages. The array of Slovenian beer bottles dropped by the troops on their way to the lines harks back to the days when there were over 100 brewers in Slovenia. There are also rooms for rent in the house for those wanting to stay with the colourful owner, though he speaks only Slovene and German.

Other collections include the **Museum of the 87th Regiment** (*Kot 56;* ✆ *05 388 6249; http://prohereditate.com/sl/museum/C0013; Ivo Ivančič,* 🕓 *by arrangement*) and **A Farewell to Arms** (*Klanc 1;* ✆ *05 388 6259; http:// prohereditate.com/sl/museum/C0013; Sašo Prochazka,* 🕓 *by arrangement*).

The lines outside Bovec Anyone wanting to get a real feel for the war should head back north from Bovec to the section of the lines that has been opened up as an outdoor museum. Here you can walk amongst the old trenches and ramble around an old Austro-Hungarian position complete with a cramped officers' quarters, fire holes and original barbed wire. The shell crater on the summit brings back the harsh reality of what happened here, a stark contrast with the beauty of the Soča River which rushes past below.

Continue on towards the Predel Pass and you will come to the sturdy **Kluže Fortress** (*http://www.kluze.net; adult/concessions €3/€2;* 🕓 *Jun/Sep 10.00–17.00 Sun–Fri, 10.00–19.00 Sat; Jul/Aug 09.00–21.00 daily*) right by the road. This was a crucial hub for the Austro–Hungarians who built Kluže, which dates from 1882, on the site of an earlier fortress. If you plan ahead and ask at the tourist information office in Bovec you can time your visit to coincide with performances by the 1313 Troop, a group of local amateurs who dress up in original consumes and put on a show that recalls the days of company 1313, so called as they were allocated a 1,313m-high ridge during the war. The performance is in a hotchpotch of German, Slovene and Croatian, reflecting the varied ethnic mix of the Central Powers troops, but it still gives English-speaking visitors an insight into those dark days. If you are feeling sorry for yourself on a wet and chilly day spare a thought for the World War I soldiers and cast your eyes across the road to the precipitous rock walls and the rudimentary metal stairs that the men had to haul themselves up to get to their positions.

THE SOČA FRONT

The Soča (Isonzo in Italian) Front was the scene of some of the most savage and brutal warfare ever fought. Looking at the hulking, mist-shrouded peaks and sweeping snow-ravaged ridges high above the Soča River today it is hard to imagine that anyone could fight a war in this terrain, and it was the weather and terrain that often proved as vicious an enemy as the opposing army. The front, stretching all the way from Mt Rombon in the north down towards the Adriatic coast in the south, opened in May 1915 as Italy declared war on the Central Powers. Soon barbed wire had been strewn, trenches forged and heavy guns heaved into position as industrialised warfare came to Primorska. Much of the war was spent with the Italians launching offensive after offensive, which the Austro-Hungarian forces managed to repel, with little territory actually captured after the initial flush of Italian success.

The picture changed inexorably in October 1917 as the Italians went from dreams of further gains to being shoved right back across the plains of Friuli during the 'Twelfth Offensive'. The spark came from the German units who had been brought in to bolster the Austro-Hungarians. They dreamed up the 'Kobarid Breakthrough' which brought a new tactic – the *blitzkrieg* or 'lightning war'. Accompanying the usual heavy artillery onslaught came the use of gas as the Germans wiped out the opposing lines just north of Bovec in minutes. The Central Powers seized the opportunity and rushed into a rapid advance and soon the Italians were in full retreat, a disorganised scramble vividly captured by Hemingway in his novel *A Farewell to Arms* (Hemingway served as an ambulance driver and was wounded during the fighting).

The Italians had been vanquished from Primorska but by the end of the war around a million men had lost their lives in the region's mountains and many of their skeletons still lie hidden amongst the rock and ice. The tactics of the *blitzkrieg* that were pioneered during the Kobarid Offensive were to be felt by many European nations during World War II and its spectacular success was not lost on one young German soldier at Kobarid, Erwin Rommel.

ADVENTURE ACTIVITIES The area around Bovec could have been sculpted with activity holidays in mind, with an almost endless list of possibilities for those willing to get stuck in. An increasing number of operators in the UK and Germany are starting to offer niche adventure breaks, but it is usually cheaper to organise things in Slovenia for yourself – easy enough to do but you may want to call a few days ahead to make sure that there are spaces and equipment. Note that all rafters and kayakers wanting to go out on the Soča by themselves need to get a permit, which can be purchased from the Bovec tourist office. As adventure tourism takes off the network of operators (see the following *Extreme-sports operators* section) is growing and overlapping so you may find yourself booking a kayak trip through the people you have just rafted with, but with the actual trip run by another operator, or vice versa. As competition grows prices are becoming flexible so look out for flyers offering good deals and ask around. Also keep an eye open for adrenaline packages that allow you to tackle three or four activities in one packed day if you are short of time. Safety is a real concern on the wild Soča River after a number of fatalities in recent years – the general rule of thumb is that if the locally trained Slovenian guides are not venturing out then you would be wise to follow suit. Note that spring is the best time for really testing conditions; as the season progresses the river level tends to drop.

Kayaking The Soča River is perfect for white-water kayaking (in the stubby short kayaks rather than the longer and slimmer sea kayaks). At any time there are challenging stretches to tackle for experienced kayakers, but after heavy rain the Soča really comes into its own and soon has less hardy paddlers scurrying upstream for respite. Kayak trips and one-to-five-day kayak courses are readily available. Courses € 50–250, kayak trip around € 40.

Canyoning The idea of hauling your way up through the gushing waterfalls and rocky pools of Učja, Sušec or Mlinarica may not seem too appealing, but this fun sport is open to any fit adult. You will be kitted out with a life jacket and helmet, and safety standards are generally high. From € 35.

Hydrospeed This is an adventure sport that is not as well known as its rafting or kayaking cousins, but if anything it gets you far closer to the water. Kitted out with a wetsuit, helmet, flippers and flotation board, you hurl yourself into the waters for an unforgettable adrenaline rush. From € 30.

Potholing Slovenia is a world-class potholing destination and Bovec makes a good base for tackling the caves of the Kanin and Rombon lake basins. Descents are possible to depths of 1.5km, but conditions can change rapidly so local advice should always be sought; it is also advisable to go with a local operator who has detailed knowledge of the caves. From € 35.

Tandem paragliding Tandem paragliding from the lofty heights of Mangart and Kanin is one of Slovenia's most exhilarating experiences, a genuinely unforgettable adventure that has people raving for the rest of their lives about the views from the Julian Alps right down to the Gulf of Trieste. A tandem flight takes around 25 minutes and costs around € 85 with Alpe Šport Vančar (see *Extreme-sports operators*).

Mountain biking The sport is still in its infancy in Slovenia, but Outdoor Freaks (see *Extreme-sports operators*) in Bovec now has a first-rate stock of bikes and the experience to tailor some excellent trips into the surrounding mountains, as well as ad hoc tours that depend on the weather and track conditions. A new permanent track opened on the slopes of Kanin in 2005. Bike hire is from € 5 per hour and € 15 per day.

Skiing The main ski fields, with the highest slopes in Slovenia at up to 2,220m, are on the slopes of Mt Kanin, where good ski conditions start in December and can linger right on into late May. The ATC Kanin ski resort (*Dvor 43;* \ *05 389 6310;* f *05 388 6930;* e *kanin@siol.net; www.bovec.net/kanin*) boasts over 9km of sledding tracks and a ski school, while passes allow skiers to use slopes that extend into Italy and Austria. Ski guides will also take skiers on tours into the neighbouring Krnica Valley. The four-person cable cars (*€ 8.50/€ 11.50 single/return;* ⊕ *08.00–16.00*) that transport skiers to the upper ski station operate in July and August, providing a great way for walkers and mountain bikers to reach the higher altitudes. Group and private tuition available.

Other winter sports Snowboarding and other types of skiing, such as cross-country and telemark skiing, are also available on Kanin and these activities can be organised through ATC Kanin (see *Skiing* above). Sledging, snow rafting and ice climbing are also becoming increasingly popular (see *Extreme-sports operators*).

Walking and hiking In summer the Kanin cable car is the most obvious way to open up the views quickly. From the terminus there are myriad options. One of the most popular walks is to the Boka Waterfall, widely regarded as the most powerful and impressive in Slovenia, while a large number of trails climb Mt Kanin, Mt Rombon and other peaks. As with any high-altitude hiking it is advisable to hire the services of a qualified guide, who will accompany you on trips that last a day through to a week – seek advice at the tourist office or from one of the extreme-sports tour operators.

White-water rafting The Soča River, usually rated as grade three to four, is a serious white-water rafting river and should not be treated lightly. Rafts and other gear can be hired, but only experienced visitors should even consider going unaccompanied as there are real dangers, as has been demonstrated by recent fatalities. Going out with one of the increasing number of local operators is the safest and often the most fun option as they look after you for the whole trip (usually one to two hours on the river) and the guides know the river well – if they do not consider conditions suitable they will adapt their plans and choose another point of entry. Mini-rafts for two (known locally as 'outsiders') are also available. Prices start at €20 per person, but can rise to €40 or more for a one–two-hour trip depending on the duration and number of people taking part.

Bungee jumping Flinging yourself off a bridge with only a rubber band for company is a relatively new phenomenon to Slovenia. From April to October there are regular jumps from the 55m-high Solkan Bridge, a long way down to the mighty Soča. From €35.

Extreme-sports operators

Outdoor Freaks Klanc 9a; ☎ 05 389 6490; e outdoorfreaks@siol.net; www.freakoutdoor.com. Offer mountain biking, mountain-bike rental, rafting, kayaking, tubing, hydrospeed, canyoning, & guides for those with their own equipment.

Soča Rafting Sports Centre Trg Golobarskih Žrtev; ☎ 05 389 6200; f 05 389 6202; e info@socarafting.si; www.socarafting.si. Offering rafting trips, canyoning, a kayak school, kayaking, canoeing, hydrospeed, caving & mountain biking. In winter they run a ski & snowboard school, rent skis & organise tobogganing. The centre also arranges accommodation & excursions.

Sport Mix Trg Golobarskih Žrtev 18; ☎ 05 389 6160; e traft@siol.net; www.sportmix.traftbovec.si. Arrange rafting, mini-rafting, canyoning & kayak tuition, as well as bicycle & scooter rental.

Alpe Šport Vančar Golobarskih Žrtev 20 trg; ☎ 05 389 6350; f 05 389 6351; e info@bovecsport.com; www.bovecsport.com. Organise rafting, mini-rafting, kayak lessons,

hydrospeed, canyoning, tandem paragliding & winter sledding.

Avantura m 041 718 317; e bovecavantura@hotmail.com; www.avantura.org. With tandem paragliding, tandem parachute jumps, caving, canyoning & summer tobogganing. In winter they offer tobogganing, ski touring & ice climbing.

Bovec Rafting Team Mala Vas 106; ☎ 05 388 6128; e bovec.rafting.team@siol.net; www.brt-ha.si. Kayak school, rafting, hydrospeed, canyoning, cycling tours, bike & equipment hire, mountain guides & free-climbing school. Snow rafting in the winter months.

Top Extreme Rafting Trg Golobarskih Žrtev 19; m 041 620 636; e info@top.si; www.top.si. Offer bungee jumping, hydrospeed, kayaking, rafting, mini-rafting, canyoning & mountain biking.

Sport Extreme Stresova 1; ☎ 05 388 5308; e x.point@siol.net. Arrange watersports, provide a guide service & organise dog-sled rides for children. Sport Extreme also offer tourist-agency services.

KOBARID

Immortalised by Ernest Hemingway in his epic *A Farewell to Arms*, Kobarid is a modest town in the Soča Valley whose name is inexorably bound up with World

War I and the horrors of the savage Soča Front (see box *The Soča Front*, page 126). These days it is a sleepy, unassuming and charming little place without the worst elements of other tourist resorts like Bovec and Kranjska Gora, with a fairly quiet main square, some of the best fish restaurants in the country and a fold of tree-clad hills on all sides. The war, though, is never far away and visitors looking to delve into its history will not be disappointed with the world-class Kobarid War Museum and a ramble of military positions to explore in the surrounding forests. There is also a number of private war museums in Kobarid. Today it is food that makes Kobarid famous, with Slovenes, Italians and Austrians making regular sojourns to this culinary Mecca. As it is so close to Bovec and the Soča River, Kobarid is a good alternative base for adventure-sports enthusiasts.

HISTORY Although World War I is the period most associated with this modest Soča Valley town, human settlement in the region actually dates back to at least the Iron Age; however, the first written mention of Kobarid, as Canoretum, was only made in 1184. Roman artefacts have been found dotted around the town and the remains of a Roman fort have also been discovered on the hillsides above. Evidence of its rich history is still being unearthed on the hills surrounding Kobarid and especially at Tonocov Castle, the site of a number of fortifications down the centuries. After World War I the Italians occupied Kobarid, the Slovene language was banned and the linden tree in Kobarid's main square, a national symbol of Slovenia, was torn down. In World War II Kobarid once again rose to prominence when partisans established the Kobarid Republic in defiance of the German occupation of Yugoslavia.

GETTING THERE Regular buses link Kobarid with Nova Gorica (45 minutes), Bovec (30 minutes) and Tolmin (20 minutes), while less frequent services from Ljubljana (3 hours), Cerkno ($1^1/_2$ hours) and Idrija (1 hour 50 minutes) also stop at the town.

TOURIST INFORMATION

🗺 **Tourist Information Centre** Gregorčičeva 8; ✆ 05 380 0490; f 05 380 0483; e info.kobarid@ lto-sotocje.si; www.lto-sotocje.si; ⊕ Jul/Aug 09.00–20.00 Mon–Fri, 09.00–12.30 & 15.30–20.00 Sat; Sep–Jun 09.00–12.30 & 13.30–19.00 Mon–Fri, 09.00–13.00 Sat

WHERE TO STAY

🏠 **Hiša Franko** (12 rooms) Staro Selo 1; ✆ 05 389 4120; e info@hisafranko.com; www.hisafranko.com. This boutique hotel with neat design touches & a minimalist feel is our favourite place to stay in Kobarid. Some rooms have massage baths & or private terraces. $$$–$$$$

🏠 **Hotel Hvala** (31 rooms) Trg Svobode 1; ✆ 05 389 9300; f 05 388 5322; e topli.val@siol.net; www.topli-val-sp.si. Welcoming 4-star hotel run by the Hvala family. Guestrooms are light & spacious with attractive design touches. The hotel also boasts one of Slovenia's finest restaurants, the Topli Val, & a Finnish sauna. $$$

🏠 **Restavracija Kotlar** (6 rooms) Trg Svobode 11; ✆ 05 389 1110; f 05 389 1112; e kotlar.restavracija@siol.net; www.kotlar.si. Stylish & understated dbl rooms with a small indoor pool, Turkish bath & solarium. $$$

🏠 **ApartMa-Ra** Gregorčičeva 6c; m 041 641 899. This welcoming B&B located close to the museum is a good budget option. $$

Camping

⛺ **Kamp Koren** Drežniške Ravne 33; ✆ 05 389 1311; e info@kamp-koren.si; www.kamp-koren.si. Well-equipped 4-star campsite with a laundry, sauna, shop, internet access, climbing wall, children's playground & bar, located just beneath the Napoleon Bridge, 500m north of Kobarid. Space for 40 tents. Choose your spot well & you will have views of the Soča River or Mt Krn. Rates are pp. $

WHERE TO EAT

✖ Hiša Franko (see *Where to stay*) ⊕ 12.00–22.00 Tue–Sun. Just out of town this is another excellent & creative restaurant that manages to serve up the likes of *sushi* as well as traditional 'slow food' Slovenian dishes. Much younger & funkier feeling than Kobarid's other dining options. **$$$$**

✖ Restaurant Topli Val Trg Svobode 1; ↘ 05 389 9300; www.topli-val-sp.si; ⊕ 12.00–22.00 daily. With a culinary tradition spanning 3 decades the Hvala family has earned itself a well-deserved reputation for first-rate seafood. This is definitely the place for a splurge with exquisite sea bass & tunafish tartar, lobster & mouth-watering fish platters for 2. Knowledgeable staff are on hand to help you choose the perfect wine to accompany your meal. **$$$**

✖ Kotlar Trg Svobode 11; ↘ 05 389 1110; www.kotlar.si; ⊕ 12.00–23.00 Thu–Mon. Whilst the food at the Kotlar may not quite match that served at the Topli Val, it is very good indeed. The restaurant has been serving simple fish dishes for over a decade. Creative touches include the likes of scallops encased in cheese. Freshwater trout with potatoes & spinach is a more traditional local speciality. **$$$**

✖ Gostilna Breza Mučeniška 17; ↘ 05 389 0040; ⊕ 12.00–23.00 Tue–Sun. Traditional Slovenian food is on offer in this popular & unpretentious eatery. **$$$**

ENTERTAINMENT AND NIGHTLIFE

♀ Bar Pri Gotarju Krilanova 3; ↘ 05 388 5743. Kobarid's liveliest bar attracts a young crowd with its cheap draught beer (Union & Laško) & funky music. The interior of the bar itself is smoky & nothing special, but the outdoor terrace is a pleasant enough place to sit on a warm night.

OTHER PRACTICALITIES

✉ **Post office** Trg Svobode 2; ⊕ 08.00–09.30, 10.30–15.30 & 16.00–18.00 Mon–Fri, 08.00–12.00 Sat

$ **Nova KMB Banka** Trg Svobode 2; ⊕ 08.00–18.00 Mon–Fri, 08.00–12.00 Sat

WHAT TO SEE

Kobarid War Museum (*Kobariški Muzej; Gregorčičeva 10;* ↘ *05 389 0000;* f *05 389 0002;* e *info@kobariski-muzej.si; www.kobariski-muzej.si; adult/concession €4/€3;* ⊕ *Apr–Sep 09.00–18.00 Mon–Fri, 09.00–19.00 Sat/Sun; Oct–Mar 10.00–17.00 Mon–Fri, 09.00–18.00 Sat/Sun*) The excellence of the museum was recognised by a Council of Europe award in 1993. Opened in 1990 just as Yugoslavia was about to descend into its own bout of savagery the museum calmly and thoughtfully explores a range of aspects of the Soča Front, from the grim realities of the front line to the sufferings in the military hospitals further back, all without being over-emotional or judgemental. The highlight is the excellent section on the Kobarid Breakthrough. The white room describes the awful winter conditions, while the black room features some graphic images of the badly injured and dead. Staff at the museum can also arrange various guided walks.

Church of St Anthony (Cerkev Sv Antona) Haunting the slopes above the town is a legacy of Italian fascism and a poignant tribute to the Italian fallen during World War I. The harsh columned ossuary that surrounds the Church of St Anthony was commissioned by Mussolini in the 1930s during the Italian occupation and the remains of over 7,000 Italians lie here. The main staircase is dedicated to the unknown soldiers, while the names of the others are sculpted into the walls that encircle the church.

World War I walking tour Delving into the hills where thousands of Italian troops manned their positions before being wiped out by the Kobarid Breakthrough is an excellent way of getting a real feel for what happened. Pick up the free 'Kobarid Historical Walk' leaflet from the Kobarid War Museum. Do not be fooled by the fact that it is only 5km as the crow flies or by promises that it is an easy walk, as in reality this circular walk will take you a good three hours if you want to take in everything, and when it rains the slippery, steep paths and trenches can be hazardous and energy-sapping. It is well worth the effort, though, both for the military history and the sweeping views of the Soča Valley opened up *en route*.

As you have already covered stop No 1 of the walk in the museum, and there is little to see at the old Roman settlement of Gradič, it is perhaps best to start from the **Italian Charnel House** (stop No 3). Although the path is waymarked (a splotch of paint – the symbol of the War Museum) it can be tricky to follow and you may end up having to double back to correct wrong turnings, so keep your wits about you. The trek north to **Tonocov Castle** (Tonocov Grad) takes you through some dense forest and over a gurgling stream before circling back on a steep ascent to the 'castle'. There is little to actually see in what has been a fortification since the Stone Age, with attempts to preserve the site currently blocking access. The crude pulley system that is being used to transport equipment up the hillside harks back to World War I when the Italians fortified the slopes in the same manner.

From Tonocov retrace your steps and cut right along the walkway, following the wooden handrail that leads to the **Italian third line**, which meanders down the hillside in search of the Soča below. A series of bunkers and cleared trenches precedes a set of steep concrete stairs down to the road. Take care when crossing and rejoining the path to the left as cars scream around what is essentially a blind bend. On the final approach to the Soča is a littering of front-line positions where your imagination may start to run away with you, especially on a gloomy windswept day.

The crossing of the Soča is quite dramatic, on a 52m swing bridge that was only completed in 1998, though it is on the exact site of its predecessor where troops crossed in World War I. If the water is too high (check with walkers coming the other way) and you do not want to get wet then there is little point in making the excursion up to the **Kozjak Waterfall** (Slap Kozjak) as it is virtually impossible to negotiate the last section of the path without having to plunge into the water. A steep path marked only in Italian and Slovene scrambles up the hillside back by the bridge. This was the site of a machine-gun position and the observation deck provides a great view of the Soča thundering past. The walk back towards Kobarid is the least interesting section, except for the Napoleon Bridge, where the French emperor's forces once crossed, though the original was destroyed at the start of World War I by retreating Austrian soldiers. Follow the road and you will soon be back in Kobarid with an appetite that only a Soča Valley trout can satiate.

TOLMIN

There is little reason to visit the administrative hub of Tolmin itself, 16km from Kobarid. However, **Maja Outdoor Centre** (*Padlih borcev 1;* ✆ *05 380 0530;* ℺ *05 380 0531;* e *info@maya.si; www.mayan.si*) offer kayaking, white-water rafting (four–eight people), hydrospeed, canyoning and mini-rafting (two–three people) on the Soča River. Their land-based activity programmes include cycling, hiking in the southwestern section of Triglav National Park, caving, free climbing and an Adrenaline Park that comes complete with bridges and obstacles suspended in the trees 8–10m above the ground. If you are going to do a watersport you will need to take a bathing suit, towel and dry T-shirt with you. Similarly to go hiking you will need the appropriate gear. For those with time to kill in Tolmin there is a modest town museum and a decent restaurant.

GETTING THERE Tolmin can be reached by bus from Bovec (50 minutes) or Kobarid (20 minutes).

TOURIST INFORMATION

Tourist Information Centre Petra Skalarja 4; ☎ 05 380 0480; e info@lto-sotocje.si; www.lto-sotocje.si; ⊕ Jul/Aug 09.00–12.30 & 13.30–20.00 Mon–Fri, 09.00–13.30 & 16.30–20.00 Sat/Sun; Sep–Jun 09.00–12.30 & 13.30–16.00 Mon–Fri, 09.00–13.00 Sat/Sun. Stocked with maps & leaflets; the staff can also help you book private accommodation.

WHERE TO STAY

Hotel Krn (48 rooms) Mestni trg 3; ☎ 05 382 1100; f 05 382 1128; e hotel.krn@siol.net; www.hotel-krn.com. If you're planning to stay in Tolmin for an activity-based holiday, or simply to use the unassuming town as a base then the hotel is a good bet, though it tends to be favoured by groups. The hotel also has its own restaurant serving up typical Slovenian dishes. 74 slot machines & a roulette wheel have also been installed in the hotel's new casino. $$$

Pension Rutar (9 rooms) Mestni trg 7; ☎ 05 080 0500; f 05 381 1701; e info@pension-rutar.si; www.pension-rutar.si. If you're looking for something a bit more characterful then you won't go too far wrong with this attractive pension. $$–$$$

Camping

Vili Campground Volarje 9, Volarje; m 031 711 288; e campvili@siol.net. This 20-pitch campsite 6km from Tolmin is a good budget option. Rates are pp. $

WHERE TO EAT

Pension Rutar (see Where to stay) ⊕ 12.00–23.00 Tue–Sun. This is the place to head for tasty Italian food. $$$

Pri Kranjcu Trg I maja 3; ☎ 05 388 182; ⊕ 11.00–23.00 Tue–Sun. Dishing up standard Slovenian fare. $$$

WHAT TO SEE

Tolmin Museum (*Tolminski Muzej; Mestni trg 4; ☎ 05 381 1360; e muzej@tol-muzej.si; www.tol-muzej.si; €2.50; 09.00–16.00 Tue–Fri, 13.00–17.00 Sat–Sun*) At the time of writing three new permanent exhibitions were coming online. When these are complete they will focus on archaeology, history and art history. The museum also administers the Archaeological Museum in Most na Soči, Simon Gregorčič's Birth House in Vrsno, Ciril Komsač's Homestead in Slap ob Idrijci and Simon Rutar's House in Krn.

GORIŠKA BRDA

This corner of Slovenia, surrounded and heavily influenced by Italy on three sides, is one of the country's relative travel secrets. Few British or American visitors to the country are aware of this Slovenian Tuscany, which is less than an hour's drive from Kobarid and easily accessible from the coastal resorts (via Solkan), but a sprinkling of Italian and German gastronomes are already in on the secret. Turning west across the Soča River from the main Bovec–Nova Gorica road at Plave, the road soon starts to climb and the landscape changes. Forests wrap themselves around the rolling Mediterranean hills and streams gurgle down the ridges as the Italian plains of Friuli unfurl in the distance. Soon you will be dawdling amongst sprawling vineyard-covered slopes, cherry and peach orchards and tiny villages clad in orange roof tiles, most topped by bleached white churches. With crisp alpine winds from the north to add flavour and milder Mediterranean breezes to enhance body, this is perfect wine-growing country and many of the country's most famous wine producers such as Movia (apparently Bill Clinton's favourite during his foray into Goriška Brda) and Simčič are based here. Keep your passport handy if you are driving around as it is all too easy to find yourself, by mistake, at one of the five minor border crossings into Italy.

TOURIST INFORMATION

⊠ Tourist Information Centre Trg 25 Maja 2, Dobrovo; ☎ 05 395 9594; f 05 395 9595;   e obcina.brda@guest.arnes.si; www.obcina-brda.si; ⊕ 08.00–16.00 Mon–Thu

🏠 **WHERE TO STAY** The Goriška Brda region provides a real opportunity for a get-away-from-it-all rural retreat. Accommodation is available on tourist farms, in *gostilnas* and in private rooms. Owners will often advertise the fact that they have rooms to let; otherwise the Tourist Information Centre in Dobrovo will be able to help you organise accommodation.

🏠 **Bužinel** Medana 16; ☎ 05 304 5082; e sobe@gostilna-buzinel.si; www.gostilna-buzinel.si. This wine-cellar-cum-restaurant in Medana has light & modern guestrooms in nearby Plešivo, 1.5km from Medana. $$–$$$

🏠 **Tourist Farm Breg** Breg pri Golem Brdu 3; ☎ 05 304 2555; e mirelaperesin@tiscali.it; www.turizembreg.com. Accommodation in a typical farmhouse on the western outskirts of the Goriška Brda region. Serving traditional Hungarian- & Italian-influenced Slovenian food such as goulash, white polenta & *pršut*. $$–$$$

🏠 **Tourist Farm Klinec** Medana 20; ☎/f 05 304 5092; e klinecs5.net; www.klinec.si. Wine cellar with modern rooms in annexe across the street. $$–$$$

✗ **WHERE TO EAT AND DRINK** Roadside *gostilnas* serving traditional cuisine are a good option, as are the restaurants in Dobrovo and Šmartno listed below.

✗ **Dobrovo Castle (Grad Dobrovo)** Grajska 10; ☎ 05 395 9506; ⊕ 12.00–23.00 Tue–Sun. The restaurant accompanies its fine wines with smooth service & high-quality cuisine. Tempting starters include homemade salami, while mains include the likes of veal in Gorgonzola & cream sauce or a seafood platter of squid, sea bass & mussels. Desserts are equally mouth-watering. $$$$

✗ **Turn Šmartno – Inn Cerkin** Smartno 62; ☎ 05 304 1311; ⊕ 11.00–22.00 Tue–Sun. An atmospheric place to try the local cuisine, which is, not surprisingly, strongly influenced by Italy with gnocchi, pasta & polenta (white not yellow) featuring heavily. $$

✗ **Vinoteka Brda** Grajska 10, Dobrovo; m 031 342 369; f 05 395 9211; e info@vinotekabrda.si; www.vinotekabrda.si; ⊕ 11.30–21.00 Tue–Sun. *Pršut* & cheese are always on hand to accompany a seemingly endless list of top-quality wines in this *vinoteka* located in the cellar of Dobrovo Castle. If you call ahead more substantial meals can be arranged. The owner can also help you select wines to take home. Wines on sale range from cheap-&-cheerful efforts through to Simčič Duet at over €30 a bottle.

WHAT TO SEE

The Brda Wine Road As Goriška Brda boasts some of the country's finest chocolate-box scenery, it is made for touring. Over the last few years the local authorities have started to invest in tourism and you can pick up a couple of leaflets at the tourist office in the town of Dobrovo, one outlining the highlights in the various villages and towns and the other pointing out the bountiful vineyards, *gostilnas* and restaurants that await your custom. Calling ahead is always a good idea when visiting a vineyard, especially if you want to eat there as well, but in season you can just pop in and you will usually be welcomed with open arms and furnished with a free sample. It is considered polite to buy at least a bottle – given the high quality in the region this should not be too much of a problem. Just look out for the signs that point off from the main roads heralding the various local producers. Wine tourism here is on the up, as evidenced by the extensions and outhouses being built as local families look to add dining rooms and accommodation to their vineyards.

Despite its small size Goriška Brda accounts for over 10% of all Slovenian wine production, with the split 60/40 in favour of white wines. There are high-quality whites and reds, but the general rule of thumb is that you will get a better quality of white for your money. The actual volume of wine production has dipped over the last decade; this is not a sign of decline in the local industry but rather a reflection of the damage caused by mass production in the 1950s and 1960s and also of the current drive for quality over quantity. Over the last decade or so modern equipment has been brought in to refine production, but things often remain on a pleasingly low scale with pesticide use and artificial input far less prevalent than in many wine-producing countries. Some of the most established grapes are Rebula, Merlot, Beli Pinot and Pinot Blanc.

Dobrovo Castle (Dobrovo Grad) Just a couple of hundred metres on from the tourist information centre in Dobrovo, at Grajska 10, is the rectangular Dobrovo Castle, which was built on the foundations of an earlier fortification at the start of the 17th century. Today it is home to a modest museum and art gallery, with various temporary exhibitions. The real reason to come here is to eat and drink, as there is an excellent restaurant inside the castle itself and a first-rate *vinoteka* in the bowels of the castle (see *Where to eat* above).

Šmartno Of the cute villages that grace the Brda region little Šmartno is our favourite. The majority of Šmartno's fortified walls are still intact with its several hundred residents managing to rebuild their homes in their original styles after a serious earthquake in the 1960s. The 16th-century Turn Tower now houses a restaurant and café (see *Where to eat* above).

The residents of Šmartno are proud of their village's historical importance, and another sight worth visiting is the biggest parish church in Brda, the **Church of St Martin** (Cerkev Sv Martin), whose enormous belltower started life as a watchtower, part of the fortifications. The interior of the church is a bit faded, although the frescoes by Slovenian artist Tone Kralj are worth looking at. Šmartno also has a handful of traditional stone buildings, identified by plaques on their doors, including the Gothic house whose late-Gothic portal today leads to the cellar. The 19th-century renovations saw the expansion of the living space and the addition of a *gunk* (balcony), typical of the Brda region.

IDRIJA

From the Soča Valley most travellers make a beeline for Primorska's Karst and coastline, but if you follow suit you will miss out on the Idrija region and the winding rivers and gorges that made ideal terrain for partisan resistance during World War II.

Mention Idrija to most Slovenes and they will immediately think of two things: mercury and lace. This town of 6,000 inhabitants was once a buzzing hub of mercury production, the second largest in the world after Almaden in Spain; and intricate lace produced by local women is still a much-sought-after handicraft. Idrija may not win any awards for its aesthetics (it also has a somewhat subdued feel, largely thanks to the closure of the last of its mercury mines in 1995), but it has a handful of interesting sights and makes a good base for exploring the region, especially if you want to splash out and stay at the Kendov Dvorec, one of Slovenia's finest hotels. Unlike many former mining towns around Europe, Idrija's economy is still flourishing with local companies now churning out car parts for global customers, and low unemployment.

HISTORY According to legend mercury was first discovered in 1490 by a local who scraped off some of the highly toxic metal when cleaning a tub in a stream, supposedly on the spot where the Church of the Holy Trinity now stands.

Eighteen years later came the discovery of cinnabar. Idrija then grew as one of the richest mercury towns in Europe, with a maze of around 700km of shafts dug to a depth of 400m. The mine even functioned through the two world wars and during the German occupation when a third of the workers joined the partisans. By the 1970s, the mine was one of the most modern in the world, with safety standards that the early miners could only have dreamt of, but it became a victim of environmental awareness as the trend turned against the use of mercury and the price dropped rapidly from US$800 to US$80 a flask. The mine was closed temporarily in 1976 as a result and although it reopened in the 1980s the writing was on the wall and it was wound up and completely closed in 1995. Many of the old shafts were filled in during 2006.

While the men of Idrija toiled in the darkness of the mineshafts that spread their tentacles beneath the town, the women began to make snow-white lace as a way of supplementing the low wages that their menfolk brought home from the mine. Today the tradition of lacemaking is kept alive by Idrija's older generation, with some younger women learning this skilled art at the town's dedicated lacemaking school. Idrija lace is on sale in tourist shops around the country, but here you can buy direct at lower prices.

GETTING THERE You can drive to Idrija from Ljubljana, Škofja Loka or Nova Gorica in an hour or less, and from Tomlin in 45 minutes. Frequent buses also run to Idrija from Cerkno (25 minutes), Tolmin (1 hour), Ljubljana (1¹/₂ hours), Bovec (1¹/₂ hours) and Kobarid (2 hours).

TOURIST INFORMATION/ LOCAL TOUR OPERATORS

⓵ **Tourist Information Centre** Vodnikov 3; ℡ 05 374 3916; e ticidrija@icra.si; www.idrija-turizem.si; ⏰ Jul/Aug 09.00–18.00 daily; Sep–Jun 09.00–16.00 daily

Kompas Lapajnetova 37; ℡ 05 372 2700. Also organises private rooms from €20 pp.

WHERE TO STAY

⌂ **Kendov Dvorec** (11 rooms) Na Griču 2, Spodnja Idrija; ℡ 05 372 5100; f 05 375 6475; e info@kendov-dvorec.com; www.kendov-dvorec.com. A sublime 5-star hotel that does everything with panache & one of our favourite places to stay in Slovenia. Gloriously luxurious rooms (which are cheaper than you might expect), full of period pieces & antiques, great food & smooth service make this one of Slovenia's finest hotels & well worth the expense. $$$$

⌂ **Gostišče Barbara** (6 rooms) Kosovelova 3; ℡/f 05 377 1162; e joze.medle@siol.net. Decent rooms with a prime location above the mine museum. $$$

⌂ **Kmetija Želinc** (15 rooms) Staža 8, Zelin; ℡ 05 372 4020; f 05 372 4021; e info@zelinc.com; www.zelinc.com. If you have your own transport this farmhouse located by the Idrijca River is an excellent place to stay & eat. You can also indulge in a spot of fishing or take a dip in the outdoor pool. Choose from rooms in a 500-year-old farmhouse or in a more modern building. $$

⌂ **Dijaški Dom Nikolaj Pirnat** (300 beds) IX Korpusa 6; ℡ 05 377 1052. A student dormitory-cum-summer youth hostel. Rates are pp. $

⌂ **Gostilna pri Škafarju** Sv Barbare 9; ℡ 05 377 3240. Centrally located restaurant with 3 small rooms. $$

WHERE TO EAT

✗ **Kendov Dvorec** (see *Where to stay*) ⏰ 12.00–22.00 daily. A restaurant as decadent as the hotel with an ever-changing menu backed up by myriad Slovenian wines. Dine & be treated like a king, a real indulgence. Great service too. On our visit the sommelier arranged for us to visit his friend's vineyard the next day. $$$$$

✗ **Gostilna Mlinar** Žirovska 4, Spodnja Idrija; ℡ 05 377 6316; ⏰ 12.00–22.00 Wed–Sat, 12.00–20.00 Sun. Welcoming *gostilna* serving delicious *žlikrofi* – a local speciality comprising homemade pasta stuffed with potatoes, herbs & a small amount of bacon, served with meat or cheese. Also decent fish & game dishes. $$$

Primorska IDRIJA

5

✗ Gostilna Kos Tomšičeva 4; ☎ 05 372 2030; ⊕07.00–15.00 Mon, 07.00–22.00 Tue–Sat. Unfussy *gostilna* serving tasty pork dishes & excellent homemade *žlikrofi*. The menu is small, so you know your food is fresh. **$$$**

✗ Gostilna pri Škafarju (see *Where to stay*) ⊕10.00–22.00 Mon/Wed/Thu/Sun, 10.00–23.00

Fri/Sat. Serving *žlikrofi*, other regional specialities & pizza. Look out for the tile stove. **$$$**

🍴 Mercator Lapajnetova 45. If you are just desperately in search of that elusive cheap snack, the friendly staff behind the deli counter will usually make you a sandwich.

BUYING LACE While the small shop within Gewerkenegg Castle (see *What to see*) sells lace there is a number of bigger outlets on Mestni trg. One of the best places to buy local lace products is the Galerija Idrijske Čipke (*Mestni trg 17*), which also has an outlet in Ljubljana (*Gornji trg*). Idrija's young girls are all still introduced to lacemaking at school and there is also a dedicated Lace School (*Prelovčeva 2;* ☎ *05 373 4572*), with its own shop, in the town. During the annual International Idrija Lace Festival (June) you can also have a go at lacemaking.

OTHER PRACTICALITIES

$ Nova KMB Banka Lapajnetova 43; ⊕07.30–18.00 Mon–Fri, 07.30–12.00 Sat

✉ Post office Lapajnetova 3; ⊕08.00–19.00 Mon–Fri, 08.00–12.00 Sat

WHAT TO SEE

Anthony's Shaft (*Antonijev Rov; Kosovelova 3;* ☎ *05 377 1142; www.rzs-idrija.si; €4.50; tours* ⊕ *10.00 & 16.00 Mon–Fri, 10.00, 15.00 & 16.00 Sat/Sun*) Roll call was at 04.00 when you were briefed on the day's work and given a number from the 'death clock' (failure to return it indicated that you were trapped below, in serious trouble). Then with only your normal clothes on and no head protection you delved down into the netherworld of one of Europe's oldest mines. This was the scene for many of the workers who toiled in Idrija's mines, but thankfully today at the museum things are a little more relaxed: although the clock says 04.00 the first tour actually starts at 10.00 and you have both an overcoat and a hard hat, not to mention a torch-wielding guide.

Dating from 1500, Anthony's Shaft is the oldest part of the Idrija mine. The tours take in a good section of the mine, which manages to tread a fine line between providing safe access for tourists and retaining many of its original features. It starts with an informative 20-minute video, which illuminates both the mine and the history of the town. Models of miners through the ages give a sense of what life was like. There is even a small chapel, reputed to be the only one in Slovenia not funded by the Church as it was crafted by the miners themselves. It features an image of St Barbara, the patron saint of miners. The trail delves down to a depth of 100m and passes blind shafts, backfilled areas and ore transporters. Fortunately these days you do not have to conquer the 1,000 steps up and down that the miners had to, and you are soon back safely above ground.

Echoes of Idrija's mining past The history of Idrija's days as a mining hub litters the town and its surrounds. Other sights worth visiting include **Frančiška's Shaft** (Frančiškov jašek), the **Idrija Miner's House** (Rudarska Hiša), the **Kamšt waterwheel** and the **Klavže water dams**.

The entrance building to Frančiška's Shaft is another of Idrija's prized technical museums (*contact the Town Museum;* ☎ *05 372 6600; www.muzej-idrija-cerkno.si for entry*), this one capturing the history of the town through a display of restored machinery that was recovered from the mine. The Idrija Miner's House (contact the Town Museum) is a typical 19th-century wooden dwelling built to cater for the large number of miners. Owing to the lie of the land around Idrija it is built into the hillside and clearly intended to house as many workers as possible, normally around 16. Although it looks quite spacious from the outside the cramped reality was that most families had just two beds for themselves and however many kids they had, so drawers and straw beds were brought into play.

The two-century-old Kamšt (*key available from Vodnikova 22, or from the Town Museum;* €*1.50; see below*) meanwhile conveys the sheer scale of the mercury operation as this is the largest wooden waterwheel in Europe with a diameter of 13.5m, a gargantuan feat of engineering that harnessed the local water to produce a surge of power for the works underground. Further upstream, about 20km from Idrija, are the Klavže, the dams, known locally as the 'Slovenian Pyramids'. Completed in 1770, these were used to build up water pressure and then fire logs downstream for use at the mercury mines in Idrija.

Gewerkenegg Castle and Town Museum (*Grad Gewerkenegg in Mestni Muzej; Prelovčeva 9;* ✆ *05 372 6600; www.muzej-idrija-cerkno.si; adult/concession* €*2.50/*€*1.50;* ⊕ *09.00–18.00 daily*) The austere-looking Gewerkenegg Castle is one of the few castles in Slovenia that was never presided over by feudal lords, as it was built by the mercury industry and served as a fortified store and administrative offices and, of course, as the director's residence. Painstaking reconstruction work since the 1980s has brought it back into shape and earned it a European Technical Museum of the Year award in 1997.

The castle also houses a municipal history museum. If you have already been down the Anthony Mine the mining section may not hold your interest for too long, though it certainly goes into the subject of mercury in much greater detail. The municipal section is, however, fascinating, tracing the history of the town; its 'Milestones of the 20th Century' exhibition was opened in 2003. World War I is touched upon before the period of Italian rule between the wars is explored, with exhibits including signs proclaiming that the Slovene language was banned. The World War II period, when Idrija was occupied by first the Italians and then the Germans, and which was central to Slovenia's strong partisan resistance, is also explored in detail.

A strikingly huge hammer and sickle, which originally hung proudly above the mine shaft, is now hung low to symbolise the fall of Yugoslav socialism. Look out for the series of photos from the Idrija Lace School, which demonstrate Idrija's ability to flourish regardless of the political climate. Photographs taken inside the school show portraits of Emperor Franz Josef – and later Mussolini – hanging in the classrooms, before Yugoslav hardman Tito usurped the Italian dictator. For lovers of lace the museum also houses a display of the intricate work of the local women, who traditionally took up the art to supplement their husbands' meagre income from the mine. The most interesting display is a huge piece of work that was meant for Tito's wife, but never received as the political climate changed yet again.

Nearby there is also a small and less slick display covering the Pavla Partisan Hospital, which treated more of the World War II wounded (an estimated 1,678) than its Franja sibling (see *Cerkno*, page 138). The simple displays show the bravery and determination of Dr Pavla Jerina and her colleagues, with one photo showing her with Dr Franja, who was a close friend.

Partisan Printing Workshop (*Partizanska Tiskarna; tours* ⊕ *Apr–Oct 09.00 &* 16.00) If Slovenia's partisan movement has caught your imagination then you might also want to check out the Partisan Printing Workshop. Here you can delve back in time to World War II and the highly dangerous production of a newspaper promoting resistance against Nazi occupation – reputed to be the only such production in wartime Europe. The daily tours help bring this small workshop alive. Hidden in the hills the museum is, by design, hard to find, so contact the Town Museum (✆ *05 372 6600; www.muzej-idrija-cerkno.si*) who will provide directions. The reward for taking the tour is an apt one: a freshly stamped leaflet.

Wild Lake (Divje Jezero) Anyone expecting a sweeping expanse of water will be sorely disappointed by what on the surface is little more than a pond. The real interest lies below in the mysterious creation of this lake, which despite its small appearance emits a continuous stream of water. Hidden deep beneath the surface a network of caves snakes away to an elusive source. The Wild Lake has become something of a holy grail for Slovene cavers and divers; headstones around the lake, the most recent from 2001, demonstrate the dangers of delving below the emerald veneer. So far 87m of the cave system has been mapped with the rest of the hidden depths (estimated to be around 120m) sure to tempt others into risking their lives in future, though you would be well advised not to be one of them. A trail of small wooden boards outlines local flora and fauna on the path around the lake. The trail was designed to be circular, though at times the far side is submerged in water and you have to double back and cross the bridge to access the other side of the lake. Look out as you cross for the gushing Jezernica River below; fittingly for its bijou source lake, the Jezernica is the shortest river in the country. If you have more time you can walk to the lake from Idrija by following a 'Science and Discovery Path', also known as the 'Rake', alongside a narrow water channel.

AROUND IDRIJA

CERKNO Cerkno is an unassuming town on the main road between the Soča Valley and Idrija, but it is home to two important museums and the Cerkno Hills are good for walking. If you visit during spring you might also be lucky enough to see the 'Laufarji' men dressed from head to foot in hay like walking scarecrows. Wintertime visitors come to ski.

Getting there Buses run to Cerkno from Idrija (35 minutes), Ljubljana (1½ hours), Tolmin (1½ hours), Kobarid (1½–2½ hours) and Bovec (2½–3 hours).

Where to stay

Hotel Cerkno (180 beds) Sedejev trg 8; ✆ 05 374 3400; f 05 374 3433; e hotel.cerkno@siol.net; www.hotel-cerkno.si. Large faceless hotel popular with skiers & coach parties. Redeeming features include a good-sized indoor swimming pool, sports hall, tennis courts & sauna. The hotel also issues ski passes. $$–$$$

Gačnik v Logu (9 rooms) ✆ 05 372 4005. The en-suite dbl rooms at this *gostilna* are a pleasant accommodation option. $$

Tourist Farm Grapar (3 rooms) Planina pri Cerknem 47; ✆ 05 372 4117; e kmetija.grapar@ email.si; www.kmetija-grapar.com. Modern rooms combined with warm hospitality make this a good option if you have a bicycle or car. Planina is 5km from Cerkno on the road to Škofja Loka. $$–$$$

Where to eat

Gačnik v Logu (see *Where to stay*) ⊕ 09.00–23.00 daily. This *gostilna* has an incredibly long menu. The salads & pastas are of a decent standard, with tasty Karst noodles & *žlikrofi*. $$$

Tourist Farm Grapar (see *Where to stay*) ⊕ 11.00–22.00 daily. Serving up a wide range of traditional food. Good home cooking. $$$

Other practicalities Cerkno doesn't have a dedicated tourist office, but the staff at the Hotel Cerkno (see *Where to stay*) will be happy to provide you with information and literature. There is a bank and a mini market on Glavni trg at the base of the road that leads you to the museum.

What to see
Cerkno Museum (*Cerkljanski Muzej; Bevkova 12;* ☎ *05 372 3180; www.muzej-idrija-cerkno.si; adult/concession €1.70/€1.25;* ⏰ *10.00–13.00 & 14.00–18.00 Tue–Sun*) No-one quite seems to have decided whether the revamped Cerkno Museum is home to the oldest musical instrument in the world or to some prehistoric artefact that just happens to have a few holes through it. Either way it is worth having a look, not least because the museum also houses exhibits on the local Laufarija carnival including masks worn by participants. The museum also explores the area's fascinating World War II history.

Franja Partisan Hospital (*Partizanska Bolnišica Franja; Dolenji Novaki pri Cerknem;* ☎ *05 372 3180; www.muzej-idrija-cerkno.si; adult/concession €3/€2.50;* ⏰ *Apr–Oct 09.00–18.00 daily; Mar/Nov 09.00–16.00 daily;Dec–Feb 09.00–16.00 w/ends*) This former partisan hospital in the Pasica Gorge, north of Cerkno, is one of the most fascinating war museums in Europe. It is a testament to the determination of the local people to overcome Italian fascism and then Nazi suppression that they were willing to risk life and limb to tend to the local partisans, along with the Austrian, Polish, French, British and American combatants, who were treated at the main hospital. The only way to avoid the brutal attentions of the occupiers was to wedge the straggle of rudimentary hospital buildings high up the rugged gorge, an amazing feat considering construction had to be clandestine and everything had to be brought in and out through the hostile terrain that formed a natural barrier against attack. A system of bunkers and mines helped nature repel two German attacks, in April 1944 and March 1945. The location also helped with the hospital's main power source: hydro-electricity.

The hospital (named after Dr Franja Bojc Bidovec, its most renowned director) opened as a museum straight after the war. You can see that little has changed with many of the original artefacts, including stretchers, bunks, posters of Tito, an X-ray machine and, chillingly, the stark operating table and accompanying surgical instruments, left intact. You can walk through the various wards, kitchen, washroom and isolation room, though the upper shelter and burial ground are not always open. Despite the challenging conditions the hospital's record was impressive with only 52 of the 522 badly injured patients who were brought here succumbing to their injuries. Given the steep ascents and slippery rock steps on the 15-minute trail from the car park, disabled access is not possible. To get to the hospital just follow the plentiful signs from Cerkno.

ACTIVITIES AROUND IDRIJA AND CERKNO
Skiing In winter the road from Cerkno to the Partisan Hospital continues to climb on to the Cerkno ski field, not exactly world-class skiing but, if you are in the area, worth trying out. The **Cerkno Ski Centre** (*Sedejev trg 8;* ☎ *05 374 3400;* f *05 374 3433;* e *hotel.cerkno@siol.net; www.hotel-cerkno.si*), 10km from Cerkno, offers decent conditions for downhill skiing with pistes up to 1,300m. The centre also has a ski school, rents equipment and has a variety of chair and ski lifts. If there is not enough snow there is even a snow-making machine. There are also cross-country runs at the **Javornik Ski Centre** (*Lome;* ☎ *05 377 7544*).

Hiking Hiking in the Cerkno Hills (Cerkljansko Hribovje) is a popular local pastime. An English-language walking map is available from the Hotel Cerkno and its eight walks include a hike to the Franja Partisan Hospital.

VIPAVA VALLEY

One of Slovenia's most famous wine regions is fairly well set-up for receiving visitors and it is also easy to get here over the hills from Idrija and Cerkno, by the fast road from Nova Gorica and also from the coastal resorts. The first wine co-operative in Slovenia was founded here in 1894, though some locals reckon that wine was savoured here as early as Roman times. Getting around the small towns and villages is only really practical if you have a car. The scenery is dramatic, with the Karst starting to rise to the south and heavily wooded hills to the north, with the verdant valley in between awash with vineyards. White wines have traditionally been the mainstay of the valley, but in recent years local producers have ventured into red wine with some considerable success (though try telling that to the Goriška Brda connoisseurs who insist that their reds are always the finest in Primorska).

There are numerous producers and the local tourist office has put together a guide to local vineyards on the **Vipava Valley Wine Road** (Vipavska Vinska Cesta) that are open to visitors. Look out for *vinska klet* signs, though calling ahead is always advisable, especially outside July and August.

The Vipava Valley also has some worthwhile sights. The town of **Vipava** itself enjoys a dramatic location and is overlooked by a ruined castle. The castle was

---

VISITING A VIPAVA VALLEY VINEYARD

The Tilia (Linden Tree) vineyard (*Potoče 41, Kukanje, 5623 Dobravlje;* \|f *05 364 6684;* e *tilia@lemut.net*) is run by a friendly English-speaking couple, Matjaž and Melita Lemut. Their three children ensure that the 6ha vineyard is one of the few in Europe where the largest stretch of vines is accompanied by a playground. After a tour through the modern but charmingly small-scale winemaking equipment (the total annual production has never been more than 30,000 litres since the vineyard started bottling in 1996), Matjaž will guide you down to his cosy cellar for the serious business of tasting.

There will usually be some homemade bread and cheese, maybe with some walnut oil for dipping, to accompany the wines – if you are looking for something more substantial call ahead and they can rustle up a wholesome meal or even get in a local chef.

Tilia specialises in young wines and we sampled an excellent fruity Pinot Grigio (*sivi pinot* in Slovene) and a passable Chardonnay. The Sauvignon Blanc was quite complex given the young age of the vineyard and the dessert wine was of such quality that it was being served in the five-star Kendov Dvorec Hotel in Idrija when we ate there. In total over 50% of the wines are exported, more through a network of personal contacts than through importers, to Austria, Croatia, Sweden, Switzerland and Denmark. Matjaž even produces a wine for Alan Ducasse in New York that sells at US$150 for half a bottle – you can pick it up here for a few euros! On a recent visit to Vinoteka Dvor in Ljubljana, they were also offering Tilia wines.

Vipava may not always be renowned for its reds and while Tilia's Merlot is not their greatest product, their stab at Cabernet Sauvignon has an impressive body, with smoky overtones. Matjaž's hospitality and *joie de vivre* can be addictive so make sure to peel yourself away after buying a few bottles before he wheels out the 'cheeky young brandy' that is one of his newer pet projects. Another development may soon see a couple of rooms opened up so that you can indulge without worrying about who will drive you back to your hotel.

once owned by the powerful Lantheiri family and their 18th-century Baroque mansion still sits in town, with the **Church of St Stephen** (Cerkev Sv Štefan), built in the same century, a further testament to the golden era before it became today's charmingly sleepy town. The town is also home to one of the valley's largest producers.

In the hills above Vipava is **Zemono Palace** (*Zemono Dvorec; Zemono;* ↖ *05 368 7007;* ⊕ *12.00–19.00 Mon–Fri, 09.00–14.00 Sat*), a Renaissance mansion now reincarnated with an epicurean oasis, **Gostilna Pri Lojzetu** (⊕ *12.00–midnight Wed–Sun; $$$$*), which draws in gastronomes from all over Slovenia and further afield. Other places worth dropping into are the largest settlement in the valley, **Ajdovščina**, with its Roman history; **Log**, with its 18th-century Nazarene frescoes; and **Vipavski Križ**, a tiny village that stands on the foundations of a prehistoric predecessor and is now a protected cultural monument in its own right.

TOURIST INFORMATION

🔲 **Ajdovščina Tourist Information Centre**
Lokarjev drevored 8b; ↖ 05 365 9140;

e tic.ajdovscina@siol.net; www.tic-ajdovscina.si;
⊕ 09.00–17.00 Mon–Fri, 10.00–14.00 Sat

THE KARST (KRAŠ)

The Karst straddles Primorska and the western edge of neighbouring Notranjska, dividing Slovenia's alpine north from the Adriatic in a flurry of rugged limestone. The region gave the world the geological term 'Karst', and it is an epic land where rivers simply disappear, vast caverns delve deep into the bowels of the earth and hidden waterways rush below. Dotted around the wooded hillsides are pretty orange-roofed towns and villages, many of them offering views south towards the Adriatic.

During World War II the Karst was the centre of fierce partisan resistance and during the savage German revenge attacks whole villages were burned down and their inhabitants sent off to concentration camps. In a sense the area has not really recovered, with only state aid, European Union funding and the promise of tourism providing hope of a renaissance. The Karst is renowned, though, for its culinary produce with the most famous exports being *pršut*, richly flavoured ham (similar to Spanish *jamon serrano* or Italian *proscuitto*) that is dried by the bitter *burja* winds, and the robust Teran red wine. Spending a few days rolling between the various beautiful chocolate-box hill towns, enjoying snatched glimpses of the Adriatic, the Italian Alps and the Vipava Valley, washed down with *pršut* and Teran, is perhaps one of the most enjoyable experiences Slovenia has to offer.

Fans of chunky cooking, sturdy wines and crumbling villages and caves fit to house a James Bond villain will enjoy the Kraš as much as us.

ŠKOCJAN CAVES (*Škocjanske Jama; Škocjan 2* ↖ *05 708 2110;* f *05 708 2111;* e *psj.info@psj.gov.si; www.park-skocjanske-jame.si; adult/concessions/children* €*11/* €*7.50/*€*4; tours* ⊕*Jan–Mar and Nov/Dec 10.00 &* *13.00 Mon–Fri, 10.00, 13.00 &* *15.00 Sat/Sun; Apr/May/Oct daily 10.00, 13.00 &* *15.30; Jun–Sep daily 10.00–17.00 hourly*) The only downside of visiting the Škocjan Caves is that most of the other caves that you visit around the world afterwards will pale in comparison. This UNESCO World Heritage-listed marvel is a truly remarkable place and is well worth the trip no matter how little time you have in Slovenia. If Hollywood producers could get their hands on this unique landscape it would make a perfect setting for a *Lord of the Rings*-style epic or the next Bond movie. The first written mention of the caves came in the 2nd century BC and there is evidence of Iron Age religious ceremonies at the site, but they were never fully explored until the 19th century. Before you delve underground on a guided tour – the only way to access the caves unless you are on a scientific research project – go up to the lookout point, which is signposted from the visitors' centre. From this lofty vantage point the scale of Škocjan becomes clear as the Reka River is swallowed into the abyss below, not to reappear for another 34km across the border in Italy.

The Škocjan Caves were formed over millions of years by the corrosive actions of the tautologous Reka River (literally meaning River River), which helped create today's subterranean world. This is a constantly changing landscape and the complex is still being actively studied and surveyed by speleologists today. The myriad Karstic features include small and large caves, stalagmites and stalactites, with the caves also home to rare and endangered species of bat as well as stone martens and spiders. Water levels vary throughout the year and other seasonal variations include the striking ice stalactites that can be found in winter.

Škocjan Caves tour The 1½-hour tour begins with a ten-minute hike to the entrance, through an artificial tunnel. The park authorities have mercifully resisted the temptation to jazz things up and the 2km main trail is a narrow and simple one with no frills – the caves speak for themselves. You will see a network of other paths that snake tantalisingly in and around the Reka, but these are off-limits for tourists.

First up on the walk is the **Silent Cave**, where some of the largest and most impressive stalactites and stalagmites that you are ever likely to see combine to conjure up a scene that the guides aptly call 'paradise'. The trail moves on and groups tend to stretch out as stragglers attempt to take photos, which has been recently banned by the park authorities. The next section is even more dramatic as the vastness of the **Great Hall** unfurls like something from a science-fiction movie, a huge space over 100m wide with a ceiling hanging around 30m overhead. You do not need any tacky soundtrack as the rumble of the Reka beckons from its nearby gorge.

For vertigo sufferers the next part can be an ordeal as a dimly lit path descends through the Tolkienesque netherworld of the **Murmuring Cave** and then crosses the narrow Cerkvenik Bridge over the Hankejev Kanal, which looks like something out of an *Indiana Jones* movie, though it is sturdy enough and was rebuilt in 2003. If you can bear to peer over, the views of the Reka bursting through the cavern are stunning. The path follows the Reka for a while before it snakes back around past the **Gours**, a series of rock pools, a kind of small-scale version of Pamukkale in Turkey – if you are lucky after heavy rain there may be some water in them – and then emerges at the vast opening of the **Schmidl Hall** that used to be the main entrance to the caves. A walkway leads around to a funicular that spirits you back up to the path below the visitors' centre – if you did not have a chance to look over the caves from the viewpoint you can do so now. There is a modest café and *gostilna* at the visitors' centre. Plans have been mooted to open a hotel for those wanting to stay overnight near the caves, though they will have to get past UNESCO first.

LIPICA

The chances are that you will have heard of Lipica's most famous residents, the graceful white Lipizzaner horses, which attract hordes of visitors to this small Karst town each year. The name of the horses, Lipizzaner, is derived from the name 'Lipica' which translates into English as 'a small linden tree'. Dating back to

1580, today Lipica's stud farm extends over 300ha of fields. If you are not content to merely watch the horses on the guided tour then you can have riding lessons (by arrangement), take a horse-drawn carriage ride or hire a horse to explore the surrounding countryside. If it is raining when you visit the stud farm, then you can always ride in the indoor arena. Try to time your visit to coincide with one of the intricate displays of the Classic Riding School (call ahead to verify times – see *What to see* below). There is no escaping the fact that Lipica these days is unashamedly touristy, but if you are passing it is still worth popping into.

GETTING THERE There are no public transport services to Lipica. A taxi from Sežana costs from €7. Sežana can be reached from Ljubljana by either train (1½–2 hours) or bus (1½–2 hours).

WHERE TO STAY

▲ **Hotel Maestoso** ✆ 05 739 1580; e info@lipica.org; www.lipica.org. Situated at the heart of the stud farm with comfortable rooms, an indoor pool, sauna, casino, restaurant & conference centre. $$$–$$$$

▲ **Hotel Klub** ✆ 05 739 1580; e info@lipica.org; www.lipica.org. Also located within the grounds of the stud farm & with a fitness centre, sauna, bar, restaurant & club rooms. $$$

✗ WHERE TO EAT

✗ **Letni Vrt** ⊕ Apr–Sep 11.00–20.00 daily. With a name that literally means 'summer garden', it is not surprising that this self-service grill only opens when the weather is good. $$$

✗ **Maestoso** ⊕ 07.00–23.00 daily. Cosy little café-restaurant open year round. $$$

ENTERTAINMENT AND NIGHTLIFE

☆ **Grand Casino Lipica** Lipica 5; ✆ 05 731 0600; e marketing.lipica@casino.si; www.casino.si/lipica; ⊕ until 03.00/04.00 nightly. If you do not feel you have spent enough money already then head to this swish casino with slot machines, poker tables, blackjack & roulette.

WHAT TO SEE

Lipica Stud Farm (*Kobilarna Lipica; Lipica 5;* ✆ *05 739 1580;* f *05 734 6370;* e *lipica@siol.net; www.lipica.org; the timetable for events at the Lipica Stud Farm is complicated and subject to change*) Many people are surprised to learn that you can find the world-famous Lipizzaner horses outside of Vienna, although the Karst village of Lipica has been the proud home to a Lipizzaner stud farm for over four centuries. It was established by the Austrian Archduke of Vienna in 1580, after experts informed him that the Karst provided all the necessary conditions for a successful stud farm, making Lipizzaners one of the oldest breeds of horse in the world. Kobilarna Lipica remained the property of the Viennese court until the end of World War I.

The brilliant-white Lipizzaner horses (which are actually grey or black when they are born), which were once trained to manoeuvre during battle, now entertain visitors from across Slovenia and all over the world. Perhaps ironically the horses originally trained for conflict were relocated during time of war – moving to Hungary on three occasions during the Napoleonic Wars and then to Vienna in World War I. The horses were threatened once again during World War II when they were seized by the Germans, with only a small number ever returned.

Lipizzaner horses are very distinctive – broad, muscular and standing around 1.6m tall. Apparently walking on the Karst also gives them very hard hooves. They have a gracious gait, thick and silky tails and manes. The characteristic whiteness

5

that people associate with the horses develops over time, so a dazzling white Lipizzaner is at least six years old.

There is more to keep you occupied at Lipica, though, than just its magnificent horses. Countryside trails around the village are good for walkers and cyclists, while the golf course (↘ 05 739 1724) and tennis courts provide other ways to keep fit. Adults staying in one of Lipica's hotels can also find plenty to keep them occupied in the Grand Casino. Children can also take 15-minute horse rides. Four-person horse-drawn carriage rides are also available and cost €20/€40 for 30 minutes/one hour.

Stud Farm Tours ⊕Jan–Mar & Nov/Dec hourly 10.00–15.00 Tue–Sun; Apr–Jun & Oct/Nov hourly 09.00–17.00 Tue–Sun; Jul/Aug hourly 09.00–18.00 Tue–Sun. Additional tours: Mar 16.00 Sun; Apr–Jun & Oct/Nov 18.00 Sun
Classical Riding School Display ⊕Apr–Oct 15.00 Tue/Fri/Sun 15.00

Classical Riding School Training Display Apr–Oct 10.00–12.00 Tue–Sun
Pony Riding for Children Apr–Oct 10.00–12.00 & 16.00–18.00 Tue–Sun
Carriage Rides Apr–Oct 10.00–12.00 & 13.00–18.00 Tue–Sun

ŠTANJEL

This stunning little Karst town is a real find, the sort of place that no-one you know will ever have been to and that everyone will want to visit when you tell them about it. Wrapped across a vine-clad hillside is an orange-roofed hill town, complete with its own castle and church, art galleries and places to stay. All around are expansive views of Slovenia and Italy, something not lost on man throughout the centuries: as far back as Roman times there was a fort on the site. Check out the typical Karst house that is now open as a museum. The **Ferrair Garden**, designed by one-time mayor Max Fabiani, is another charming diversion.

On the third Sunday of every month a small but lively market fills up the main square as you enter through the town gate. Everything is on sale here from bottles of sturdy Teran wine and massive jars of local honey, right through to all sorts of Yugoslav-era paraphernalia and even leftovers from the two world wars including bullets, helmets and (when we visited) a set of British-army-issue dungarees. On our last visit there were signs that Štanjel was finally waking up to its tourist potential, so get there before the sprinkling of tourists becomes a steady trickle.

GETTING THERE Štanjel is a brisk 15-minute walk from Kobdilj railway station. Buses drop passengers on the main road.

TOURIST INFORMATION
🛈 **Tourist Information Centre** ↘ 05 769 0056; e tic.stanjel@komen.si; http://vodnik.kras-carso.com; ⊕11.00–16.00 Mon/Wed/Sat, 14.00–17.00 Sun. Located up the stairs next to the castle.

🏠 **WHERE TO STAY** The tourist information centre (see above) can help arrange private accommodation in and around Štanjel.

✖ **WHERE TO EAT AND DRINK**
🍷**Stranarjev Hram** Štanjel 29. This small bar with an even smaller terrace located opposite the Mala Galerija is a great place to enjoy a drink.
🍴**Okrepčevalnica** Grad Štanjel; ↘ 05 769 0118; ⊕summer 10.00–22.00 Tue–Sun; winter 09.00–18.00 Tue–Sun. Café-bar located within the castle, serving snacks.
✖ **Gostilna Zoro** Štanjel 42; ↘ 05 769 0101; ⊕11.00–23.00 Fri/Sat, 11.00–22.00 Sun/Mon. $$

OTHER PRACTICALITIES

There is a small **souvenir shop** housed in the old tower & you can buy honey from Jožef & Marija Švagelj at Štanjel 6a.

ELSEWHERE IN THE KARST

Other notable Karst attractions include **Hrastovlje**, an unassuming town that is home to the Church of the Holy Trinity, renowned for its frescoes of the *Dance of Death*, which date back over 500 years and include some of the earliest examples of the Slavic Glagolithic script ever found. **Rihenberg Castle** (Rihenberg Grad), with a chequered history laced with Habsburgs, Slovene counts and Nazi troops, is the largest and oldest castle in Primorska and its ramparts boast sweeping views out over the Karst. If you are lucky it will just be you up here appreciating this unique and compelling landscape. Take in the sunset before heading for the welcoming arms of a *gostilna* and a soothing glass of Teran.

Lynx

6

The Slovenian Adriatic

While neighbouring Croatia's sweeping 1,185-island-studded coastline tends to overshadow Slovenia's more modest 47km slice of the Adriatic – even many Slovenes head south to Croatia rather than to their own coast – there are plenty of reasons to swoop south, not least the more languorous Mediterranean climate and lifestyle. The Venetians from just across the water have left an architectural bounty from their years in charge with the old cores of the towns of Koper, Izola and – especially – Piran the highlight of a visit to Slovenia's coastline. Then there is Piran's brash sibling, Portorož, an unsubtle but fun beach resort with plenty of tacky trimmings. Given its location the Slovenian coastline unsurprisingly bears many similarities to Italy, a connection that manifests itself in the use of Italian, the seafood and the architecture, which is the most visual legacy of the long period of Venetian rule.

Between the world wars the entire coast was occupied by Italy, and Mussolini's administration set about a process of Italianisation by banning the use of Slovene and its teaching in schools, as well as renaming streets and bringing in Italian settlers. 'Zone B' was handed to Yugoslavia after World War II and, although many Italians did choose to leave, the Italian community in coastal Slovenia is still vibrant; Italian words and accents can be heard all over and street signs are bilingual. Croatian influences emerge too, which is not too surprising as Slovenia shares its tiny corner of the Istrian Peninsula with Croatia. The Slovenian Adriatic still feels very much at a crossroads and, sitting down to an alfresco dinner in Piran, the bright lights of the Italian city of Trieste blink to the north while the shadowy hulk of Croatia looms just to the south. A border feud simmers on the coast between Slovenia and Croatia, with the Croatians said to be threatening to cut off Slovenia's access to the open sea, which would be disastrous for the Slovenian port of Koper.

KOPER

Many Slovenes dismiss the nearest the coast has to a city due to its unattractive port. It is easy to write it off as any approach reveals a welter of heavy industry and docklands, but delve beyond this and the shabbily attractive Venetian heart of Koper unfurls. Koper's glory days were during Venetian times when it took on a role as a major port. Koper slipped into decline under the Austro-Hungarians as Trieste and Rijeka both took much of its trade away; ironically today the successful port thrives on business from Austria and Hungary. One problem for visitors is that many restaurants and bars close early as most locals make a beeline for the coastal resorts or stay home.

GETTING THERE Frequent buses run from Izola (15 minutes), Piran (30 minutes), Strunjan (20 minutes) and Portorož (25 minutes) on the coast to Koper. Services

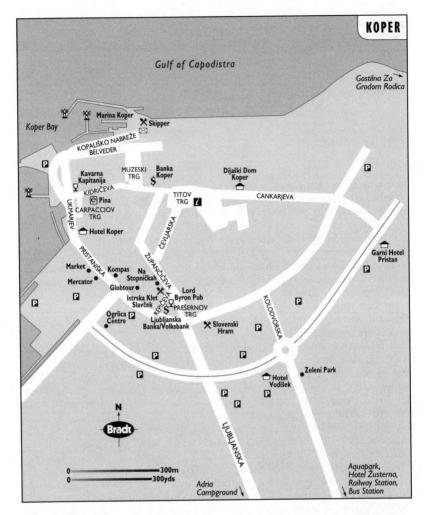

Gulf of Capodistra

Gostilna Za
Grodom Rodica

Koper Bay

Marina Koper

Skipper

KOPALIŠKO NABREŽE
BELVEDER

MUZESKI
TRG

Banka
Koper

Dijaški Dom
Koper

Kavarna
Kapitanija

KIDRIČEVA

Pina

CARPACCIOV
TRG

TITOV
TRG

CANKARJEVA

UKMARJEV

Hotel Koper

PRISTANIŠKA

CEVLJARSKA

ŽUPANČIČEVA

Garni Hotel
Pristan

Market

Kompas

Na
Stopničkah

Mercator

Globtour

Istrska Klet
Slavček

REPIČEVA

Lord
Byron Pub

PREŠERNOV
TRG

KOLODVORSKA

Ogrlica
Centre

Ljubljanska
Banka/Volksbank

Slovenski
Hram

N

Zeleni Park

Hotel
Vodišek

Bradt

LJUBLJANSKA

0 ————— 300m
0 ————— 300yds

Adria
Campground

Aquapark,
Hotel Žusterna,
Railway Station,
Bus Station

also run from Ljubljana (2½ hours), Postojna (1½ hours), Celje (3½ hours), Maribor (5½ hours) and Murska Sobota (6½ hours). Train services are less frequent, but there are trains to/from Postojna (1½ hours) and to/from Ljubljana (2½ hours). Koper also has a marina that welcomes visiting yachts.

Bus station Kolodvorska 11; ✆ 05 639 5269
Railway station Kolodvorska 11; ✆ 05 639 5263

Marina Koper Kopališko nabrežje 5; ✆ 05 662 6100; f 05 662 6161; e info@marina-koper.si; www.marina-koper.si

GETTING AROUND Local buses leave from the bus station.

🚗 **Taxi Morje** ✆ 05 628 1111

TOURIST INFORMATION/LOCAL TOUR OPERATORS
𝑖 Tourist Information Centre Titov trg 3; ✆ 05 664 6403; f 05 664 6406; e tic@koper.si;

www.koper.si; ⏰ 09.00–17.00 Mon–Sat, 13.00–17.00 Sun

Globtour Pristaniška 23; ☎ 05 626 0017;
e globtour.koper@globtour.si

Kompas Pristaniška 14; ☎ 05 660 3580;
e kompas.koper@siol.net; www.kompas.si. Services
include accommodation, car rental & onward travel.

⌂ WHERE TO STAY

⌂ **Hotel Koper** (65 rooms) Pristaniška 3; ☎ 05
610 0500; f 05 610 0594; e koper@terme-catez.si;
www.terme-catez.si. Our favourite place to stay in
Koper overlooks the sea on the fringe of the Old
Town, with huge bedrooms & plush public areas.
You can also use the gym, pool & spa facilities at
the Aquapark Žusterna across the bay.
$$$–$$$$

⌂ **Hotel Vodišek** (32 rooms) Kolodvorska 2;
☎ 05 639 2468; f 05 639 3668; e info@hotel-
vodisek.com; www.hotel-vodisek.com. Rooms
sleeping 1–4 people are simply furnished with
wooden floors & white bedding. The hotel also has
its own rustic restaurant. $$$

⌂ **Aquapark Hotel Žusterna** (117 rooms)
Istrska 67; ☎ 05 663 8000; f 05 663 8010;
e zusterna@terme-catez.si; www.terme-catez.si.

Definitely one for families, this hotel has an
impressive array of leisure facilities including
indoor & outdoor swimming pools, gym, Roman-
Irish baths & a fitness centre. Guest rooms are on
the small side. Check for special offers.
$$$–$$$$

⌂ **Garni Hotel Pristan** (18 rooms) Ferraska
30; ☎ 05 614 4000; f 05 614 4040; e hotel@
luka-kp.si; www.pristan-koper.si. Newish hotel
geared towards businesspeople, with rooms & apts.
$$$

⌂ **Dijaški Dom Koper** (380 beds) Cankarjeva 5;
☎ 05 627 3250; f 05 627 3182; e ddkoper-
recepcija@guest.arnes.si; www.d-dom.kp.edus.si. This
large student dormitory transforms into an HI-
affiliated youth hostel from mid Jun–mid Aug with
affordable beds in trpl rooms. Rates are pp. $

Camping

⌂ **Adria Campground** Jadranska 25, Ankaran;
☎ 05 663 7350; f 05 633 7360; e adria.tp@siol.net.
Pitch amongst the trees in this large seaside
campsite just outside Koper. This well-equipped 500-
pitch site boasts a diverse range of facilities that

include an Olympic-size outdoor swimming pool,
indoor pool, laundry, shop, restaurant & bicycle
rental, alongside a host of water- & land-based
sports. Rates are pp. $

✗ WHERE TO EAT
Restaurants are thin on the ground in Koper's Old Town. Fast
food comes in the form of the bureks on sale at Kidričeva 8.

✗ **Gostilna Za Gradom Rodica** Kraljeva 10;
☎ 05 628 5505; ⊕ 12.00–22.00 Tue–Sat. Focusing
on Istrian specialities & fresh Adriatic fish this
restaurant is well worth the taxi ride out of town.
$$$$$

✗ **Skipper** Kopališko nabrežje 3; ☎ 05 626 1810;
⊕ summer 11.00–22.00 daily; winter 11.00–22.00
Mon–Sat, 11.00–18.00 Sun. Second-floor restaurant
with terrace overlooking the marina. A lively
atmosphere, fresh fish & tasty grills make this one of
the best dining spots in town. Try the scampi soup or
seafood salad. $$$$

✗ **Istrska Klet Slavček** Županičeva 39; ☎ 05 627
6729; ⊕ 07.00–22.00 Mon–Fri. Old World restaurant
selling hearty Slovenian specialities. Try the bean &

sausage soup, followed by Hungarian goulash or roast
pork knuckle & washed down with wine from the
vineyards near Koper. $$$

✗ **Slovenski Hram** Taclev 8; ☎ 05 626 2701;
⊕ 11.00–22.00 Mon–Sat. Decent eatery with a
varied menu of pasta, fish, meat & veggie dishes.
$$$

✗ **Market** Pristaniška (adjacent to Mercator).
Stallholders sell fresh food ⊕ 07.00–20.00 Mon–Fri,
07.00–11.00 Sat.

✗ **Mercator** Centrally located stores include
Prešernov trg 1, Pristaniška 2 & Titov trg 2. The last
is also open on Sun mornings.

✗ **Na stopničkah** Županičeva 37. Deli that makes
sandwiches & is also open on Sun mornings.

ENTERTAINMENT AND NIGHTLIFE
If you are looking for a lively night out you
won't usually find it in Koper's Old Town. Locals travel to the neighbouring
resorts for nightlife. However, there are a number of pleasant venues for a quiet
drink.

Kavarna Kapitanija Ukmarjev 8. This mellow café near the marina has a large outdoor terrace.
♀ Lord Byron Pub Repičeva 2. Welcoming British-style pub tucked away off Prešernov trg with Guinness, Caffreys, Staropramen & Tennent's Super on draught.

If you are still looking for a party and don't mind leaving the Old Town then try Papas or Abar at **Zeleni Park**; the latter is open until 02.00. The **Ogrlica Centre** also has some late-night bars.

SHOPPING Koper's Old Town is a decent place to go shopping especially if you are hankering after a new pair of shoes, attractive jewellery or just like to window shop in galleries and boutiques. The best streets to indulge in a spot of retail therapy are Čevljarska and Kidričeva.

OTHER PRACTICALITIES
$ **Banka Koper** Kidričeva 14; ⊕08.00–12.00 & 15.00–17.00 Mon–Fri, 08.00–12.00 Sat
$ **Ljubljanska Banka** Pristaniška 43; ⊕08.30–13.00 & 15.30–17.00 Mon–Fri
$ **Volksbank** Pristaniška 45; ⊕08.30–13.00 & 15.30–17.00 Mon–Fri

✉ **Post office** Muzeski trg 3; ⊕08.00–19.00 Mon–Fri, 08.00–12.00 Sat
🖥 **Pina** Kidričeva 43; ⊕09.00–22.00 Mon–Fri. This great internet café has high-speed connections, affordable prices & modern PCs.

WHAT TO SEE
Exploring the historic quarter A good place to start a walking tour of Koper is in the central square, one of the few important public spaces in Slovenia to keep its socialist-era name of Titov trg. The local authorities seem to be torn between allowing this charming Venetian-era square to breathe and letting it become part of a choking bus road. Hopefully the cars will be absent when you visit.

Head for the 36m **campanile** (*Titov trg; €2; ⊕09.30–13.30 & 16.00–18.00 daily*), which was modelled on the campanile across the water in Venice, for a bird's-eye view of the city and you will see the tight warren of streets that make up the Old Town stretching out below. The rather austere **Cathedral of the Assumption** (Stolnica Marija Vnebovzetja) lies below the belltower. The square is also home to the 12th-century **Rotunda of John the Baptist** (Rotunda Janeza Krstnika) baptistery, which you will see if you look north. Elsewhere on Titov trg is the most dramatic building in Koper: the **Praetorian Palace** (Pretorska Palača). What used to be the home of the Venetian-era mayor now houses a tourist information centre and also functions as a cultural hub with temporary exhibitions and shows. At the opposite end of the square is the well-preserved **loggia** (Loža), which dates back to the 15th century. The Loggia Café is now housed within the loggia, offering a unique experience as you sip your *bela kava* amidst the hub of Venetian Koper and admire the square. Upstairs is a modest art gallery, **Galerija Loža** (*Titov trg 1; ⊕15.00–22.00 Tue–Sat, 20.00–22.00 Sun*).

Head east out of Titov trg onto Kidričeva, a narrow pedestrianised thoroughfare which has connected the square to the Adriatic for centuries. You will soon come to the **Koper Regional Museum** (*Pokrajinski Muzej; Palača Belgramoni, Kidričeva 19; ✆ 05 663 3570; f 05 663 3571; €1.50; ⊕Jun–Aug 08.00–13.00 & 18.00–20.00 Mon–Fri, 08.00–13.00 Sat; Sep–May 08.00–15.00 Mon–Fri, 08.00–13.00 Sat*) at No 19 on the left, which is housed in the 16th-century Belgramoni Palace. Inside you will find a variety of exhibits, including a copy of the *Dance of Death* that you may already have seen in the Karst in Hrastovlje. Continue along Kidričeva and you will soon come upon two medieval houses at Nos 31 and 33, with raised painted timbered upper levels, unlike anything else that you will find on the coast. Opposite on the right is the **Totto Palace** (Palača Totto) sporting the unmistakable Venetian lion, symbol of the Divine Republic. Further down is a trio of faded churches, indicative of a city whose Old Town needs a major refurbishment. At No 29 is the simple façade of the 16th-century **Church of St Nicholas** (Cerkev Sv Nikolaj), with the 18th-century **Church of the Holy Trinity** (Cerkev Sv Trojice) at No 23. If you want to take a minute to check your emails and have a coffee then pop into **Pina** at No 43, a great wee internet café (see *Other practicalities* above).

Kidričeva soon opens out into the expanse of Carpacciov trg with its shops and cafés. Look out for the Roman well and also the Column of St Justin, the latter commemorating the part Koper played in fighting the Turks during the landmark tussle against the Ottomans in 1571 at the Battle of Lepanto. From here the Adriatic beckons and there is a long walkway just across the Belvedere (the waterfront road) with plenty of benches to relax on and take in the sun. A branch of the Mercator supermarket chain is located just behind the walkway if you want to grab a drink or rustle up a picnic.

ACTIVITIES

Aquapark Žusterna Istrska 67; ☎ 05 663 8000; f 05 663 8010; e zusterna@terme-catez.si; www.terme-catez.si. Open to non-residents this is a great place to indulge in a spot of pampering.

A 30-min massage costs from €20, use of the gym €6 & 2 hrs' use of the swimming pools €6.50 depending on the day of the week.

IZOLA

Most visitors make a beeline south for Piran, but consider at least stopping off for lunch in unpretentious Izola, 5km to the south of Koper, as it offers some of the finest seafood in Slovenia, the bounty from its own fishing fleet. The most dramatic approach to the town is from the south, as Izola rears up from the sea like a mini-Piran and proudly shows off its Venetian-style architecture – approach from the north and you may well want to skip past the hulking dry dock that welcomes you. The Romans and the Venetians have both played their part in Izola's history, while these days tourism is increasingly shaping the town, as Izola smartens itself up in an attempt to win much-needed visitors. The whole seafront is currently being revamped and 2004 saw a new and alternative film festival arrive in Izola, which focused on films made by African, Asian, Latin American and eastern European producers. This event combines film with outdoor screenings on Manzioli trg, camping and even Bollywood projections on the beach. The four-day event takes place at the end of May each year (*www.isolacinema.org*).

GETTING THERE Coastal buses connect Portorož (10 minutes), Strunjan (10 minutes), Koper (15 minutes) and Piran (20 minutes) with impressive frequency. More limited services run to/from Ljubljana (2½ hours), Celje (4 hours), Maribor (5½ hours) and Murska Sobota (6½ hours).

GETTING AROUND

Taxi Bo-Bo ☎ 05 060 2602

Ritoša Kajuhova 28; ☎ 05 641 5337. For bicycle hire.

TOURIST INFORMATION/LOCAL TOUR OPERATORS

☑ **Tourist Information Centre** Sončno nabrežje 4; ☎ 05 640 1050; f 05 640 1052; e tic.izola@izola.si; www.izola.si; ⊕ Jul–Aug 09.00–21.00 Mon–Sat,

08.00–12.00 Sun; Sep–Jun 07.00–18.00 Mon–Fri, 07.00–12.00 Sat. Limited tourist information, but can help you find private accommodation.

Bele Skale Cankarjev drevored 2; ℡ 05 640 3555; f 05 641 8200; e beleskale@siol.net; www.beleskale.si. Centrally located tourist agency that organises private accommodation, car & bicycle rental.

Turist Biro Simonov Zaliv Morova 6a; ℡ 05 660 3100; f 05 641 8402; e simonov.zaliv@sansimon.si; www.htp-simonov-zaliv.si. A couple of streets back from the Marina behind the Delfin Hotel. Arranges accommodation & a range of sporting activities.

WHERE TO STAY

Hotel Marina (52 rooms) Veliki trg 11; ℡ 05 660 4100; f 05 660 4410; e marina@belvedere.si; www.hotelmarina.si. Located at the heart of the Old Town, this hotel has decent rooms with minibars, satellite TV & AC. The health spa offers a choice of jacuzzi, sauna, massage & thalassotherapy. $$$–$$$$

Hotel Delfin (225 rooms) Tomažičeva 10; ℡ 05 660 7000; f 05 660 7420; e delfin.recepcija@

siol.net; www.hotel-delfin.si. Large waterfront hotel geared towards tour groups & located 1km from town. $$$

Hotel Belvedere (119 rooms) Dobrava 1a; ℡ 05 660 5100; f 05 660 5171; e belvedere@belvedere.si; www.belvedere.si. Standard 3-star hotel with good-value apts (if you are planning to stay for at least 3 nights) sleeping 2–3 people. $$$

Camping

Camping Belvedere Dobrava 1a; ℡ 05 660 5100; f 05 660 5171; e belvedere@belvedere.si; www.belvedere.si. Adjacent to the Belvedere Hotel, 3km from town on a hill overlooking the Bay of Trieste, this campsite has a capacity for 500 tents. Rates are pp. $

Campsite Jadranka Pole 8; ℡ 05 640 2300; f 05 641 8358; e freetimedoo@siol.net. Beachfront campsite 1km east of the Old Town. Rates are pp. $

WHERE TO EAT

Parangal Sončo nabrežje 20; ℡ 05 641 7440; ⏰10.00–midnight daily. This deservedly popular restaurant offers excellent fish & has a terrace that spreads out along the waterfront. The 'first class' fish platter cannot be beaten, although there is a slightly cheaper option using unappetising sounding 'second class' seafood, which is still perfectly palatable. $$$$

Gostilna Ribič Veliki trg 3; ℡ 05 41 8313; ⏰08.00–01.00 daily. Held in equal esteem to

Parangal by the locals. The car park that sits between this fish restaurant & the sea can be off-putting for visitors. $$$$

Sidro Inn Sončo nabrežje 24; ℡ 05 641 4711; ⏰08.00–midnight daily. Another of Izola's great waterfront seafood restaurants. $$$$

Gušt Devored 1 Maja 3; m 041 675 953; ⏰08.00–01.00 daily. If you don't fancy fish then head to this friendly little pizzeria. $$

ENTERTAINMENT AND NIGHTLIFE

☆ **Gavioli** Located amidst Izola's industrial zone & only open at weekends, Gavioli is a favourite of the 'hands in the air' Slovene dance crowd. Entrance € 10–15.

☆ **Club Belvedere** (see *Where to stay*) The Belvedere's nightclub is a cheesier & cheaper option. Entrance from € 5.

♀ **Wall Pub** Sončno nabrežje. Lively waterfront pub.

OTHER PRACTICALITIES

✉ **Post office** Cankarjev drevored 1; ⏰08.00–19.00 Mon–Fri, 08.00–12.00 Sat

$ **Banka Koper** Drevored 1 Maja 5; ⏰08.30–12.00 & 15.00–17.00 Mon–Fri, 08.30–12.00 Sat

$ **A Banka** Pittonijeva 1; ⏰08.00–12.00 & 16.00–18.00 Mon–Fri, 09.00–12.00 Sat

WHAT TO SEE There are few real sights in Izola with the highlights just lazing away the afternoon in one of the seafood restaurants, wandering around the small web of Venetian streets and dawdling around the coast. Attractions as such include the **Church of St Maurus** (Cerkev Sv Mavricija) whose detached belltower rises high above the town and the Rococo **Besenghi degli Ughi Palace**, where you can hear the efforts of local music students and admire the fine stuccowork on the façade. The local authorities have dabbled with renovating the waterfront past the marina with a landscaped park, but turn the corner and a concrete pier at the town's main beach lies cracked in two. One positive move has been to tempt Slovene artists into Izola with cheap rents and the Old Town now has a sprinkling of little studios where you can pick up some truly unique works as well as slightly cheesy images of the coastal towns. A tourist train is on hand to whisk you around. Simon's Bay is the best local beach, though most sun-worshippers have no idea a Roman port once lay on the site. The **Parenzana Museum** (*Alme Vivode 3;* ✆ *05 640 1050; free entry;* ✆ *09.00–12.00 & 18.00–21.00 Tue–Sun*) commemorates the opening of the railway line between Trieste and Poreč, illustrating the history of the line with photos and documents. The highlight, though, are the model trains from around the globe.

PIRAN

Piran is by far the most attractive town on Slovenia's bijou coastline, the sort of oasis that you cannot pull yourself away from and where you will end up wanting to buy a house. You will not be alone as property prices are accelerating in the Old Town as the city's young people are nudged out to nearby Lucija – EU accession has hastened this move as in the first few months of membership around a dozen Old Town dwellings were snapped up by foreigners as holiday homes. Piran sits dramatically on its own peninsula with the Adriatic lapping all around, while Trieste is clearly visible to the north and Croatia to the south. Preserved as a national monument its narrow, cobbled streets hark back to the days of the mighty Venetian Republic, which bequeathed Piran many of its most elaborate and attractive buildings. Piran does also have its downsides, such as a car park on its most striking square and a glut of overpriced restaurants. Sitting today on the waterfront at sunset, savouring fresh seafood and a chilled glass of locally produced Malvazija wine, with the lights of Trieste twinkling to the north and the shadowy hulk of Croatia looming to the south, Piran is a truly magical place to be.

HISTORY While the Venetian legacy is the most striking, the name 'Piran' probably comes from the Greek word *pyr*, meaning fire, when the extremities of Piran were illuminated to ward off passing ships. Early in its history, both the Romans and the Slavs breezed through Piran before 'La Serenissima' wrapped itself around the town in the 13th century and held on to it for the best part of five centuries. Under the Austro-Hungarians in the 19th century, Piran sprawled out along the coast towards Portorož but these days development has moved inland and the hills in the hinterland are awash with holiday homes, though the central core remains intact and protected. Between the world wars Piran was firmly under Italian rule and a wave of settlers flocked in to bolster the fascist attempts to Italianise the town by banning the use of the Slovene language and its teaching in schools. Although some Italians did flee when Piran was handed to Yugoslavia there is still a lively Italian community today with no fewer than four Italian elementary schools. Sadly some of Piran's older buildings are in a sorry state as few businesses or residents can manage to make the sums add up when it comes to renovating them and sticking to the strict preservation rules at the same time; something that passing visitors do not need to worry about as it only adds to the charm of the town.

GETTING THERE Regular buses connect Piran to Portorož (5 minutes), Strunjan (10 minutes), Izola (20 minutes), Koper (30 minutes), Postojna (1½ hours),

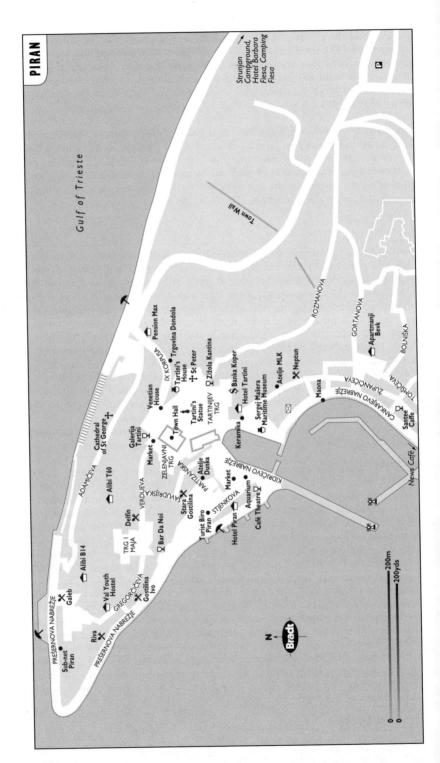

PIRAN

Gulf of Trieste

Strunjan
Campground,
Hotel Barbara
Fiesa, Camping
Fiesa

Town Wall

ROZMANOVA

GORTANOVA

Apartmanji
Bevk

BOLNIŠKA

TOMŠIČEVA

ŽUPANČIČEVA

CANKARJEVO NABREŽJE

Santee
Caffe

News Café

KIDRIČEVO NABREŽJE

Maona

Neptun

Atelje MLK

Sergej Mašera
Maritime Museum

Hotel Tartini

Banka Koper

Žižola Kantina

St Peter

Tartini's
House

Trgovina Dondola

Pension Max

IX KORPUSA

Venetian
House

Town Hall

Tartini's
Statue

TARTINIJEV
TRG

Keramika

Aquarium

Hotel Piran

Café Theatre

Market

Atelje
Dunka

PRATZIJANSKA

STJENKOVA

Turist Biro
Piran

Star X
Gostilina

Bar Da Noi

Delfin

TRG 1
MAJA

Alibi B14

Galb

Val Youth
Hostel

Gostilina
Ivo

GREGORČIČEVA

PREŠERNOVA NABREŽJE

Riva

Sub-net
Piran

PREŠERNOVA NABREŽJE

Galerija
Tartini

Market

ZELENJAVNI
TRG

ŠAVUDRIJSKA

VERDJEVA

Alibi T60

ADAMIČEVA

Cathedral
of St George

N

Bradt

0   200m
0   200yds

154

Ljubljana (2½ hours), Celje (4½ hours), Maribor (5½ hours) and Murska Sobota (6½ hours).

Amazingly locals are allowed to park on historic Tartinijev trg (see *A walking tour*, page 157); tourists are directed to the public car park at Formače towards Bernardin, from where you can either walk (15–20 minutes) or hop on a free shuttle bus.

GETTING AROUND
🚖 **Taxi Piran** ↘ 05 673 0700

TOURIST INFORMATION/LOCAL TOUR OPERATORS
🄸 **Tourist Information Centre** Tartinijev trg 2; ↘ 05 673 4040; e ticpi@portoroz.si; www.portoroz.si; ⊕Sep–Jun 09.00–16.00 Mon–Fri, 09.00–12.00 Sat; Jul/Aug 09.00–13.00 & 15.00–21.00 daily. Recently revamped.
Turist Biro Piran Tomažičeva 3; ↘ 05 673 2509; f 05 673 2507; e info@tuirsbiro-ag.si; www.turistbiro-ag.si

Maona Cankarjevo nabrežje 7; ↘ 05 673 4520; e maona@siol.net; www.maona.si
Sub-net Diving School ↘ 05 673 2218; e info@sub-net.si; www.sub-net.si. Offers a variety of diving courses, including PADI, & dives. Explore a shipwreck or Slovenia's only marine reserve. Prices start at €25 for a guided dive from the shore.

⌂ WHERE TO STAY
⌂ **Hotel Piran** (78 rooms) Stjenkova 1; ↘ 05 676 2520; e marketing@hoteli-piran.si; www.hoteli-piran.si. Welcoming hotel on the seafront. Modern rooms have a minibar & satellite TV. Try to book a sea-facing room with a balcony. The hotel also has some car-parking spaces. The restaurant is also above average; make sure to book a window table. $$$–$$$$
⌂ **Hotel Tartini** (43 rooms) Tartinijev trg 15; ↘ 05 671 1000; e info@hotel-tartini-piran.com; www.hotel-tartini-piran.com. Stylish modern hotel with individual rooms. Although they do not have the sea views of the Hotel Piran, square-view rooms have an appeal of their own, though standards vary between rooms. $$$–$$$$
⌂ **Pension Max** IX Korpusa 26; ↘ 05 673 3436; e info@maxpiran.com; www.maxhotel-piran.com. Friendly & welcoming pension on the way up to the Cathedral of St George (Stolna Cerkev Sv Jurija). $$$

⌂ **Hotel Barbara Fiesa** (44 rooms) Fiesa 68; ↘ 05 617 9000; f 05 617 9010; e hotel.barbara@siol.net; www.rlv.si/fiesa. Located in nearby Fiesa the hotel offers good-value rooms with sea views & balconies. 4 of the rooms sleep 4 people. $$
⌂ **Alibi B14 Hostel** (6 rooms) Bonifacijeva 14; ↘ 05 673 0141; www.alibi.si/b14/index.html. Bright & welcoming dormitory rooms sleeping 4–6 people. Rates are pp. $
⌂ **Alibi T60 Hostel** Trubarjeva 60; ↘ 05 673 0141. Hostel accommodation in dbl & twin rooms. Reception at Alibi B14. $$
⌂ **Apartmanji Bevk** Marxova 13; ↘ 05 162 3682; e info@bevk.si; www.bevk.si. Offering 3 attractive self-catering apts at the heart of Piran's Old Town. $$
⌂ **Val Youth Hostel and Garni Hotel** (22 rooms) Gregorčičeva 38a; ↘ 05 673 2555; f 05 673 2556; e yhostel.val@siol.net; www.hostel-val.com. Simple 2–4-bed rooms with shared bathroom facilities on each floor. Rates are pp. $

Camping
Ⅺ **Camping Fiesa** Fiesa 57b; ↘ 05 674 6230. This Fiesa campsite is very busy in Jul/Aug. Rates are pp. $
Ⅺ **Strunjan Campground** Strunjan 23; ↘ 05 678 2076; f 05 678 2344; e amd-piran@siol.net; www.amdpiran-drustvo.si. With 200 pitches spread

over 1.5ha this campsite, overlooking Strunjan Bay, can feel a bit crowded in Jul/Aug. Arrive early & you might be lucky enough to find a pitch with views back towards Piran. Wooden bungalows sleeping 4 are available to rent. Bungalows $$$, camping $

✗ **WHERE TO EAT** Most locals avoid the flurry of tourist-oriente restaurants dotted along the waterfront. In these you pay more risk of sacrificing quality. These waterfront restaurants do views out across the Adriatic.

✕ Neptun Župančičeva 7; ☎ 05 673 4111; ⏰11.00–23.00 daily. Ask most locals where the best place to eat seafood is & they will send you here. An intimate dining space & good service form part of the appeal, but the winning ingredient is excellent food. The gnocchi with cheese & shrimps is divine. The only things Neptun doesn't have are sea views & a terrace. **$$$$**

✕ Gostilna Ivo Gregorčičeva 31; ☎ 05 673 2233; ⏰11.00–23.00 daily. As good as it gets on the waterfront strip. This unfussy seafood trattoria-style set-up does the likes of grilled squid & sea bass well, with a generous platter for 2 also available. **$$$$**

✕ Galeb Pusterla 5; ☎ 05 673 3225; ⏰11.00–22.00 daily. Another local favourite. In the summer the restaurant spills out onto the waterfront terrace. Serves seafood specialities & grills. **$$$**

✕ Riva Gregorčičeva 43; ☎ 05 673 2225; ⏰09.00–midnight daily. Combining great seafood & sea views – what more could you want? **$$$**

✕ Stara Gostilna Savudrijska 2; m 041 640 240; ⏰09.00–23.00 daily. Tasty grills, fresh fish & friendly staff make Stara a good option. **$$$**

✕ Delfin Kosovelova 4; ☎ 05 673 2448; ⏰11.00–23.00 daily. Another fish restaurant favoured by locals, just off Trg 1 Maja. **$$$**

ENTERTAINMENT AND NIGHTLIFE

☕ Café Teatre Piran The place to see & be seen in Piran. Great café-bar with a polished wooden interior, mellow music & great sea views from the terrace. The only downside is the seriously dodgy Guinness. Housed in Piran's bright-yellow theatre, you cannot miss it.

♀ Bar Da Noi Another waterfront bar with friendly staff & a good-sized garden. The music can be a bit iffy though.

♀ Zižola Kantina Tartinijev trg 10. Tiny bolthole with a terrace overlooking the main square. Blink & you miss it.

☕ News Café Obala 4f, Bernardin; ⏰until 02.00. Good food – including b/fast, open sandwiches, gnocchi, pasta & enormous salads – & regular live music all make the walk here worth the effort (if you are not staying in Bernardin). Decent cocktail list & range of beers too in a huge venue. Just follow the sea around the coast from Piran in the direction of Portorož.

☕ Santeé Caffe Župančičeva 18; Bright & modern café-bar selling tasty ice cream.

☕ Galerija Tartini Zelenjavni trg 10. Stylish café-cum-art gallery that spills out onto the square in the warmer months.

SHOPPING

Atelje Dunka Partizanska 2. Contemporary ceramics including funky vases & statues of cats made in the onsite workshop.

Atelje MLK Župančičeva 3. Sells handmade glass & contemporary paintings.

Keramika Cankarjevo nabrežje 1. Wide range of ceramics including artistic tiles.

Trgovina Dondola IX Korpusa 18. Handmade ceramics geared towards a tourist market.

Tourist Market You can pick up cheap jewellery, prints of Piran & other seaside souvenirs at this small market on Kidričevo nabrežje outside the aquarium.

Food For fresh food head to the market on Zelenjavni trg. On the square you will find a fishmonger, mini market, bakery & a pharmacy. If these are closed there is a **Mercator** at Levstikova 5.

OTHER PRACTICALITIES

✉ **Post office** Leninova 1; ⏰08.00–19.00 Mon–Fri, 08.00–12.00 Sat

$ Banka Koper Tartinijev trg 13; ⏰08.30–12.00 & 15.00–17.00 Mon–Fri, 08.30–12.00 Sat. Piran's most central bank.

WHAT TO SEE

A walking tour A good place to start is on the remaining stretch of the town walls high above Piran, at their most impressive at sunrise or sunset, as the town glows ... reds with the Adriatic spreading out all around. To get to the walls ... Cathedral of St George (Stolna Cerkev Sv Jurija) and follow ... Cut left through what looks like someone's garden, just ... lls, and a staircase takes you up onto the well-preserved ... talian Alps are plainly visible and you get a bird's-eye

The great composer was born in Piran on 8 April 1692, in the house that is now a museum dedicated to him and his work. His father, a merchant who later became involved in the local salt trade, came to Piran from his native Florence and married Tartini's mother, a woman from Piran, in 1685. There is some evidence that Tartini showed his musical talent at an early stage in his life, but one of the most important violinists of the 18th century was almost lost to music after he flirted with life in Naples running a martial arts school, an art he had learned during his time at the University of Padua, where he was studying law. Padua was also a crucial period in Tartini's love life as he met Elisabetta Premazore when he was still a teenager and later married her in the city in 1710.

From Padua his life took an ecclesiastical turn as he moved to Assisi to join the Franciscan brotherhood where he devoted much of his time to music. As his reputation grew he ventured further afield, playing regularly in Assisi's surrounds and also in Ancona, before moving to Venice with his wife in 1715. Tartini quickly established himself as one of the most renowned performers in Italy and when he was not composing and teaching others, he was devoted to travelling to and performing in Milan, Bologna and Naples. After a two-year period being fêted and productive in Prague Tartini settled back in his beloved Padua where he spent the rest of his life. His performances around the country were severely limited after a minor stroke and he died in Padua in 1770, a year after his wife, with a requiem being held in the city in his honour. Today Tartini is remembered as not only a great violinist, but also as a composer and musical theorist. Tartini left a more immediate legacy in the expertly trained graduates from the violin school he ran in Padua.

view of Piran – here you can appreciate just how tightly woven its medieval town plan, or lack of it, is.

From the walls, if you fancy relaxing at the beach, turn right as you walk back towards the Cathedral of St George. Follow the path that curls around the coast to the small resort of Fiesa 1km away, a real summer playground that gets packed when the mercury rises. Otherwise go into the church and have a look at the sculpture of George himself slaying the dragon. Now head back down the hill to Tartinijev trg, once actually part of the town's harbour, but now Piran's showpiece square and the hub of local life. It is a real shame that this striking square is still blighted by parked cars. Dominating the centre of the square is a **statue** by the Venetian sculptor Antonio dal Zotto of Giuseppe Tartini, the locally born composer who gives the square its name. The **Church of St Peter** (Cerkev Sv Petra) has stood on the square since the 13th century, though it has been revamped in various styles over the centuries.

The 19th-century **Town Hall** (Mestna Hiša) stands opposite on the site of the old Venetian loggia with the civic, Slovenian and European Union flags all flying proudly over the square. Perhaps the most attractive building in the whole square is the ruby-red **Venetian House** (Benečanka), which dates back to the 15th century and is still in pretty good shape. Look out for the Venetian lion and the inscription 'lassa pur dir', which translates as 'let them talk', said to be a reference to the love-struck man who commissioned the house as a testimony to his love for a local girl. Apparently, he wanted to show he was not afraid of local gossips defaming his new love.

Tartini's House (*Tartinijeva Hiša; Kajuhova 12;* ✆ *05 663 3570; entry* €*1;* ⊕ *Sep–May 11.00–12.00 & 17.00–18.00 daily; Jun–Aug 09.00–12.00 &*

18.00–21.00 daily) The house where Piran's most famous son was born now houses the Giuseppe Tartini Memorial Room, dedicated to the renowned composer. Tartini was cherished by Slovenes throughout the country; although he was born in what comprises present-day Slovenia, his family was Italian. Exhibits on display include Tartini's death mask, one of his violins and some of his original scores. The museum was opened in 1991.

Sergej Mašera Maritime Museum (*Pomorski Muzej Sergej Mašera; Cankarjevo nabrežje 3; ✆ 05 671 0040; f 05 671 0050; e muzej@pommuz-pi.si; www2.arnes.si/guest/ kppomm/index.htm; adult/concession €3.40/€3; ◷09.00–12.00 & 15.00–18.00 Tue–Sun*) Housed in the 19th-century **Gabrielli Palace** (Gabrielli Palača), located on the waterfront, the maritime museum has exhibits based around seafaring, maritime routes, trade and salt making. Highlights include the shipbuilding display and the impressive array of intricate model ships. Remember to seek out the museum's sailing ship *Galeb* which is moored in Piran harbour.

Aquarium (*Akvarij; Kidričevo Nabrežje 4; ✆ 05 673 2572; f 05 674 7242; adult/concession €2/€1.25; ◷mid Mar–mid Jun & Sep/mid Oct 10.00–12.00 & 14.00–19.00 daily; mid Jun–Aug 09.00–22.00 daily*) Piran's modest Aquarium may not be the biggest or most high-tech of its kind in the world, but it does have a good selection of local marine life and is a good option for a rainy day, especially for those with children in tow.

PORTOROŽ

The reality of Portorož may be a bit more prosaic than the 'port of roses' moniker suggests. In summer this can be some people's idea of hell as thousands of tourists descend to cram into the large hotels and squash together on the congested beaches. To be fair to Portorož, though, it is trying to clean up its old socialist-era image with refurbished hotels, numerous 'wellness centres' and a choice of new bars and restaurants that overcome the nightmare of the old-fashioned hotel buffet. Portorož these days is a fun place to put your feet up and relax for a few days. It is also becoming increasingly popular with boat show and conference organisers. Portorož also makes a good base for exploring the coast and for striking out into Croatia.

GETTING THERE
By car The main thoroughfare in Portorož, Obala, which runs along the seafront, is full of parking spaces, the majority of which are pay and display. There are also secure car parks near the Hotel Metropol and Hotel Palace.

By sea Portorož Marina (*Solinarjev 8; ✆ 05 676 1100; f 05 676 1210; e reception@ marinap.si; www.marinap.si*) has over 1,000 berths and welcomes visiting yachts. Facilities are good and include hotel accommodation, restaurants, supermarket, laundry, car rental, yacht charter and equipment, clothing and most other supplies that you might need. There is also the possibility of day returns to Venice by catamaran.

By bus Buses serve Portorož from Piran (5 minutes), Strunjan (5 minutes), Izola (10 minutes), Koper (25 minutes), Postojna (1½ hours), Ljubljana (2½ hours), Celje (4 hours 20 minutes), Maribor (6 hours) and Murska Sobota (7½ hours).

On foot/by bicycle A pleasant 40-minute walk that curls around the bay takes you from Piran via Bernadin to Portorož. On a bike the journey will be even quicker.

GETTING AROUND
Taxi Piran ✆ 05 673 0700

TOURIST INFORMATION/LOCAL TOUR OPERATORS
🛈 Tourist Information Centre Obala 16; ✆ 05 674 2220; f 05 674 8261; e ticpo@portoroz.si; www.portoroz.si; ⏱Sep–Jun 09.00–17.00 daily; Jul/Aug 09.00–13.00 & 15.00–21.00 daily

Portorož is overflowing with tourist agencies who arrange private accommodation. Those listed below are located on Obala.

Atlas Express Obala 55; ✆ 05 674 6772; e atlas.portoroz@siol.net. Also offer bicycle & scooter hire for 2–24 hrs. You must be over 18 & have a valid driving licence to hire a scooter.
Kompas Obala 41; ✆ 05 617 8000; f 05 674 7258; e portoroz@kompas.si

Maona Obala 14b; ✆ 05 674 0363; f 05 674 6423; e maona@siol.net; www.maona.si
Top Line Obala 144; ✆ 05 674 7161; f 05 674 7029; e top.line@siol.net; www.topline.si
Turist biro Obala 57; ✆ 05 674 1055; f 05 674 1056; e info@turistbiro-ag.si; www.turistbiro-ag.si

WHERE TO STAY While we wait with bated breath for the once-grand Hotel Palace to reopen (the latest estimates suggest this will happen in 2009), Portorož has plenty of alternatives.

🏠 **Hotel Riviera** (183 rooms) Obala 33; ✆ 05 692 9001; f 05 692 9003; e booking@lifeclass.net; www.lifeclass.net. Everything about this hotel is stylish from the lobby to its cocktail bar & wellness centre offering Thai massage. Large bedrooms are modern & comfortable & the hotel also has 3 heated seawater swimming pools & one of the best b/fast buffets in Slovenia. $$$$$
🏠 **Hotel Slovenija** (160 rooms) Obala 33 ✆ 05 692 9001; f 05 692 9003; e booking@lifeclass.net; www.lifeclass.net. The Riviera's sister hotel has modern & comfortable rooms with balconies, cable

BORDER BOTHER

Take a wrong turning on the Slovenian Adriatic and you may well end up in Croatia, which is not necessarily a bad thing as it has plenty to offer. Croatia's majority stake of the Istrian Peninsula tempts not just visitors as Slovenia has been locked in a dispute over where the border lies since the two countries became independent back in 1991. The crux of the issue is that Slovenia wants to at least secure its present coastline and guarantee its access to the open sea, while Croatia wants to assert its own coastal rights and solidify its dominance of this stretch of the Adriatic. The argument has been widened into the practicalities of the Dragonja River, which marks much of the border and has confused the issue by changing its course. This wrangle and other similar squabbles along the border keep rearing up and then slipping back down the agenda when both countries draw bad press from it and the only thing that you will probably notice are the flash Slovenia Policija speedboats that prance proudly up and down Slovenia's coast in a clear statement that these are firmly Slovenian territorial waters.

This ongoing problem stems from the fact that prior to 1991 there was no distinct Croatian or Slovenian territorial sea, just one uniform area belonging to Yugoslavia, which gave all of the federation's member states uniform access to international waters. Along with the independence of both countries came the question of how to divide the former Yugoslav territorial seas between them and to ensure that Slovenia continued to have access to international waters. As Croatia heads closer to EU membership the border issue looks set to rise further up the political agenda.

TV & minibars. For a real treat ask for a room with a waterbed. Guests also have direct access to the Riviera's swimming pools & spa centre. $$$$$

⌂ **Grand Hotel Metropol** (104 rooms) Obala 77; ☎ 05 690 1000; f 05 690 1900; e sales@metropolgroup.si; www.metropolgroup.si. Despite its luxurious rooms, 5-star rating & impressive list of facilities including its own casino, this immense concrete hotel may not be to everyone's taste. $$$$$

⌂ **Hotel Roža** (111 rooms) Obala 77; ☎ 05 690 2000; f 05 690 2900; e sales@metropolgroup.si; www.metropolgroup.si. The poorer sister of the

Grand Hotel Metropol has good-sized rooms with balconies & sea views. Guests can use all the facilities at the other hotel. $$$$–$$$$$

⌂ **Hotel Restaurant Tomi** Letoviska 1; ☎ 05 674 0222; f 05 674 7285; e tomi.m@siol.net; www.tomi-sp.si. This restaurant offers accommodation in a number of rooms & apts sleeping 1–4 people. $$$

⌂ **Penzion Forma Viva** Seča 159, Seča; m 040 369 003; e info@formaviva-portoroz.com; www.formaviva-portoroz.com. If the prices in Portorož itself leave you cold then try this much more affordable pension located in Seča. $$–$$$

Camping

⋀ **Lucija Campground** Seča 204, Lucija; ☎ 05 690 6000; f 05 690 6900; e camp@metropolgroup.si; www.metropolgroup.si. Campsite offering

watersports, minigolf & other sports facilities. With onsite entertainment, a restaurant & a shop. Rates are pp. $

✖ **WHERE TO EAT** There are myriad dining options in Portorož which are unashamedly geared towards tourists. This means that you can often get an inexpensive set-price meal, but the food is rarely outstanding.

✖ **Restavracija Staro Sidro** Obala 55; ☎ 05 674 5074; ◷ 11.00–23.00 daily. A stone staircase adorned with an imitation Venetian lion leads you to the restaurant's raised & secluded terrace. Away from the bustle on the main street, this is the spot in Portorož for a romantic meal. Good seafood makes up for the cheesy music & plastic furniture. $$$$

✖ **Pizzeria Figarola** Obala 14a; ☎ 05 674 2200; ◷ 10.00–22.00 daily. A light AC interior & good pizzas make this one of Portorož's most popular

restaurants. If you don't fancy a pizza then they also serve tasty pasta dishes & large salads. $$$

✖ **Restavracija Gregory** Obala 14; ☎ 05 674 2200; ◷ 10.00–22.00 daily. Located to the rear of Figarola with a typical menu of fish & grills. The food is good though. For children there is the cheekily named 'McDonald's Gregory Burger'. $$$

✖ **Stara Oljka** Obala 20; ☎ 05 674 8555; ◷ 10.00–midnight daily. Tasty Balkan grills. $$$

✖ **Mercator** Obala 53. Central branch of the omnipresent supermarket chain.

ENTERTAINMENT AND NIGHTLIFE

⌑ **Caco** Obala 14. Trendy café with a great outdoor terrace.

♀ **Mystica** Hotel Riviera. This raised terrace with stylish furniture & loungers is one of the best locations for a drink on a summer's night. Choose from the extensive list of cocktails, but make sure you get there before it closes at 22.00.

♀ **Paprika Pub** Obala 20a. Live music, a sleek interior & tree-fringed terrace overlooking Portorož make this new bar a popular spot.

⌑ **News Café** (see *Piran* listings, page 156)
Avditorij Portorož Senčna pot 10; ☎ 05 676 6700; www.avditorij.si. Keep a lookout for performances in the auditorium's open-air amphitheatre.

☆ **Grand Casino Portorož** Obala 75a; ☎ 05 676 0373; www.casino.si. Late-night gambling & entertainment.

OTHER PRACTICALITIES

$ **Banka Koper** Obala 33; ◷ 08.00–12.00 & 15.00–17.00 Mon–Fri, 08.30–12.00 Sat

✉ **Post office** K Stari 1; ◷ 08.00–19.00 Mon–Fri, 08.00–12.00 Sat

WHAT TO SEE As it's a purpose-built resort, a visit to Portorož is not so much about what to see but more about relaxing and participating in the many activities

While most visitors rumble up and down the busy coast road, the hinterland of Slovenia's slice of the Istrian Peninsula is worth visiting on a day trip or as an alternative route to save any backtracking through the coastal resorts. You will need your own wheels, though, as public transport is infrequent at best. Following the highway north from Koper you will gain altitude quickly and soon be peering down on Koper and the Adriatic with the Karst rising to the northwest. The main road here continues all the way to Croatia, but you should fork off after 15 minutes at the turn marked Šmarje. This quiet hilltop village has a Partisan Monument, with the names of local men who died fighting the Nazis, and the modest Church of the Virgin Mary. Circle back down the main road and take the right turn for Korte, a charming hamlet that boasts sweeping views of the surrounding hilltop villages and the green vine-covered slopes. The restaurant in Korte also sometimes has the elusive Slovenian truffle; most are imported from Croatia. Look out also for the *vinska klet* signs that are sprinkled around the hills – you can often arrange tastings or at the very least secure a bottle of the local produce from the various wine houses.

on offer. Nearby Sečovlje with its saltpans and unique flora and fauna is definitely worth a visit. A range of watersports is available at the resort's beaches and the **Viva Sculpture Park** is a pleasant diversion for a couple of hours. Portorož is also a good alternative base for exploring Piran.

Sečovlje Salina Nature Park Just 3km from Portorož, on Slovenia's southwestern border with Croatia, is a unique nature park covering 6.5km². The Sečovlje saltpans (*www.kpss.soline.si*) are divided into two parts, Lera in the north and Fontanigge in the south, by the Drinica Channel. In Lera salt is still being harvested from the pans, whilst this process was abandoned in Fontanigge back in the 1960s. Today the southern part is home to the **Museum of Salt Making** (*Muzej Solinarstva; adult/concession €3/€2; ⊕09.00–13.00 & 14.00–19.00 daily*), where you can still see traditional salt-harvesting methods that date back to the 14th century. Both Lera and Fontanigge are open to the public and can be explored on foot or by bicycle along well-marked routes.

The salt production alone did not earn Sečovlje the status of a nature park, which it was awarded in 2001: its distinctive and diverse fauna and flora also played a role. Shallow water with high levels of salinity, the salt-production process itself and the Mediterranean climate all combine to create the ecological conditions necessary to support a diverse and thriving fauna and flora. Sečovlje has an abundance of salt-loving plants and is home to more than 270 species of birds. The saltpans are an ornithologist's dream in the spring and autumn when migrating birds stop off *en route* to or returning from Africa or the rest of Europe. Look out for the three species of heron that have been spotted at the nature park throughout the year: the little egret, the great white egret and the grey heron.

Although they are both part of the Sečovlje Salinas Nature Park, Lera and Fontanigge are not connected by land and have separate entrances. To access Fontanigge by land you have to cross the Slovenian border checkpoint and then turn right before you reach the checkpoint on the Croatian border. Both Lera and Fontanigge can also be reached by boat with **Solinarka** (m *031 653 682; adult/concession €11/€7; pick-up from Bernardin at 09.15, Portorož at 09.30 or Piran at 09.45 in Jul/Aug*). If you don't make it to the saltpans, the shop on the ground floor of the **Venetian House** (Benečanke Hiša) on Tartinijev trg 10 in Piran sells products made from the salt harvested there.

ACTIVITIES AND EXCURSIONS
Boat trips
Burja Tours End of the main pier; www.ladja-burja.com. This company offers a variety of excursions on board a modern boat including a trip to Poreč, a fish picnic & sunset cruises. They also pick up in Koper, Izola & Piran.

Aquamarine Run trips from Bernardin harbour.

Indulgence
Wai Thai Wellness Centre Hotel Riviera, Obala 33; ↘ 05 696 8060; www.lifeclass.net. Treat yourself to a Thai massage, facial or an oriental honey wrap in the Riviera Hotel's luxurious spa. The centre's signature Wai Thai massage costs €50.

Terme Palace Obala 43; ↘ 05 696 8060; www.lifeclass.net. The Grand Hotel Palace's modern thermal pools, thalassotherapy centre, massage & a wellness centre are all great places to treat yourself. They also have a 'Sauna Park' with a variety of wet & dry stations.

Swimming If you don't fancy plunging into the sea then most of the hotels will also let you use their pools for a fee, although these are usually full of salt water too.

Postojna cave formations

7

Notranjska

The world-famous caves at Postojna, Predjama Castle and Lake Cerknica aside, much of southerly Notranjska is still undiscovered and economically undeveloped. In Notranjska's west the Karst landscape of Primorska continues with its landmark caves and disappearing rivers and lakes. To the east, though, it is a very different story as the vast forests of Slovenia's southern flank take over. This is no post-Sunday-lunch country park jaunt as amidst the pitch-black forests bears, lynx and wolves still run wild. If Hollywood is looking for a venue for shooting a follow-up to the *Blair Witch Project* they could not pick anywhere more dramatic or spooky. This unheralded region does have one major claim to fame – the locals here insist that Notranjska was the birthplace of skiing in Europe, a sport they say was born on the Bloke Plateau.

POSTOJNA CAVES (POSTOJNSKA JAMA)

(*Postojnska Jama Turizem; Jamska 30;* \ *05 700 0100;* f *05 700 0130;* e *info@ postojnska-jama.si; www.postojnska-jama.si; adult/student/child €18/€14/€10.80; tours Jan–Mar & Nov/Dec 10.00, 12.00 & 14.00 Mon–Fri, 10.00, 12.00, 14.00 & 16.00 Sat/Sun; Apr/Oct 10.00, 12.00, 14.00 & 16.00 daily; May–Sep 09.00–18.00 daily on the hour*) Slovenia's largest cave complex, and Europe's most visited, is certainly no secret and on a packed high-season day it feels like all of the 30 million-plus tourists who have visited the caves over the years are here at once. It is easy to recoil at the concrete hotel that blights the entrance, the rip-off car parking and toilet charges, as well as the factory-like processing of tourists, but the two-million-year-old caves themselves make up for it all for most visitors. A good plan, though, is to come here first for the wow factor and then hop across to the Škocjan Caves (see *Chapter 5, Primorska*, page 141), which most people find even more dramatic. For the infirm or those slightly squeamish with heights the Postojna Caves are much more manageable with solid concrete paths, few steep ascents and most of the distance covered by train.

HISTORY Like most of the caves in Slovenia's Karst region the Postojna Caves are millions of years old. The huge 21.5km-long cave complex has been known to man for centuries (the first recorded human visit to the caves was in 1213), but it was not until the 19th century that it was extensively explored after lighting was installed and the first pathways were constructed in 1818. By the 1820s the first guidebook to the caves had appeared. The Habsburg Prince Ferdinand is said to have been one of the first tourists to delve into the caves and millions have followed ever since.

Mankind's abuse of this delicate ecosystem began as soon as it was discovered, with the earliest visitors blackening the formations nearest to the entrance with torchlight and carving their names on fragile stalagmites. In 1824, this mistreatment began in earnest with the staging of the first event ever held – a

Map labels:
Cerkno
LJUBLJANA
Spodnja Idrija
Idrija
Wild Lake
A1
E70
A2
Ajdovščina
Vipava Valley
Vipava
Predjama Castle
Planinska Cave
Pivka Cave
Bloke Plateau
Lake Cerknica
Postojna Caves
Black Cave
Postojna
A1
12
9
Križna Cave
Snežnik Castle
Karst
E61
7
N
Bradt
CROATIA
0 ——————— 20km
0 ——————— 20miles
NOTRANJSKA

dance – in the modern-day **Kongresna Dvorana** (Congress Room). The first organised tour arrived in 1936 and the opening of the Vienna–Ljubljana–Trieste railway in 1857 saw the number of people visiting the Postojna Caves rise dramatically. With scant regard to conservation the caves' first railroad was constructed in 1872. Further lighting was installed in 1884 and gas-powered locomotives began operating on the caves' railway track in 1914 (in 1959 these were replaced by electric trains which preserve the air quality more effectively).

Other damage inflicted upon the caves was largely dictated by the political climate of the time and they have been used as bunkers, hideouts and for storage. During World War II the Germans even amassed fuel in the caves, a stockpile that brought devastating destruction to some areas when partisan forces set it alight. These days the tourist operation is slick and efficient and, in a bid to protect the caves, the transit of the masses of people, who, understandably, want to visit one of Slovenia's most spectacular attractions is carefully managed. The only way to see the caves is on a tour, where the paths must be adhered to and the taking of photographs is not allowed (although many visitors flaunt this rule).

FORMATION Experts estimate that the formation of the Postojna Caves dates back over four million years, with the River Pivka eroding the limestone rock to create a system of caverns. Tectonic movements facilitated the river in its work and allowed it to penetrate the caves at deeper and deeper depths. As a result the caves have three distinctive levels, with the river continuing to flow and cut its way through the rock at the lowest. Scientists believe that the oldest limestone formations first began some 40,000–100,000 years ago; sadly many of these have now dried out and are falling apart, while the larger stalagmites and stalactites on display today are believed to date back a mere 8,000 years. These other-worldly creations are formed by rainwater as it seeps through the limestone and brings deposits with it, that very slowly, drip by drip, settle on the tip of the ever-growing stalagmites or stalactites. Occurring at a rate of less than 1mm every ten years this growth is invisible to the human eye, but is given away by the splashing droplets of rain and moist surfaces. Take time to notice the slightly different colours of the formations in Postojna Caves. These variations are caused by the presence of minerals and chemicals in the rainwater, as well as the quantity of rainwater permeating the stone – the whitest structures are the most 'pure'.

THE TOUR The only way to see the caves unless you are on a scientific research trip is to go on the 1½-hour guided tour, which allows a bit of walking between two train trips. Take a look at the Pivka River below the tourist complex as it disappears into the caves, later to resurface as the Ljubljanica which flows through the Slovenian capital. You should take a waterproof jacket as it can get cold and there are drips from the cave room. The tour starts with a stampede towards the entrance where the cute toytown trains await. Do not be fooled by their innocuous appearance, though, as they rattle off downhill for 2km at a fair rate and if you pop your head up for a closer look at the stalactites you risk losing it. The line (laid in 1872) skirts myriad stalactites and stalagmites on a narrow route in. On arrival at the foot of **Great Mountain** (Velika Gora) the hordes are divided up by language and trooped off for their 1.5km walk, starting with a stroll up the Great Mountain itself and then a wander through the galleries and caverns that house a variety of sizes and shapes of stalactites, stalagmites and pillars, many with nicknames such as Spaghetti.

The trail then drops down to the sturdy Russian Bridge, built by prisoners of war during World War I, that leads through to the aptly named Beautiful Cave before entering the Winter Hall where the Brilliant and Diamond formations have become the rather phallic symbol of the caves. There is much less description of the formations than in Škocjan and you are also whisked through at a fair pace. The walking section ends – after having paid a visit to some captive *Proteus anguinus* (human fish; see the box, *The Karst's Human Fish*, page 166) – in the **Concert Hall** (Koncertna Dvorana), a voluminous space that is used for concerts, although a tacky souvenir stand, that is meant to keep you occupied while you wait for the trains out, somewhat ruins the ambience.

GETTING THERE Buses and trains call at Postojna Town, with buses from Ajdovščina (45 minutes), Koper (1½ hours), Ljubljana (1 hour), Nova Gorica (1 hour 20 minutes), Piran (1½ hours) and Maribor (4½ hours). Trains arrive from Ljubljana (1 hour 20 minutes) and Koper (1½ hours). From Postojna you can walk to the caves, 1.5km from the centre of town, or get a taxi (see *Getting around* below).

GETTING AROUND A tourist train runs between Postojna railway station and Postojna Caves (adult/child €3/€2).

THE KARST'S HUMAN FISH

Some 200 living species have been discovered in Postojna Caves, with their most famous resident being the 'human fish' or *Proteus anguinus* – a species found only in Slovenia's Dinaric Karst. These little candyfloss-pink salamanders have human-like skin, although it has no pigment in it, and can live to a ripe old age of 100 years, spending their entire lives blind with no need for sight in their entirely dark native habitat.

Known by Slovenes as *mocherils* (a word that has emerged from the phrase 'that which burrows into wetness'), *Proteus anguinus* is believed to be the only amphibian that lives in caves. Adults can grow to be some 25–30cm long, are thin and snake-like with a flat tail that aids swimming. They also have two pairs of legs: the front ones, located just below their heads, have three digits and the hind ones, near the tail fin, bizarrely have just two. Other peculiarities are its ability to breathe inside and outside the water. It does this through three pairs of bright-red gills that are located at the back of its head, rudimentary lungs and even through its skin! Scientists have also discovered fundamental differences between the human fish and other amphibians, as *Proteus anguinus* does not finish the process of metamorphosis, instead reaching its sexual maturity as a larva (but between 16 and 18 years old) – a phenomenon that science terms neoteny. Today, knowledge of the *Proteus anguinus* remains limited so it is no surprise that for centuries the local people spoke of mysterious small dragons being found in pools near the region's myriad caves.

HUMAN FISH MUSEUM (*Proteus Vivarium; adult/child/student €6/€4.80/€3.60;* ⊕*Jan–Mar & Nov/Dec 10.00–15.00 Mon–Fri, 10.00–16.00 Sat/Sun & holidays; Apr/Oct 10.00–16.00 daily; May–Sep 09.00–18.00 daily. Tours take around 45 mins, starting at 10 mins past the hour with the last tour an hour before closing*) The Postojna Caves' most famous resident, the 'human fish' or *Proteus anguinus*, is a species that is found only in the Slovenian Karst. On your cave tour the only chance you get to see it is in a brightly lit pool, but here you can learn much more about it and other cave flora and fauna in the visitor's centre dedicated to speleobiology (the scientific study of life underground). As well as exhibits there is also a multi-media show.

TOURIST INFORMATION

🛈 **Tourist Information Centre** Jamska 30; ☏ 05 700 0100; f 05 700 0130; e info@postojnska-jama.si; www.postojnska-jama.si; ⊕May–Sep 09.00–18.00 daily, Oct–Apr 10.00–16.00 daily. The TIC has a list of accommodation, restaurants & bars in the Postojna area, as well as general information about the caves. They can help you book private accommodation, though getting there may be difficult if you do not have your own transport.

WHERE TO STAY

🏠 **Hotel Jama** (220 beds) Jamska 30; ☏ 05 700 0100; e info@posstojnska-jama.si; www.turizem-kras.si or www.lifeclass-postojna.com. The only hotel at the caves catering largely to tourist groups. A recent expansion and renovation has greatly improved the hotel. $$$–$$$$

✗ WHERE TO EAT Whichever of Jamska's cafés or restaurants you choose to eat at you can guarantee that it will be expensive (€3 for a humble burger or €2 for a can of Coke) and usually disappointing, so take your own food and enjoy a picnic in the sunshine. If you are staying at Hotel Jama it has a passable restaurant, but if you have a car you would be better off finding a countryside *gostilna* instead.

OTHER PRACTICALITIES There is a **Banka Koper ATM** next to the Proteus Vivarium.

POSTOJNA TOWN

If you have your own wheels, or your cave tour finishes early enough to allow you to catch a bus out of Postojna, it is a good idea to leave, as with many more interesting places within striking distance – such as Slovenia's coastal towns or the villages of the Karst – the unattractive town of Postojna is not really worth spending the night in.

GETTING THERE Buses and tours call at Postojna Town, with buses from Ajdovščina (45 minutes), Koper (1½ hours), Ljubljana (1 hour), Nova Gorica (1 hour 20 minutes), Piran (1½ hours) and Maribor (4½ hours). Trains arrive from Ljubljana (1 hour 20 minutes) and Koper (1½ hours).

TOURIST INFORMATION/LOCAL TOUR OPERATORS
Kompas Titov trg 2; \ 05 721 1480; f 05 721 1487; e info@kompas-postojna.si; www.kompas-postojna.si. Full service travel agent booking private accommodation, excursions, transport & car hire, etc. It also dishes out tourist information.

WHERE TO STAY
Hotel & Hostel Sport (120 beds) Koldovorska 1; \ 05 720 2244; f 05 720 2240; e info@sport-hotel.si; www.sport-hotel.si. Guests at the hotel & hostel benefit from internet access, en-suite facilities, a bar, restaurant & laundry. Bicycle hire is also available. Hotel $$$, hostel $

Hudičevec (9 rooms) Razdrto 1, Hruševje; \ 05 703 0300; f 05 703 0320; e hudicevec@siol.net; www.hudicevec.com. Pleasant tourist farm 8km from Postojna with dbls, quads & an apt sleeping 6. Rates are pp. $

Camping
Kamp Pivka Jama Veliki Otok 50; \ 05 726 5382; f 05 726 5348; e avtokamp.pivka.jama@siol.net; www.venus-trade.si. Camping & 4-person bungalows with an onsite restaurant 4km northwest of Postojna. Facilities include washing machines, shop, restaurant & bicycle hire. Bungalows $$$, camping $

WHERE TO EAT
Restavracija Milena Hruševje 4, Hruševje; \ 05 756 1063; ⊕ 11.00–23.00 daily. Located 8km from the caves, this charming restaurant offers typical dishes from Slovenia as well as wines from the Karst & Vipava Valley. $$$

Zmajev Hram \ 05 700 0181; ⊕ 09.00–18.00 daily. Serving up reasonable set menus near the entrance to Postojna Caves. $$$

Minutka Ljubljanska 14; \ 05 726 5720; ⊕ 11.00–23.00 daily. Decent & large pizzas cooked in a wood-fired oven. $$

Restavracija Jadran Titov trg 1; \ 05 720 3900; ⊕ 09.00–22.00 daily. Housed in a large white building on Postojna's central square, this restaurant serves good grills & fish dishes, with seating inside & on its outdoor terrace. $$

ENTERTAINMENT AND NIGHTLIFE You will find a sprinkling of bars and cafés on Ljubljanska and Tržaška. Two of the best include Riziko (*Tržaška 9*) and Boem Bar (*Ljubljanska 11*)

OTHER PRACTICALITIES
$ **Banka Koper** Tržaška 2; ⊕ 08.00–17.00 Mon–Fri, 08.00–12.00 Sat
$ **SKB Banka** Ljubljanska 5a; ⊕ 08.00–17.00 Mon–Fri, 08.00–12.00 Sat

⊠ **Post office** 1 Maja 2; ⊕ 08.00–18.00 Mon–Fri, 08.00–12.00 Sat

OTHER CAVES NEAR POSTOJNA

The area around Postojna is awash with caves and underground rivers. None is as geared to the needs of tourists as Postojna, though, which is not necessarily a bad thing for adventurous visitors prepared to don some boots and do without the luxuries of electric lighting. Conditions and access vary greatly, although the caves are generally becoming easier to visit as interest grows. **Otoška Cave** (Otoška Jama) is less than 2km from Postojna on the road to Predjama Castle. This cave was once linked to the Pivka River, and hence to Postojna, but is now dry. Check at the Postojna tourist information office to arrange access – note that there are no electric lights. A short distance north of Postojna you will find two caves in close proximity: **Pivka Cave** (Pivka Jama) and **Black Cave** (Črna Jama). These caves, like Postojna Caves, were formed by the Pivka River, have a variety of wet and dry sections and can be visited together (*tours Jun–Sep 09.00, 13.00 & 15.00 daily; 1¹/₂ hrs*). Booking ahead is essential (contact Postojna TIC in advance of your visit).

On the road to Lake Cerknica is **Planinska Cave** (*Planinska Jama;* m *041 338 696*), where the Pivka and Rak rivers meet, the largest wet cave in Slovenia. This is a challenging cave complex where access very much depends on water levels and only experienced cavers should head here.

PREDJAMA CASTLE (PREDJAMSKI GRAD)

(\ *05 700 0100; adult/student/child €7/€5.60/€4.20;* ⊕ *Jan–Mar & Nov/Dec 10.00–16.00 daily; Apr/Oct 10.00–18.00 daily; May–Sep 09.00–19.00 daily*) One of the most striking castles in Europe, never mind Slovenia, stands out proudly from the rugged hillside 10km west of the Postojna Caves. The tourist operation at the 700-year-old castle is stepping up a gear and there are now medieval pageants, with combination tickets sold in conjunction with the Postojna Caves and guided tours. Dubious plans to construct a faux medieval village in front of the castle are currently under discussion.

As you approach through the car park look at the tree to the left, which is said to be the spot where Slovenia's answer to Robin Hood was finally buried after years of robbing the rich to give to the poor. In reality it appears Erasmus Lueger may have been more a Rob Roy than the Robin Hood of children's stories; a romantic but ruthless rogue who proved a thorn in the side for more than just the region's various competing ruling elites. While his castle lay under siege he took full advantage of the porous local landscape and sneaked in and out through an underground cave. You cannot help, though, feeling sorry for a man who met his maker as he was thumped by a cannonball while he sat on the place where even folk heroes have to go sometimes.

After you pass the ticket kiosk the drama of the castle really unfolds as it rises high above, stretching impossibly up the 123m sheer cliff face. Look out to the right for the jousting arena that has been re-created complete with a royal box for the very popular re-enactments as well as the catapult that all too vividly demonstrates how the besieging forces used to attack Predjama. You can just buy a ticket and use the information booklet to navigate your own way around the castle, but a guided tour is a better option as the tall stories of its most famous resident are often more interesting than what is actually on show.

PREDJAMA CAVE (PREDJAMSKI JAMA)

(\ *05 700 0100; adult/student/child €7/€5.60/€4.20; tours Apr/Mar & Nov/Dec 10.00, 12.00 & 14.00; Apr/Oct 10.00, 12.00, 14.00 & 16.00; May–Sep 09.00–18.00 on the hour*) If you have not yet had your fill of caves then you can pop beneath the castle and explore the cave that used to provide a lifeline for Erasmus Lueger, on a 45-minute tour. Rubber boots are available for hire just after the main ticket desk for the castle. You will, however, need a torch as there are few frills in this dark lair. The four-level cave was formed by the action of Lokva River which still runs through it. On the second level down, look out for the graffiti that has been left over the centuries by various visitors, while the fourth level down is the active section where the Lokva is continuing its mysterious work. The waters from Predjama eventually snake their way out again in the fertile Vipava Valley. Experienced cavers can delve down deeper than the normal guided excursion.

✖ WHERE TO EAT

✖ **Gostilna Požar** Predjama 2; ☎ 05 751 5252. The only restaurant at Predjama Castle is worth visiting if you can get a seat on the outdoor terrace where the views make up for any inadequacies in the food. Busy days at the height of season are a bit of a scrum.

LAKE CERKNICA

Slovenia's largest lake does not exist for much of the year. The vast freshwater lake that spreads south of the town of Cerknica, just off the Ljubljana–Koper motorway, vanishes completely in the summer as its waters evaporate and seep down into the Karst caverns and underground channels below. Cerknica has always been a source of amazement for man and over the centuries the local people have tried, unsuccessfully, to drain the lake to make agricultural land and prevent flooding, or to trap it for irrigation. A greater understanding of the machinations of the disappearing lake came with Baron Janez Vajkard Valvasor (see page 38) whose seminal work won him a fellowship of the Royal Society in London. Of the lake Valvasor proclaimed: 'There is no lake as remarkable in Europe or in any other of the three corners of the world.'

Today the lake still retains much of its mystery, whether you visit when the lake unfurls for miles and canoeists, swimmers, anglers and boaters flock to its shores, or when the water vanishes leaving a dried-up moonscape, or even in the depths of winter when sheets of ice form in the shallow waters as ice skaters take full advantage.

To appreciate the scale of the meandering lake you can either drive or cycle around the unsealed roads that are raised above the waters. *En route* there are soaring birds of prey, ducks and butterflies which are part of the 2,000 animal and plant species that live in and around the impermanent lake. From the unspectacular town of Cerknica head down the 2km road to Dolenje Jezero, which sometimes lies right on the edge of the lake. The **Lake Cerknica Museum** (*Muzej Jezerski Hram;* ☎ *01 709 4053;* e *jezerski.hram@siol.net; www.jezerski-hram.si;* ⊕ *by appointment for groups of 7 or more – with tours in Slovene,*

7

English, German or Italian) here delves deeper into Slovenia's most intriguing lake. There are guided tours of the museum that last just over an hour, as well as a multi-vision show. If the museum is closed the adjacent bar will probably still be open and this is a good place to grab a drink and some advice. There is also a relief map by the bar outside that gives a good idea of the layout of the lake – fittingly it has dried up and cracked in the middle. Continue on from Dolenje Jezero and you will soon be on the unsealed section of road with the lake on either side. The village of Otok, 'island' in Slovene, as the name suggests is right in the heart of the lake. From here you can circle back up through Gorenje Jezero to Grahovo where you can rejoin the main Cerknica–Dolenjska road.

GETTING THERE Buses from Ljubljana (1½ hours) stop in Cerknica. The lake is located 2.5km south of the town.

TOURIST INFORMATION
🗎 **Tourist Information Centre** Cesta 4 maja 51; ☏ 01 709 3636; e tdrustvo@volja.net; ⏰ 07.30–15.00 Mon–Fri. Staff at the TIC can help you find private accommodation.

WHERE TO STAY
⌂ **TeliCo** (2 rooms) Brestova 9; ☏ 01 709 7090; f 01 709 7092; e drago.telic@siol.net. This pleasant B&B located 500m east of the town centre has an outdoor pool & rooms that offer good views of the lake. They also rent out bicycles. $$

✗ WHERE TO EAT
✗ **Valvasorjev Hram** Partizanska 1; ☏ 01 709 3788; ⏰ 11.00–22.00. Simple eatery serving up equally simple & hearty Slovene dishes. $

KRIŽNA CAVE (KRIŽNA JAMA)

(*Guided tours: Bloska Polica 7;* m *041 632 153;* e *krizna_jama@yahoo.com; www.krizna-jama.si; 1hr visits adult/concession €6/€4 (min charge €16); 4hr tours to Kalvarija 2/3/4 people €31/€27/€25*) A 10km drive south of Lake Cerknica is the Križna Cave, a very active subterranean environment which offers the unique chance to cruise through a cave complex aboard a rubber raft, admiring the stalactites and stalagmites of wet caves (with lakes) sporting intriguing names like the Pirate's Ship, Venice's Port and the First Lake from an unusual vantage point. Cave bears used to haunt the many underground lakes and these days their legacy is thousands of fossilised remains. The 8km-long caves were not fully explored until the 1920s and today visitors are welcome to venture into one of the least known – amongst tourists anyway – of the cave systems in Slovenia. There are two types of tour available: a one-hour walk through dry caves including the Great Hall, or a four-hour paddle on the cave lake. Access, though, can sometimes be limited after heavy rainfall when the water level surges throughout the network of caves. It is advisable to arrange your visit as far as you can in advance, as bids to conserve the caves mean that only one group (maximum four people) per day is allowed to raft through the caves, while the 60-minute tours of the dry part of the cave only operate on Sundays at 15.00 between May and October.

SNEŽNIK CASTLE (SNEŽNIK GRAD)

Continue just over 5km south from Križna towards the Croatian border and you come to Snežnik Castle (*Kozarišče 67;* ☏ *01 705 7814; free entry;* ⏰ *Apr–Oct*

10.00–12.00 & 15.00–18.00 Wed–Fri, 10.00–18.00 Sat/Sun) This ornate Renaissance creation lies across a charming little bridge. Inside, many of the 19th-century furnishings remain. From the castle it is possible to head off for a spot of trekking in the wilds of the Snežnik Plateau, though mind the bears (seriously). The peak of Snežnik (1,796m) is also an enjoyable challenge for adventure types.

PARK OF MILITARY HISTORY (PARK VOJAŠKE ZGODOVINE)

One of Slovenia's newest attractions is the Park of Military History in Pivka (*Kolodvorska 51;* ↘ *05 721 2180; www.tank.pivka.si; adults/concession/child €6/€4.80/€3.60; Oct–Apr 10.00–15.00 Sat/Sun, May–Sep 10.00–17.00 daily*) Opened on the site of a former military base, at present 17 old tanks (all over 50 years old), armoured vehicles, cannons and other military memorabilia are amongst the museum's key exhibits. One of the most interesting aspects for visitors is the exhibition and film that document Slovenia's 1991 war of independence. The collection is set to expand in the near future.

Brown bear

8

Dolenjska and Bela Krajina

Dolenjska is the region that stretches east from Notranjska skirting the Croatian border at first to the south and then to the east. This is a land of rolling hills that is laden with history in the form of crumbling castles and musty monasteries. Dolenjska is also intrinsically linked to the development of the Slovene language. When Primož Trubar laid the foundations of the language back in the 16th century, it was based upon the dialect spoken by the inhabitants of Dolenjska. There is the historic city of Novo Mesto, well worth visiting, a sprinkling of health spas (or *termes*) and the Kolpa and Krka rivers. Tagged onto the southeastern fringe of Dolenjska is tiny Bela Krajina. The temptation is to just lump them together as a 'Greater Dolenjska', but that would not be doing justice to Bela Krajina, culturally distinct and a vibrant part of the country where folk music is far more than just pub background music.

KOČEVJE AND KOČEVSKI ROG

This protected oasis is one of the wildest parts of Europe, never mind Slovenia. Here when you are trampling through the heavily wooded slopes you are as likely to see a bear as you are another human. There is much more to Kočevski rog, though, than its rugged beauty, and the wider Kočevje area has a fascinating history. During the Middle Ages the region was populated by a group of peasants who had migrated south from present-day Germany. Over the centuries the inhabitants of Kočevje's villages developed their own distinct culture, dialect and identity which, while it was influenced by the land that they inhabited, remained essentially German. The advent of World War II brought Italian occupation, under the control of Nazi Germany, to the Kočevje area and Hitler ordered the Kočevje Germans to relocate to Slovenia's German-occupied territory. There they were offered estates and homes from

CVIČEK

One of Dolenjska's most popular tipples is definitely an acquired taste, one that a large number of Slovenes throughout the country seem to have developed. The signature wine of the region, *Cviček*, is a blend of red and white grapes with a dry acidic flavour and a low alcohol content (usually around 10%). A washed-out ruby colour, it is often compared to rosé, though it is distinctly different in both its appearance and taste. Locals extol the virtues of this unique beverage, claming that it is light and refreshing, yet lively, which might explain why it is consumed in such substantial quantities. *Cviček* is traditionally a cheap wine, which goes well with cold meats like *pršut*. For your first taste try the Matinčič brand, which is usually dependable.

which Slovenes had been forcibly removed and packed off to Serbia, Germany and elsewhere in Europe.

At the end of the war some of the Kočevje Germans returned to their former residences, but they too chose, or were forced, to leave and the wider area of Kočevski rog became an off-limits military area. The Yugoslav army then set about constructing a system of intricate, and supposedly nuclear-proof, underground shelters, in order to safeguard Slovenia's communist leadership in the event of another war (ask at the tourist office for information about guided tours). Those moving in the higher echelons of Yugoslavia's socialist regime were also given exclusive access to the natural park of Kočevski rog, and it became a popular hunting and holiday destination amongst officials. One of the most tragic consequences of the militarisation of the wider Kočevje area and the establishment of an exclusive playground, was the destruction of much of the region's heritage, with villages and more than 40 churches razed to the ground.

An even more sinister event occurred in the area of Kočevski rog immediately after the war, when those troops who had been fighting against Tito's partisans during the conflict were prevented from escaping into Austria and sent back to Yugoslavia by British forces. Some historians estimate that up to 12,000 former members of the Slovenian Home Guard were slaughtered by the communist authorities in the woods of Kočevski rog. The dead were then unceremoniously dumped into mass graves, which were in turn blown up in a bid to eradicate any evidence of this evil act. While he was never formerly implicated, many believe that the massacre occurred at the request, or at least with the approval of, Tito. The relatives of the dead were also prevented from visiting the site until Slovenia secured its independence in 1991. Today a small church commemorates the thousands of men who died even though the war had already ended.

Returning to the dark days of World War II, visiting Kočevski rog it is easy to see why it was such a perfect hideaway for partisan forces, including the famous **Base 20** (Baza 20), from where hundreds of partisans once ran their operations. It may not be as well preserved as the Franja Partisan Hospital (Partizanska Bolnišica Franja) near Cerkno, but it is nonetheless dramatic as your mind conjures up images of the partisans risking life and limb to resist their Nazi occupiers. Today the site is a national monument, though many of the original buildings have long since disappeared and the ones that remain are not in great condition. Considering the importance of Base 20 this is nothing short of a scandal, though given the shift in the political climate away from Yugoslav socialism perhaps not too surprising.

There are two small partisan hospitals in the Kočevski rog that you can visit: Jelendol and Zgornji Hrastnik. Jelendol, just north of Base 20, opened in 1943 and went on to treat 330 patients, saving the lives of an impressive 309 of these. The bodies of the 21 people who died lie in a nearby graveyard. Zgornji Hrastnik, to the south of Base 20, also accepted its first patients in 1943 and unlike many of the Kočevski rog wartime hospitals it was not dug into a dark hollow, but instead built in an elevated position. Of the 400 wounded who were treated 69 died, with a small cemetery nearby a poignant reminder. To visit the memorial rooms at the hospitals you will have to arrange it in advance with the tourist office in Novo Mesto.

GETTING THERE Kočevje can be reached by bus from Ljubljana (1½ hours) and Novo Mesto. Base 20 is 8km from Dolenjske Toplice (see below) – heading south for 1km you will come to the mountain road, which has a car park located 7km along it. From the car park Base 20 is a 15–20-minute walk.

TOURIST INFORMATION

Tourist Office Trg zbora odposlancev 72; ☎ 01 893 1460; ⊕ Apr–Aug 07.00–19.00 daily; Sep–Mar 08.00–15.00 Mon–Fri

OTHER PRACTICALITIES

✉ **Post office** Ljubljanska 19; ⊕ 08.00–18.00 Mon–Fri, 08.00–12.00 Sat

WHAT TO SEE

Kočevje Regional Museum (*Pokrajinski Muzej Kočevje; Prešernova 11; ☎ 01 895 0303; f 01 895 0305; e muzej@pmk-kocevje.si; www.pmk-kocevje.si; adult/concession.child €3/€2.50/€2; ⊕ 09.00–12.00 Mon/Tue, 09.00–12.00 & 16.00–18.00 Thu–Sat*) An exhibition of the life, history and culture of Kočevje's former German population.

DOLENJSKE TOPLICE

If Base 20 has left you feeling emotionally drained then 8km away to the east is one of Slovenia's most popular spa complexes, a perfect stop-off if you are heading further east to Novo Mesto. Surrounded by forests and hills this is a great place to relax for a few days. Unlike some of the country's more modern spa towns, Dolenjske Toplice has a touch of class with some 19th-century buildings dating from the days when the stressed-out citizens of Vienna sought refuge here. Today the therapeutic treatments are worth travelling for and the town also makes a good base for exploring the Kočevje area on foot or by bike.

GETTING THERE Regular buses run from Novo Mesto (20 minutes) to Dolenjske Toplice. There is also a daily bus from Ljubljana (1½ hours).

TOURIST INFORMATION/LOCAL TOUR OPERATORS

Tourist Information Centre Zdraviliški trg 8; ☎ 07 384 5188; f 07 384 5191; e tic.dtoplice@volja.net; www.dolenjske-toplice.si; ⊕ 10.00–17.00 Mon–Fri, 10.00–12.00 & 15.00–18.00 Sat, 10.00–12.00 Sun

K2M Pionirska 3; ☎/f 07 306 6830; e info@k2m.si; www.k2m.si. This tourist agency located near the tourist office can arrange accommodation, kayaking, rafting & 8-day guided cycling trips. It also rents out bicycles.

WHERE TO STAY

Kristal Hotel (66 rooms) Zdraviliški trg; ☎ 07 391 9400; f 07 306 5662; e booking.dolenjske@terme-krka.si; ww.terme-krka.si. Pleasant & comfortable rooms come equipped with minibars & other mod cons. $$$$

Vital Hotel (102 rooms) Zdraviliški trg; ☎ 07 391 9400; f 07 306 5662; e booking.dolenjske@terme-krka.si; www.terme-krka.si. The larger of the resort's hotels benefits from 3 indoor swimming pools. $$$$

Camping

Doljenske Toplice Campground Zdraviliški trg; ☎ 07 391 9400; f 07 306 5662; e booking.dolenjske@terme-krka.si;

www.terme-krka.si. Campers have access to all of Dolenjske Toplice's facilities. Rates are pp. $

WHERE TO EAT

Gostilna Rog Zdraviliški trg 22; ☎ 07 391 9421; ⊕ 09.00–22.00 Sun–Thu, 09.00–midnight Fri/Sat. Slovenian home cooking, game & good fish dishes

make this a good dining option. Pizzas are also on the menu. If you visit at the weekend you might even be treated to folk music & dancing. $$$

OTHER PRACTICALITIES

✉ **Post office** Zdraviliški trg 3; ⊕ 10.00–12.00 & 15.00–18.00 Mon–Fri, 10.00–12.00 Sat

$ **Nova Ljubljanksa Banka** Zdraviliški trg 8; ⊕08.00–12.00 & 15.00–17.00 Mon–Fri

WHAT TO DO The indoor and outdoor pools at Dolenjske Toplice's lagoon (*Zdravliški trg 7;* ☏ *07 391 9400;* f *07 306 5662;* e *booking.dolenjske@terme-krka.si; www.terme-krka.si; adult/child from €7/€5;* ⊕*09.00–21.00 Sun–Thu, 09.00–23.00 Fri/Sat*) come complete with underwater massages, waterfalls and water jets. In addition to its therapeutic waters the *terme* also offers a combination of dry and wet heat in its Oasis Centre, while a unique facility is the Japanese sweat bath (a hot pool and waterfall heated to 40°C). If you are feeling brave you can even take a traditional Finnish sauna on the spa's nudist terrace. Shiatsu massage, reflexology, aromatherapy massage and hot-stone therapy are also on offer in the Aura Centre.

NOVO MESTO

The largest city in Dolenjska has a booming economy, with a major Renault factory, the national flagship pharmaceutical company, Krka, and a number of other industrial companies providing plenty of employment. All the more sad then that many of the historical buildings that crowd the old centre are in a shabby state and the Old Town is all too often choked with traffic. Still, when the traffic congestion eases and you troop into town across the Krka River, which curves around the Old Town in a looping horseshoe, Novo Mesto can be one of the most attractive cities in Slovenia. Evidence of human settlement here dates back as far as the Bronze Age, but it was not until the 14th century that Novo Mesto first became a city.

GETTING THERE Buses run to Novo Mesto from Otočec (15 minutes), Dolenjske Toplice (20 minutes), Ljubljana (1 hour) and Brežice (1 hour 10 minutes). The city is also connected by train to Črnomelj (1 hour), Metlika (1¹/₂ hours) and Ljubljana (1¹/₂ hours).

Bus station Topliška 1; ☏ 07 332 1123

Railway station Kolodvorska 1; ☏ 07 298 2100

GETTING AROUND

🚗 **Taxi** ☏ 07 332 5777

Bicycle hire is available at the **Hotel Krka** (see Where to stay below).

TOURIST INFORMATION/LOCAL TOUR OPERATORS

🛈 **Tourist Information Centre** Novi trg 6; ☏ 07 393 9263; f 07 332 2512; e tic@novomesto.si; www.novomesto.si. Helps arrange accommodation & offers bicycle hire.

Globtour Rozmanova 19; ☏ 07 337 4022; e globtour.novomesto@globtour.si
Kompas Novi trg 10; ☏ 07 393 1520; e kompas.nm@siol.net

 WHERE TO STAY

🏠 **Hotel Krka** (53 rooms) Novi trg 1; ☏ 07 394 2112; f 07 331 3000; e booking.hotel.krka@terme-krka.si; www.terme-krka.si. Fairly standard business hotel in a hard-to-beat location. $$$$
🏠 **Gostilna Pri Belokranjcu** (13 rooms) Kandijska 63; ☏ 07 302 8444; f 07 302 8445; e gostilna.pri.belokranjcu@insert.si; www.pribelokranjcu-vp.si. Located around 1km from Novo Mesto's Old Town on the main road heading

west, this welcoming *gostilna* has light & simply furnished rooms & serves regional fare in its restaurant. $$
🏠 **Apartmaji-Sobe Ravbar** (2 rooms, 5 apts) Smrečnimova 15–17; ☏ 07 373 0680; f 07 373 0681; e uros.ravbar@siol.net; www.ravbar.net. Friendly family-run guesthouse close to the centre of town, with tidy rooms & apts that sleep 2–6 people. $$

WHERE TO EAT

✕ **Gostišče Dežmar** Ljubljanska 65; ☎ 07 337 9300; ☻10.00–22.00 daily. Offering Slovenian & regional specialities including venison & freshwater fish dishes. Located a short distance out of town, follow the road east from the railway station. Dežmar also has accommodation for up to 6 people. **$$$**

✕ **Gostišče Loka** Župančičevo sprehajališče 2; ☎ 07 332 1108; ☻12.00–22.00 Mon–Sat,

12.00–20.00 Sun. Fish restaurant overlooking the River Krka. **$$$**

✕ **Kvarna Tratnik** Glavni trg 11; ☎ 07 497 5079; ☻07.00–22.00 daily. Centrally located café-cum-pizzeria. **$$**

✕ **Pizzerija and Spaghettarija Don Bobi** Kandijska 14; ☎ 07 338 2400; ☻09.00–23.00 Mon–Sat. Popular pizzeria 10 mins' walk from the Old Town (cross the Kandijski Bridge & head west). **$$**

ENTERTAINMENT AND NIGHTLIFE Like Novo Mesto itself, the city's nightlife scene is a little jaded. There is a sprinkling of bars on Glavni trg and Novi trg.

♀ **Bar Boter** Kandijska 9. During the warmer months the riverside terrace offers great views back across to the Old Town – well worth the short walk.
♀ **Lokal Patriot** Novi trg 6. This laidback student club might appeal to more youthful visitors.
♀ **Pri Vodnajaku** A decent pub option on Glavni trg.
♕ **Kulturni Centre Janeza Trdine** (Cultural Centre Janez Trdina) Novi trg 5; ☎ 07 393 0390; f 07 393 0392; e info@kulturnicenter.com;

www.kulturnicenter.com. Has a programme of theatre, concerts & exhibitions. The Cultural Centre actually has 2 locations: on Novi trg & the **Dom Kulture** (House of Culture) hall on Prešernov trg. The latter is also a cinematic venue.
Planet Tuš Topliška 2; ☎ 07 373 7480; e info@planet-tus.com; www.planet-tus.com/novomesto. Multi-screen cinema & supermarket complex just west of Šmihelski Bridge (on the south side of the Krka River).

OTHER PRACTICALITIES

✉ **Post office** Novi trg 7; ☻07.00–20.00 Mon–Fri, 07.00–13.00 Sat

$ **Banka Koper** Novi trg 5
$ **SKB Banka** Novi trg 3 & Glavni trg 10

WHAT TO SEE

A walking tour A good place to start a walking tour of Novo Mesto is at the grey **town hall** (Mestna Hiša), whose façade has recently been given a revamp. Look behind it and you will come across the pale-yellow **Church of St Leonard** (Cerkev Sv Lenarta), which was built by Franciscan monks from Bosnia, though the exterior on show today is from the 19th century. To the church's left is the **Franciscan Monastery** (Frančiškanski Samostan). If you fancy taking a break in a café head back to Glavni trg, though if the traffic is busy you may not want to bother given the congestion and pollution.

The next stop on the tour is the **Dolenjska Museum** (*Dolenjski Muzej; Muzejska 7;* ☎ *07 373 1130;* f *07 373 1112;* e *dolenjski.muzej@guest.arnes.si; www.dolmuzej.com; adult/concession* €3/€2; ☻*Apr–Oct 09.00–17.00 Tue–Sat, 09.00–13.00 Sun; Nov–Mar 09.00–16.00 Tue–Fri, 09.00–13.00 Sat/Sun*), which is easily identified by the decommissioned guns that sit outside it. Inside are various artefacts from as far back as the Bronze Age as well as leftovers from the days when Celtic tribes breezed through the region. Moving on from the museum, further up the hill you come to the **Church of St Nicholas** (Cerkev Sv Nikolaja), which is a bit of an architectural hotchpotch. A unique design feature is the altar that is built at a right angle to the main body of the church. Look out for traces of Baroque and Gothic architecture and the painting of St Nicholas himself by Italian master Tintoretto. Novo Mesto looks at its best from the other side of the Krka River so head for the bridge over the river by the train station to see a sweep of the Old Town. On the way look for the old section of town walls that still stands. Turn left once you have crossed the river away from

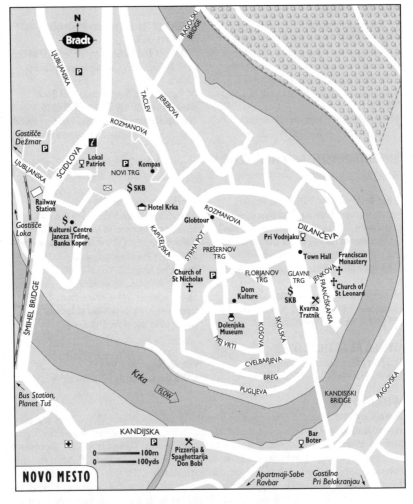

NOVO MESTO

the new shopping mall and follow Kandijska – the Old Town will keep peeking through the buildings and vegetation. After ten minutes you will come to Bar Boter (see *Entertainment and nightlife* above) so if you are thirsty, pause for a drink before heading back across the **Kandijski Bridge** (Kandijski Most) to Glavni trg and the town hall.

BACK TOWARDS LJUBLJANA

If you are short of time then you can head back up towards Ljubljana by rail or road. If you have your own wheels, make sure to stop off at **Žužemberk Castle** (*Žužemberk Grad; Občina Žužemberk, Grajska trg 33;* ✆ *07 388 5180;* €*4.50; Jul/ Aug 09.00–19.00 Fri, 10.00–18.00 Sat or by arrangement*) and then **Stična Monastery** (*Stična Samostan; Stična 17;* ✆ *01 787 7100;* ℻ *01 787 7570*). The former is a chunky castle overlooking the Krka River that has never really recovered from being savaged during World War II. You still get some idea of its grand scale from its remaining towers and in summer it is a great place to be when often free outdoor concerts are held here. However, until the local authorities get serious about the refurbishment then the castle will not really look its best again. Stična, meanwhile, like Pleterje further to the east, is one of the oldest monasteries in Slovenia, dating back to the 12th century. If it looks more like a fortress than a monastery it is because of the sturdy defences that were necessary to keep out the Ottomans. The monastery has taken on various design features over the centuries with Baroque, Gothic, Renaissance and Romanesque all woven into the structure. Although you can visit the religious museum, which is spread across two floors, the refectory and the library, as well as the Abbey Church, this is no fusty old museum as around a dozen monks still live and pray onsite.

ABBEYS AND CASTLES EAST OF NOVO MESTO

East of Novo Mesto, Dolenjska still manages to squeeze in a flurry of castles and health spas, as well as a monastery, before the Croatian border, which is now connected by motorway to Novo Mesto and on to Ljubljana.

OTOČEC CASTLE (OTOČEC GRAD) This castle, on its own island just outside Novo Mesto, is home to one of the most famous hotels in Slovenia. The rumbling express road above can be a bit of a pain, but it really is a special place as the castle rests in the midst of the Krka River surrounded by a park, with a cheaper hotel on one bank and a campsite on the other. Wherever you are staying, or if you just want to visit on a day trip, you can meander around the small islet watching the swans and ducks vying for attention with the rowing boats that the Hotel Grad rents out. The castle may look like an original Renaissance building, but most of it is actually the result of post-World War II reconstruction.

 Where to stay

 Otočec Castle Hotel (34 rooms) Grajska 2; \ 07 384 8600; f 07 384 8605; e booking.otocec@terme-krka.si; www.terme-krka.si. Period rooms & an undeniably romantic location hold a certain appeal. The hotel now also boasts its own golf course & its restaurant is often excellent. $$$$$

Hotel Šport (160 beds) Grajska 2; \ 07 384 8600; f 07 384 8605; e booking.otocec@terme-krka.si; www.terme-krka.si. Actually comprising a hotel, motel & self-catering bungalows, the Šport is a more affordable option than the castle itself. Sports facilities include tennis courts & an aerobics studio. $$–$$$$

✗ Where to eat
✗ **Otočec Castle Hotel** (see *Where to stay* above)

Activities A map detailing hiking trails and cycle paths is available from either of the hotels at Otočec. There are also horseriding stables at Struga Castle, which is a 20-minute walk from Otočec.

ŠMARJEŠKE TOPLICE Only 5km from Otočec is this decent health spa (*Šmarješke Toplice 100*; \ *07 384 3400*; f *07 307 3107*; e *booking.smarjeske@terme-krka.si*; *www.terme-krka.si*; *adult/child from €7/€5*; *07.00–21.00 Mon/Wed/Thu/Sat, 07.00–18.00 Tue, 07.00–22.00 Fri, 08.00–20.00 Sun*) also handy for Novo Mesto. In addition to its pools Šmarješke Toplice offers a diverse range of health treatments in its Vitarij Centre – including a complete relaxation programme based around the four elements (air, water, earth and fire) that incorporates aromatherapy, body wraps, venotonic baths (using thermal water, sea salt and herbal extracts), personalised cardiovascular training programmes, relaxation methods, colonic irrigation and cryomassage (using ice).

Where to stay

⌂ **Šmarjeta** (108 rooms) Šmarješke Toplice; ☎ 07 384 3400; f 07 307 3107; e booking.smarjeske@terme-krka.si; www.terme-krka.si. Completely refurbished in 2006 the hotel now offers modern & comfortable accommodation. $$$$–$$$$$

⌂ **Vitarium** (72 rooms) Šmarješke Toplice; ☎ 07 384 3400; f 07 307 3107; e booking.smarjeske@terme-krka.si; www.terme-krka.si. The terme's new

hotel offers plush rooms & Wi-Fi throughout. For a special occasion push the boat out on the Presidential Suite. $$$$–$$$$$

⌂ **Toplice** (47 rooms) Šmarješke Toplice; ☎ 07 384 3400; f 07 307 3107; e booking.smarjeske@terme-krka.si; www.terme-krka.si. Rooms with balconies are the best at this smaller & cheaper hotel. $$$

PLETERJE MONASTERY (SAMOSTAN PLETERJE) Set in the rolling hills of Dolenjska with white-robed monks flitting behind the sturdy walls Pleterje Monastery (*Drča 1, Šentjernej;* ☎ *07 337 7680*) is an intriguing place to visit. You can visit the shop and take in the multi-vision show – call ahead – but you cannot delve into the inner sanctum, which just adds to the mystery and appeal of Pleterje. There is an hour-long walk that meanders through the forest around the exterior wall, offering tantalising glimpses into the monastery and taking in the vineyards and orchards. The monastery's shop sells its famous wines and brandies, the most interesting being the pear brandy that comes complete with a real pear inside – they slip the bottle around when the pear is hazelnut-sized and when it matures they snip it off and add the brandy. You will probably find this on sale at Ljubljana's airport if you don't want to drag around a bottle from the monastery for the rest of your trip – though it has become something of an expensive souvenir.

KOSTANJEVICA NA KRKI

Blink and you will miss Slovenia's smallest town. It may not really be deserving of the term 'town' as it is only really two streets and has a population that would pack into one of the houses, but it makes for a good day trip, especially if you combine it with a visit to the nearby cave. The town straddles the Krka River with a sprinkling of things to see and do, including visiting a brace of Gothic churches, the former **Cistercian Monastery** (Cistercijanski Samostan) and the **Božidar Jakac Gallery** (*Galerija Božidar Jakac; Grajska 45;* ☎ *07 498 7333;* f *07 498 7335;* e *info@galerija-bj.si; www.galerija-bj.si; adult/concession €3/€1.50;* ⊕ *Apr–Oct 09.00–18.00 Tue–Sun; Nov–Mar 09.00–16.00 Tue–Sun*), with its eclectic display of works on various media, some of them culled from Jakac's days as a partisan. Other Slovene artists also get a look in with a surprisingly extensive collection given the small size of the town.

KOSTANJEVICA CAVE (KOSTANJEVIŠKA JAMA)

It may not be as impressive as the caves that you will see in Notranjska and Primorska, but this small cave (*Grajska 25;* ☎ *07 498 7542;* e *brane.cuk@email.si; www.kostanjeviska-jama.com; adult/student/child €5/€3/€2; tours mid Apr–Oct 10.00, 12.00, 14.00, 16.00 & 18.00 daily*) which penetrates 20m underground, is one of the most accessible in Slovenia. Illuminated trails take in some interesting shapes that have been affectionately named the Teddy Bear, Santa Claus, the Rainbow, Christ and the Sabre. There is also a smattering of wildlife inside the cave including horseshoe bats. The deeper recesses of the cave system are only open to properly equipped cavers.

TERME ČATEŽ

Terme Čatež (*Topliška 35;* \ *07 493 5000;* f *07 493 5520;* e *info@terme.catez.si; www.terme-catez.si; adult/child from €6.50/€5.00;* ☉*09.00–21.00 daily*) lays a fair claim to being the most impressive thermal spa in the country. If you are looking to relax for a few days or to indulge in some serious pampering then head here. Slovenia's largest spa resort boasts a range of therapeutic and leisure facilities from Finnish saunas, Turkish baths and jacuzzis through to myriad indoor and outdoor thermal pools with a total surface area of 13,000m², some heated to 36°C and others specifically geared up for children, with water slides, waves and a slow river ride under waterfalls. The highlight for many visitors is the Irish-Roman baths. For around €30 you and a loved one, or a travelling companion for that matter, can forget about reality for two hours and enter spa heaven. Although it is fairly private (there are never more than six people using the facilities at any one time), the experience may not be for the prudish as it all takes place in your birthday suit (you can cover up with a toga between stations). The session includes an aromatherapy scrub and massage after you plunge into a variety of hot and cold pools and saunas. A pleasant touch takes the form of a glass of bubbly, or a fruit elixir, in a jacuzzi before your massage and then it all finishes with a half-hour sleep on an airbed. Thermal pools are not Čatež's only attraction – you can also play golf and tennis, take a boat out or fish in the Sava River, go horseriding or try your hand at archery.

Where to stay

🏠 **Hotel Terme** (150 rooms) Topliška 35; \ 07 493 7000; f 07 493 5520; e terme.catez@terme.si; www.terme-catez.si. The fitness studio, health & beauty spa & swimming pools (both indoor & outdoor) geared towards adults make this hotel a winner with singles & couples. Large modern guestrooms have minibars, satellite TV, balconies & baths. If you are planning to stay in Čatež for a couple of days the HB or FB options are a good idea. Keeping with the tradition of health spas in Slovenia, Čatež also has its own health centre & offers a variety of therapeutic programmes, which incorporate the thermal water. $$$$–$$$$$

🏠 **Hotel Toplice** (139 rooms) Topliška 35; \ 07 493 7000; f 07 493 5520; e terme.catez@terme.si; www.terme-catez.si. The indoor thermal pool complex or Winter Thermal Riviera, is attached to the Hotel Toplice; as such the hotel tends to attract families. Rooms are modern & comfortable. $$$$–$$$$$

🏠 **Čatež** (186 rooms) Topližka 35; \ 07 493 7000; f 07 493 5520; e terme.catez@terme.si; www.terme-catez.si. The former Zdravilišče has opened as this newly renovated 3 star. $$$–$$$$

🏠 **Apartment Village and Camping** Topliška 35; \ 07 493 5010; f 07 493 5005; e camp@terme-catez.si; www.terme-catez.si. Modern apts sleeping 3–5 people, with kitchens, 2 bedrooms & a parking space. Just make sure you remember which of the 400 apts is yours. The campsite has space for tents, camper vans & caravans. Each pitch has an electricity supply. Apts $$$$, camping $

MOKRICE CASTLE AND GOLF COURSE

Right on the edge of the Croatian border on the main Novo Mesto–Zagreb road is this luxury hotel (*29 rooms; Rajec 4, Jesenice na Dolenjskem;* \ *07 457 4240;* f *07 495 7007;* e *mokrice@terme-catez.si; www.terme-catez.si*) which is housed in a Renaissance castle that once stood guard against the Ottomans. Mokrice comes complete with an 18-hole golf course that boasts some spectacular holes, especially the 10th which swings back down the hill towards the castle itself. The hotel's restaurant (**$$$**) is also worth eating at even if you are not staying here.

Guestrooms at Mokrice (**$$$$–$$$$$**) are large and furnished in period style – the suites in the turret are something to behold with huge round beds and tables big enough to hold a board meeting. Guests get free use of the facilities at Terme Čatež, as they are owned by the same people.

BELA KRAJINA

The 'White March', named after its silver birch trees, is one of Slovenia's smallest but most rewarding regions, as in this southeastern corner many of the folk traditions and cultures that have been lost elsewhere have been cherished and preserved and the locals are only too keen to share them with interested visitors. This is border country as Bela Krajina sits atop a ridge that basically separates Slovenia from Croatia and you are never more than a few miles from the Croatian border. The local tourist association has teamed up with neighbouring Dolenjska to offer a numbered trail of key towns, villages and attractions. This is especially useful in Bela Krajina as tourism is in its embryonic stages, so make sure to pick up a leaflet at the tourist offices in Metlika or Črnomelj in Bela Krajina, or in Novo Mesto in Dolenjska. Also make sure to check with the same offices for a list of current events to ensure you do not miss any of the cultural shows and festivals – the village of Adlešiči is particularly well known for regular cultural events such as concerts using traditional instruments like the lute and tamburica, instruments also used commonly across the border in Croatia. The tourist offices in Metlika and Črnomelj tend to co-ordinate the local attractions and can fill you in on where to pick up keys for churches and also on current opening hours as these can be fluid in these laidback parts of the country. Taking a car or renting a bike is the best way to explore Bela Krajina and the tourist offices in both Metlika and Črnomelj can usually arrange bicycle hire.

METLIKA

Though it plays second fiddle in size to its great rival Črnomelj to the south, Metlika is a much more appealing place to visit with a compact Old Town hidden inside the less appealing outskirts. The local tourist office is very helpful and should be your first port of call – as well as dishing out as many brochures as you can handle and myriad words of advice they have also been known to furnish visitors with the odd fresh local strawberry. If you can time your visit here to coincide with the three-day wine festival that swings through Metlika in late May all the better.

HISTORY Metlika's history is long and eclectic with evidence of Stone Age settlement before the Romans fortified the town. Later it became a key bulwark against the Ottomans and was attacked 19 times and sacked more than once

---

THE BELA KRAJINA WINE ROAD

The tourist offices in Črnomelj, Metlika and Semič have put together a wine-road map that covers the vineyards in the three subdistricts. You risk a fate worse than death if you try to order a *Cviček* here as there is a great rivalry between the Dolenjska wine and Bela Krajina's finest Metliška Črnina. You can just tour around looking for the wine cellars (*vinska klet*) using the trail handed out by the tourist offices in Bela Krajina or even get them to call ahead for you and arrange a tasting programme. The Vinska Vigred wine festival that takes place in Metlika every May is another good place to learn about the region's wines. One producer who opens his doors to visitors is Peter Malenšek who owns **Domačija Pecel** (*Maline 17, Semič;* ⊀ *07 306 7022;* f *07 306 7778;* e *peter.malenske@siol.net*). He also has a five-person apartment and restaurant that can accommodate groups of up to 60 people.

before they were finally sent on their way. In the 20th century, Metlika paid heavily for backing the partisans when its Italian occupiers razed many buildings to the ground. Metlika has always been a survivor, though, and it has managed to pick itself back up and celebrate its rich history through a range of festivals and cultural events. The economy moved from agriculture before World War II into viniculture and textiles (such as the successful Komet underwear manufacturer) and workers now come in daily from all over Bela Krajina, Dolenjska and Croatia.

GETTING THERE Buses from Črnomelj (20 minutes), Novo Mesto (50 minutes) and Ljubljana (1½ hours) stop at Metlika, as do trains from the same places – Črnomelj (20 minutes), Novo Mesto (1 hour) and Ljubljana (2½ hours).

TOURIST INFORMATION

Tourist Information Centre Mestni trg 1; 07 363 5470; f 07 363 5471; e tdvigred.metlika@siol.net; www.metlika.si; ⊕ Jun–Oct 08.00–15.30 Mon–Fri; Nov–May 08.00–17.00 Mon, 08.00–14.00 Tue–Sat

WHERE TO STAY
Private accommodation can be arranged at the tourist information centre.

Hotel Bela Krajina (24 rooms) Cesta Bratstva in Enotnosti 28; 07 305 8123; f 07 363 5281. Metlika's only hotel is just a couple of mins' walk from the Old Town. The rooms are a little on the tatty side. $$

Camping

Kamp Primostek 07 305 8123; e gostinstvo.sodec@siol.net. Riverside campsite 2km from Metlika welcomes tents, campers & touring caravans. It also has accommodation in a handful of bungalows that sleep up to 8 people. The onsite restaurant has an outdoor terrace. Rates are pp. Camping $, bungalows $

Kamp Podzemelj ob Kolpi, Podzemelj 16b; 07 306 9572; e gostinstvo-turizem@gtm-metlika.si. Larger campsite around 7km from the centre of Metlika, only easily accessible if you have your own car or a bike. Rates are pp. $

WHERE TO EAT

Pri Bartusu Mestni trg 6; ⊕ 10.00–22.00 daily. Centrally located restaurant overlooking the Church of St Nicholas (Cerkev Sv Nikolaja). $$$

Gostilna Budački Belokranjskega odreda 14; 07 363 5200; ⊕ 08.00–22.00 Mon–Thu, 08.00–midnight Fri/Sat, 12.00–15.00 Sun. Filling & tasty Slovenian dishes are the order of the day at this pleasant *gostilna* 500m south of the Old Town. $$$

Gostišče Veselič Podzemelj 17; 07 306 9156; e veselic1966@hotmail.com; ⊕ 08.00–22.00 Thu–Tue. Located near the Podzemelj campsite, this popular local eatery is justifiably popular with the locals & serves up solid Slovenian dishes. It also has a handful of basic rooms ($$). $$$

Pizzerija Lipa Cesta Bratstva in Enotnosti 83; 07 363 5130; ⊕ 07.00–22.00 daily. Good pizza with all the usual suspects on the menu. $$

ENTERTAINMENT AND NIGHTLIFE

Grajska Točilnica 07 305 8999. Located at the castle this café-bar is a good place to sample local wines.

Vinoteka Pinot Trg Svobode 28. This cosy cellar bar close to the tourist office is another good place to sup local wine.

OTHER PRACTICALITIES

$ **Nova Ljubljanksa Bank** Trg Svobode 7; ⊕ 08.00–12.00 & 15.00–17.00 Mon–Fri

The Metlika Wine Co-operative began production back in 1909 and is still at the backbone of the industry today. From its very modest beginnings it now boasts 25ha of vineyards as well as pooling the production of its members who cover much of Bela Krajina's 700ha of vineyards. While they do produce the Zdravica red, reputed to have health-giving properties, the excellent Modra Frankinja red and a passable Riesling, Chardonnay, a champagne-style sparkling wine and a dessert wine, their most renowned product is the Metliška Črnina, a red unique to Bela Krajina that you should try at least once during your visit. The co-operative has looked on enviously as Cviček across in Dolenjska has grown and grown in popularity and been given special status by the EU. In recent years the popularity of Bela Krajina's wines has also been rising, and the co-operative now has an outlet in Ljubljana. It has also branched out into food products. The Metliška Črnina varies from 10.5–11.5% alcohol content with a full body and dry finish and it goes particularly well with local game.

WHAT TO SEE

Metlika Castle and Bela Krajina Museum (*Metliški Grad in Belokranjski Muzej; Trg Svobode 4;* ✆ *07 306 3370;* f *07 305 8177;* e *belokranjski.muzej@guest.arnes.si; adult/concession €2.50/€1.70;* ◷ *09.00–17.00 Mon–Sat, 09.00–12.00 Sun*) Metlika Castle and its courtyard, rebuilt in the 18th century, are home to weddings, a gallery, summer concerts, a viniculture collection and also the excellent Bela Krajina Museum. The museum offers a 15-minute video on the history of Bela Krajina and its towns, villages and churches, before you enter the main exhibits which cover its history from prehistoric times right through to the end of World War II. It starts with the bounty from local archaeological digs which includes tools, bracelets and vases, before moving on through Roman times, local arts and crafts, including a fine collection of the brightly coloured wooden Easter eggs for which the region is famous. The World War II exhibits are fascinating with photographs of active partisan brigades in Bela Krajina as well as various weapons and pieces of kit.

Fire Brigade Museum (*Slovenski Gasilski Muzej; Trg Svobode 5;* ✆ *07 305 8697; free entry;* ◷ *09.00–13.00 Mon–Sat, 09.00–12.00 Sun*) The locals are very proud of the fact that the first-ever fire brigade in Slovenia was formed in Bela Krajina in 1869, so proud in fact that they opened this museum in two buildings close to the castle in 1969 to commemorate the fact. If you are visiting the castle anyway the museum is worth seeing as entry is free and you can learn about the history of the fire services in Bela Krajina complete with uniforms, photos and even disused fire engines, as well as some very early models consisting of a wooden cart with a couple of water barrels slung on the back.

Trg Svobode Sprouting out of the middle of the square is a small park that is dominated by a grenade-sporting partisan – nothing unusual for a Slovenian town – but next to the heroic fighter is a bust of Tito, much more of a rarity as he has been deposed in most villages and towns across the country. This perhaps reflects the rich ethnic mix of Bela Krajina, itself a rarity in homogeneous Slovenia, as Slovenes, Croats and Serbs all share this border region. Look out also for the trio of busts that commemorate the local dead from World War II when Črnomelj was briefly the capital of the independent Slovenian state.

Mestni trg Just a short walk along past the tourist office from Svobode trg is Mestni trg, a pleasant public space that is dominated by the **Church of St Nicholas** (Cerkev Sv Nikolaja), built in the 18th century on the site of a church that was burned to the ground in 1705. The model was Križanke's Church of St Mary in Ljubljana so if you are headed back to the capital you can compare the two.

Kolpa River Just a few kilometres outside Metlika is the Kolpa River, the place to be in summer as it is renowned as the warmest river in Slovenia, perfect for swimming, canoeing or just lazing by its banks. Good places to take a dip include around the campsites at Primostek and Podzemelj. The river is also easily accessible to the south near Črnomelj.

Three Parishes of Rosaline (Tri Fare Rosalnice) Just outside Metlika are three impressive Gothic churches, a trio of pilgrimage churches that sit dramatically together inside the same walls. It is still unclear as to why and exactly when the three churches were built on the site; what is clear is that the site has been an important pilgrimage venue for centuries, at least as far back as the 13th century when it was mentioned in print for the first time and that they later fell under the ownership of the Teutonic Knights.

The **Church of Our Lady of the Sorrows** (Žalostna Matere Božja), with its buttressed exterior, is reckoned to be the oldest, though today's incarnation owes much to 17th- and 18th-century makeovers. Look out for the particularly elaborate late Baroque altar and pulpit. The middle building, the **Ecce Homo** (Cerkev Glej Človeka), is a church dedicated to Ecce Homo meaning 'Behold the Man' and features an octagonal interior, while the **Church of Our Lady of Lourdes** (Lurške Matere Božje) was mentioned by Valvasor (see page 38) in the 17th century, though the church's graffiti dates it at least as far back as 1565. The conversion from a single to triple vane was not made until the 19th century. Easter is a good time to be here for the Way of the Cross procession. Another important event is St Bartholomew's Day on 24 August.

Walking and Mirna Gora Bela Krajina is an excellent area for walking with a surfeit of unspoilt rolling hills. Mirna Gora is the highest peak in the region and you can see most of Bela Krajina from up here as well as a swathe of Croatia. Before World War II there was a Franciscan church up here, but it was burnt down by the Italians, though there have been recent attempts to bring it back to life. The trail up through the birch trees is a great way to spend an afternoon and there is also a mountain hut on Mirna Gora, as well as a restaurant and picnic area. Pick up the leaflet from the tourist office in Metlika which details four walks, from 3.5km to 10.5km, around the slopes and forests.

ČRNOMELJ

Metlika's big rival, also bigger in population, makes much of the fact that, unlike its northern upstart, it never succumbed to the Ottomans. It enjoys a strategic and scenic position between the bends of the Dobličica and Lahinja rivers. Today, though, it looks far shabbier than Metlika with crumbling footpaths and façades, though it is worth visiting given its equally interesting history. Local archaeological digs suggest that settlement dates back as far as the early Iron Age and there is also evidence that the Romans occupied the area, before it received its municipal charter at the same time as Metlika in the 15th century. Sturdy fortifications and a moat, which was only filled in in the 19th century, kept out the Turks. The Italians, however, did succeed in taking the town during World War

The popular St George's Day, or *Jurjevanje*, cultural and folk festival was first held in Črnomelj in 1964 and despite the saint's name its origins go back to much earlier days when the local people thanked the Slavic deities for the arrival of spring. This day used to be celebrated in many other parts of Slovenia, but it has long since been forgotten, only to live on in culturally vibrant Bela Krajina. Many of the traditions surrounding the festival, such as the dunking of Green George (Zeleni Jurij), a young lad clad from head to toe in birch tree leaves and branches, in the Lahinja River may have vanished, but each year bonfires are still lit on the eve of St George's Day and people still get dressed up in the traditional stark white costumes to perform folk songs and resurrect their ancient dance, the *Kolo*. Another highlight is the procession of Green George from house to house.

II and after their capitulation the partisans took over. In June each year the town comes alive with the **St George's Day** (Jurjevanje) celebrations (see box, *St George's Day Festival*, above).

GETTING THERE Buses run to Črnomelj from Metlika (20 minutes), Novo Mesto (40 minutes) and Ljubljana (2½ hours), as do trains from Metlika (20 minutes), Ljubljana (2¼–2¾ hours) and Novo Mesto (45 minutes).

TOURIST INFORMATION

Tourist Information Centre Trg Svobode 3; ☎ 07 306 1100; e tic.crnomelji@ric-belakrajina,si; www.crnomelj.si; ⊕ 07.30–15.30 Mon–Fri, 09.00–12.00 Sat

WHERE TO STAY

Hotel Bojana (10 rooms) Koldovorska 60; ☎ 07 306 2900; f 07 306 2903; e info@redex.si. An overhaul of the faded Hotel Lahinja has brought 10 decent new rooms to Črnomelj, & a new name for the hotel. $$$

Gostilna Müller (4 rooms) Ločka 6; ☎ 07 356 7200; www.gostilna-muller.si. Offering rooms with AC, minibars & satellite TV. $$

✗ WHERE TO EAT AND DRINK

✗ **Gostilna Müller** (see *Where to stay*) ⊕ 09.00–23.00 Tue–Sat, 11.00–22.00 Sun. Popular eatery with outdoor terrace & vast interior dining space. Rich creamy sauces are the order of the day; try the Bela Krajina *žlikrofi* or the gnocchi with boletus mushrooms & cream. Disappointingly its nightclub is currently only open to large pre-booked groups. $$$

✗ **Gostilna Skubič** Pod Lipo 4; ⊕ 11.00–22.00 Mon–Sat. The restaurant's rear terrace overlooking the river is the nicest setting for a meal in town. Hearty grills & some fish dishes feature on the menu. $$$

✗ **Pri Klepcu** Otona Župančiča 6; ☎ 07 356 7470; ⊕ 09.00–23.00 Mon–Sat, 16.00–22.00 Sun. If you're in a hurry you could do worse than this cheap & centrally located pizzeria.

⊒ **Odeon Café** na Utrdbah 2. Trendy café located close to the castle & overlooking the river.

🍴 **Mercator** Kolodvorska 39

OTHER PRACTICALITIES

✉ **Post office** Koldovorska 30; ⊕ 07.00–19.00 Mon–Fri, 07.00–12.00 Sat

$ **Dolenjska Banka** Trg Svobode 2
$ **Ljubljanska Banka** Pod lipo 4a

WHAT TO SEE Črnomelj Castle (Črnomaljski Grad), built originally in the 12th century, may look a bit tatty and in need of a revamp these days but this was once the grand headquarters of the Teutonic Knights in the area. Here you will find the local tourist information centre and a modest museum with some images of the town through the ages. The expansive fresco of the eponymous saint beckons you towards the **Church of St Peter** (Cerkev Sv Petra), but there is not much to see inside this Baroque place of worship. The **Church of the Holy Spirit** (Cerkev Sv Duha) is crying out for a decent refurbishment. If you want to sample or buy some of the local wines the best place to head is to the **Črnomaljska Klet** wine information centre (*Ulica Mirana Jarca 2, near the castle and tourist office;* ↘ *07 306 1100*).

HUNGARY

Moravske
Toplice
Terme
3000
Murska Sobota

Grad

Terme
Radenci

Ščavnica

Mura

Pesnica

Ptuj

Drava

Bori Castle

CROATIA

N

Bradt

25km

25 miles

Maribor

Dravinja

Rogaška
Slatina

Podčetrtek
Castle

Podsreda
Castle

Pohorje

Terme Zreče

Rogla
Ski Centre

Celje

Laško

Terme Laško

Sotla

Savinja

Sloveni
Gradec

Velenje

Drava

Savinja

Dravograd

AUSTRIA

Sava

Kamniške-Savinje Alps

Logar Robanov Kot
Dolina

Kamnik

Begunje

Brezje

Kranj

Cmgrob

Suha

Škofja
Loka

Kropa

LJUBLJANA

9

Štajerska and Prekmurje

Ljubljančani often like to make fun of Štajerska, dismissing it as one big industrial farm, but Slovenia's largest region has plenty to offer tourists, from two impressive cities, Maribor and Celje, and what is arguably the most attractive town in Slovenia, Ptuj, through to castles and parks and, of course, perhaps the country's finest beer, Laško. Spas are big here too with thermal water spurting out of the ground and people frolicking in it everywhere you look. You would be well advised to join them in a region where the stresses and strains caused by sightseeing can so easily be erased by relaxing in a spa. Another highlight of the Štajerska region is Logarska Dolina, a stunning valley eulogised as the 'Jewel of the Alps' that brings all Slovenes out in a proud smile when you mention it. Then there is Prekmurje, a picturesque region of rolling hills, hearty cuisine and sturdy castles that is heavily influenced by Hungary across the border, which is as distinct from the rest of Štajerska as Bela Krajina is from Dolenjska.

MARIBOR

Maribor is not the sort of place to accept the 'second city' tag lying down, especially now that it has its own budget air link from London with Ryanair. Impressively located on the banks of the Drava River with the waters sweeping past an extensively pedestrianised Old Town, Maribor may not be as populous as Ljubljana, but this vibrant city is laden with things to do and see. In summer when the Lent Festival buzzes through and the city comes to a virtual standstill, as its residents indulge in the myriad shows and a jug or two of Laško, this is the place to be. Maribor is, in fact, a bit of a playground all year round: in winter the slopes of the nearby Pohorje Massif beckon with everything from beginner runs through to World Cup-standard thrills, while in summer the river and the Pohorje are obvious places to relax for a while. That Maribor is not yet more popular as a city-break destination may be as much to do with the admirable modesty of its inhabitants as anything else. Go now before Maribor really is 'discovered'.

HISTORY Archaeological finds dating back as far as 2400BC suggest that Slovenia's second city has been inhabited for almost 4,500 years. Copper Age settlers, Illyrians, Celts, Romans and Huns all number amongst the city's former residents, but it only really began to flourish in the middle of the 13th century when Maribor (or Marchburg as it was known then – later becoming Markburg) was first mentioned in historical documents. This recognition also prompted the townspeople to erect a defensive city wall, which was 2km in length and marked the boundary of the present-day Old Town, and four defence towers to stave off Turkish attacks. The 15th century was blighted by ethnic cleansing, when the large and influential Jewish population was banished from the town. A similar fate was to greet the Protestant minority in 1600 when the Catholic Church ordered their removal.

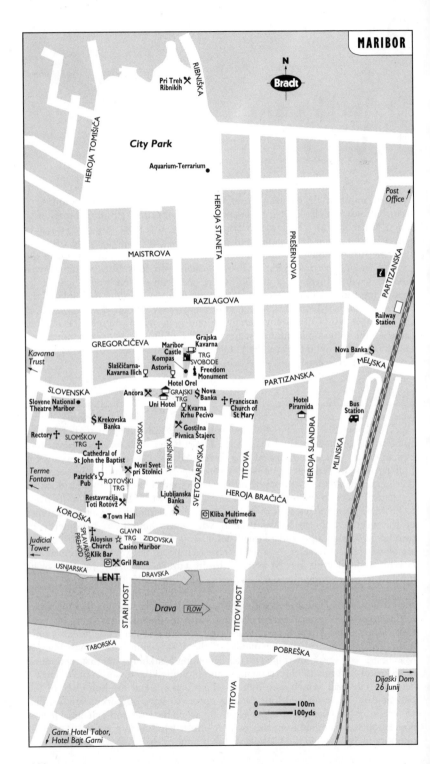

MARIBOR

N

Bradt

City Park

RIBNIŠKA

HEROJA TOMŠIČA

Pri Treh Ribnikih ✕

Aquarium-Terrarium

HEROJA STANETA

MAISTROVA

PREŠERNOVA

Post Office

PARTIZANSKA

Railway Station

RAZLAGOVA

GREGORČIČEVA

Kavarna Trust

Slaščičarna-Kavarna Ilich

Slaščičarna-Kavarna Ilich

SLOVENSKA

Slovene National Theatre Maribor

Krekovska Banka $

Rectory †

SLOMŠKOV TRG

Cathedral of St John the Baptist

Terme Fontana

Patrick's Pub

Restavracija Toti Rotovž ✕

KOROŠKA

Judicial Tower

SPLAVARSKI PREHOD

Aloysius Church

Klik Bar

✕ Gril Ranca

USNJARSKA

LENT

DRAVSKA

Drava FLOW

TABORSKA

STARI MOST

Maribor Castle

Kompas

Astoria

Hotel Orel

Ancora ✕

Uni Hotel

GOSPOSKA

GRAJSKI TRG

Kvarna Krhu Pecivo

✕ Gostilna Pivnica Štajerc

Novi Svet pri Stolnici

ROTOVŠKI TRG

Town Hall

Ljubljanska Banka $

VETRINJSKA

SVETOZAREVSKA

Grajska Kavarna

TRG SVOBODE

Freedom Monument

Nova Banka $

Franciscan Church of St Mary

PARTIZANSKA

Nova Banka $

Hotel Piramida

HEROJA SLANDRA

TITOVA

HEROJA BRAČIČA

e Kliba Multimedia Centre

GLAVNI TRG ZIDOVSKA

Casino Maribor

MLINSKA

MELJSKA

Bus Station

Nova Banka $

TITOVA

TITOV MOST

POBREŠKA

Dijaški Dom 26 Junij

0 ——— 100m
0 ——— 100yds

Garni Hotel Tabor, Hotel Bajt Garni

Mother Nature succeeded where the Ottomans failed and in the late 17th century around a third of Maribor's population was wiped out by the plague; she has in fact devastated the city on numerous occasions, with fires in 1513, 1601, 1648 and 1699. The next defining events in the city's history include brief periods of French occupation (1805 and 1809) and the construction of the Vienna–Trieste railway (completed in 1857), which was accompanied by a surge of industrial development. Maribor continued to prosper and emerged from World War I relatively unscathed and with a strong textile industry. Its fortunes during World War II were in stark contrast to the earlier conflict, when industry in occupied Maribor came to a standstill and Allied air raids all but demolished parts of the city. In the post-war years Maribor has made an impressive recovery and while recent years have seen its industrial output decline, the city is fighting back by establishing itself as a centre for tourism and other services. The new budget route from London Stansted, which started in summer 2007, looks set to boost Maribor's tourist industry.

GETTING THERE Regular trains from Ptuj (45 minutes), Celje (1 hour) and Laško (1½ hours) stop at Maribor. There are also direct services from Ljubljana (1½–2½ hours), Murska Sobota (2 hours), Postojna (3 hours 20 minutes) and Koper (4–5 hours). Daily international trains from Venice, Trieste, Zagreb, Vienna, Graz and Budapest also come to the city. Buses from Ptuj (30 minutes), Murska Sobota (1½ hours), Celje (1 hour 20 minutes) and Ljubljana (3 hours) also serve Slovenia's second city.

Railway station Partizanska 50; ✆ 02 292 2100. The station has self-service left-luggage lockers at €2 for 24 hrs. If you lose the key you will have to fork out €20 to replace it. There is also an ATM & information point at the station.
Bus station Mlinska 1; www.certus.si

GETTING AROUND A comprehensive and easy-to-follow **bus** map can be obtained from the tourist information centre with almost all of the city's 20 services running through the centre of Maribor. Lines are colour coded. There are **taxi ranks** at Trg Svobode, the railway station, Partizanska and Heroja Bračiča.

TOURIST INFORMATION/LOCAL TOUR OPERATORS
🛈 **Tourist Information Centre** Partizanska 47; ✆ 02 234 6611; f 02 234 6613; e zzt@maribor.si; www.maribor-tourism.si; ◷ 09.00–18.00 Mon–Fri, 09.00–13.00 Sat. Located 5 mins' walk from Maribor's historic core & opposite the railway station. Friendly staff dish out tourist leaflets & can help you find accommodation. They can also arrange tourist guides, but generally need advance notice for this.
Kompas Tivolta 2a; ✆ 02 234 6950

WHERE TO STAY Some of the best accommodation options in Maribor are in Maribor Pohorje, just a ten-minute drive from the city. Details are listed in the *Maribor Pohorje* section, page 196.

🏠 **Hotel Orel** (71 rooms) Grajski trg 3a; ✆ 02 250 6700; f 02 251 8497; e orel@termemb.si; www.termemb.si. This recently revamped 3-star hotel has well-equipped rooms & a very central location. Guests have free use of many of the recreational facilities at Terme Fontana west of the city centre. $$$
🏠 **Hotel Piramida** (81 rooms) Heroja Šlandra 10; ✆ 02 234 4400; f 02 234 4360; e piramida@ termemb.si; www.termemb.si. Centrally located 7-storey business hotel. Good-sized rooms have minibars, satellite TV & private bathrooms. Only 5 mins from the main railway station. Guests here can also use many of the facilities at Terme Fontana free of charge. $$$–$$$$
🏠 **Garni Hotel Tabor** (58 rooms) Heroja Zidanška 18; ✆ 02 421 6410; f 02 421 6440; e hoteltabor@podhostnik.si;

www.hoteltabor.podhostnik.si. Pleasant medium-sized & family-owned hotel, with modern & functional rooms, located 10 mins' walk from the south bank of the Drava River & 15 mins' walk from the Old Town. The hotel also has private parking & its own restaurant. $$$

🏠 **Hotel Bajt Garni** Radvanjska 106; \/f 02 332 7650; e info@hotel-bajt.com; www.hotel-bajt.com. Family-run hotel located in the suburb of Nova Vas, just south of the city centre, with simple, but stylish rooms. $$

🏠 **Uni Hotel** (53 rooms) Grajski trg 3a; \ 02 250 6700; f 02 251 8497; e uni.hotel@termemb.si.

Very centrally located & recently renovated hostel, which is generally used for long-term stays by students. Casual visitors can stay here but due to the high demand reservations are recommended. Rates are pp. $

🏠 **Dijaški Dom 26 Junij** Železnikova 12; \/f 02 480 1710; e info@dd26junij.si; www.dd26junij.si. Maribor's other youth hostel doubles up as student dormitories & is only open in Jul & for the first 3 weeks of Aug. Located 3km from the centre, the hostel can be reached by Bus 3, which takes you within 300m. Rates are pp. $

✗ WHERE TO EAT

✗ **Novi Svet pri Stolnici** Slomškov trg 5; \ 02 250 0486; www.novi-svet.com; ⏲ 10.00–midnight Mon–Fri, 11.00–midnight Sat, 11.00–21.00 Sun. For a seafood splurge this is the place to come. Feast on fresh Adriatic fish with squid, lobster & fabulous fish platters all on the menu. In season this is also a good place to sample truffle dishes. $$$$

✗ **Pri Treh Ribnikih** Ribniška 9; \ 02 234 4170; ⏲ 10.00–22.00 Mon–Sat, 10.00–20.00 Sun.. Historic restaurant with a stunning brick-vaulted wine cellar & leafy terrace in the heart of Maribor's city park. Immaculate service & good food come at a price. $$$$

✗ **Gostilna and Pivnica Štajerc** Vetrinjska 30; \ 02 234 4234; ⏲ 10.00–22.00 Mon–Thu, 10.00–midnight Fri/Sat. Great beer hall & restaurant serving schnitzels, fried chicken & a variety of Hungarian-influenced goulashes. Read the menu carefully because one of the stews is made from

horsemeat. A jug of their own recipe beer, the eponymous Štajerc, is also a must. The well-shaded terrace is great on sunny days. $$$

✗ **Gril Ranca** Dravska 10; \ 02 252 5500; ⏲ 08.00–23.00 Mon–Sat. On a balmy summer's evening the terrace of this waterfront restaurant is a great place to eat. Enjoy grilled meats amidst the hustle & bustle of the neighbouring café-bars. $$$

✗ **Restavracija Toti Rotovž** Rotovški trg 9; \ 02 228 7650; ⏲ 09.00–midnight Mon–Sat. Upmarket restaurant in a 16th-century dwelling at the heart of Maribor's Old Town. The eclectic menu offers everything from Thai, Japanese & Mexican dishes to more traditional Slovene flavours. There is also dancing in the cellar on Fri/Sat evenings. $$$

✗ **Ancora** Jurčičeva 7; \ 02 250 2033; www.sidro.si; ⏲ 09.00–midnight Mon–Thu, 09.00–01.00 Fri, 10.00–01.00 Sat & 10.00–23.30 Sun. Busy pizzeria & bar. $$

ENTERTAINMENT AND NIGHTLIFE

Maribor is overflowing with lively café-bars and the city takes on a Parisian feel as the locals move onto the streets during the warmer months. Poštna, south of the cathedral is particularly charming.

🍽 **Grajska Kavarna** Grajski trg 2. On a sunny day the café that spills out onto the square from the castle has a hard-to-beat location, especially if the monthly organic market is open. Admire the 15th-century fortifications & watch life pass by in this central square as you sip a *bela kava*.

🍽 **Astoria** Slovenska 2; \ 02 251 5250. On the fringe of Grajski trg this café is a great place for people-watching.

🍽 **Kavarna Krhu Pecivo** Grajski trg 6; \ 02 251 4842. Grab a snack in this café immediately behind the statue of St Florian, protector of firemen & wine.

☆ **Kavarna Trust** Gosposvetska 84; \ 02 235 0126; www.trust.si. Heading west on the street that

continues on from Slovenska you will arrive at this popular student haunt. The café also has a nightclub that is open daily until 03.00, but some residents are trying to rein in the opening hours.

♀ **Patrick's Pub** Poštna 10; \ 02 251 1801. On balmy summer evenings the pubs that line the Lent waterfront are the place to be. This Irish theme pub is an especially lively venue.

🍽 **Slaščičarna-Kavarna Ilich** Slovenska 6; \ 02 250 2408. Frequented by locals who reckon this café has the best ice cream in Maribor.

☆ **Casino Maribor** Glavni trg 1; \ 02 230 1300; www.casino-maribor.si. Housed in an attractive building in the centre of town the casino has gaming machines on the ground level & black jack & roulette on the 1st floor for more serious gamblers. The casino also has a decent restaurant & its own 'Clip Bar' with a terrace overlooking the Drava. Gaming rooms open daily until 03.00; the bar & restaurant close at 23.00.

🏛 **Slovene National Theatre Maribor (Slovensko Narodno Gledališče Maribor/SNG Maribor)** Slovenska 27; ☎ 02 250 6100; f 02 252 1207; e sng.maribor@sng-mb.si; www.sng-mb.si.

Maribor's National Theatre actually comprises 3 buildings, with the 1st auditorium & former casino dating from 1851. The oldest part of the theatre boasts an attractive neo-Classical façade & an ornate concert hall. The new buildings date from 1979–94. As well as hosting a packed annual calendar of theatrical, operatic & musical performances the theatre is also the hub of the annual Borštnik Festival – a fortnight of top-quality dramatisations – held in mid–late Oct.

OTHER PRACTICALITIES

✉ **Post office** Partizanska 1; ⊕08.00–19.00 Mon–Fri, 08.00–12.00 Sat
✉ **Post office** Partizanska 54; ⊕07.00–19.00 Mon–Fri, 07.00–18.00 Sat, 08.00–12.00 Sun
🖥 **Kliba Multi-media Centre** Kneza koclja 9; ☎ 02 229 4022; 09.00–18.00 Mon–Fri, 16.00–20.00 Sat/Sun. Centrally located internet centre just east of Glavni trg.

🖥 **Klik Bar** Dravska 10. One of a handful of café-bars situated on the north bank of the Drava, immediately west of the Stari Most, with free internet access.
$ **Ljubljanska Banka** Vetrinjska 2
$ **Krekovska Banka** Slomškov trg 18
$ **Nova Banka** Trg Svobode 6 & Partizanska 42

SHOPPING

Kiosks Selling bread, cakes, ice cream & meat are concentrated at the beginning of Partizanska between Trg Svobode & Prešernova.
Mercator Glavni trg 10 & Partizanksa 7
Mladinska Kinga The bookshop has several outlets in the city including those at Partizanksa 9 & Gospoka 24/28.
Abruni Gallery Ventrinjska 5; ☎ 02 252 6473. Great for window shopping or shelling out on works by contemporary Slovene & African artists.
Galerija Dum Židovska 10. Another gallery showcasing modern work by Slovene painters.
Vinag Wine Cellar Trg Svobode 3; ☎ 02 220 8111; www.vinag.si. If you don't have time to explore the vineyards around Maribor, you could do worse than visit Vinag in the centre of town. Your tour will take you into the cellar where 5.5 million litres of wine are stored in huge wooden barrels, & even larger steel barrels. The cellar fell victim to thirsty German troops during World War II, & today the oldest wine in their collection dates back to 1946. Apparently a bottle of this vintage will set you back around €7,000. There are around 30 types of far more affordable wines for sale in the shop upstairs including White Riesling, Chardonnay, Pinot Grigio, Sauvignon Blanc & 3 varieties of sparkling Penina Royal. Around 90% of the wine produced by Vinag is white, & this is reflected in the bottles on sale.

WHAT TO SEE

A walking tour Maribor is easy to get around on foot and a good place to start is across the Drava River on the opposite side to the Old Town where you can see how the historic core shapes up with its orange roof tiles. Cross **Old Bridge** (Stari Most) and you will be in Lent district. Head down on the left-hand side of the bridge and you will soon be amongst the busy bars and cafés of this lively part of town. As you walk west you will come across a building smothered with a tentacle of vines. Unusually for the Maribor region these are red wine grapes and even more unusually they are reputed to be the oldest vines in the world (as recognised by the *Guinness Book of Records*), having grown here for almost 500 years. When they are harvested only 20 litres of wine are produced and it is precious stuff indeed, retailing at around €70 for a 20cl bottle. If you are a visiting dignitary you may be in with a better chance of snaffling some as Pope John Paul II was amongst the luminaries given a bottle as a unique souvenir of the city.

Looking west along the river you will see the **Judicial Tower** (Sodni Stolp), one of four towers that hark back to the days when the city's walls stood strong.

Turn north now and you will pass **Aloysius Church** (Alojzijeva Cerkev) and come out in Glavni trg, one of the city's most important squares. The striking **Plague Memorial** (Kužno Znamenje) in the middle dazzles with its gold. One of the most notorious visitors to the **Town Hall** (Mestna Hiša) was Adolf Hitler, who stood on the balcony in 1941 and claimed Maribor for the Third Reich.

Duck under the arch and you will be in Rotovški trg where a pavement café is open in the warmer months if you are getting thirsty. Head a block further north and you will be in Slomškov trg, a leafy square that is dominated by the city's vast cathedral. The **Cathedral of St John the Baptist** (Cerkev Sv Janez Krstnik) is an architecture student's dream. The Romanesque base has been added to over the ages, as the city's wealthier citizens tried to keep up with all the new fads with Baroque, Rococo, Renaissance and neo-Classical styles all on show. Other majestic buildings that front the square include the headquarters of Maribor University – the **Rectory** (Rektorat) – the main office of the city's postal service and the **Slovene National Theatre** (Slovensko Narodno Gledališče).

Head back east now towards another of the city's main squares, Grajski trg, home to **Maribor Castle** (Mariborska Grad), which looks more like a palace. Have a look at the **Franciscan Church of St Mary** (Frančiškanska Cerkev Sv Marija) to the southeast, the red-brick one, whose construction is the subject of a bizarre local urban myth. It is said that local women who had sinned were asked to donate two bricks each and if you imagine how many bricks are in this voluminous building then that is a lot of sinning for a place of Maribor's modest size! If you want to indulge a bit yourself continue slightly further north to Trg Svobode where the **Vinag Wine Cellar** awaits with 5.5 million litres of wine, of which 90% is white. A more sobering sight outside is the haunting dark sphere, cruelly named 'Kojak' by some of the city's youth who use it as a meeting point, which is the **Freedom Monument** at the heart of Freedom Square (*svobode* means 'freedom'). On it are images of 167 locals who were executed by the occupying Germans during World War II and equally touching is the inscribed letter at its base of a partisan's parting note to his wife and family before he was shot.

If you want to escape the centre for a while just go a few blocks further north and you will come to the **City Park**, which is a haven with plenty of space for strolling around and taking it easy away from the bustle.

Aloysius Church (Alojzijeva Cerkev) Constructed in 1769 this late Baroque church is the design of local architect Johannes Fuchs. Its most notable features include attractive Rococo railings and ornate colonnades on the main altar. A more unusual aspect of the church is the panoramas of Celje, Ptuj and Maribor that can be found in the altar painting, where St Maximilian is depicted in Celje, St Viktorin in Ptuj and St Aloysius himself in Maribor.

Plague Memorial (Kušno Znamenje) Around a third of Maribor's citizens were wiped out as the plague ravaged the city in the 17th century. The immense gratitude that the survivors felt when the disease finally left the city led them to erect the Kužno Znamenje in 1681, a memorial that took the form of a column topped by a figure of the Virgin Mary. The monument that visitors see today is an 18th-century structure, the work of Jožef Štraub who, using a degree of artistic licence, added the six saints that surround the virgin mother.

Town Hall (Mestna Hiša) This late Gothic structure dates from 1515, but was re-mastered in an Italian Renaissance style in 1565 – the balcony was also added at this time. On the front of the building you will be able to spot Maribor's coat of arms and an unusual onion-dome-topped tower, while inside the Baroque wedding hall is also worth seeking out. During the 19th century the authorities, somewhat misguidedly, gave the town hall a makeover and it gained a late Classicist appearance; fortunately it was restored to its 16th-century appearance in the 1950s.

Cathedral of St John the Baptist (*Cerkev Sv Janez Krstnik; Slomškov trg 21;* \ *02 251 8432; free entry;* ⊕*belltower 09.00–18.00*) This former church acquired its cathedral status back in 1859 when Bishop Anton Martin Slomšek (after whom Slomškov trg is named) moved the seat of the diocese to Maribor. Almost 250 years later the Slovene bishop is on his way to becoming the country's first modern saint. Like France Prešeren, Slomšek was a powerful force in terms of the preservation of Slovenian literature and culture during the 19th century. The bishop's most celebrated acts are, as already mentioned, the transference of the see of the bishopric to Maribor from Styria, at a time when German nationalism dominated life in Slovenia, and his establishment of the Mohorjeva Society. The latter was a publishing house, which Slomšek used to promote both Catholicism and the development of Slovenian literature in general. Works produced by Slovenia's oldest surviving publishing house found their way into the majority of Slovenian homes in the early 20th century, with over 90,000 subscribers by 1914, a fact made more impressive when you consider that it occurred against a backdrop of growing German nationalism.

Dating from the 12th century the cathedral was originally constructed in Romanesque style and gained its present-day Gothic appearance in the 14th and 15th centuries, with the belltower being added in 1623. Mother Nature changed the appearance of the cathedral in the late 18th century when the campanile was reduced from its lofty 76m to its present-day 57m as a result of the destruction inflicted upon it by a bolt of lightning – fortunately this shortened version still makes a good vantage point from which to survey the Old Town. Inside the cathedral visitors can admire the choir benches whose 18th-century reliefs depict the life of St John the Baptist, a replica of Rubens's *Descent from the Cross* and stained-glass windows illustrating the work of Bishop Slomšek. The cathedral is particularly atmospheric during one of the frequent organ recitals.

Maribor Castle and Provincial Museum (*Mariborska Grad in Pokrajinski Muzej;* \ *02 228 3551;* f *02 252 7777;* e *info@pmuzej-mb.si; www.pmuzej-mb.si;* €*2.50;* ⊕*Apr–Dec 09.00–17.00 Tue–Sat, 10.00–14.00 Sun*) Like many of the historic buildings in Maribor's Old Town, the 15th-century castle exhibits a number of architectural styles including its medieval fortifications, flamboyant Rococo staircase and the Baroque Loretska Chapel. Today the castle is but a mere shadow of its former self – city planners gradually removed three defensive towers, the main portal and its gate during the 19th century – and most of the castle's rooms are occupied by exhibits of the Provincial Museum. English-language handouts guide you through the museum's ethnological and archaeological collections – exhibits of traditional costume, gemstones, apothecary and church artefacts. For many visitors the most interesting displays are those covering the town's history and culture. As you walk around look out for the wonderfully outsized ceiling frescoes in the first-floor Knight's Hall – Johan Glebler's 1763 depiction of clashes between Christian and Turkish forces.

Franciscan Church of St Mary (Frančiškanska Cerkev Sv Marija) Constructed at the turn of the 20th century according to the plans of Viennese architect Richard

Jordan, the Franciscan Church of St Mary stands on the spot of a former convent and 18th-century church. The austere structure that stands today is covered entirely in red bricks, which locals claimed were transported here by women wishing to receive atonement for two sins (each is said to have carried two bricks).

Maribor City Park (Maribor Mestni Park) Located just north of the city centre, on Tomšičeva, you will find this 5ha green oasis. First landscaped between 1872 and 1896 the present-day park is home to three fish ponds, colourful flowerbeds, ornate fountains, a children's playground and a maze of footpaths. In the warmer months musicians play from the pavilion, while the aquarium-terrarium (akvarij-terarij) is a useful distraction for those travelling with kids on a rainy day. For most the real reason to visit the park is to scale the Piramida, a 386m hill that offers good panoramas over the city and the Pohorje Mountains.

Aquarium-Terrarium (*Akvarij-Terarij;* ✆ *02 251 2295;* e *akvarij-terarij@florina.si; www.florina.si/akvarij-terarij/index.html; adult/child €3/€2.50;* ◷ *08.00–19.00 Mon–Fri, 09.00–12.00 & 14.00–19.00 Sat/Sun*) The older aquarium dating from 1953 is home to more than 100 species of fish including brightly coloured tropical fish, piranhas and those indigenous to Slovenia's Adriatic coast. The more modern terrarium houses a large number of amphibians, insects and reptiles including a rattlesnake, cobra, python and boa constrictor, turtles, crocodiles and lizards.

Terme Fontana (*Koroška 172;* ✆ *02 234 4100;* f *02 234 4114;* e *fontana@ termemb.si; www.termemb.si; adult/child from €7/€5;* ◷ *09.00–21.00 Sat–Thu, 09.00–23.00 Fri*) The emphasis at this *terme* is firmly on health and rehabilitation, with a diagnostic centre and treatments ranging from massage and acupuncture to personal fitness programmes and magnetic therapy. For the more casual user, though, Fontana also has indoor and outdoor thermal pools, underwater massage jets and jacuzzis heated to temperatures between 33°C and 37°C. Fontana also has a fitness centre, saunas, a steam bath, solariums and massage programmes.

MARIBOR POHORJE

It may not boast the skyscraping peaks of the Julian Alps to the west, but the Pohorje is a pleasure-filled playground for all sorts of activities right on the edge of the city. Here you can head off for a spot of skiing or mountain biking, paintballing or horseriding. The Pohorje makes a useful alternative base if you love your skiing or walking as it is still easy to get into town by bus or taxi. Leafy suburbia up here gives way to World Cup-run ski slopes and a multitude of things to do.

GETTING THERE Bus 6 runs between the centre of Maribor and the Pohorje at frequent intervals.

WHERE TO STAY There is plenty of accommodation available in the Pohorje offering everything from basic hostel-style accommodation to five-star luxury, mountainside ski lodges and private rooms.

Habakuk (137 rooms) Pohorska 59; ✆ 02 300 8100; f 02 300 8128; e habakuk@termemb.si; www.termemb.si. If your budget will stretch to a 5-star hotel then stay here at one of Slovenia's best hotels. Indoor & outdoor thermal pools & whirlpools with a water temperature that hovers around 33°C, sauna, Turkish bath, fitness centre, squash courts & a variety of spa treatments are the hotel's biggest lures. Out of season (spring & early summer) you may well have all these things to yourself. Well-equipped guestrooms are large & comfortable. $$$$$$

🏠 **Bellevue** (50 rooms) Na slemenu 35; ☎ 02 607 5100; f 02 607 5128; e bellevue@termemb.si; www.termemb.si. A major renovation has transformed this former youth hostel into a luxury 4-star property. Standing 1,050m above sea level next to the upper cable-car station on the Maribor Pohorje the elegant rooms boast magnificent views. The hotel also has a wellness centre with saunas & a laconium. $$$$-$$$$$

🏠 **Apartments Martin** (4 apartments) Hočko Pohorje 103; ☎ 02 220 8841; f 02 220 8849. These 3-bed apts are located on the ski slopes close to the upper cable-car station. Simple chalet-style bedrooms sleep 3–7 people. $$$-$$$$$

🏠 **Hotel Areh** (25 rooms) Lobnica 62; ☎ 02 220 8841; f 02 220 8849. 3- & 4-bed rooms are available in this ski lodge located at the Areh peak summit. The hotel also has its own restaurant & hires out ski equipment. $$$

🏠 **Villa Divji Petelin** (6 rooms) Pohorska 41; ☎ 02 614 0153; f 02 614 0154; e divji.petelin@siol.net; www.divjipetelin.com. Offering B&B in simply decorated, but stylish & comfortable rooms. The villa also has private parking & serves food. $$

ACTIVITIES

Skiing The main reason to visit Maribor Pohorje in season is to ski. This is one of the country's biggest ski resorts, which boasts 63km of ski slopes that are well served by a cable car and ski lifts, with a large variety of runs that lend themselves to all levels of skier, from the beginner to the advanced. The Pohorje also has its own ski and snowboard schools. For two days each January Maribor Pohorje plays host to the Women's Alpine Skiing World Cup. One of its more unusual features is the fact that 7km of the ski slope are illuminated at night, allowing you to experience night skiing. For more information contact **Športni Centre Pohorje** (*Pohorska 60; ☎ 02 603 6553; f 02 603 6565; www.pohorje.org*).

Adrenaline Park Pohorje When the ski season is over activities offered by the Adrenaline Park Pohorje (☎ *02 220 8843; f 02 220 8849; e info.park@sc-pohorje.si; www.pohorje.org*) take over the region. Visitors can choose from a range of activities.

High ropes course This is basically an obstacle course that takes place 8m above the ground. Challenges include crossing from one high platform to another as you walk across narrow ropes, tackling the elevated rope climbing wall and swinging on a series of suspended tyres. The course is located on Trikotna jasa and is accessible on foot or by chair lift. A four-hour programme costs from €35.

Downhill mountain biking The Pohorje's challenging downhill track is open all year round and descends 500m from the starting point at Bolfenk. Only for experienced mountain bikers and those with specially adjusted bikes. Helmets and body armour are also a must. The Pohorje boasts plenty of other options for all skill levels.

Summer sledding Sledding in the Pohorje is not just confined to winter and in the summer months a 5km track (€10 per hour) takes you from the top of Bellevue's cable-car station back to the base – descending 725m in total. Be warned, this is not for the faint-hearted as the sleds can go as fast as 50km/h. Alternatively you can take a two-hour trip from Trikotna jasa into the valley (€15).

Paintball Adrenaline-pumping simulated warfare takes place in the summer season at an altitude of 580m (near the High ropes course). The aim of the game is to capture the opposing team's flag, while preventing yours from being captured by them. The only snag is that if you are 'killed', or rather struck by a high-speed paintball as it is propelled from another player's gun, then you are out. Still there is always the next game (€10–15 for two hours depending on group size).

Walking For those who like to take their exercise at a more leisurely pace the Pohorje's hills, which have a variety of marked trails, are great for rambling in. A good mountain map is also essential to keep you on the right track. Routes include walks to the **Slap Šumik** (Šumik Waterfall), **Črno Jezero** (Black Lake) and the virgin forest Pragozd. The Rozika forest trail, from next to the Bellevue to the Church of St Bolfenk, offers some stunning views. The Areh Hotel is another good place to begin an exploration of the Pohorje's walking paths.

ZREČE AND ROGLA

GETTING THERE The easiest way to reach both Rogla and Zreče is by car. From Murska Sobota or Maribor head southwest towards Ljubljana and Celje for 30km, taking the Slovenske Konjice exit and from there following the road to Zreče and then Rogla. From Ptuj head for Kidričevo, Slovenska Bistrica and continue southeast to Slovenske Konjice before travelling on to Zreče and/or Rogla.

GETTING AROUND Regular buses connect the *terme* to the ski centre.

TERME ZREČE (✆ *03 757 6155; www.terme-zrece.si; adult entrance to the thermal pools €8.50–10 depending on the day of the week*) About 17km away from the ski slopes you will find this modern health spa with five swimming pools whose healing thermal waters are naturally heated to temperatures of 26°C to 35°C. Zreče also has a fitness centre, Turkish bath and dry saunas. A range of massages and other treatments are also offered. Accommodation is provided in two hotels, the Dobrava 2000 Hotel and the Dobrava Hotel and the self-catering Terme Zreče Villas ($$$$–$$$$$).

ROGLA Rogla (✆ *03 757 6155; www.rogla.si*), one of Slovenia's premier ski resorts offers skiing, snowboarding and telemark skiing on 12km of downhill pistes and 18km of cross-country tracks; snow-making machines ensure that there is always enough snow for the winter sports to take place. Only 2km of the pistes are classified as easy, but those with some skiing experience can take advantage of advanced lessons in the ski school. After a hard day on the slopes why not go for a ride in a snowmobile, or take a scenic helicopter tour. Skiing competitions, night skiing and full equipment hire are also offered.

The Olympic Centre itself has a large sports hall with badminton, tennis, volleyball, squash, handball and basketball courts, as well as a swimming pool, massage and sauna facilities and a fitness centre. Outside there is a football pitch, running track and courts for tennis, basketball and handball.

Accommodation is available in the resort's Planina, Brinje and Rogla hotels, the Koca na Jurgovem Apartments and the Gaber Bungalows ($$$$–$$$$$).

VELENJE

A thoroughly modern city that grew up around the coal industry, Velenje is an interesting, if not exactly attractive, place to visit. It is also home to Gorenje, one of the most successful Slovenian companies, which exports kitchen appliances around the world. Its original name of Titovo Velenje came when it was 'born' in 1959. During the heyday of Yugoslav socialism a city in each of the sectors that made up Yugoslavia was adorned with the Tito moniker, and was held up as a successful example of socialism. In Slovenia this honour was bestowed upon Velenje. The two main reasons to visit are the the the **Coal Mining Museum of Slovenia** (Muzej Premogovništva Slovenije) and **Velenje Castle and Regional Museum** (Velenjski Grad in Pokrajinski Muzej).

GETTING THERE Velenje can be reached by bus from Slovenj Gradec (40 minutes), Celje (45 minutes), Dravograd (1 hour) and Ljubljana (1½ hours). Trains from Celje also stop in Velenje (50 minutes).

WHERE TO STAY Velenje can easily be visited in a single day and there is nothing in the town that really merits an overnight stay.

WHAT TO SEE
Coal Mining Museum of Slovenia (Muzej Premogovništva Slovenije; Stari Jašek–Koroška; \f 03 587 0997; e trgovina@rlv.si; www.rlv.si/muzej; adult/concession/child €8.50/€7.10/€6; ⊕09.30–17.00 Tue–Sun) The mine that was once the driving force of the town is not the all-encompassing giant it once was, though the onsite museum is well worth visiting all the same. The museum allows an actual tour of sections of the mine, which takes 1½ hours. Following the path of the first shaft sunk into the mine in 1887, the tour takes you past fairly realistic models of miners hacking out the lignite as the chamber fills with wailing sirens and the clanging of the mechanised shaft and work tools. A presentation covers the issues of environmental pollution and the decline of Slovenia's coal-mining industry. If your time in the pit has made you peckish then you can also visit the canteen and eat like a real miner. Located 1.5km from the centre of town in Škale.

Velenje Castle and Regional Museum (Velenjski Grad in Pokrajinski Muzej; Ljubljanska 54; \ 03 898 2630; f 03 898 2640; www.muzej.velenje.org; adult/child €2.50/€2; ⊕09.30–17.00 Tue–Sun) Dating from the 13th century, the present-day castle owes its appearance largely to additions that were made 300 years later. Today visitors can explore the castle's keep with its vaulted cellar, defensive walls and round tower. The museum exhibits are, however, the real reason to visit. Nine permanent collections include Baroque artwork taken from the **Church of St George** (Cerkev Sv Jurij) in Škale, more than 1,000 artefacts from Africa and 20th-century paintings by various Slovene artists, as well as the unique reconstructions of a 1930s inn and an early 20th-century general store. The shop and inn are not just stuffy museum pieces and visitors are invited to quench their thirst or purchase souvenirs.

Trawling through the heavy industry on the outskirts of Celje, your first instinct may be to leave Slovenia's third-largest city instantly, especially if you are thrown into the maelstrom of the local traffic system with honking horns, frenetic junctions and one-way streets. Endure beyond the morass, though, and one of Slovenia's most attractive and historic Old Towns awaits, whose green and hilly surrounds offer plenty of opportunities to escape the traffic and industry. Celje is not yet firmly on the tourist trail so you will probably have it largely to yourself, though things may change with the new budget flights to Maribor.

HISTORY Celje has a long history, with archaeological finds suggesting settlement here dates as far back as the Iron Age. After this time Celje was settled by the Celts then the Romans, the latter elevating it to the status of a town in the 1st century AD under the name Claudia Celeia. Barbarian raids 400 years later saw the end of Roman rule and left Celje in ruins. It took another 600 years for Celje to recover its former prominence and by the 15th century it had become an important and powerful administrative, economic and urban centre under the Counts of Celje, who later became dukes. This was Celje's golden age when the dukedom was the strongest in this part of Europe and it is a period that many locals still fondly hark back to. The achievement of the counts is also recognised in the Slovenian national coat of arms, where you will find three yellow stars that came from the emblem of the Dukes of Celje. This mighty feudal dynasty came to an abrupt end when the last duke, Count Ulrich II, was murdered in 1456 and the city has been playing catch-up ever since.

GETTING THERE Buses run to Celje from Ljubljana (1½ hours), Maribor (1½ hours), Ptuj (2 hours) and Murska Sobota (2¼–2¾ hours). Trains from Laško (10 minutes), Velenje (50 minutes), Rogaška Slatina (45 minutes–1 hour), Maribor (45 minutes–1 hour), Ptuj (1 hour) and Ljubljana (1–1½ hours) also stop there.

Railway station Krekov trg 1

Bus station Aškerčeva

GETTING AROUND There is a taxi rank on Krekov trg near the Hotel Evropa. You can also call taxis on the following numbers:

- 🚖 **Maxi-taxi Speedy** ✆ 03 491 3990
- 🚖 **Radio Taxi** ✆ 03 548 300
- 🚖 **Taxi Plus** ✆ 03 492 2280

TOURIST INFORMATION/LOCAL TOUR OPERATORS

ℹ Tourist Information Centre Krekov trg 3; ✆ 03 428 936; ⊕ Nov–Mar 09.00–17.00 Mon–Fri, 09.00–13.00 Sat; Apr–Oct 08.00–18.00 Mon–Fri, 11.00–17.00 Sat/Sun

Kompas Glavni trg 1; ✆ 03 428 0308
Globtour Razlagova 1; ✆ 03 490 1560

🏠 WHERE TO STAY

🏠 **Hotel Evropa** (28 rooms) Krekov trg 4; ✆ 03 426 9000; f 03 426 9620; e info@ hotel-evropa.si; www.hotel-evropa.si. This friendly 3 star is centrally located near the train station & has bright & modern rooms with showers. Even with the windows closed some of the rooms get a lot of noise from the street & the nearby church bell. The rooms on the 1st & 2nd floors are the best. $$$

🏠 **Štorman** (45 rooms) Mariborska 3; ✆ 03 426 0426; f 03 426 0395; e recepcija.storman@siol.net; www.gostilne-hotel-storman.com. A 9-storey business hotel close to the bus station. $$$

🏠 **Turška Mačka** (26 rooms) Gledališka 7; ✆ 03 548 4611; f 03 544 2908; e info@majolka.si; www.majolka.si. Like the hotel itself the rooms are small, but clean. $$–$$$

🏠 **Hotel Astor** (30 rooms) Ljubljanska 39; ✆ 03 545 2018; f 03 545 1401; e merx@merx-gt.si; www.astor-hotel.net. The outdoor swimming pool, private garage & pleasant location near the Savinja River almost make up for the 15-min walk to Celje's Old Town. $$$

🏠 **Dijaški Dom** Ljubljanska 21; ✆ 03 426 6600; f 03 426 6621. Student dorm providing cheap accommodation for visitors in Jul/Aug. A 10-min walk from the tourist office. Rates are pp. $

✖ WHERE TO EAT

✖ **Istska Konoba** Gledališka 7; ✆ 03 548 4611; ⊕07.00–22.00 Sun–Thu, 07.00–midnight Fri/Sat. The seafood restaurant at the Turška Mačka hotel is a good central option. $$$

✖ **Restavracija and Pivnica Koper** Gubečeva 3; ⊕09.00–23.00 daily. It may not be the tastiest food you will ever eat, but the pasta, pizzas & grilled-meat dishes are good value. $$

🛒 **Mercator** Prešerenova 1. Selling a wide selection of food & drinks.

ENTERTAINMENT AND NIGHTLIFE

🖵 **Kulturni Club Ivan Cankar** Galvni trg 7. Lively café-bar housed in an ornate Art Nouveau building with a dark wood interior & outdoor terrace.

♀ **Branibor Pub** Satnetova 27; ✆ 03 492 4144; ⊕until 01.00–02.30 every night. With regular live music performance, this is one of Celje's most popular bars.

♀ **Local** Trg celjskih knezov 10. Lively cellar bar with regular live music & DJ nights.

OTHER PRACTICALITIES

✉ **Post office** Krekov trg 9; ⊕07.00–20.00 Mon–Fri, 07.00–13.00 Sat. There is an ATM outside.

$ **Volksbank** Prešerenova 27; ⊕08.30–16.30 Mon–Fri

$ **Nova Ljubljanska Banka** Krekov trg 4; ⊕08.30–12.00 & 14.30–17.00 Mon–Fri

WHAT TO SEE

A walking tour A good place to start is by Hotel Evropa where you can enjoy a fortifying *bela kava* before you set off. The first sight is **Celje Old Castle** (*Stari Grad Celje; free entry;* ⊕*summer 09.00–21.00 daily; winter 10.00–17.00 daily*) which is a good 45-minute trek, so if you are short of time or feeling a bit lazy you can catch a taxi from the rank by the hotel. If you are on foot from Krekov trg turn to the right of the railway station and follow the tracks to the underpass, which leads to a bridge over the Savinja River. Once across the bridge leave the road and take the footpath to the right along the riverbank before descending and taking the pedestrian crossing over Cesta na Grad. After the small sports stadium a shortcut leads up through the forest – only take this if you are covered up and have some insect repellent as the bugs are ferocious. Either way your final approach to the castle will be back on the winding Cesta na Grad with good views of Slovenia's largest castle.

Originally constructed at the beginning of the 13th century, the castle that visitors see today has undergone a series of changes under its various residents and more recently faced years of decline. The castle wall and northern defence tower were added at the end of the 13th century, while the 14th century saw the Lords of Žovnek (who later became the Counts and then the Dukes of Celje) mould the interior of the fortress to residential quarters; the dukes also added the four-storied Frederick's Tower. Other defining events include the 1348 earthquake, a 15th-century extension of the living space and the enlargement of the wall the following century. As the power of the Dukes of Celje declined and the castle lost its strategic position it was abandoned and fell into ruin by the 17th century. Over the last decade serious attempts have been made to restore parts of the immense

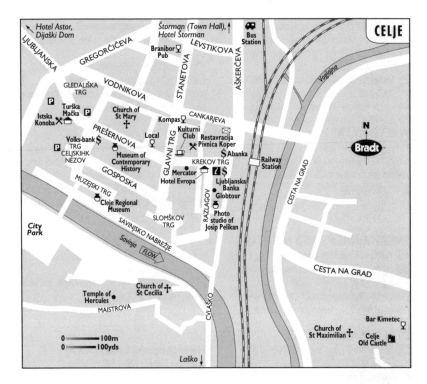

fortress, which has suffered a barrage of looting down the years – including the pilfering of the roof and the best stones for construction elsewhere and its exploitation as a quarry – and today it is just slowly returning to its former glory. Standing on the solid ramparts staring out over the hills and the city you can conjure up the days when the Dukes of Celje were masters of all they surveyed. There is also a **Children's Gallery** (*Stari Grad Celje;* m *041 615 274;* ⊕ *10.00–18.00 daily*) in the castle, a tourist information point and a pub called Hermanova Krčma (m *031 227 353*), although you shouldn't count on either of the last two places being open.

If you are thirsty after the steep ascent to the castle then check out **Bar Kimetec**, located on the road that branches away to the left as you near the castle; a wooden carving of a man holding a jug of Laško beer will help you find the way. If you want to come back down to continue the tour then just retrace your steps or if the walk has whetted your appetite for a spot of hiking there are several options from up here (see *Activities*, page 203). Cross the bridge back over the river and take the underpass before breaking right to take a quick look at the **Church of St Maximilian** (Cerkev Sv Maksimiljana), built on a site where some sources claim Bishop Maximilian was beheaded in the 2nd century.

From the church, walk back to Krekov trg and take Razlagova past the defence tower and water tower, before you come out by the river. From here go over the bridge to your right and head up the welter of stairs to the **Church of St Cecilija** (Cerkev Sv Cecilija). Nearby is a throwback to Roman times – the reconstructed **Temple of Hercules** (Heraklejev Tempelj). Head back down through the leafy **City Park** (Mestni Park), a favourite drinking venue for the city's wayward youth, and cross the footbridge to the stretch of grass that harbours a preserved stretch of the Old Town walls as well as a bundle of Roman remnants. One street inside the Old Town is Muzejski trg with its choice of museums before you end up on Trg Celjskih Knezov. Turn right onto pedestrianised Prešernova and follow it along towards Krekov trg. On the way you will come across the **Church of St Mary** (Cerkev Sv Marije), which no longer houses the bones of the Dukes of Celje, but is still worth sticking your head in. Cut right before you get to Krekov trg and you will end up in Glavni trg, the city's finest square, which is home to a plague pillar and a charming collage of 18th- and 19th-century buildings, as well as a sprinkling of cafés for you to relax in and reward yourself with a drink.

Celje Regional Museum (*Pokrajinski Muzej Celje; Muzejski trg 1;* ☎ *03 428 0950;* f *03 428 0966;* e *info@pokmuz-ce.si; www.pokmuz-ce.si;* €*3.50;* ⊕*Mar–Oct 10.00–18.00 Tue–Sun*) The Dukes of Celje are crucial to the city's history and this exhibition space delves into their story – a rather gruesome array of skulls that is on display is said to be those of the famed dukes, an interesting way to treat the city's finest. Other things to look out for are rooms done in various architectural styles, such as Art Nouveau and Baroque, as well as the *Celje Ceiling*, a lavish mural that depicts images from Roman and Greek mythology.

Celje Museum of Contemporary History (*Muzej Novejše Zgodovine Celje; Prešernova 17;* ☎ *03 428 6410;* f *03 428 6411;* e *info@guest.arnes.si; www.muzej-nz-ce.si; adult/concession* €*2.50/*€*1.70;* ⊕*10.00–18.00 Tue–Fri, 09.00–12.00 Sat, 14.00–18.00 Sun*) If you want to follow the story of Celje down the ages, well since the beginning of the 20th century at least, this is the place to come and fittingly the exhibits are housed in the old town hall. Opened in 1963, the museum's permanent collection includes artefacts that illuminate the history of dentistry in Slovenia, workmen's tools, weapons used by soldiers in World War II, enamel kitchenware (this has been produced at the EMO Enamel Factory since 1894) and even weighing scales. For visitors, letters saying farewell to their loved ones written by those imprisoned in Stari Pisker during the Nazi occupation of the city, may be of more interest. Another highlight is a mock-up of an old street renovated to look like 20th-century Celje with typical shops of the time. Elsewhere postcards and posters illuminate changes that have occurred in Celje and Štajerska during the course of the 20th century. Incorporated into the museum is the children's museum **Herman's Den** – the only museum in Slovenia designed for kids.

The Photo Studio of Josip Pelikan (*Razlagova 5;* ☎ *03 548 5891;* ⊕*10.00–14.00 Tue–Fri, 09.00–12.00 Sat, 14.00–18.00 Sun*) In a separate building you will find what is arguably the Museum of Contemporary History's most interesting collection: Josip Pelikan's photographs of Celje. The Celje-born photographer's images include studio shots, landscapes, photographs of the city's industry sector and people relaxing in nearby *termes*, all of which combine to give a pictorial history of the city and its environs between 1919 and 1977.

ACTIVITIES The verdant hills that surround Celje are a great place for walking. A handful of easy walks are signposted from the castle end of Cesta na Grad and should take you between 1½ and 2½ hours. These include a two-hour hike to Tovsti Vrh at 834m, a two-hour walk to Grmada at 718m and a 1½-hour trail to Celjska Koča at 651m. The insects in the woods can be ferocious in spring and summer so remember to bring your insect repellent. It is also important to take the usual walking safety precautions.

LAŠKO

Just 11km from Celje, Laško is popular with day trippers. Laško first appeared in written documents in 1227 as a market town, but archaeologists believe that humans settled in the area centuries before, including the Celts and the Romans. Laško's important trading role diminished under the Austro-Hungarians and it didn't regain its town status until its 700th anniversary in 1927. Today much of the town's architecture is modern and largely unattractive with few tourist sights. Instead visitors are lured here by its recently revamped spa and the beer that is produced by the very popular Laško Brewery. The best time to visit is during the beer festival in June.

GETTING THERE Trains from Celje (10 minutes) and Maribor (1½ hours) stop at Laško.

TOURIST INFORMATION

ⓘ Tourist Information Centre Trg Svobode 8; ✆ 03 733 8950; f 03 733 8956; e turisticno.drustvo.lasko@siol.net; www.turisticnodrustvo-lasko.si; ⊕ 08.00–17.00 Mon–Fri, 08.00–12.00 Sat

WHERE TO STAY

⌂ **Hotel Vrelec & Zdraviliški Dom** (210 rooms) ✆ 03 734 5122; f 03 734 5298; e info@zdavilisce-lasko.si; www.zdravilisce-lasko.si. The *terme*'s plush onsite hotel accommodation comes with an equally impressive price tag. $$$$$
⌂ **Hotel Hum** (28 rooms) Trg Svobode 1; ✆ 03 573 1499; f 03 573 1736; e hotel.hum@zdravilisce-lasko.si; www.zdravilisce-lasko.si. This pleasant 3-star hotel is located near the tourist information centre. $$$–$$$$
⌂ **Penzion Park** (26 beds) Zdraviliška 22; ✆ 03 573 16 10; e camloh@siol.net; www.penzionpark.si. This pleasant pension on the outskirts of town has clean rooms, café & tennis courts. $$

✕ WHERE TO EAT

✕ **Restavracija Špica in Pizzerija** Trg Svobode 7; ✆ 03 734 3330; ⊕ 10.00–23.00 daily. With trout, grilled meats & around 30 different pizza toppings Spica caters to most tastes. $$$
✕ **Pivnica Pačnik** Aškerčev trg 10; ✆ 03 573 0452; ⊕ 11.00–23.00 daily. Welcoming tavern serving regional cuisine & wine. $$$

WHAT TO SEE

Laško Brewery (*Pivovarna Laško; Trubarjeva 28;* ✆ *03 734 8000;* f *03 573 1817;* e *info@pivo-lasko.si; www.pivo-lasko.si; group tours by appointment*) Laško have been brewing beer since 1825 and they have recently bought stakes in their main rival Union to become Slovenia's leading beer producer. The company's best-known brand is the blond Zlatorog, which is available in bottles or on draught in almost every bar in the country. Other products include Temno Laško (dark beer), Lahko Laško (light beer), Zlatorog Club, Pils and Roler (see box, *Beer Battles*, in *Chapter 3*, page 64).

Terme Laško (*Zdraviliška 4;* ✆ *03 734 5111;* f *03 734 5298;* e *tajnistvo@zdravilisce-lasko.si; www.zdravilisce-lasko.si*) The spa at Laško is becoming as big a business as the brewery these days with an impressive recent renovation really improving things. The spa offers everything from therapeutic spring waters at temperatures of 32°C to 35°C, medical consultation and rehabilitation to aerobics and relaxation classes. The treatments offered in its wellness centre including hot- and cold-stone therapies, facials and body massages are a real highlight. Terme Laško also has an impressively large sauna centre with a range of dry and wet rooms. If you can't bear to drag yourself away then accommodation is available (see *Where to stay* above).

LOGARSKA DOLINA

When Austrians cross the border to come and savour your mountain scenery it has to be a sign that you have something special indeed. Logarska Dolina, or 'Logger's Valley', is indeed special: a stunning glaciated valley where the green meadows give way to papier-mâché mountains that loom improbably into the heavens above. The views are sublime and rival any stretch of mountain scenery in Europe, but there is a lot more to do in Logarska Dolina than just ogle at the landscape as facilities are well set up so you can get in and about it all. All of Logarska Dolina is a protected park (*www.logarska-dolina.si*) and entrance to it is controlled through a gate, where a €5 charge is levied on cars (payable each time you leave and re-enter). Two kilometres further on the scenery really opens up as you approach an information kiosk that has a good map of the area and can also dish out plenty of literature. This is where you will find the Plesnik Hotel, *the* place to stay and eat within the valley.

GETTING THERE Reaching Logarska Dolina on public transport is not that easy, especially outside the main tourist season. Most buses will take you as far as Gornji Grad from where there is one daily service to Mozirje (45 minutes). Buses to Gornji Grad come from Ljubljana (1 hour 50 minutes) and Kamnik (1 hour). It is also possible to reach the settlements of Solčava, Ljubno ob Savinji and Luče from Velenje and Celje, but services are irregular and you would be well advised to ask locally before setting out.

TOURIST INFORMATION

🔲 **Tourist Information Centre** Logarska Dolina 9; ✆ 03 838 9040; f 03 838 9003; e info@ logarska.si; www.logarska-dolina.si; ⏱ May–Oct

09.00–13.00 daily. Located in a hut at the foot of the driveway leading to the Plesnik Hotel. Out of season the staff at the hotel will help you.

🏠 WHERE TO STAY

🏠 **Hotel Plesnik and Vila Palenk** (32+11 rooms) Logarska Dolina 10; ✆ 03 839 2300; f 03 839 2312; e hotel@plesnik.si; www.plesnik.si. This oasis feels a world away from 21st-century life. The main building is a comfortable retreat with a swimming pool & sauna in the basement – though be aware that a lot of guests choose to dispense with their clothes in the pool, sauna & on the sunbeds. The Vila Palenk to the back is run by the same people, with very cosy rooms where you can burn your own log fire & relax on your balcony. The views from the valley-facing rooms in the main hotel are, however, more impressive. Whether you are staying or not a meal here is worth it too, though try to avoid weekends in summer when weddings can take over. $$$$
🏠 **Pension Na Razpotju** (10 rooms) Logarska Dolina 14; ✆ 03 839 1650; f 03 584 7017;

e razpoje@siol.net; www.plesnik.si. Attractive guesthouse with balconied rooms, just 500m from the Plesnik Hotel. $$$
🏠 **Tourist Farm Plesnik** (5 rooms) Logarska Dolina 13; ✆ 03 838 9009; f 03 838 9010; e nina.plesnik@gmail.com; www.plesnik.si. More affordable accommodation 200m from the Plesnik Hotel. $$
🏠 **Tourist Farm Juvanija** (4 rooms) Logarska Dolina 8; ✆ 03 838 9080; e juvanija@email.si. Offering pleasant accommodation near the park entrance in a traditional farmhouse. $$
🏠 **Tourist Farm Lenar** (4 rooms) Logarska Dolina 10; ✆ 03 838 9006; f 03 838 9003; e tk.lenar@siol.net. Another pleasant farmhouse located well within the park. $$

✖ WHERE TO EAT

✖ **Hotel Plesnik** Logarska Dolina 10; ✆ 03 839 2300; ⏱ 08.00–22.00 daily. The hotel's restaurant is

undoubtedly the best place to dine in the valley. In the summer months the prime seats are on the outside terrace, but similar views of the valley can be had from the windows. The fixed-price menu, which most diners opt for, is surprisingly good value at around €10 pp & is decent. For a real treat splash out on the à la carte dishes & choose a more expensive bottle of wine from their sizeable list. $$$

✕ **Rinka Inn** Logarska Dolina 15; 🕾 03 838 9036; ⊕ 08.00–22.00 daily. Much further up the valley on the way to Rinka Waterfall, this *gostilna* is a popular weekend lunch venue for Slovene families. $$$
✕ **Pension Na Razpotju** Logarska Dolina 14; 🕾 03 839 1650; ⊕ 08.00–22.00 daily. The guesthouse terrace is a pleasant place for a relaxed & informal meal. Look out for the spit-roast pork. $$$

ACTIVITIES Logarska Dolina has many outdoor activities to help you really enjoy and discover one of Slovenia's most stunning landscapes. Activities can be arranged at the tourist information centre; if this is closed ask at your accommodation.

Mountain biking One of the best ways to explore the 7km expanse of the valley is to hire a bike; however, Logarska Dolina has quite a steep incline and is certainly not a place to practise if you have never ridden a bike before. There are plenty of trails for those looking to strike out independently, but you can also embark on guided tours. Rental costs €2.50 an hour or €10 a day, although your hotel or pension may let you use a bike for free.

Walking and hiking Hiking up to the **Rinka Slap** (Rinka Waterfall) is easy enough, but if you want to tackle any of the 2,000m-plus peaks around here make sure you have all the necessary gear and a good map, as well as letting someone know your intended route. If you are looking for a more leisurely experience there is a sprinkling of *gostilnas* and cafés dotted around the valley, which are especially good on weekends. If you like your rambling to be more social then you can join a guided tour; this is charged according to the size of the group with a minimum charge of €68 for groups smaller than 20 people.

Other activities The extensive list of activities that you can book at the tourist office, which take place in or around the valley itself, also include horseriding (€15 for a one-hour guided tour), tandem paragliding (€60 per hour), rock climbing (€25/€137 per hour/day), archery (€10 per hour) and kayaking or rafting (both from €25). More leisurely pursuits are available in the form of a horse-drawn carriage ride (€25 per hour), ride in a hay cart (€5 per hour), a dip in the Plesnik's pool and the use of its sauna (€13, free for guests).

ROBANOV KOT AND MATKOV KOT

If you are staying for a few days and have your own wheels you can travel through to the neighbouring valleys of Robanov Kot or Matkov Kot. These are much less developed than Logarska, and while maybe not quite as attractive they are still stunning. Tourism is far less developed here so you get to enjoy the epic scenery often on your own.

PTUJ

Ptuj is the most complete historical town in Slovenia, a rhapsody of well-preserved medieval, Romanesque, Gothic and Renaissance architectural styles that is still built around a medieval plan which feels far removed from the modern world. Stretching out across the Drava River with its castle dominating the Old Town above, Ptuj invites comparisons with Prague, though things are on a much more compact and manageable scale. Strolling through the town often feels like leafing through the musty pages of a historical novel, and standing on the castle ramparts looking over the Drava River most visitors are charmed by Ptuj, even though few can pronounce it (try saying 'putuy' with your lips pursed and you will come close enough). Ptuj has not yet become too crowded, though there are some big plans for more hotels and the turning of the dammed section of the Drava that forms Ptuj Lake into a leisure park.

HISTORY Ptuj's rich history flits through a period when the Mithraic cult was dominant in the area. Roman times were also important for Ptuj as the river port of Poetovio, when it was the largest Roman settlement in Slovenia. Centuries later Ptuj's landmark castle served as a bulwark against the Turks and also held off the attentions of the Hungarians. Ptuj lost its role as Štajerska's most important town when the railway arrived in its rival Maribor in the 19th century, which is good news for today's tourists as the lack of industrial development has aided the preservation of this architectural gem.

GETTING THERE Frequent bus services connect Ptuj to Maribor (30 minutes) and Ljubljana (3½ hours). Trains from Maribor (45 minutes–1 hour), Celje (1 hour), Murska Sobota (50 minutes–1 hour 10 minutes) and Ljubljana (2–3 hours) also stop in Ptuj.

Railway station Osojnikova 2; ⤞ 02 292 4734   **Bus station** Osojnikova 11; ⤞ 02 771 1491

TOURIST INFORMATION
🛈 **Tourist Information Centre** Slovenski trg 5; ⤞ 02 779 6011; e info@ptuj-tourism.si; www.ptuj-tourism.si; ⊕ 09.00–20.00 daily

🏠 WHERE TO STAY
🏠 **Terme Ptuj** (129 rooms) Pot v toplice 9; ⤞ 02 782 7821; f 02 783 7771; e info@terme-ptuj.si; www.terme-ptuj.si. You can stay in the new 4-star Grand Hotel Primus, bungalows & apts sleeping up to 6, or camp at the *terme*, a 15–20-min walk from the Old Town. Hotel $$$$$, apts $$$, bungalows $$$, camping $

🏠 **Garni Hotel Mitra** (23 rooms) Prešerenova 6; ⤞ 02 787 7455; f 02 787 7459; e info@hotel-mitra.si; www.hotel-mitra.si. Located right at the heart of Ptuj's Old Town the hotel has been welcoming visitors since 1870 & it is our favourite

place to stay in the town. Spacious rooms & traditionally styled public spaces all add to the hotel's charm. If you have your own car, the only bugbear will be the absence of parking spaces. The car park by the castle is free. $$$

🏠 **Hotel Poetovio** (29 rooms) Vinarski trg 5; ⤞ 02 779 8201; f 02 779 8241. A step down from the Garni Hotel Mitra, with acceptable rooms. $$

🏠 **Kurent Youth Hostel** (55 beds) Osojnikova 9; ⤞ 02 771 0814; f 02 771 0815. This centrally located hostel, just 250m from the bus station & 500m from the train station, has 2–6-bed rooms. Rates are pp. $

✕ WHERE TO EAT
✕ **Ribič** Dravska 9; ⤞ 02 749 0635; ⊕ 11.00–23.00 Mon–Thu & Sun, 11.00–midnight Fri/Sat. If you eat out only once in Ptuj make it here. Smooth service, great fresh fish & seafood, as well as nice serving touches like soup served in a hard bread roll make the bill easier to stomach. The waiting staff will tell you about the daily specials – trout is a frequent highlight. If the weather is good the terrace next to the Drava is an unbeatable setting. $$$$

✕ **Gostilna Amadeus** Prešerenova 36; ⤞ 02 771 7051; ⊕ 12.00–22.00 Mon–Sat, 12.00–16.00 Sun. Another decent dining option serving good-quality Slovenian dishes at more affordable prices than Ribič. $$$

✕ **Café Evropa Pub** Mestni trg 1; ⤞ 02 771 0235; ⊕ 07.00–23.00 Mon–Thu, 08.00–04.00 Fri/Sat, 14.00–22.00 Sun. The menu comes in the form of a newspaper – like the News Café in Bernardin – &

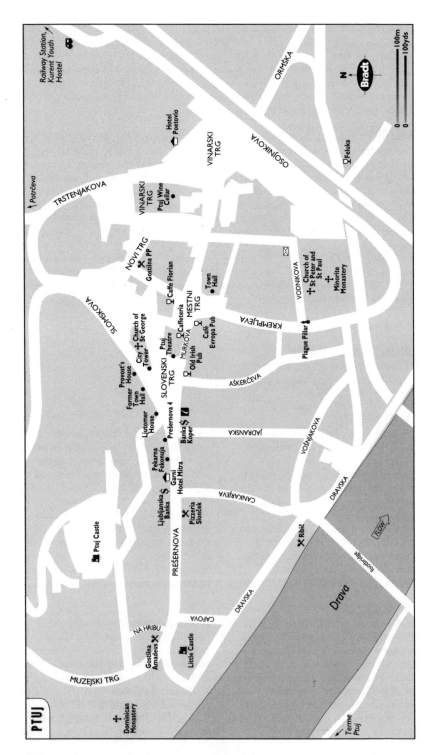

PTUJ

Railway Station, Kurent Youth Hostel

Patrčeva

TRSTENJAKOVA

ORMŠKA

OSOJNIKOVA

N

Bradt

0   100m
0   100yds

Hotel Poetovio

VINARSKI TRG

VINARSKI TRG

Ptuj Wine Cellar

Feluka

NOVI TRG

Gostilna PP

Caffe Florian

Town Hall

VODNIKOVA

Church of St Peter and St Paul

Minorite Monastery

SLOMŠKOVA

Church of St George

City Tower

Ptuj Theatre

MURKOVA

Cafeteria

MESTNI TRG

Café Evropa Pub

Old Irish Pub

KREMPLJEVA

Plague Pillar

Prowost's House

Former Town Hall

SLOVENSKI TRG

AŠKERČEVA

Ljutomer House

Prešernova 4

Banka Koper

JADRANSKA

VOŠNJAKOVA

DRAVSKA

Pekarna Fekonuja

Gerni Hotel Mitra

Ljubljanska Banka

CANKARJEVA

Ptuj Castle

Pizzeria Slonček

PREŠERNOVA

Ribič

DRAVSKA

CAFOVA

NA HRIBU

Drava

footbridge

ELON

Gostilna Amadeus

Little Castle

MUZEJSKI TRG

Dominican Monastery

Terme Ptuj

features a wide range of alcoholic beverages as well as cheap & tasty pizzas. Stick with the *malo* (small) size pizzas unless you are sharing. When the pizzeria closes this becomes one of the town's most popular bars. $$

✗ **Gostilna PP** Novi trg 2; \ 02 749 0622; ⏲09.00–19.00 Mon–Sat, 12.00–16.00 Sun.

Inexpensive set lunches cost from €3.50. The Sun buffet brunch is also very popular with locals. However in terms of quality & taste, you get what you pay for. $$

✗ **Pizzerija Slonček** Prešerenova 19; \ 02 776 1311; ⏲09.00–22.00 Mon–Sat. Standard but cheap pizzas. $$

ENTERTAINMENT AND NIGHTLIFE Ptuj's historic core is bursting with café-bars with the biggest concentrations running along Prešerenova to Murkova and then onto Mestni trg.

♀ **Café Evropa Pub** (see *Where to eat* above)
⎵ **Caffeteria** Murkova 6. Great little teahouse serving up myriad blends & herbal brews.
♀ **Feluka** Čučkova 6a. Popular with the local in-crowd; few tourists make the effort to seek out this bar as it is not in the centre of town.

♀ **Old Irish Pub** Murkova 5; \ 02 782 3261. Draught Guinness, a vaulted brick ceiling, friendly staff & a small terrace are all part of the winning formula.
♀ **Bar Caffe Florian** Mestni trg 4; \ 02 787 8542. Popular spot with outside tables & watched over protectively by the statue of St Florian, patron saint of fire & firemen.

OTHER PRACTICALITIES

✉ **Post office** Vodnikova 2; ⏲08.00–19.00 Mon–Fri, 08.00–13.00 Sat
$ **Banka Koper** Slovenski trg 3

$ **Ljubljanska Banka** Prešerenova 6
✚ **Health centre** Potrčeva 19a; \ 02 771 2511
✚ **Emergency dentist** Potrčeva 19a; \ 02 771 2511

WHAT TO SEE
Ptuj Castle and Ptuj Regional Museum (*Grad Ptuj and Pokrajinski Muzej Ptuj; Na Gradu 1;* \ *02 748 0360; tour adult/concession €3.50/€2.50; admission €1.50;* ⏲*mid Oct–Apr 09.00–17.00 daily; May–mid Oct 09.00–18.00 daily, with extended opening hrs at w/ends 09.00–20.00 Jul/Aug*) The 12th-century Ptuj Castle came under state ownership at the end of World War II after a chequered history which, at one point, saw it presided over by a Scottish family, the Leslies, from 1656 through to 1802 (see the family coat of arms on the first floor). Today the first thing that you will notice when you visit the castle is the sweeping view over the Old Town and the Drava River. You can explore the regional museum on your own, but it does not cost much more, and it is infinitely more interesting, to book yourself onto a guided tour in advance – they are in very high demand and you are unlikely to be able to just turn up and join one.

The first stop on the guided tour is the armoury, where weapons dating from the late 14th century to the end of World War II are displayed behind glass cabinets. This surprisingly contemporary space is more interesting for its architectural detail; one of the preserved stone walls dates from the 12th century when curators think it was probably a stable, while the Romanesque window and vaulted ceiling suggest that this room was later used as a residential space. The rest of the ground floor is home to a smorgasbord of costumes and furniture, largely dating from the 16th to the 19th century. A narrow medieval turret leads up to the first floor, which functions as one large gallery. If you are on a self-guided visit take time to really explore this level of the castle. Highlights of the building itself include the colonnades that overlook the courtyard and the Baroque Festival Hall – dating from the 17th century, this is a particularly atmospheric place to watch a performance. This room is worth visiting to see the huge collection of Turkerie portraits. The exotic ladies in them are not really as dainty as they may at first look, as these paintings were shockingly risqué at the time with underwear hinted

KURENTOVANJE FESTIVAL

The Kurentovanje is one of Slovenia's most vibrant and alluring festivals, taking hold of the town of Ptuj every year in the run-up to Shrove Tuesday. The festival originates from early Slavic times when it emerged as a ritual designed to fend off winter and its evil spirits. The most colourful part of the action is when the local men dress in extravagant costumes with masks to become 'kurents' – the demons coming from the other side – who you cannot miss as they rollick around rattling their cow bells. Their handmade costumes feature massive feathery headgear and scary masks top off the outfits. At the height of the festival over 300 young men can be heard hollering around the town trying to win the favour of local maidens, who traditionally throw handkerchiefs to show their approval, though apparently in recent years the tradition has moved on with G-strings replacing handkerchiefs on more than one occasion. Look out for the other character at the head of the processions, who is one of the devils that the festival is trying to chase out of town.

at and suggestive use of fruit. The largest painting is of a harem, which is particularly daring when you consider it in the context of the 17th century.

Other highlights in the museum's collection include the 'soft Gothic' statues from the early 15th century and the collection of modern art by celebrated Slovene artist France Mihelič. Meanwhile the salon, Chinese salon and ladies' salon are interesting as the proprietors have endeavoured to restore their 18th-century appearance. Also look out for the colourful displays showing masks and costumes from the local Kurentovanje Festival (see box, above), which are part of the ethnological collection. Worth checking out as well is the separate musical section, which delves into the instruments found from local digs, including a Roman flute from the 2nd century that the curators reckon may be the oldest in existence. This interactive space is especially appealing to children; music comes on to accompany the displays as you walk around and you can even have a go on the snare drum if your skills are up to it.

A small café operates within the castle with a few tables outside in summer if you are thirsty after your drumming.

A walking tour Strolling around Ptuj could not be easier as the tourist office issues a good map and most of the main attractions have a multi-lingual information board, including English, with a paragraph on each stop to make things easier. A good place to start a walking tour of Ptuj is from the castle itself as you can easily make out the layout of the town as it unfolds below and plan out your route.

First up just below the castle ramparts (take Na Hribu) is the **Dominican Monastery** (*Dominikanski Samostan; Muzejski trg 1;* ✆ *02 787 9421; adult/concession €3/€1.70;* ⊕*Apr–Nov 09.00–17.00 daily*), which rests in a small park below the castle to the right when you are facing the river. A glass screen leads through to a fine collection of Mithraic shrines that were unearthed in and around Ptuj at Spodnja Hajdina. From here head downhill and you will be near the river on Dravska; strike out for the footbridge and continue on past the Ribič Restaurant and you will come to Minoritski, site of a **Minorite Monastery** (*Minoritski Samostan, Minoritski trg;* ✆ *02 771 3091;* ⊕*by appointment*). The **Church of Sts Peter and Paul** (Cerkev Sv Petra in Pavla) was mauled in an Allied air attack during World War II and is only now being rebuilt.

As you head up back towards the castle and away from the river up Krempljeva look out for the **plague pillar**, a gleaming gold image of Mary and Jesus. You are now in the heart of the Old Town and soon you will spill out into Mestni trg, which is home to a couple of interesting buildings and a smattering of bars. Take a look at the **Town Hall** (Mestna Hiša) on the right, a relative newcomer for Ptuj as it was only added at the start of the 20th century.

Follow Murkova up the hill and you are now in Slovenski trg, a pretty square with a triangular ramble of cobbles forming an island in the middle. The brightly coloured façade to the right is **Ptuj Theatre** (Gledališče Ptuj), which demonstrates Ptuj's cultural vibrancy by playing host to cutting-edge theatre rather than sticking with safer classics. Dominating the square above is the **City Tower** (Mestni Stolp). Lurking behind is the **Church of St George** (Cerkev Sv Jurija). The lump of stone outside is a 2BC chunky Roman leftover, which looks a bit faded especially as it is exposed to the elements here. It depicts scenes from the *Orpheus* story, but it has other stories to tell as it was once also used for public beatings. Other notable buildings in the square include the **Ljutomer House** (Ljutomer Hiša), the **Provost's House** and the **former town hall**. Take Prešernova ulica, one of Ptuj's prettiest streets and also home to the **oldest building in Ptuj** at No 4; if you want a break take a seat at one of the sprinkling of cafés in this street, before wrapping up the tour with a stop at the **Little Castle** (Mali Grad).

Terme Ptuj (*Pot v toplice 9*; ☎ *02 749 4100*; f *02 749 4520*; e *info@terme-ptuj.si; www.terme-ptuj.si; entrance to the thermal complex* €*11*; ☼*07.00–22.00 Sun–Thu, 07.00–23.00 Fri/Sat*) The recently revamped *terme* is a good place to come and relax. It is a 15–20-minute walk from town across the Drava and is perfect for soothing limbs aching after tackling Ptuj's Old Town.

Ptuj Mountain (Ptujska Gora) From Ptuj Castle on a clear day you can easily make out Ptuj Mountain and the Church of St Mary (Cerkev Sv Marija) which lie 13km across the Drava. One of Slovenia's most important churches, Cerkev Sv Marija serves as the main pilgrimage church for the Štajerska region and attracts pilgrims from all over Slovenia. In fact, in terms of Catholic pilgrimage, Ptujska Gora comes second only to Brezje in Gorenjska. As you approach look out for the plague pillar that was erected to mark the drastic epidemics of the 17th century. A church has stood on the mountain since the 14th century. The walls are buttressed and the interior comprises three aisles. One of the highlights is the relief of the Virgin Mary herself, which is famous because it depicts people from diverse economic and cultural backgrounds all seeking refuge under the Madonna's coat.

ŠTAJERSKA CASTLES

BORL CASTLE (*Borl Grad*; e *info@borl.org; www.borl.org*) A frontier castle located 12km from Ptuj in Haloze (follow the road for Zavrč), Borl Castle dates back to the turn of the 12th century when Frederick of Ptuj lived here, although the castle belonged to King Bela IV of Hungary. Some sources suggest that settlement on the site of today's impressive castle dates back as far as Neolithic times and over the centuries various masters have presided over this strategic hillock overlooking the Drava River, including the Romans and the Hungarians. Borl has had its fair share of setbacks including a devastating earthquake in the 16th century and a fire in the 18th, but one of its darkest periods came during World War II when it was used as a staging post for Nazi victims *en route* to the concentration camps. From the end of the war until 1948 the castle lay empty, then became a refugee camp before being partially renovated in the early 1950s. Further renovation saw the addition of a restaurant and the castle was transformed into a hotel, but years of underinvestment and the collapse of the access bridge across the Drava River saw this close in 1981. Since 1994 various artistic programmes have been taking place within the castle; however, like many of Slovenia's castles Borl Castle still requires a lot of renovation work.

PODČETRTEK CASTLE (Podčetrtek Grad) In the border village of Podčetrtek, 15km from Rogaška Slatina, you will find one of many eye-catching Slovenian castles. The 12th-century fortification draws the eye with its impressive shape dominating a strategic position, though this time there is not actually that much to see when you head for a closer look. Damage sustained in the 1974 earthquake and years of neglect have left the castle in a sorry state and while you can easily walk up to it (as countless passers-by do) the castle is not actually open to the public.

PODSREDA CASTLE (*Podsreda Grad; Podsreda 45;* \ *03 800 7100;* f *03 800 7108;* e *kozjanski-park@kp.gov.si; adult/concession* €*2.50/*€*1.70;* ⊕ *Oct–Apr 10.00–18.00 Tue–Sun*) Located in Kozjansko (Kozjanski) Park at Podsreda some 20km southwest of Podčetrtek Castle, this Romanesque castle dates back to the beginning of the 13th century, although much of its present-day incarnation is the result of careful restoration work. Its main attractions are the small chapel and defence tower, both frequently held up as some of the best examples of Romanesque architecture in Slovenia. It is possible to visit alone or as part of a guided tour and while the exhibition of Rogaška glass is nothing special, the collection of prints dedicated to the Štajerska region is interesting enough.

In addition to the castle, this national/nature park has a number of walking trails ranging from 2km to 32km in length. Guided walks and hikes can be booked through the information centre. An enjoyable way to get to the castle is to hike uphill from the nearest village of Podsreda.

TERME RADENCI

(*Zdraviliško naselje 12;* \ *02 520 2770;* f *02 520 2723;* e *terme@terme-radenci.si; www.terme-radenci.si; adult/child from* €*6/*€*4.50;* ⊕*09.00–21.00 daily*) Right on the edge of Prekmurje at Radenci, and very close to the border with Austria, is one of Slovenia's most famous spas, the source of the 'three hearts' mineral water that you will see all over the country. Radenci has been a popular spa resort since the 19th century and is said to have been a favourite retreat of Emperor Franz Ferdinand amongst others. The spa operation is becoming increasingly slick here with prices in euros and everything available from a three-hour play in the pools

---

HALOZE WINES

To the south of Ptuj are the Haloze Hills, which produce a range of excellent wines. If you are short of time in Ptuj you will find the **Ptuj Wine Cellar** (*Ptjuska Klet; Vinarski trg 1;* \ *02 787 9810;* e *tanja.vinkler@perutnina.si; www.ptujska-klet.si*), where you can go on an hour-long tour (booking in advance is essential) and explore the wine cellars, watch a video and then, of course, try some of the produce including Riesling, Chardonnay, Muscat and Pinot Noir. The wine vats themselves are huge (around 3.5 million litres of wine is stored here) and the cellars are all the more atmospheric for their minimal lighting. Look out for the old hidden storage area, which has fine wines dating back as far as 1917 that are housed in a fortified section designed to keep out the attentions of the German occupiers in World War II.

for €7.50 right through to a seven-day detox and slimming programme from around €400. You can just turn up and use the pools with that three-hour ticket, though remember to bring a towel as they do not hire them out and you will have to beg nicely to scrounge one from a member of staff. Inside there is a 25m swimming pool that is cool enough to lane-swim in, and a more relaxed fun pool that includes a water-jet system that grabs unsuspecting bathers and deposits them outside where steam rises from the hot pool. There are lots of nooks and crannies here with bubbling jacuzzis and water sprays as well as sun loungers. Radenci also has a smaller outdoor pool that attracts mainly adults and is an oasis of calm on a busy summer day when hordes of children descend on the complex. For real spa addicts there is even an onsite museum to fill you in on the history of this impressive spa. Accommodation comes in the form of two four-star hotels: **Hotel Izvir** and **Hotel Radin** ($$$$).

PREKMURJE

This tiny enclave of northeastern Slovenia, so named as it lies 'beyond' the strategic Mura River, is one of the most distinctive parts of the country and many travellers find it one of the most enjoyable to visit. Historically Prekmurje is the region of Slovenia that has been most influenced by Hungary. Even today the area of Lendava is home to a constitutionally recognised Hungarian minority; here the children learn Hungarian at school and anyone who wants to join the civil service must be fluent in both Slovene and Hungarian. Around 6,000 Hungarians live in and around Lendava and their national tongue is the region's official second language. This Hungarian minority also has a sufficiently powerful vote to return one MP to the Slovenian Parliament (there is a total of 90 seats). Today's picture of ethnic harmony couldn't be further removed from that of less than a century ago when during Hungarian rule in Prekmurje the Slovene language was actively subjugated. World War I saw Prekmurje become part of the new Yugoslavia, yet this small corner of Slovenia found itself subjected to Hungarian oppression once again during the occupation in 1941.

It is easy to say that Prekmurje is the Hungarian part of Slovenia given its proximity to Hungary, the similarities in much of its architecture, cuisine (goulash is one of the most popular dishes) and crafts, but this does not give the whole picture. Little Prekmurje, a land of fertile plains and vineyards is neither entirely Slovenian nor Hungarian – for example even under Hungarian rule many people still spoke Slovene and today while most locals are happy to be Slovene they are still proud of their Magyar traditions. The best way to explore it is just to get on a bike or in your car and meander around the country lanes, stopping off at any of the villages you find interesting. In many villages you will see more tractors and bicycles than cars and find a pace of life that is more 19th than 21st century. Drifting through the narrow lanes as the signature white storks set off from the field next to you and the little churches twinkle all around, Prekmurje manages to surprise many travellers. With EU accession has come a drive for tourism with signs for *sobes*, restaurants and the like popping up all over the place and property speculators moving to snap up holiday homes in a region that lies supremely well located in the northeastern corner of Slovenia and bordered by Austria, Hungary and Croatia.

Despite this strategic location Prekmurje was for a long time hindered by its geography – something of a surprise when looking at a map as it occupies such a strategic position in central Europe. The map does not tell the whole story as Prekmurje was previously isolated from the south by the lack of a bridge over the Mura River and much of its terrain is awash with flooded pools and marshes.

Štajerska and Prekmurje PREKMURJE

9

Over the centuries the list of the civilisations who have rattled through Prekmurje reads like a who's who of European history with the Illyrians, Celts, Romans, Slavs and the Hungarians all playing a part.

MURSKA SOBOTA It may be the largest town in Prekmurje, but the regional centre is not an instantly lovable place with a smattering of modern buildings and industrial developments blighting the few more promising districts.

Getting there Buses from Radenci (15 minutes), Maribor (2 hours), Celje (2½–2½ hours) and Ljubljana (4 hours) all stop at Murska Sobota. Trains from Ptuj (50 minutes–1 hour 10 minutes), Maribor (1½ hours) and Ljubljana (3½ hours) also call there.

Bus station Slomškova 40; ↘ 02 530 1666

Railway station Arhiteka Novaka 33; ↘ 02 292 5802

Tourist information
🔲 **Tourist Information Centre** Kiosk outside Slovenska 37; ↘ 02 534 1130; ⊕09.00–17.00 Mon–Fri, 08.00–12.00 Sat

🏠 Where to stay
🏠 **Hotel Diana** (95 rooms) Slovenska 52; ↘ 02 524 1200; f 02 532 1097. Fortunately the interior of the hotel is much nicer than its monstrous concrete exterior. Geared firmly towards business visitors, rooms are functional rather than luxurious. The hotel offers various dining choices including its popular pizzeria, & also has a fitness centre, pool tables, squash courts & its own thermal pool. At weekends the hotel's nightclub attracts Murska Sobota's younger citizens. $$$

🏠 **Hotel Dobray** (28 rooms) Trg zmage 8; ↘ 02 514 1200; f 02 514 1245. The Diana's sister hotel is located just 200m away. $$$

✖ Where to eat
✖ **Restavracija in Pivnica Zvezda** Trg zmage 8; ↘ 02 514 1861; ⊕07.00–23.00 Mon–Thu & Sun, 07.00–01.00 Fri/Sat. This restaurant & beer hall serves up lashings of domestic brews & hearty Slovene cuisine. $$$

✖ **Gostilna Rajh** Soboška 32; ↘ 0254 93 9098; www.rajh.si; ⊕ 10.00–23.00 Tue–Sat, 10.00–16.00 Sun. This restaurant 4km out of town is no competition for anything in Murska Sobota itself. The menu features dishes characteristic of the Prekmurje region like goulash, sausages, buckwheat porridge & crackling. $$$

✖ **Hotel Diana** Slovenska 52; ↘ 02 524 1200; ⊕08.00–22.00 daily. The hotel's busy pizzeria serves decent pizzas. $$

✖ **Mercator** Slovenska 40

For a quick snack join the locals queuing at the bustling bakeries and *slaščicarna* (ice-cream parlours) on Kodjeva.

Other practicalities
$ **Ljubljanska Banka** Slovenska 41 & Trg zmage 7; ⊕08.00–17.00 Mon–Fri

$ **Banka Koper** Slovenska 27; ⊕08.00–16.00 Mon–Fri

✉ **Post office** Trg zmage 6; ⊕07.00–19.00 Mon–Fri, 07.00–13.00 Sat

What to see It is worth visiting Murska Sobota's **Town Park**, a green lung that unusually for Slovenia refuses to hide its socialist-era past with an imposing war memorial complete with two howitzers, heroic soldiers and Cyrillic script. This monument commemorates the bravery of the Soviet soldiers who liberated the area at the end of World War II. Interestingly enough this is the only Soviet monument in Slovenia, and Prekmurje is the only area where the Soviet Red Army actually ventured into as a part of the Allied liberation operation at the end of the war. Head behind the monument to cross into the largest section of the park where a small pond leads on to **Sobota Castle** (*Grad Sobota; Trubarjev drevored 4;* ☏ *02 527 1706;* f *02 521 1155;* e *Pok-muzej-ms@guest.arnes.si; www.pok-muzej-ms.si;* €*2.50;* ☉ *10.00–17.00 Tue–Sat, 10.00–13.00 Sun*), which is home to the **Regional Museum of Murska Sobota** (Pokrajinski Musej Murska Sobota). The castle has its origins in the 16th century, though it was given a major Renaissance makeover and later opened as a museum in 1955. The well-presented first-floor display space was refurbished in 1997 and the museum these days does much more than tell the story of the town and its immediate surrounds, as it spills over into more general Prekmurje themes from prehistoric times right through to the early 21st century.

EXPLORING PREKMURJE It's a good idea to seek local advice and pick up some literature at the tourist information centre in Murska Sobota. Armed with a tourist map of Prekmurje and the ever-increasing amount of flyers promoting restaurants, hotels and the like – most of them are in Slovene or German only – head out of the town and soon you will descend into the bucolic escape that is much of the region. Planning where to go is up to you and if you have time just venture out and see what you come across, but keep your passport handy as it is all too easy to wind up at an international border by mistake in these parts.

The flat Prekmurje plain is ideal for cycling. A collection of leaflets detailing seven waymarked cycling routes titled *Cycling Around Prekmurje* will help you in your exploration. The trails vary in length from 14km to 50km and are graded from easy to difficult. A 44km trail starts at the Lipa Hotel in Lendava and extends south to the forest of Murska Šuma and east to Kapca before returning to the starting point. We picked up our leaflets at the tourist information centre in Maribor, but the offices in Murska Sobota and Lendava (*Kranjčeva 4;* ☏ *02 578 8390*) should also be able to help you. The longest tour crosses into Hungary, so again you will need to remember to take your passport with you. Make sure to try the local goulash and gorgeous *gibanica* cake you will find served all over Slovenia.

GRAD If you only have a day strike north from Murska Sobota for Grad, where Slovenia's largest Baroque castle awaits. Dating from the early 13th century the castle's layout is noteworthy for its almost triangular shape. After decades of neglect – refurbishing a castle with a largely Hungarian heritage was not close to the top of the Yugoslav government's priority list – European Union money is finally helping to turn this sleeping giant around. For now only parts of the castle have been revamped with a number of museum rooms now open to the public including a pottery, herbalist and the old kitchen on the first floor, while on the second floor you can see the old living quarters which are now used for local weddings. Look out also for the scale model of how the castle may once again look and also for the helpful English-language signs, which help add a bit of background. There are usually guides on hand to give you a quick tour for the princely sum of €2. A variety of plans have been mooted for Grad and hopefully this vast place will soon ring with life once again.

From Grad you can head back east dodging storks, tractors and octogenarians on bicycles through vineyards and tiny villages accompanied by churches that lie within the Goriška Park.

Hotel accommodation in Slovenia tends to be concentrated in its big cities and towns. As a result most hotels cater to a business crowd and rooms are often scarce, expensive or very average. In many interesting historical locations like Kranj (the fourth-largest city in Slovenia) there is often just one centrally located hotel. Savvy visitors, however, are beginning to take advantage of private rooms in rural villages, or just outside main urban centres. This system of rural accommodation, or agritourism, in Slovenia is well organised and farm or agricultural properties offering tourist services are called tourist farms. Farm stays give guests the opportunity to visit some of Slovenia's most beautiful areas, experience real Slovenian hospitality, try traditional foods and get active in the countryside. The Slovenian Tourist Board (*www.slovenia.info*) lists almost 300 tourist farms and their contact details on its website. It is advisable to book this type of rural accommodation in advance. There are tourist farms throughout Slovenia, but the majority are located in Gorenjska, in and around Triglav National Park with its stunning Julian Alps, and in the regions of Prekmurje, Dolenjska and Bela Krajina. Again, many offer regional foods, so in Prekmurje you are in line for fiery goulash dishes and *gibinica*, the delightful dessert for which the region is renowned.

MORAVSKE TOPLICE AND AROUND In the southeastern corner of Prekmurje you will find Lake Bukovnisko, a good place to relax on a sunny day, though your hire car will not thank you for rattling it down the last section of the unsealed road to the lake. From here dip down to the pretty village of Bogojina – there are many villages as charming as this, though none can boast as stunning a church by ubiquitous Slovene architect Jože Plečnik. Lying on the edge of fields in a sleepy village where the residents often call out a greeting as you pass, this dramatic edifice comes as something of a surprise.

Continue west on through Tesanovci, which has a flurry of local potteries, with the more commercial ones displaying signs on the main streets as you pass. Soon you will be at Moravske Toplice, just short of Murska Sobota, home to Terme 3000, one of the country's largest and most impressive spas. For an alternative afternoon there is also a golf club and if you really want to kick back there are hotels as well so you can spend a few days here and try some of the health treatments.

TERME 3000 (*Kranjčeva 12;* ✆ *02 512 2200;* f *02 548 1607;* e *info@terme3000.si; www.terme3000.si; adult/child from €9/€7;* ⊕ *09.00–21.00 daily*) The facilities here are impressively modern and extensive. You can smell the sulphur as you approach and soon you will be bathed in the bubbling thermal waters. There are indoor and outdoor sections with lanes for swimming, jacuzzis, sunbeds and even flumes if you fancy something a bit different – beware that although these are mainly for kids the green one is not for the faint-hearted as it plummets in a near-vertical drop as we found out in a heart-thumping moment! Bicycle hire is also available from the *terme*'s bike centre (✆ *02 512 2186*). The 18-hole golf course and tennis courts are other distractions.

🏠 **Where to stay** All Terme 3000 accommodation can be booked through the central reservations number (see contact details above).

Hotel Livada Prestige (122 rooms) The newest & swankiest accommodation option at the *terme* opened its doors towards the end of 2007. $$$$$

Hotel Ajda (157 rooms) This 4 star has pleasant rooms. $$$$

Camping
Terme 3000 Campground Kranjčeva 12, Moravske Toplice; ☎ 02 512 1200; f 05 512 1148; e recepcija.camp2@terme3000.si; www.terme3000.si. Facilities at this 5ha, 400-pitch

Hotel Termal (139 rooms) Another decent 4-star option. $$$$

Tourist Village Bungalows (4 dbl/twin rooms) Sleeping 8. $$$

Prekmursa Vas Village Apartments Accommodating 2–5 people. $$$–$$$$

site include laundry, internet access & a shop. Campers also have access to the pools & recreational facilities at Terme 3000. Rates are pp. $

Wolf

10

Koroška

Historically, Koroška (Carinthia) and Štajerska (Styria) have shared a regional identity with their Austrian neighbours – at one time a historic site near Klagenfurt (Celovec in Slovene) was the seat of the early Slovenian state of Carinthia (Carantania), and the modern-day Austrian provinces of Carinthia and Styria both have sizeable Slovene minorities. This common heritage has given Slovenia's northwestern corner architecture and a way of life that is broadly similar to that in Kaernten (Steiremark) across the border. While it may closely resemble Austria, plucky little Koroška in Slovenia's north defiantly rejected the advances of its powerful neighbour after World War I when its citizens chose to be part of the Kingdom of Serbs, Croats and Slovenes instead of being absorbed by Austria. The choice of the people to the north of the Kobansko Hills to throw their lot in with Austria still rankles with many people in Koroška who feel passionately Slovene. Koroška also stood up to the might of the Yugoslav army in 1991 when they put up fierce resistance and hampered the army's attempts to secure the border posts with Austria. It may not quite have the drama of the mountainscapes to its west, but it offers easy access to the Pohorje Massif and is largely made up of rolling tree-shrouded hills that are bisected by the broad sweep of the Drava, Slovenia's second-longest river, which cuts through Koroška from west to east on its route to joining the even mightier Danube. The drive to or from Maribor is picturesque as the road follows the Drava with floating cafés and restaurants to rest at on your way, although the odd hydro-electric power station does detract from the ambience slightly. Cycling is also a good way to explore the smattering of small towns and villages *en route*, though the main highway can be busy and potentially dangerous for those on two wheels.

SLOVENJ GRADEC

The largest town in Koroška is a pleasant enough place to spend a few days and is also a good base for exploring the region with convenient transport connections. Everything you are likely to need is on two streets in the Old Town: Meškova and Glavni trg, which run parallel to each other and are connected by Trg Svobode. A sprinkling of cafés, bars and restaurants dot all three in summer and there is also a number of worthwhile sights to cover even if you are desperate to get out into the hills and explore. Winters can be bitter in these parts and not for nothing is Slovenj Gradec known as the coldest town in Slovenia. Slovenj Gradec's cultural scene does help liven up the darkest of days as this was the home of composer Hugo Wolf, the Baroque painter Franc Strauss as well as today being home to a modern art gallery and a sprinkling of street sculptures. The town is keen to forge its links with the outside world and in 1989 it was bestowed the title of 'Peace Messenger City' by the United Nations. During the Balkan conflicts of the 1990s it was actively involved in the peace movement and in

SLOVENJ GRADEC

N

Gostilna Murko

FRANCETOVA

Suhodolnica River

ŠOLSKA

POŠTNA

P

P

CANKARJEVA

MEŠKOVA

Regional Museum of Koroška, Koroška Gallery of Fine Arts

GLAVNI TRG

TRG SVOBODE

P

Koroška Banka

Sedmica ✗

Soklič Museum

✝ Church of St Elizabeth

Probanka

Hotel Slovenj Gradec

✝ Church of the Holy Spirit

Stari Trg

Hotel Aerodrom Mislinjska Dobrava

VORANČEV TRG

P

0 ————— 100m
0 ————— 200yds

organising aid convoys into the region. Two days of festivities are given over to commemorate this honour and promote world peace each year – with the Peace Festival filling Glavni trg on 23 October, and the town's residents also celebrating United Nations Day on 24 October.

HISTORY Like the rest of Koroška Slovenj Gradec has always been a town torn between different cultures and even today it feels both Germanic and Slovene. Evidence of civilisation extends as far back as Roman times when it was known as Colatio. During the days of the Ottomans Slovenj Gradec had to hold fast against their repeated attacks. While the Ottomans could not snuff out the town fire almost did in 1903, but slowly Slovenj Gradec staggered back to its feet. Under the communist regime Slovenj Gradec and Koroška often felt dismissed and ignored by Belgrade as being 'too German', but the upside is that heavy industrial development never really took hold here and you will struggle to find any building over a couple of storeys high.

GETTING THERE Slovenj Gradec is served by buses from Dravograd (20 minutes), Velenje (40 minutes) and Ljubljana (2½ hours).

TOURIST INFORMATION
🄸 Tourist Information Centre Glavni trg 24;
📞 02 881 2116; f 02 881 2117; e tic@

slovenj-gradec.si; www.slovenj-gradec.si;
🕐 09.00–18.00 Mon–Fri, 09.00–12.00 Sat/Sun

WHERE TO STAY
🏠 Hotel Aerodrom (12 rooms) Mislinkjska Dobrava 110, Šmartno pri Slovenj Gradec; 📞 02 885

0500; f 02 885 0522; e hotel@aerodrom-sg.si; www.aerodrom-sg.si. You will find the best accommodation option in Slovenj Gradec at the Aerodrom (airstrip), a 10-min drive south of the centre towards Velenje. This modern hotel housed by the runway has its own restaurant & bar, as well as modern, spacious & high-tech rooms. The real winner though is its pleasant location amongst the forested hills that surround the city. If your budget won't stretch to 4-star hotel prices they also have bungalows & a campsite. Look out for occasional shows & car racing. $$$

🏠 **Hotel Slovenj Gradec** Glavni trg 43; ✆ 02 884 5285; e vabo@siol.net. The town's most centrally located hotel has cheap rooms, but offers standards to match the low prices. $$

✖ WHERE TO EAT There are few central options for dining in the centre of town.

✖ **Gostilna Murko** Francetova 24; ✆ 02 883 8103; ◷ 08.00–22.00 daily. If you don't mind a short stroll (500m) then this tourist-orientated *gostilna* just north of the centre offers more traditional Slovenian cuisine. $$$

🏠 **Sedmica** Trg Svobode 7; ✆ 02 884 5109; ◷ 09.00–22.00 daily. Popular pizzeria with outdoor seating in the summer months. $$

OTHER PRACTICALITIES

✉ **Post office** Francetova 1; ◷ 08.00–18.00 Mon–Fri, 08.00–12.00 Sat

$ **Probanka** Cankarjeva 1
$ **Koroška Banka** Glavni trg 30

WHAT TO SEE Housed in the old town hall are both the Regional Museum of Koroška and the Koroška Gallery of Fine Arts. In the same building on ground level is the tourist office so pop in there before you head upstairs if you want some more information on the town.

Koroška Gallery of Fine Arts (*Koroška Galerija Likovnih Umetnosti; Glavni trg 24;* ✆ *02 884 1283;* f *02 882 2130;* e *galerija@glu-sg.si; www.glu-sg.si; adult/ concession €2/€1.50;* ◷ *09.00–18.00 Tue–Sun*) On the first floor is the art gallery, a *Tardis*-like space with a large hall for temporary exhibitions added onto the back of the original Fine Arts Gallery that deals exclusively in modern art. It was first opened as part of an international arts exhibition in 1966. Of the permanent collections the work of Ljubljana-born abstract artist Bogdan Borčić is perhaps the most interesting. Borčić has taught in Ljubljana and Belgium and has held over 100 solo exhibitions around the world, but these days he calls Slovenj Gradec home. Outside the museum is another striking work, the strangely shaped *Venetian Horse* by Oskar Kogoj, a favourite meeting place for the town's youth.

Regional Museum of Koroška (*Koroški Pokrajinski Muzej; Glavni trg 24;* ✆ *02 884 2055; adult/concession €2/€1.50;* ◷ *09.00–18.00 Tue–Sun*) The Regional Museum upstairs is by no means a high-tech or flashy experience, but for its simplicity it is worth having a look around. It focuses mainly on the fire in 1903

ŠTIRJE KOVAČI

The 'Four Blacksmiths' were all, as the name suggests, blacksmiths from in and around Slovenj Gradec. They came together in 1954 and ever since have been churning out cheesy folk tunes to appreciative audiences in Slovenia and across the border in Austria and Germany. Their accordion ditties take over the airwaves on Slovenian radio stations on Sundays when families are having their traditional Sunday dinners. They have toured the world and can be heard in Slovenian outposts from Sydney to Cleveland.

which devastated Slovenj Gradec on a Sunday morning while its citizens were at church. On display are old fire trucks and equipment with the most interesting exhibits the photos showing what the town looked like before and then after being engulfed by the flames. In 1992 the museum added an archaeological collection with many finds from Roman Colatio the highlights of a range of exhibits that also includes sections on the prehistoric, early Slavic and medieval periods. There are also regular temporary exhibitions such as those dedicated to Slovenj Gradec folk band Štirte Kovači (see box, above), but the museum, like all of the cultural attractions in Slovenj Gradec, is firmly in need of some investment to realise its full potential.

Soklič Museum (*Sokličev Muzej; Trg Svobode 5;* ✆ *02 884 1505; free entry;* ⊕ *by appointment*) This private museum housed in the former residence of the town's priest is a gem; however, it faces an uncertain future as it needs serious investment to really function properly. There have been rumours that the Bishop of Maribor is more than a little interested in acquiring the unique collection and shifting it off to Štajerska, with the museum reverting to its original function as clergy living quarters. Jakob Soklič was a great patron of the arts until his death in 1972 and his quarters house a stunning array of artefacts, sculptures and paintings from various periods, though a few of the paintings are of dubious quality and all too many are portraits of the local composer Hugo Wolf. There is a number of portraits of various bishops including one by Zoran Music, now one of Slovenia's most famous artists, who lived with his patron here in his early days. Other interesting things to look out for include a black-and-white photo of Soklič taking a stroll through town with a certain Tito and a scale model of the **Church of St Elizabeth** (Cerkev Sv Elizabeta). To get into the museum ask at the tourist office, who can also arrange a guided tour.

Church of St Elizabeth (Cerkev Sv Elizabeta) Slovenj Gradec, a town that has been torn between Protestantism and Catholicism over the centuries, today boasts no fewer than four churches. St Elizabeth's, in the heart of town on Trg Svobode, is the oldest building in Slovenj Gradec. The church was refurbished at the start of the new millennium and is now back to something approaching its best. Look out for the Gothic ceiling and the Baroque altar. On the right is a large tombstone, taken from the graveyard that used to rest on the site, which was once the family stone of a local Protestant family before they decided to flee north. Above is a window that was dedicated to local painter Hugo Wolf by his mother. The painting behind the altar is by local Baroque artist Franc Mihael Strauss – see if you can spot the image of the artist himself staring back at you. Strauss was no artistic pauper scraping two pennies together as when he painted this work his other role was as the mayor of the town. Behind the church look out for the small section of town walls that is all that is left of the original fortifications.

Church of the Holy Spirit (Cerkev Sv Duha) If the building is locked don't just walk away as you can still see inside one of the most interesting churches in Koroška. This 15th-century church's main attractions are the scenes of *The Passion of Christ* with the images on the archway showing a sobering depiction of the *Last Judgement*. All are Baroque.

Stari Trg Just a short walk out of the centre of Slovenj Gradec is Stari trg, where settlement has been traced as far back as prehistoric times. This is the site of Colatio, the old Roman town that once stood on the important road north. Archaeological digs have unearthed a graveyard and numerous artefacts, from

Roman coins right through to ceramics, though there is very little to actually see these days. Continue on from here and you can explore the Church of St Pancras, with its 17th-century defences.

Mislinjska Dobrava (*Mislinkjska Dobrava 110, Šmartno pri Slovenj Gradec;* \ *02 885 0500;* f *02 8875 0510;* e *info@aerodrom-sg.si; www.aerodrom-sg.si*). This adventure playground just to the south of Slovenj Gradec lies around the banks of the Mislinjska River with wooded slopes all around. It makes an alternative regional base to Slovenj Gradec with a funky hotel and campsite at the Slovenj Gradec Aerodrom. The busy little flying club here offers scenic flights at very reasonable rates with everything from ten-minute spins around the environs of the airfield through to more expansive trips south over the Pohorje. They are pretty flexible and can cater to most requests if you call ahead. A ten-minute trip costs from € 17 per person, 15 minutes from € 23, 20 minutes from € 38 and one hour from € 63. If you want to travel further afield you can negotiate this with the pilots. The vicinity of the airport is also a great place to go horseriding, walking or cycling (though it is a good idea to seek advice from the tourist information centre in Slovenj Gradec first) and explore the surrounding countryside, while the aerodrom's campsite has tennis courts. If you are feeling a little more sedentary the café/restaurant at the aerodrom is a good place to sit and watch the planes zip around.

KOPE

Keen skiers may want to head off to the slopes at Kope (*Glavni trg 41, Slovenj Gradec;* \ *02 882 2740;* f *02 883 8806;* e *info.kope@sc-pohorje.si; www.phorje.org*), 16km from the centre of Slovenj Gradec, where there is often snow from November through to late spring. A variety of runs are geared towards both the beginner and the more experienced skier with the longest piste spanning 1,400m with a descent of 500m. In all the Kope ski centre has 8km of alpine ski runs – with around half of them pitched at the intermediate skier – and 15km of cross-country trails. Those who have never skied before can enrol with the ski school, while more experienced skiers can test their skills on the competition course. Equipment rental, snowboarding and night skiing are also offered. Adult ski passes cost from € 23 for one day to € 161 for ten days. Outside winter the Pohorje mountain range is a great place for hiking. Accommodation is available.

GETTING THERE Head south from Slovenj Gradec on the Velenje road. After 3km head east and you will find the ski centre at the end of the road another 13km away. Buses run from Slovenj Gradec to Kope when there is enough snow for skiing.

DRAVOGRAD

As the name suggests this town rests on the banks of the lifeblood Drava River, where it meets the Meža and Mislinja rivers, in a strategic spot just across from the Austrian border. Many people speed through *en route* from Maribor to Logarska Dolina or Slovenj Gradec, but it is well worth stopping off to take a look at the town, not least to admire its location.

GETTING THERE Buses from Slovenj Gradec (20 minutes), Velenje (1 hour) and Ljubljana (2½ hours) run to Dravograd, as does the train from Maribor (1½ hours).

TOURIST INFORMATION

i Tourist Information Centre Trg 4 julia 57;
↘ 02 871 0285; e info@dravograd.si;
www.dravograd.si; ⊕May–Oct 09.00–18.00 daily

🏠 WHERE TO STAY

🏠 **Hotel Hesper** (44 rooms) Koroška 48; ↘ 02 878 4440; f 02 878 4443; e info@hesper.si; www.hesper.si. Modern hotel that looks like a motel & has its own café-bar & restaurant. The décor in the bedrooms is a little busy, but they are comfortable & a good size. There are also apts with their own kitchens that sleep up to 4 people. The hotel also has a pleasant restaurant. $$

✕ WHERE TO EAT

✕ **Gostilna Lovski Rog** Trg 4 julia 37; ↘ 02 878 3288; ⊕05.30–23.00 Mon–Fri, 05.30–01.00 Sat, 07.00–20.00 Sun. Hearty Slovenian food. $$$

✕ **Restavracija Kaiser** Trg 4 julia 27; ↘ 02 878 3104; ⊕08.00–22.00 daily. Centrally located café-restaurant serving a variety of snacks & meals. $$

✕ **Pizzeria Kapra** Meža 24; ↘ 02 872 0236; ⊕13.00–22.00 Mon–Fri, 15.00–22.00 Sat/Sun. Popular pizzeria located just south of the Drava on the road towards Slovenj Gradec. $$

OTHER PRACTICALITIES

✉ **Post office** Trg 4 julia 1

$ **Koroška Banka** Trg 4 julia 42

WHAT TO SEE The **castle** that gave the town the other half of its name is now in ruins, but you can take a look by an easy path up from town. There are two interesting churches to explore as well: the **Church of St Vitus** (Cerkev Sv Vida) and the **Church of St John** (Cerkev Sv Janeza). The former is a Romanesque church dating back to the 12th century, while the latter just outside the town centre is Baroque. A string of dwellings dating from the 17th to the early 19th century is also of interest, as are the dam of the Dravograd Hydro-electric Power Station and the marshland behind it; both of these are home to a large number of birds (some migratory) and unusual flora. Bird enthusiasts should keep their eyes peeled for sandpipers, egrets and various gulls.

PODZEMLJE PECE

(*Glančnik 8;* ↘ *02 870 0180;* f *02 870 0165;* e *podzemljepece@rscm-gm.si; www.podzemljepece.com; adult/child €2;* ⊕*09.00–15.00 Thu–Sun; mine tours 09.00, 11.00, 13.00 & 15.00 or by appointment; adult/child €7/€5*) Cycling down a mine shaft might sound like a bizarre idea, but that is exactly what is on offer here. The experience is unusual to say the least, but also a fun way of exploring the old lead and zinc mines in the north of Koroška under the Peca and Uršlja mountains. Lead has been mined here since Roman times and at one point there were over 800km of tunnels snaking beneath the surface. The tours run for 5km along the old routes taken by the ore transporters. You will have to book ahead and if you need a bike let them know as they will generally presume you have your own. All riders are given the necessary helmets and headlamps. Tours usually start from outside the Hotel Club Krnes in Črna na Koroškem. Non-cyclists can arrange two-hour walking tours of the mine and museum in the nearby town of Mežica, with a trip on an old mining train all part of the fun.

Many of the activities available in and around Logarska Dolina (see *Chapter 9, Štajerska and Prekmurje,* page 206) are also available from Črna na Koroškem in Koroška. The area is also one of the best in the country for cycling above as well as below ground.

Appendix I

LANGUAGE

The official language of the Republic of Slovenia is Slovene, a Slavic language that has a lot in common with the languages spoken by Slovenia's Croatian, Serbian, Bosnian and Montenegrin neighbours. Slovenes use a version of the Roman alphabet with 25 letters: a b c č d e f g h i j k l m n o p r s š t u v z ž. Many letters are pronounced as they are in English, but there is a number of key exceptions.

PRONUNCIATION
Vowels

a	short pronunciation like 'a' in 'hat'
a	long pronunciation like 'a' in 'rather' (to confuse things it can also sound like the 'u' in 'hut')
e	short pronunciation like the 'e' in 'vet'
e	long pronunciation like the 'ea' in 'wear'
i	short pronunciation like the 'i' in 'pink'
i	long pronunciation like the 'ee' in 'seem'
o	short pronunciation like the 'o' in 'off'
o	long pronunciation like the 'aw' in 'paw'
u	like the 'oo' in 'foot'

Consonants

c	like the 'ts' in 'rats'
d	like the 'd' in 'dog'
g	like the 'g' in 'gold'
j	like the 'y' in 'yacht'
l	like the 'l' in 'leak'
r	Slovenes roll the letter 'r', pronouncing it from the tip of their tongue, in the same way as the French and the Scots
v	can sound like the 'v' in 'vodka', but more often takes the form of the 'w' in 'water'

Consonants with carons

č	like the 'ch' in 'chomp'
š	like the 'sh' in 'sham'
ž	like the 'su' in 'treasure'

BASICS

hello	*zdravo*	yes	*da/ja*
good day	*dober dan*	no	*ne*
good morning	*dobro jutro*	please	*prosim*
good evening	*dober večer*	thank you	*hvala*
goodbye	*nasvidenje*	(very much)	(*lepa*)

here you are	*izvolite*	Miss	*gospodična*
excuse me	*dovolite mi, prosim*	what	*kaj*
sorry	*oprostite*	why	*zakaj*
Mr	*gospod*	when	*kdaj*
Mrs	*gospa*	who	*kdo*

Conversation

How are you?	*Kako ste?*
Very well thank you	*Zelo dobro, hvala*
My name is…	*Imenujem se…*
What's your name?	*Kako vam je ime?*
I am English/Scottish/Welsh/Irish/ American/Canadian/Australian	*Sem Anglež/ Škot/ Vališan/ Irec/ Američan/ Kanadčan/ Avstralec*
Where are you from?	*Od kod ste?*

Family

aunt	*teta*	husband	*mož*
brother	*brat*	mother	*mama*
daughter	*hči*	sister	*sestra*
father	*oče*	son	*sin*
grandfather	*stari oče*	uncle	*stric*
grandmother	*stara mama*	wife	*žena*

Language

Do you speak English?	*Ali govorite angleško?*
I don't speak Slovene	*Ne govorim slovensko*
Please speak more slowly	*Govorite počasneje prosim*
I understand	*Razumem*
I don't understand	*Ne razumem*
Please write it down	*Prosim zapišite*
How do you say…?	*Kako rečete…?*

Accommodation

half board	*polpenzion*
Can I see the room?	*Ali lahko vidim sobo?*
I have a reservation	*Imam rezervacijo*
Do you have a single/double room?	*Ali imate prosto enoposteljno/ dvoposteljno sobo?*
with a bath/shower	*s kadjo/prho*
Could you wake me at…?	*Ali me lahko zbudite ob…?*
I'd like a…	*Rad bi… (male) Rada bi… (female)*
How much is it per night/per person?	*Koliko stane na noč/po osebi?*
Is breakfast included?	*Ali je zajtrk vključen?*

Health and emergencies

police	*policija*	blood	*kri*
hospital	*bolnišnica*	chest	*prsni koš*
ambulance	*rešilec*	hand	*roka*
chemist/pharmacy	*lekarna*	head	*glava*
dentist	*zobozdravnik*	leg/foot	*nog*
doctor	*doktor*	shoulder	*rama*
ache/pain	*bolečina*	stomach	*želodec*
arm	*laket*		

Directions

Where is the...?	*Kje je...?*	opposite	*nasproti*
turn left/right	*obrnite levo/desno*	here/there	*tu/tam*
near/far	*blizu/daleč*	north	*sever*
go straight ahead	*pojdite naravnost naprej*	south	*jug*
		east	*vzhod*
behind	*zadaj*	west	*zahod*
in front of	*spredaj*		

Driving/transport

airport	*letališče*	garage	*mehanična delavnica*
aeroplane	*letalo*	petrol	*bencin*
bus	*avtobus*	petrol station	*bencinska črpalka*
train	*vlak*	motorway/highway	*avtocesta*
railway station	*železniška postaja*	road	*cesta*
platform	*peron*	puncture	*preluknjana zračnica/ avtomobilska guma*
bus station	*avtobusna postaja*		
bus stop	*avtobusno postajališče*	map	*zemljevid*
timetable	*vozni red*	bicycle	*kolo*
car	*avto*	ferry	*trajekt*

A one-way ticket to ... please	*Enosmerno vozovnico za ... prosim*
A return ticket to ... please	*Povratno vozovnico za ... prosim*
Can I reserve a seat?	*Ali lahko rezerviram sedež?*
What time does the bus/train leave?	*Kdaj odpelje avtobus/vlak?*
Stop here please	*Ustavite tukaj prosim*

Signs

entrance/exit	*vhod/izhod*	prohibited	*prepovedano*
open/closed	*odprto/zaprto*	(male/female)	*(moško/žensko)*
arrivals/departures	*prihod/odhod*	toilets	*stranišče*
information	*informacije*		

Places

bank	*banka*	laundry	*pralnica*
bay	*morski zaliv*	market	*tržnica*
beach	*plaža*	monastery	*samostan*
bridge	*most*	mountain	*gora*
castle	*grad*	museum	*muzej*
cathedral	*stolnica*	Old Town/City	*stari del mesta*
cave	*jama*	port	*pristanišče*
centre	*središče*	post office	*pošta*
chapel	*kapelica*	river	*reka*
church	*cerkev*	school	*šola*
city	*veliko mesto*	sea	*morje*
fair	*sejem*	shop	*trgovina*
field	*polje*	shopping centre	*nakupovalni center*
forest	*gozd*	(main/old/upper/ town) square	*(glavni/stari/gornji/ mestni) trg*
fountain	*vodnjak*		
garden	*vrt*	street	*ulica*
hill	*hrib, grič*	therapeutic spa	*toplice*
house	*hiša*	tower	*stolp*
island	*otok*	town	*mesto*
lake	*jezero*	town hall	*mestna hiša*

| valley | dolina | waterfall | slap |
| village | vas | | |

Eating and drinking

| restaurant | restavracija | good appetite | dober tek |
| taverna | gostilna | | |

Fish

dorada	orada	salmon	losos
fried fish	ocvrta riba	sea bass	brancin
grilled fish	riba na žaru	shrimps	škampi
lobster	jastog	sole morski	list
mussels	školjke	squid	lignji
octopus	hobotnica	trout	postrv
prawns	rakci	tuna	tuna

Meat

air-dried ham	pršut	mixed grill	meso na žaru
beef	govedina	pork	svinjina
chicken	piščanec	rabbit	zajec
foal	žrebiček	sausage	klobasa
goulash	golaž	turkey	puran
ham	šunka	veal	teletina
lamb	jagnjetina	venison	divjačina

Fruit and vegetables

apple	jabolko	basil	bazilika
apricot	marelica	beans	fižol
banana	banana	cabbage	zelje
cherry	češnja	carrots	korenje
grape	grozdje	courgette	bučke
lemon	limona	cucumber	kumara
melon	melona	garlic	česen
orange	pomaranča	mushrooms	gobe
peach	breskev	(black) olive	(črne) olive
pear	hruška	onions	čebula
pineapple	ananas	peas	grah
plum	sliva	pepper	paprika
raspberry	malina	potato	krompir
strawberry	jagoda	ruccola	rukola
watermelon	lubenica	(green/mixed) salad	(zelena/mešana) solata
		spinach	špinača
artichoke	artičoke	tomato	paradižnik
asparagus	beluši		

Dessert

cream cake/slice	kremna rezina	traditional Slovenian cake	potica
ice-cream	sladoled		
strudel	štrudelj		
traditional Prekmurje dessert	gibanica		

Drinks

beer	*pivo*	(mineral) water	*(mineralna) voda*
coffee	*kava*	tea (with milk/	*čaj (z mlekom/*
milky coffee	*bela kava*	lemon)	*z limono)*
espresso with milk	*macchiato*	wine	*vino*
fruit juice	*sok*	(white, red, rosé)	*(belo, črno, roze)*

Miscellaneous

beef/mushroom/bean/vegetable/fish soup	*goveja/fižolova/gobova/zelenjavna/ribja juha*
bread	*kruh*
cheese	*sir*
(sour) cream	*(kisla) smetana*

egg — *jajce*
omelette — *omleta*

Meals and useful words

breakfast	*zajtrk*	bowl	*skleda*
lunch	*kosilo*	cup	*skodelica*
dinner	*večerja*	fork	*vilica*
baked	*pečen*	glass	*kozarec*
boiled	*kuhano*	knife	*nož*
fried	*ocvrto*	plate	*plošča*
grilled	*na žaru*	spoon	*žlica*
roast	*pečenka*		

USEFUL WORDS AND PHRASES

The bill, please	*Račun prosim*
Where is the toilet?	*Kje je stranišče?*
What's the time?	*Koliko je ura?*
How much does this cost?	*Koliko stane?*
Not much	*Komaj da/ne veliko*
You're welcome	*Prosim/ni za kaj*
married	*poročen/poročena* (male/female)
maybe	*mogoče*
good	*dober*
bad	*slab*

big — *mala*
small — *velika*
money — *denar*

Numbers

0	*nič*	15	*petnajst*
1	*ena*	16	*šestnajst*
2	*dve*	17	*sedemnajst*
3	*tri*	18	*osemnajst*
4	*štiri*	19	*devetnajst*
5	*pet*	20	*dvajset*
6	*šest*	30	*trideset*
7	*sedem*	40	*štirideset*
8	*osem*	50	*petdeset*
9	*devet*	60	*šestdeset*
10	*deset*	70	*sedemdeset*
11	*enajst*	80	*osemdeset*
12	*dvanajst*	90	*devetdeset*
13	*trinajst*	100	*sto*
14	*štirinajst*	1,000	*tisoč*

Time, days and months

What is the time?	*Koliko je ura?*	today	*danes*
It is...	*Ura je...*	yesterday	*včeraj*
two o'clock	*dve*	tomorrow	*jutri*
nine o'clock	*devet*	morning	*zjutraj*
eight thirty	*pol devetih*	noon	*poldan*
quarter to five	*tričetrt na pet*	afternoon	*popoldne*
quarter past eleven	*enajst in četrt*	evening	*večer*
day	*dan*	night	*noč*

Monday	*ponedeljek*	Friday	*petek*
Tuesday	*torek*	Saturday	*sobota*
Wednesday	*sreda*	Sunday	*nedelja*
Thursday	*četrtek*		

January	*januar*	July	*julij*
February	*februar*	August	*avgust*
March	*marec*	September	*september*
April	*april*	October	*oktober*
May	*maj*	November	*november*
June	*junij*	December	*december*

Colours

black	*črno*	green	*zeleno*
white	*belo*	blue	*modro*
red	*rdeče*	orange	*oranžno*

Appendix 2

FURTHER INFORMATION

MAGAZINES AND NEWSPAPERS
Entertainment

Ljubljana Calling is a monthly listings magazine, which can be hard to find in its printed version but is available at some of the city's hotels.

Ljubljana Life is a quarterly magazine with plenty of tourist information and some longer articles. It is available at tourist information centres and hotels throughout the city.

News and current affairs

Slovenia News is a weekly colour magazine with features on personalities and cultural events. Look out for copies at TICs, cafés and hotels throughout the city.

Slovenia Times is an excellent English-language monthly newspaper that covers politics, the economy and also has occasional tourist supplements. Again this can be picked up at TICs and hotels.

BOOKS
Architecture

Gooding, Mel and Music, Marko and Fiennes, Mark *National & University Library, Ljubljana, Slovenia, 1936–39, by Jože Plečnik* (Architecture in Detail Series) Phaidon Press, 1997. In-depth examination of what many consider to be Plečnik's finest architectural achievement.

Hrausky, Andrej and Koželj, Janez *Architectural Guide to Ljubljana: 100 Selected Buildings* Rokus, 2002. Insightful guide to Ljubljana's impressive architecture. Hard to buy outside Slovenia.

Fiction

Bartol, Vladimir (translated by Michael Biggins) *Alamut* Scala House Press, 2005. Historical fiction, commonly regarded as the most popular book ever written by a Slovene. Set in 11th-century Iran, the book has parallels with the rise of fascism in the 20th century and the fundamentalist terrorism in the 21st.

Blatnik, Andrej *Skinswaps* (*Writing from an Unbound Europe*) Northwestern University Press, 1998. Sixteen short stories by the popular Slovene post-modern writer.

Debeljak, Ales *The City & the Child* White Pine Press, 1999. Anthology of contemporary poems by the popular Slovene poet.

Holton, Milne and Taufer, Veno (translators) *Waterlings* Northwestern University Press, 2000. Six epic Slovenian poems about mythical water beings, translated into English.

Jančar, Drago (translated by Michael Biggins) *Mocking Desire* Northwestern University Press, 1998. The story of a creative writing teacher who takes a job in New Orleans and who, as a Slovene in America, remains very much an outsider, a stranger who can't get used to the unfamiliar customs and people, most of whom have never heard of where he is from.

Mozetič, Brane *Butterflies* Meeting Eyes Bindery, 2004. Poetry anthology.

History

Benderley, Jill and Craft, Ivan *Independent Slovenia* Palgrave Macmillan, 1997. In-depth study of Slovenia's political and economic development during the years following independence.

Benderley, Jill *Independent Slovenia: Origins, Movements, Prospects* Palgrave Macmillan, 1996. Decent introduction to Slovenia and the country's recent political and economic history.

Carmichael, Cathie and Gow, James *Slovenia & the Slovenes* Indiana University Press, 2001. Thorough examination of history, economics, politics and culture in 20th-century Slovenia.

Fink-Hafner, Danica and Robbins, John, R *Making a New Nation: Formation of Slovenia* Dartmouth, 1996. Examining the role of Slovenia in the Socialist Federal Republic of Yugoslavia and its emergence as an independent country.

Mrak, Mojmir and Rojec, Matja and Rojec, Marika (Editors) *Slovenia: From Yugoslavia to the European Union* World Bank, 2004. Weighty but informative read focusing on the reasons for the dissolution of Yugoslavia and Slovenia's political and economic development since 1991, including its integration into the EU.

Prunk, Janko *A Brief History of Slovenia: Historical Background of the Republic of Slovenia* Zalozba Mihelac, 1994. Useful introduction to Slovenia and its history. Can be a little too general at times.

War in Slovenia: From first 'attacks' on YPA to final victory over the Yugoslav Army Ljubljana International Press Centre, 1991. Fascinating insight into Slovenia's ten-day war of independence with Yugoslavia. Limited availability.

Mountaineering/hiking

Brown, Simon *Walking in the Julian Alps* Cicerone Press, 1993. Now something of a classic, a range of easy-to-follow walks for all levels of fitness and experience.

Collomb, Robin *Julian Alps Mountain Walking* West Col Productions, 1998. Giving details of more routes in the Julian Alps.

Mihelič, Tine *Mountaineering in Slovenia: The Julian Alps and Kamnik and Savinja Alps* Cordee, 2003. Comprehensive guide for those interested in tackling Slovenia's mountains.

Newbury, Mike *A Guide to Walks & Scrambles in the Julian Alps Based on Kranjska Gora* Zlatorog Publications, 2003. Excellent rambling guide with trails suitable for everyone from the novice to the experienced walker.

Robertson, David and Stewart, Sarah *Landscapes of Slovenia* Sunflower Books, 2003. Essentially a book for hikers, Robertson and Stewart also present six itineraries for exploration by car and highlight great picnic spots alongside their 41 main walking trails.

Travel

McKelvie, Robin and Jenny *Ljubljana: The Bradt City Guide* Bradt Travel Guides, 2005

Wildlife

Gorman, Gerard *Central & Eastern European Wildlife* Bradt Travel Guides, 2008. Full-colour visitors' guide to the wildlife of the region, including Slovenia.

Other

Dolenc, Milan *Lipizzaner: The Story of the Horses of Lipica* Control Data Publishing Co, 1986.

MAPS

Geodetski Zavod Slovenije dd (*www.gzs-dd.si*) produce the majority of maps to Slovenia. Their maps are available in hotels, TICs and bookstores in Slovenia. Bookstores and online retailers outside Slovenia should also stock maps produced by the same company.

Julian Alps (*Walking Maps*) Freytag & Berndt 2000. Detailed walking maps.

Kod & Kam (*Trg Francoske Revolucije 7;* \ *01 200 2732*). Stock a wide range of maps and road atlases.

WEBSITES
Tourist information
Slovenia Tourism www.slovenia.info

Ljubljana Tourism www.ljubljana-tourism.si

Slovenian Landmarks www.burger.si

Slovenia Holidays.com www.SloveniaHolidays.com. Providing general tourist information, as well as links to accommodation and activities.

SloveniaBike.com www.Sloveniabike.com. Website dedicated to cycling in Slovenia.

SloveniaSki.info http://SloveniaSki.info. Website giving detailed information about skiing in Slovenia.

General information
State Portal of the Republic of Slovenia http://e-uprava.gov.si/e-uprava/en/portal.euprava

Daily newspapers
Delo www.delo.si

Dnevnik www.dnevnik.si

Večer www.vecer.si

English-language news
Republic of Slovenia Public Relations and Media Office www.uvi.si/eng

Sinfo www.uvi.si/eng/slovenia/publications/sinfo

Slovenia Bulletin http://www.geocities.com/ljubljanalife/News.htm

Slovenia Business Report www.businesspatrol.com

Slovenia Business Week www.gzs.si

Slovenia Magazine www.zdruzenje-sim.si

Slovenia News www.uvi.si/eng/slovenia/publications/slovenia-news

Slovenia Times www.sloveniatimes.com

Lifestyle and culture
Slovenian Ministry of Culture www.kultura.gov.si

Slovenian Queer Resources Directory www.ljudmila.org/siqrd

WIN £100 CASH!

READER QUESTIONNAIRE

Send in your completed questionnaire for the chance to win £100 cash in our regular draw

All respondents may order a Bradt guide at half the UK retail price – please complete the order form overleaf.

(Entries may be posted or faxed to us, or scanned and emailed.)

We are interested in getting feedback from our readers to help us plan future Bradt guides. Please answer ALL the questions below and return the form to us in order to qualify for an entry in our regular draw.

Have you used any other Bradt guides? If so, which titles? ....
....

What other publishers' travel guides do you use regularly? ....
....

Where did you buy this guidebook? ....

What was the main purpose of your trip to Slovenia (or for what other reason did you read our guide)? eg: holiday/business/charity etc........................
....

What other destinations would you like to see covered by a Bradt guide?
....

Would you like to receive our catalogue/newsletters?

YES / NO (If yes, please complete details on reverse)

If yes – by post or email? ....

Age (circle relevant category) 16–25   26–45   46–60   60+

Male/Female (delete as appropriate)

Home country ....

Please send us any comments about our guide to Slovenia or other Bradt Travel Guides. ....
....
....
....

Bradt Travel Guides

23 High Street, Chalfont St Peter, Bucks SL9 9QE, UK
☏ +44 (0)1753 893444 **f** +44 (0)1753 892333
e info@bradtguides.com
www.bradtguides.com

CLAIM YOUR HALF-PRICE BRADT GUIDE!

Order Form

To order your half-price copy of a Bradt guide, and to enter our prize draw to win £100 (see overleaf), please fill in the order form below, complete the questionnaire overleaf, and send it to Bradt Travel Guides by post, fax or email.

Please send me one copy of the following guide at half the UK retail price

Title		Retail price	Half price
...	....	....	....

Please send the following additional guides at full UK retail price

No	Title		Retail price	Total
...	....		....	....
...	....		....	....
...	....		....	....

Sub total . . . .
Post & packing . . . .
(£2 per book UK; £4 per book Europe; £6 per book rest of world)
Total . . . .

Name . . . .

Address . . . .

Tel . . . .   Email . . . .

☐ I enclose a cheque for £ . . . . made payable to Bradt Travel Guides Ltd

☐ I would like to pay by credit card. Number: . . . .

  Expiry date: . . . / . . .   3-digit security code (on reverse of card) . . . . .

  Issue no (debit cards only) . . . . .

☐ Please add my name to your catalogue mailing list.

☐ I would be happy for you to use my name and comments in Bradt marketing material.

Send your order on this form, with the completed questionnaire, to:

Bradt Travel Guides SLO2
23 High Street, Chalfont St Peter, Bucks SL9 9QE
☎ +44 (0)1753 893444   f +44 (0)1753 892333
e info@bradtguides.com   www.bradtguides.com

Bradt Travel Guides

www.bradtguides.com

Africa

Africa Overland	£15.99
Algeria	£15.99
Benin	£14.99
Botswana: Okavango, Chobe, Northern Kalahari	£15.99
Burkina Faso	£14.99
Cameroon	£15.99
Canary Islands	£13.95
Cape Verde Islands	£13.99
Congo	£15.99
Eritrea	£15.99
Ethiopia	£15.99
Gabon, São Tomé, Príncipe	£13.95
Gambia, The	£13.99
Ghana	£15.99
Johannesburg	£6.99
Kenya	£14.95
Madagascar	£15.99
Malawi	£13.99
Mali	£13.95
Mauritius, Rodrigues & Réunion	£13.99
Mozambique	£13.99
Namibia	£15.99
Niger	£14.99
Nigeria	£17.99
Rwanda	£14.99
São Tomé & Príncipe	£14.99
Seychelles	£14.99
Sudan	£13.95
Tanzania, Northern	£13.99
Tanzania	£16.99
Uganda	£15.99
Zambia	£17.99
Zanzibar	£12.99

Britain and Europe

Albania	£15.99
Armenia, Nagorno Karabagh	£14.99
Azores	£13.99
Baltic Capitals: Tallinn, Riga, Vilnius, Kaliningrad	£12.99
Belarus	£14.99
Belgrade	£6.99
Bosnia & Herzegovina	£13.99
Bratislava	£6.99
Budapest	£8.99
Bulgaria	£13.99
Cork	£6.99
Croatia	£13.99

Cyprus see North Cyprus	
Czech Republic	£13.99
Dresden	£7.99
Dubrovnik	£6.99
Estonia	£13.99
Faroe Islands	£15.99
Georgia	£14.99
Helsinki	£7.99
Hungary	£14.99
Iceland	£14.99
Kiev	£7.95
Kosovo	£14.99
Lapland	£13.99
Latvia	£13.99
Lille	£6.99
Lithuania	£14.99
Ljubljana	£7.99
Luxembourg	£13.99
Macedonia	£14.99
Montenegro	£14.99
North Cyprus	£12.99
Paris, Lille & Brussels	£11.95
Riga	£6.95
River Thames, In the Footsteps of the Famous	£10.95
Serbia	£14.99
Slovakia	£14.99
Slovenia	£13.99
Spitsbergen	£15.99
Switzerland: Rail, Road, Lake	£13.99
Tallinn	£6.99
Transylvania	£14.99
Ukraine	£14.99
Vilnius	£6.99
Zagreb	£6.99

Middle East, Asia and Australasia

Borneo	£17.99
China: Yunnan Province	£13.99
Great Wall of China	£13.99
Iran	£14.99
Iraq: Then & Now	£15.99
Kazakhstan	£15.99
Kyrgyzstan	£15.99
Maldives	£13.99
Mongolia	£16.99
North Korea	£14.99
Oman	£13.99
Shangri La	£14.99
Sri Lanka	£13.99
Syria	£14.99
Tibet	£13.99

Turkmenistan	£14.99
Yemen	£14.99

The Americas and the Caribbean

Amazon, The	£14.99
Argentina	£15.99
Bolivia	£14.99
Cayman Islands	£14.99
Chile	£16.95
Chile & Argentina: The Bradt Trekking Guide	£12.95
Colombia	£16.99
Costa Rica	£13.99
Dominica	£14.99
Falkland Islands	£13.95
Guyana	£14.99
Panama	£13.95
Peru & Bolivia: Backpacking & Trekking	£12.95
St Helena	£14.99
USA by Rail	£14.99

Wildlife

100 Animals to See Before They Die	£16.99
Antarctica: Guide to the Wildlife	£14.95
Arctic: Guide to the Wildlife	£15.99
Central & Eastern European Wildlife	£15.99
Chinese Wildlife	£16.99
East African Wildlife	£19.99
Galápagos Wildlife	£15.99
Madagascar Wildlife	£15.99
Peruvian Wildlife	£15.99
Southern African Wildlife	£18.95
Sri Lankan Wildlife	£15.99

Eccentric Guides

Eccentric Australia	£12.99
Eccentric Britain	£13.99
Eccentric California	£13.99
Eccentric Cambridge	£6.99
Eccentric Edinburgh	£5.95
Eccentric France	£12.95
Eccentric London	£13.99
Eccentric Oxford	£5.95

Others

Your Child Abroad: A Travel Health Guide	£10.95
Something Different for the Weekend	£9.99

NOTES

NOTES

NOTES

NOTES

NOTES

Index

Page numbers in **bold** indicate major entries; those in *italic* indicate maps

accommodation 31–2 *see also* where to
  stay in individual listings
activities 112–16, 119–20, 126–28, 139,
  151, 162, 179, 197–8, 203, 206
Adrenaline Park Pohorje 197
airports 19
archery 181, 206
Arnic, Blaž 39
art 37
arts and entertainment 37–40
ATMs 26
Avesenik Brothers 40

banks 25–6
bars *see* entertainment and nightlife in
  individual listings
Bartol, Vladimir 39
Base 20, 174
Begunje 116–17
Bela Krajina 182–7
Black Cave 168
Bled **101–7**, *102*
  activities 112–16
  entertainment and nightlife 106
  getting around 103–4
  getting there 103
  history 103
  practicalities 104
  tourist information 104
  tour operators 104
  what to see 106–7
  where to eat 105–6
  where to stay 104–5
Bohinj **107–12**, *108*
  activities 112–16
  getting around 109
  getting there 109
  history 109
  practicalities 111
  tourist information 109
  tour operators 109

Bohinj *continued*
  what to see 111–12
  where to eat 110–11
  where to stay 110
border regulations *see* red tape
Borl Castle 211
Bovec **123–8**
  activities 126–8
  entertainment and nightlife 12
  extreme-sports operators 128
  getting around 123
  getting there 23
  practicalities 125
  tourist information 124
  tour operators 124
  what to see 125–6
  where to eat 124
  where to stay 124
Brezje 101
budgeting 38–9
bungee jumping 140
business 42–3
buying property 43

camping 32 *see also* where to stay in
  individual listings
canoeing 112
canyoning 113, 127, 131
castles
  Borl 211
  Dobrovo 134
  Ljubljana 68–9
  Maribor 195
  Morkice 181
  Otočec 179
  Podčetrtek 212
  Podsreda 212
  Ptuj 209
  Snežik 170–1
  Žužemberk 178

caves
   Black 168
   Kostanjevica 180
   Križna 170
   Otoška 168
   Pivka 168
   Planinska 168
   Postojna 163–7
   Predjama 168–9
   Škocjan 141–2
Celje **200–3**, *202*
   activities 203
   entertainment and nightlife 201
   getting around 200
   getting there 200
   history 200
   practicalities 201
   tourist information 200
   tour operators 200
   what to see 201–3
   where to eat 201
   where to stay 200–1
Cerkno 138–9
classical music *see* music
climate 2, **3–4**
climbing 104, 109, 112, **114–15**, 120
conservation 12
credit cards 27–8
crime *see* safety
Crngrob 90–1
Črnomelj 185–7
cultural etiquette 43
currency 25
currency exchange 27
Cviček 173
cycling 113, 114, 131, 215, 225 *see also*
   mountain biking

debit cards 27–8
disabled visitors 24
diving 52, 155
Dobrovo Castle 134
Dolenjska **173–81**, *172*
Dolenjske Toplice 175–6
Dravograd 223–4
duty-free *see* red tape

eating and drinking 32–4 *see also* where to
   eat in individual listings
   drinks 34
   prices 34
   wine 33
economy 8–9

education 11
embassies 18–19
exchange rates 25
extreme-sports operators 128

family travel 24
female travellers *see* safety
festivals 35–7
Fink, Bernarda 40
fishing 113
flag 11
folk music *see* music
food *see* eating and drinking
further reading 233–4

Gallus, Jakob 39
gay and lesbian travellers 24–5
geography *see* climate
getting around 29–31
   by bus 29–30
   by car 29, 30
   by train 31
getting there and away 19–21
   by air 19
   by bus 20
   by car 20–1
   by sea 21
   by train 19–20
golf 13, 82, 104, 113, 144, 179, 181, 216
Gorenjska **83–121**, *84*
Goriška Brda 132–4
gostilna see eating and drinking
gostišče see eating and drinking
government 7–8
Grad 215

Haloze wines 212
handicrafts 38
health 21–3
highlights 14
hiking **15**, 114–15, 128, 131, 139, 179,
   206, 234
history 4–7 *see also* history in individual
   listings
horseriding **115**, 179, 181, 196, 206
hotels 31 *see also* where to stay in
   individual listings
Hrastovlje 145
human fish 166
hydrospeed 115, **127**, 131

ice skating 116
Idrija 134–8

internet cafés 41 *see also* practicalities in
   individual listings
Ipavec, Benjamin 39
Izola 151–3

Jančar, Drago 38
Jelendol 174
Jurjevanje 186

Kamnik 83–6
Karst 141–5
kayaking 112, 127, 131, 206
Kobarid 128–31
Kočevje and Kočevski rog 173–5
Kope 223
Koper **147–51**, *148*
   activities 151
   entertainment and nightlife 149–50
   getting around 148
   getting there 147–8
   practicalities 150
   shopping 150
   tourist information 148
   tour operators 148–9
   what to see 150–1
   where to eat 149
   where to stay 149
Koroška **219–25**, *218*
Kostanjevica Cave 180
Kostanjevica na Krki 180
Kranj 96–101, *97*
   entertainment and nightlife 97–8
   getting around 96
   getting there 96
   history 101–2
   tourist information 96
   tour operators 98
   practicalities 99
   what to see 99–101
   where to eat 97
   where to stay 97
Kranjska Gora 117–20
   activities 119–20
   entertainment and nightlife 118
   getting around 117
   getting there 117
   history 101–2
   tourist information 117
   tour operators 117, 120–1
   practicalities 119
   what to see 119
   where to eat 118
   where to stay 118

Kraš 141–5
Križna Cave 170
Kropa 94–6
Kurentovanje 210

Lake Bohinj 107–9
Lake Cerknica 169–70
language 10, **225–30**
Laško 204–5
Laško beer 64
Laško Brewery 204
Lent 198
linden tree 9
Linhart, Anton Tomaž 93
Lipica 142–4
Lipovšek, Marjana 40
literature 38–9
Ljubljana **47–82**, *46, 54–5*
   activities 51–2
   banks 67
   cafés and bars 63–5
   cinema 62
   clubs 65
   entertainment and nightlife 61
   getting around 50–1
   getting there 49–50
   history 47–9
   internet cafés 67
   medical facilities 67
   music venues 62–3
   post offices 67
   practicalities 67
   shopping 65–7
   theatre **61–2**, 77, 78
   tourist information 51
   tour operators 51–2
   what to see 68–82
      churches and cathedrals 79–81
      galleries and museums 69–73
      Krakovo and Trnovo 78
Ljubljana Castle 68–9
Ljubljana Marshes 81
Ljubljanica 69
   market 74
   monuments 73–8
   NUK 77
   Slovene Philharmonic Hall 77
   Šmarna Gora 82
   squares 75–6
   Tivoli 81
   where to eat 56–60
   whcrc to stay 52–3, 56
Ljubljana Summer Festival 36, **63**

local charities 43
Logarska Dolina 205–6

maps 234
Maribor 189–96, *190*
  entertainment and nightlife 192–3
  getting around 191
  getting there 191
  history 189, 191
  practicalities 193
  shopping 193
  tourist information 191
  tour operators 191
  what to see 193–6
  where to eat 192
  where to stay 191–2
Maribor Pohorje 196–8
Matkov Kot 206
medical facilities *see* health
Metlika 182–5
Mirna Gora 185
money matters 25–9
  ATMs 26
  banks 25–6
  budgeting 28–9
  credit cards 27–8
  currency 25
  currency exchange 27
  debit cards 27–8
  exchange rates 25
  travellers' cheques 27
  wiring money 28
Moravske Toplice 216
Morkice Castle and golf course 181
mountain biking 114, 127, 197, 206 *see also* cycling
mountain huts 16
Murska Sobota 214–15
music 39–40

natural history *see* conservation
Notranjska **163–71**, *164*
Novo Mesto **176–80**, *178*

Otočec Castle 179
Otoška Cave 168
overseas embassies and consulates in Slovenia *see* embassies

paintball 219
paragliding 113, 115, 127, 206
Park of Military History 171
people 9–10

photographic tips 26–7
Piran **153–8**, *154*
  entertainment and nightlife 156
  getting around 155
  getting there 153–4
  history 153
  practicalities 156
  shopping 156
  tourist information 155
  tour operators 155
  what to see 156–8
  where to eat 155–6
  where to stay 155
Pivka 171
Pivka Cave 168
Planinska Cave 168
Plečnik, Jože 47, **48**, 49, 68, 69, 70, 71, 72, 74, 75, 76, 77, 78, 79, 80, 81, 82, 85, 89, 100, 101, 117, 216, 233
Pleterje Monastery 180
Podčetrtek Castle 212
Podsreda Castle 212
Podzemlje Pece 224
politics *see* government
Portorož 158–63
post offices 41 *see also* practicalities in individual listings
Postojna Caves 163–7
Postojna town 167
potholing 127
Predjama Castle 168
Predjama Cave 168–9
Prekmurje *188*, **213–17**
Prešeren, France 68, 79, 96, **99**, 100, 103, 117
press 40–1
Primorska **123–45**, *122*
private rooms 32 *see also* where to stay in individual listings
Proteus anguinus 166
Ptuj **206–11**, *208*
  entertainment and nightlife 209
  getting there 207
  history 207
  practicalities 209
  tourist information 207
  what to see 209–11
  where to eat 207, 209
  where to stay 207
Ptuj Castle 209
Ptuj Mountain 211
public holidays 34–5

radio 41
Radovljica 92–4
rafting 113, 128, 131, 206
rail passes 20
red tape 18
religion 11
restavracija see eating and drinking
Rihenberg Castle 145
Robanov Kot 206
Robba, Francesco 75, 79, 80
Rogla 198–9
rules of the road *see* getting around

safety 23–4
Savica Falls 111
Sečovlje Salina Nature Park 12, **161–2**
shopping 37 *see also* individual listings
skiing 115–16, 119–20, 127, 139, 163, 169, 197, 198, 224
Škocjan Caves 141–2
Škofja Loka **86–90**, *87*
sledding, summer 197
Slovenian Adriatic **147–62**, *146*
Slovenian embassies overseas *see* embassies
Slovenj Gradec 219–23, *220*
Šmarješke Toplice 179–80
Šmartno 133, **134**
Snežik Castle 170–1
snowboarding 119, 127, 198, 224
Soča Front 126
spas
　　Dolenjske Toplice 175–6
　　Šmarješke Toplice 179–80
　　Terme 3000 216–17
　　Terme Čatež 181
　　Terme Fontana 196
　　Terme Laško 205–6
　　Terme Ptuj 211
　　Terme Radenci 212–13
　　Terme Snovik 85
　　Terme Zreče 198
special events *see* festivals
Štajerska **189–213**, *188*
Štanjel 144–5
Stična Monastery 178–9
student dormitories *see* where to stay in individual listings
suggested itineraries 14
Suha 91

Tartini, Giuseppe 157
telephones 41–2
television 41

Terme 3000 216–17
Terme Čatež 181
Terme Fontana 196
Terme Laško 205–6
Terme Ptuj 211
Terme Radenci 212–13
Terme Snovik 85
Terme Zreče 198
Three Parishes of Rosaline 185
ticket discounts *see* rail passes
Tolmin 131–2
Tomšič-Srebotnjak, Dubravka 40
tour operators 16–17 *see also* individual listings
tourist farms 32, **216** *see also* where to stay in individual listings
tourist information *see* individual listings
travel clinics 23
travellers' cheques 27
Triglav, Mount
　　tackling 114–15
Triglav National Park 12, 104
　　walking 113

Union beer 64

vaccinations *see* health
Valvasor, Janez Vajkard 38
Velenje 199
Vintgar Gorge 107
Vipava Valley 140–1
visa requirements *see* red tape
Vrba 117
Vršič Pass 120–1

walking *see* hiking
water park 112
websites 235
what to take 25
when to visit 13–14 *see also* climate
white-water rafting *see* rafting
wildlife 12
wine **33–4**, 132, 133–4, 140, 141, 161, 173, 180, 182, 184, 194, 212
winter sports 117, 119, 127, 198
wiring money 27

youth hostels 32 *see also* where to stay in individual listings

Zgornji Hrastnik 174
Zupan, Jakob 39
Žužemberk Castle 178